A
CHANGING
IMAGE:
American
Perceptions of
the Arab-Israeli Dispute

by
RICHARD H. CURTISS

Published by the
American Educational Trust

For Raymond Holden Curtiss
1963 – 1981

A brave and concerned idealist
whose causes were those of compassion, not of anger

A CHANGING IMAGE:
American Perceptions of the Arab-Israeli Dispute

Acknowledgments

At a Christmas party in 1955 in Germany, during a discussion with other foreign service people, I found myself saying that after living in Europe, the Far East and Latin America, I looked forward to assignments anywhere in the world except the Middle East. Afterward, I wondered what had so turned me against the thought of service in that one troubled area. The next year I decided to find out. I told the U.S. Information Agency's Middle East personnel officer that I would go anywhere he chose to send me. It was the beginning of 24 continuous years of living in or dealing with the Middle East that were frequently rewarding, sometimes frightening, occasionally tragic, and never dull.

In the fall of 1956, while preparing in Washington for my first Middle Eastern assignment, I underwent the "revelation" familiar to nearly every American who becomes involved in Middle Eastern affairs. In a year that encompassed U.S. withdrawal of support for Egypt's Aswan Dam, President Nasser's nationalization of the Suez Canal, and the subsequent tripartite Israeli, French and British attack on Egypt, I was stunned by the contrast between what I read in the U.S. press on the one hand and in the diplomatic telegraphic traffic from the Middle East on the other. Even more surprising was the contrast between the scholarly orientation material I was reading on the Middle East, and virtually all of my preconceptions. I had imagined an area of hostile, volatile people dominated by viciously anti-American mobs. I learned instead about more than a century of uniformly harmonious and productive cooperation between Americans and Arabs that had brought great benefits to both. I had not merely been ignorant about the region, I had been shockingly misinformed.

Upon arrival in the Middle East, I found that my American foreign service colleagues there bore special burdens. In my previous experience, colleagues had generally approved of American policies in the areas in which they served. Helping to explain and carry out such policies had been something of a holy crusade for us all. In the Middle East, however, the atmosphere was totally different. Patriotic American foreign service officers there considered our developing policies a prescription for disaster, and their best efforts were devoted to compiling evidence that U.S. policy should be reconsidered and revised in Washington. Though there was not unanimity of assessment of the responsibility for the tragic cycle of violence that already had claimed so many Arab and Jewish lives in the Middle East, there was general agreement that knee-jerk American partisanship on the side of the Israelis was complicating efforts to settle the problems. Most unsettling to Americans in the Middle East at that time was the one-sided picture of events that Americans at home received from the American media, and sometimes from official American statements, particularly during national election campaigns.

Some foreign service officers, not liking what they saw, simply completed their tours and transferred to other areas. Others, however, steeped themselves in knowledge of the area so that, while they might be ignored, they could not be refuted when they spoke out to correct American public misperceptions of the area, its peoples, and their problems. Long association with such foreign service officers in the Middle East, who repeatedly have put their country's interest ahead of their own career advancement, has been one of the most inspiring aspects of my foreign service career. Conversations with such associates, and with the American educators, businessmen, missionaries and journalists in the Middle East who fought similar battles within their own disciplines, reinforced my own deep misgivings and strengthened my determination not to acquiesce silently in actions that I perceived to be against the best interests of the people of the United States.

It is, therefore, all those thoughtful and patriotic colleagues and associates who have inspired this book. Unfortunately, to name them would in many cases do them a disservice. They know who they are. I am deeply indebted to them all, as all Americans should be.

A major part of this manuscript took shape during my assignment by the U.S. Information Agency (at that time designated the U.S. International Communication Agency) to the Department of State's Executive Seminar in National and International Affairs during the 1979–1980 academic year. I visited government departments, media offices, universities, think tanks, the Israeli and several Arab embassies, and lobbying groups for both sides. Particularly useful were the summaries of various public opinion polls prepared over many years by the Bureau of Public Affairs of the Department of State. Thanks to recommendations and introductions developed during those off-the-record conversations in Washington, I then was able to visit similar Middle East and public opinion specialists throughout the United States for more off-the-record conversations.

The resulting case study, *Too Often Promised Land—American Public Opinion and the Arab-Israeli Dispute, 1973–1980,* was published in 1980 by the Foreign Service Institute. It was made possible by the director of the U.S. International Communication Agency, Ambassador John Reinhardt, who assigned me to the seminar; the seminar coordinator, Ambassador James Blake, who helped me to define the topic; Shirley Brown, of USICA, who cheerfully typed it all through many revisions; my wife, Donna Bourne Curtiss, who accompanied me on all the travel, discussed and analyzed with me the information developed, and did innumerable helpful things to get the study finished on time; and finally by my mother and our children who, while sharing our home, had to make do for themselves through much of that hectic period.

In the final months before my retirement in late 1980 as USICA Chief Inspector, a number of my USICA and State Department colleagues read the manuscript and offered many helpful and encouraging comments. John C. Kimball, Chief of the Department of State's Editorial Division, helped to make the study available to still more of our colleagues.

Two of those colleagues, Isa Khalil Sabbagh and George Amel Naifeh, subsequently retired from the Foreign Service and founded the American Arab Affairs Council. They encouraged me to expand and update the study so that it could be published in book form. I am grateful to them for such encouragement and subsequent assistance. Again my wife Donna provided advice on content and editorial style, typed the entire first draft under great pressure, and prepared the index. Joyce Bouvier typed the second draft, and Steven Naifeh, Rosemary Behney and Erik Peterson handled many editorial details as the book assumed its present form. Ambassadors Edward Henderson and Andrew Killgore, co-founders of the American Educational Trust, made possible the actual publication of the book.

Like the case study on which it is based, the book represents my own conclusions. It is in no way an expression of official U.S. government policy. It is, however, as objective as I can make it and I expect it will satisfy most of those Americans, official and unofficial, who have shared my experiences in the Middle East. Partisans of the Arabs may disagree with my position that the original injustices suffered by the Palestinians displaced in 1948, though inexcusable, have nevertheless been largely offset by the *de facto* exchange of populations that brought hundreds of thousands of Oriental Jews from the Arab lands to live within the pre-1967 borders of Israel.

Partisans of Israel may be equally critical, and I am mindful of the caution by James Reston of the *New York Times* that any criticism of Israel will be described as "anti-Semitic" by those who choose to do so. Some critics may cite incidents of terrorism instigated from the Arab side that I have not mentioned. In response I can only point out that I have limited the narrative to items I considered directly relevant to U.S. perceptions of the dispute. If I mentioned only one of several senseless and brutal skyjackings perpetrated by the Popular Front for the Liberation of Palestine (and that only because it was the event that precipitated Jordan's "Black September"), it was because others were not central to the theme of this book. If I discussed the "Lavon affair" and the assault on the *Liberty* at length, but failed to dwell on the Irgun massacre of Arab villagers at Deir Yassin or the Irgun hanging of British hostages, it was for the same reason. It should not be news to anyone in the United States that there have been hundreds of savage and barbaric acts committed by cruel fanatics in both camps. That is not the point of this book, which concerns the making of American perceptions, and the relationship of these perceptions to possible solutions to the problem.

Friends have asked me why I undertook a task that, based on the experiences of other Americans, may expose me and members of my family to harassment. I can only answer that had I not been strongly encouraged as well as assisted at every turn by my wife, this book would not have been possible at all.

All four of our children spent some of their formative years in the Middle East, and all came to terms with the fact that their foreign friends often blamed the United States for tragedies that occurred around them. Each, however, remained aware of the extraordinary, and perhaps unique, basic decency and fairness of the American public. If Americans at home perceived Middle Eastern events differently than did Americans who grew up in the Middle East, our children were willing to ascribe the differences to lack of accurate information, not to lack of human compassion.

Our youngest son, Denny, having lived most of his first 13 years overseas, had developed an intense patriotism that perhaps only other young expatriates can fully understand. He hoped for a military or civilian career with the U.S. government. Having personally experienced some of the tragedy of lives and dreams wasted in the Lebanese Civil War, he was also an extraordinarily concerned and idealistic person. He directed his hard-earned dollars to the causes of wildlife conservation and wilderness preservation, and his thoughts and actions to the creation of international understanding to avert future wars.

In high school in Virginia he was bothered by the fact that even his closest American friends had some of the same biases and hostilities toward Arabs that his Middle Eastern friends had had toward Americans. He brought some of those American high school students to talk with me about it. After one such session, to prepare Denny and his friends to represent Jordan in a mock United Nations debate, they told him it was the first time they had realized there really were two sides to the Israeli-Palestinian problem, and that there were some moderate and reasonable people on both sides.

"Dad," Denny said that night, "you should write a book so that other people can read some of the things you told my friends."

"I'll try," I promised, "when I have the time to do it."

"Okay," he answered, "but what if by then it's too late?"

By now it is too late for Denny to read this book, but perhaps not for other Americans like the concerned friends who meant so much to him. So this book is for Denny: A promise kept, and perhaps not altogether too late.

Contents

CHAPTER I

Why Perceptions Matter

"Since the war in 1973 the United States has agreed to over $10 billion in military and economic support for Israel. Under the Carter Administration, one fifth of all our economic and military assistance around the world has come to this nation. In next year's budget, nearly half of all our sales credits and grants will go to Israel. This is an unprecedented amount, but we have no regrets."[1]

Vice President Walter F. Mondale,
July 5, 1978 (address in Jerusalem)

"Four Arab-Israeli wars have not only brought bloodshed and untold suffering to the peoples of the Middle East, they have also cost the United States and the rest of the world incalculable billions. At several points the conflict has threatened world peace itself."[2]

Ambassador-at-Large Alfred L. Atherton, Jr.,
April 3, 1979 (address in Pittsburgh)

"From the time of Israel's founding, the United States has served as its indulgent protector. In the past four years alone we have provided assistance exceeding $11 billion. Our current annual subsidy of over $2 billion (the equivalent of more than $3,500 a year for each Israeli family of five) is . . . one of our few sacrosanct budget items. In addition to official aid from American taxpayers, Israel receives massive sums from its generous American friends."[3]

Former U.S. Under Secretary of State George Ball,
June 15, 1981 (in the *Washington Post*)

"One miscalculation and the flames of war could sweep the entire Mideast region. And it is not known how far the sparks of this fire could scatter."[4]

Leonid I. Brezhnev, May 22, 1981
(In address from the Georgian Soviet Republic)

1

These statements illustrate the extraordinary nature of America's relationship with Israel, and hint at its significance to American relationships with the rest of the world. Although, as Ambassador Atherton says, the Arab-Israeli wars have cost the United States and the rest of the world "incalculable billions," the costs of direct U.S. government assistance to Israel *can* be calculated. Between 1949 and September 30, 1982 Israel, with some 3 million Jewish citizens, will have received more than $24 billion ($24,239,200,000) in direct U.S. government grants and loans. This means that every man, woman and child in the U.S. has contributed just over $110 toward a total of $8,080 per Israeli. Or, to follow George Ball's example above, each American family of five has contributed $550 to subsidize each Israeli family of five to the tune of $40,400.

These figures do not include the substantial losses to the U.S. treasury from tax-free contributions by U.S. citizens to Israel, probably a larger item in Israel's earlier years than were direct U.S. treasury grants and loans. Neither do these totals reflect the rapidly accelerating rate of U.S. payments to Israel. Of the $24 billion allocated to Israel in the first 33 years of its existence, more than $20 billion was allocated within the last nine years, and of that more than $11 billion within the last four years. This brings the average annual direct U.S. government contribution over each of those four years to just under $1,000 per Jewish Israeli.

The 1980 election campaign was conducted against a background of local tax revolts. It culminated in massive efforts to balance the federal budget by cutting non-military expenditures. It might seem remarkable, therefore, that during that campaign, no presidential and few Congressional candidates mentioned that a country with less than one tenth of one per cent of the world's population was, in the last year of the Carter administration, receiving more than 22 per cent of total direct U.S. foreign assistance, and substantial additional amounts via various government subsidies and tax-exempt donations. Instead, after the advent of the Reagan Administration, Israel's military aid total was significantly increased at the same time that the world-wide total of U.S. aid was further reduced. Clearly, the relationship with Israel flows outside the current of normal partisan politics. Throughout the past decade each administration, whether Republican or Democratic, has regularly increased Israel's aid total, while also increasing its assistance to neighboring countries willing to keep the peace with Israel, particularly Jordan and Egypt. This in turn brings the percentage of U.S. aid devoted directly to Israel or to its immediate neighbors close to 40 per cent of the total world-wide American effort.

What is the explanation for this uncomplaining acceptance by taxpayers, and their elected representatives, of a heavy, rapidly-increasing, and obviously perilous burden of support for Israel? Most Americans would unhesitatingly answer that they support Israel because it is the right thing to do. In fact, over the years many—perhaps most—Americans have maintained that the U.S. has a "moral obligation" to protect Israel, regardless of cost, from destruction at the hands of its neighbors.

There have always been some American critics of Israel who question both the morality of and the obligation for American support. They contend that the Jewish state in Palestine was founded with total disregard for the rights and welfare of the Arab majority which then inhabited the land, and that the sense of obligation has been built up in the United States only by many years of intense media manipulation and political pressure. When such objections to the idea of a U.S. "moral obligation" are raised, Israel's defenders are less likely to defend the premise than to shift to a second rationale for extensive U.S. support of Israel. For many years this rationale concerned Israel's image as an embattled "friendly democracy" surrounded by hostile and unstable dictatorships. Very recently, and particularly under Republican administrations, it has been suggested that the U.S. has a "strategic interest" in defending Israel. The implication is that states hostile to Israel are also likely to be hostile to the U.S., and that Israel thus somehow has a role in keeping them at bay on behalf of the United States. This explanation, however, does not withstand scrutiny. The American tradition of friendly relations with all the major Arab states, as well as with the Ottoman Empire which once administered most of them, goes back without interruption for more than a century and a half. In fact, the only significant issues of contention between the U.S. and any major Arab countries in this century have all in one way or another derived from U.S. support for and Arab hostility to Israel.

What is remarkable, then, is that for 33 years Americans have willingly shouldered the burdens of supporting Israel, at steadily and rapidly-increasing costs and dangers to themselves, regardless of the shifting circumstances in the Middle East and without ever reaching a national consensus on specific reasons for this faithful, and militarily and politically perilous, support.

A foreigner, seeking to make sense of the variety of contrasting, and sometimes conflicting, explanations offered, could be forgiven for examining the common political interest or "strategic ally" explanations first. Would a great power, locked in a hideously expensive, frequently bloody, and seemingly endless struggle with the Soviet Union for world-wide power and influence, commit so much of its military and financial capability to the support of Israel except for political or military advantage? One way to approach this question is through the writings of American experts in authoritative publications over the past several years.

Perhaps predictably, a critic of Israel, Professor Alan R. Taylor of American University, asserts that America's support for Israel is not a political advantage, but a liability. He writes:

"The political cost of America's special relationship with Israel has been to place in serious jeopardy the political leverage of the United States in an area of primary strategic and economic importance. The relationship has also placed a far greater strain on the Soviet-American search for detente than any other factor in contemporary international affairs. In these respects, Israel is more of a liability than an asset and there is an imperative need for the United States to re-evaluate what it is getting—or losing—from its patronage of Israel."[5]

Even a sympathetic observer of Israel, Professor Robert Tucker of Johns Hopkins University, notes that although Israel's dependence upon the U.S. is increasing, the common political interests of the two countries are diminishing. He writes:

"The congruence of interests that might make so increasingly dependent a relationship tolerable—if never desirable—no longer exists. Indeed, it has never really existed, though it more nearly approximated the ideal in earlier years."[6]

Still more bluntly, shortly before Egyptian President Sadat's death syndicated columnist Joseph Kraft assessed the consequences to the United States of Israel's political course under Prime Minister Menachem Begin. Kraft, an occasional critic of Begin but no enemy of Israel, wrote:

"As matters now stand, Begin threatens American ties with moderate states, especially Saudi Arabia. He could drive Egyptian President Sadat away from the peace accord with Israel, and force Syria further into Soviet arms. Even war cannot be excluded."[7]

Both friends and foes of Israel seem to agree that America's popular, but expensive, special relationship with Israel is not based upon common political interests, and is in fact a growing political liability to the United States. Therefore, foreigners schooled in the maxim that in international relations there are "no friendships, only interests" may be pardoned for assuming that if the U.S. does not subsidize Israel for political advantages, it must do so for military purposes. Both influential Republicans and Democrats have made statements to this effect. For example, in a 1977 article, Dr. Eugene V. Rostow, Under Secretary of State in the Johnson Administration from 1966 to 1969, defined a "strategic" motive for supporting Israel:

"It is our interest that the area be secure and at peace, available on fair terms both to our military and to our commerce. So far as Israel is concerned, our interest is twofold: To achieve peace between Israel and its Arab neighbors, and to maintain Israel as a bulwark whose presence and strength discourage imperial impulses on the part of Egypt, Syria or Iraq. For a long time, as the Saudi Arabians and the Iranians understood very well, only Israel prevented Egypt under Nasser from conquering Saudi Arabia and the Persian Gulf States. And if we face, as we may, a showdown some day with the oil-producing states, Israel would be an indispensable ally. In addition, Israel is the only sure access point we have between Western Europe and our partners in the Far East, Australia, New Zealand, Korea and Japan."[8]

Edward Sheehan is an author and Middle East expert with little affinity for the kind of thinking represented by the Rostow quotation. He indicates, however, that there was a "strategic" motive in U.S. support for Israel in the minds of at least some officials of the first Nixon administration. This was from 1969 to 1972 when Henry Kissinger was President Nixon's national security adviser, before Kissinger became Secretary of State and assumed the dominant role in U.S. Middle Eastern policy. Sheehan writes:

"Kissinger accepted and in fact helped to promote the conventional strategic wisdom of the first Nixon administration—that, in the absence of fruitful negotiations, a strong Israel, militarily much superior to its Arab foes, would prevent war and serve as the surest sentinel of American interests in the Middle East."[9]

However, whatever the conventional wisdom of the era prior to the October 1973 war, by 1975 Dr. Tucker, despite his sympathy for Israel, was prepared to dismiss Israel's "strategic" value to the U.S. as categorically as he dismissed its political value. He wrote:

"In the best of circumstances Israel is not an attractive ally, and the present circumstances are evidently not the best."[10]

Four years later George Ball, Under Secretary of State in the Kennedy and Johnson administrations from 1961 to 1966 and Permanent Representative to the UN in 1968, took this view of American strategic interests in the Middle East:

"We need to keep the Middle East out of the communist orbit. That requires not only that there be peace between Israel and the Arab world, but that we avoid those divisive issues that set Arab states against one another, and thus invite them to play one superpower against the other. . . . Particularly now that the Soviets have beachheads in the Horn of Africa and South Yemen, America must do everything possible to sustain and strengthen the nations on the littoral of the Gulf, which is at the moment the strategic heart of the world. . . . In the past, there was at least one occasion—the fedayeen and Syrian attack on Jordan in September 1970—when Israeli military forces played a crucial role in preserving Middle East stability. And so long as Iran was governed by the Shah, who was friendly to Israel, it was at least arguable that the military power of Israel, in tandem with Iran's, was a general force for stability. Today, however, with Iran in a militantly anti-Israeli posture that is unlikely soon to change, there is no possibility whatever of Israel playing any useful part in the direct military or strategic sense. Last February, when Secretary of Defense Harold Brown visited Saudi Arabia and other countries to see what could be done to assist in the face of Soviet incursions . . . his mission was told in the most categorical terms that any project that involved Israeli territory or forces would be highly disruptive. The blunt fact then is that so long as it seems to be seeking to consolidate its hold on the West Bank for the long term, its impact on the stability of the Middle East will be wholly negative."[11]

Most other assessments dating to the end of the Carter administration agreed that Israel was a net strategic, as well as political, liability to the U.S. The Reagan administration, however, initially signaled a new attitude. On February 13, 1981, only a month after he assumed office, the new U.S. Secretary of State's approach to the Middle East was bluntly described in the *Washington Post* by the syndicated columnists, Rowland Evans and Robert Novak:

"Haig looks at Israel not in terms of American constituency-group politics but as an American ally with strategic strength to offer Washington, much like Saudi Arabia and other U.S. allies in the Arab world."[12]

Only three weeks later, in a CBS "Face the Nation" interview on March 8, Defense Secretary Caspar Weinberger was even more specific about the need for U.S. allies in the Middle East, but less so about Israel. He said:

"It is essential we have a presence in the Middle East or, as it is being called, Southwest Asia. We need some facilities and additional men and material there or nearby, to act as a deterrent to any Soviet hopes of seizing the oil fields or interdicting the line."[13]

The emphasis continued to shift from Israel to area strategic concerns as President Reagan's administration confronted the same Middle Eastern realities previously faced by Presidents Nixon, Ford, and Carter. On June 10, 1981, only three days after Israeli planes had bombed Iraqi nuclear facilities outside Baghdad, the *Washington Post* declared in an editorial:

"Israel has directly challenged the fundamental terms on which the United States conducts its Mideast policy. The United States must be in a position to pursue its interests with Arabs as well as Israelis. An Israeli policy that thwarts that purpose cannot be accepted."[14]

In the United Nations, the Reagan administration's newly-appointed Ambassador, Jeane Kirkpatrick, declared on June 21, 1981:

"The security of this nation and our allies is bound up with the peace and security of the Middle East. Our own broad foreign policy interests do not permit us to ignore the interests and sensibilities of Egypt, Saudi Arabia, Jordan and other states in the area. Neither do we desire to do so."[15]

Three weeks later, *Washington Post* columnist Philip Geyelin wrote:

"Sooner rather than later . . . the Reagan administration will have to figure out how tough-minded it is prepared to be in its handling of Menachem Begin. How it deals with him on the tormenting Palestinian issue will determine, in large degree, the success of its larger strategic purposes in the Middle East and the Persian Gulf."[16]

On July 14, 1981, syndicated columnist Joseph Kraft suggested in the *Washington Post*:

"American officials ought to take Begin up on his repeated insistence that everything is different now because the United States and Israel are allies. The fact is that Israel has not recently behaved as a good ally should behave. It has acted as though that alliance meant an American blank check for everything Begin considered to be in his country's national interest. It has created situations at times—notably the raid on the Iraqi nuclear installation—that were harmful to American interests."[17]

And finally, on July 24, 1981, Evans and Novak reported in the *Washington Post*:

"Some Presidential intimates have cautioned Reagan that the timing of Begin's air raid may have been deliberately planned to weaken U.S. ties with its essential Arab allies—particularly Saudi Arabia. He has listened closely. . . . Against his will, his instinct and a lifetime of emotional support for Israel, President Reagan is reappraising the U.S.-Israel connection to preserve his 'strategic consensus' in the Middle East against Soviet penetration."[18]

President Reagan's educational "reappraisal" of Middle Eastern strategic realities turned into a crash course of instruction after his administration announced its decision to sell five airborne early warning aircraft to Saudi Arabia, a plan inherited from the Carter administration. After Reagan's election victory in 1980, lame-duck Carter administration officials had offered to present the sale for Congressional approval before their term ended, on condition that the incoming Republican President-elect not oppose it and thus turn it into a partisan issue. Inexplicably, the incoming Republicans declined this politically generous offer which would have saved them from a politically exhausting Congressional battle. If nothing else the refusal indicated that at that time Reagan sincerely believed his campaign statements about Israel's strategic value to the United States.

In early 1981 while his own officials studied the $8.5 billion deal, President Reagan found himself increasingly involved in Israeli domestic politics. When Prime Minister Menachem Begin's domestic political fortunes had sunk to an all-time low, largely because of runaway Israeli inflation, his opposition forced a vote of no-confidence and early elections. As the Israeli election campaign opened, Israel began a series of confrontational military moves that included air strikes against Palestinians all over Lebanon, combat in southern Lebanon between Israel's surrogate Lebanese forces and UN peacekeeping troops, and the shooting down by Israel of two Syrian troop-carrying helicopters in northern Lebanon during fighting between Syrian soldiers and Israeli-backed Maronite Christian forces. The Reagan administration, closely supported by Saudi Arabia, found itself engaged in putting out military brush fires ignited all around Israel's borders.

When the joint U.S.-Saudi efforts apparently had succeeded in quieting the situation in Lebanon, Begin once again fanned the flames of Israeli nationalism with his sudden air raid on the Iraqi nuclear reactor, in the course of which his aircraft violated the airspace of two moderate Arab regimes friendly to the U.S. Warned by American diplomats in Israel that U.S. condemnation of Israel's actions would cause Israelis to "circle the wagons" and thus strengthen electoral support for Begin, Reagan equivocated. Pressed by American journalists to comment on Israel's seemingly reckless and aggressive actions, the U.S. President said lamely that Israel perhaps "thought" they were defensive. Within hours Reagan learned that Begin was quoting his words in election rallies as proof that the U.S. President supported his hardline policies. At the same time Begin used statements in Europe condemning the Iraqi raid as proof that European anti-Semitism was not dead. By this time in Israel a vote for Begin had become a patriotic statement. He was re-elected by a narrow margin.

Even after he had watched Begin deliberately set up a series of bloody and dangerous confrontations with the Arabs in order to come from behind to win re-election, Reagan at first seemed caught by surprise when Begin's confrontational tactics were turned against his own administration. Israel now went all out, via its supporters in the United States, to oppose the Saudi Arabian AWACS sale even though both the Carter and Reagan administrations had decided the sale was essential to overall U.S. strategic interests in the Middle East. Initially, Israeli lobby arguments were even couched in terms of U.S. interests, quoting rhetoric from the Reagan campaign and early Reagan administration statements.

The Reagan administration, however, staunchly maintained, in the words of then National Security Adviser Richard Allen, that "the five AWACS aircraft that would be sold to Saudi Arabia" were the minimum required "to maintain one AWACS (plane) continuously in the air" and that "AWACS and the other air defense equipment would make a substantial contribution to the security interest of the United States in a vital part of the world without endangering the security interests of Israel."[19]

As leaders from both political parties, including all three living ex-Presidents, came out strongly in favor of the sale, the Israeli campaign in the U.S. changed. It became shrill, with invocations of the European Holocaust and intimations that the U.S. valued Arab oil over Jewish blood and that proponents of the deal were guilty of "tactical anti-Semitism." Israel's powerful U.S. lobby charged that the United States was acting against the interest of Israel and, at least for the duration of the campaign, rejected any suggestion that the interests of the two countries were linked.

The power of Israel's persuasion was demonstrated in a 301-111 vote in the House of Representatives to disapprove the sale. Since both houses of Congress had to disapprove in order to block the sale, however, the administration concentrated its efforts on the Senate. Few senators wanted to be recorded as voting against Israel's interests. Nevertheless, the administration had felt from the beginning that when the voting began, just enough senators would be willing to support a move which major figures in both parties said was so essential to U.S. interests. Although President Reagan's faith apparently never wavered, Senator Howard Baker admitted that he was not sure of victory until a week before the vote, and most of the Washington press corps predicted a Reagan defeat until only a few hours before the resolution disapproving the sale was defeated 52-48. At the last moment a handful of senators, including some already on record against the sale, found reasons such as the assassination of President Sadat a few days earlier to reverse their public stands and to support the administration. After the votes had been counted, however, there was no one in the Reagan administration making claims that further strengthening Israel, or keeping moderate Arab regimes weak, was somehow in the national interest.

When a U.S.-Israel "strategic cooperation agreement" was announced a month later, it was Israel that had pressed hard for the agreement. It sought U.S. bases, U.S. troops, or at least pre-positioning of U.S. arms and ammunition on Israeli soil. The U.S. on the other hand negotiated hard to limit the cooperation to such matters as "joint maneuvers" and "joint consultations." The resulting agreement, clearly, was simply a reluctant U.S. payoff to induce Israel to follow through on its final Sinai withdrawal commitment under the Camp David treaty with Egypt.

On December 13, 1981, just two weeks after the agreement was signed and only hours after the declaration of martial law in Poland suddenly escalated the Communist Party-free trade union confrontation there into a global crisis, Israel stunned its new "ally" by announcing that it had annexed territory previously seized from Syria. (The incident is described more fully in Chapter 24.) President

Reagan reacted by suspending the strategic cooperation agreement. Prime Minister Begin responded by renouncing the agreement altogether in a burst of fiery rhetoric. Interestingly, the exchange brought about an admission from Israeli Foreign Minister Yitzhak Shamir on December 15 of the lack of congruence between Israeli and American interests. He said:

"Much as we want to coordinate our activities with the United States, the interests are not identical. We have to, from time to time, worry about our own interests."[20]

It was the echo of a thought being expressed increasingly in the United States. The obvious unwillingness of the U.S. to enter into anything more than a cosmetic military agreement with Israel in the first place already had indicated that the attitude of the Reagan administration had swung 180 degrees from the sentiments it had proclaimed as the President assumed office. President Reagan's crash course in Middle Eastern strategic realities had been completed in only 11 months.

Regardless of changes in both American and Israeli leadership, the strategic, military, and political facts have remained immutable for several years. Israel is a country literally too small to contain a U.S. military base that could not be neutralized in short order by Soviet weapons from adjacent Arab lands or Mediterranean waters. The Israeli army, though superbly trained, equipped, and motivated, demonstrated in 1973 that it cannot sustain a full-scale war against its Arab neighbors for more than a few days without almost total resupply from the outside. Even in the absence of open hostilities, Israel cannot maintain full mobilization for much more than a month without bringing the economy to a halt. Moreover, so long as Israel's political problems with the Palestinians and its Arab neighbors remain unresolved, American use of Israeli facilities or support of an Israeli military effort would seriously undermine U.S. relations with most or all of more than twenty Arabic-speaking states. These states extend in a 5,000-mile belt from the Straits of Gibraltar to the Straits of Hormuz, straddling air and sea routes between Europe and Africa, and between Western Europe and South and East Asia. A simple glance at the map confirms that, until Israel and its Middle Eastern neighbors compose their differences, the strategic advantages in the bilateral U.S.-Israel relationship accrue to Israel, not to the U.S.

If, then, even Israel's faithful friends admit an increasing divergence between U.S. and Israeli political interests, and cannot substantiate vague statements that the U.S. and Israel are "strategic allies" by explaining how the relationship could confer a net political or strategic advantage upon the U.S., then the real basis of American support for Israel must lie elsewhere. If it has little or nothing to do with U.S. interests in the Middle East, or in the world at large, then it must lie within the U.S. itself.

Friends of Israel might cite consistent and overwhelming support from virtually all segments of U.S. public opinion for a "beleaguered outpost of democracy" in the Middle East. Critics of Israel describe "persistent and increasing domestic political activity" by American Jewish organizations on behalf of Israel.

Both viewpoints have merit. The polls attest to the former. Candidates for national elective office attest to the latter. In every state and in a majority of Congressional districts, large blocs of influential Americans can be organized rapidly to protest in harsh and politically damaging terms any signs of wavering support for Israel. They can also reward or punish initiatives concerning Israel by increasing or withholding campaign contributions. Bloc votes in key industrial states can influence Presidential elections, sometimes decisively.

How has such overwhelming public support and political influence been developed? Is it largely due to the commitment, energy, and high achievement of America's Jewish citizens, who number a little more than six million people, but less than three per cent of a national population of some 220 million? Or can it be attributed largely to the sentiments of other Americans: Democrats and Republicans, Catholics and Protestants, old and young, Northerners, Southerners and Westerners, who rarely turn their attention to the Middle East, but who will always lean toward an Israel they perceive as having been born out of the Holocaust that wiped out European Jewry, shaped by the lonely struggle for an independent Jewish state, and tempered in four wars against seemingly overwhelming numbers?

Expert opinion supports both views. In an article in *Commentary,* the monthly organ of the American Jewish Committee, a political scientist, Earl Raab, emphasizes the support of the general public. He writes:

"The fulcrum of popular American support for Israel has nothing to do with Israel as a Jewish state; it is, rather, the belief that Israel is a small democratic nation which is trying to preserve its independence."[21]

Also writing in *Commentary,* Professor Seymour Martin Lipset, a long-time close observer of U.S. public attitudes toward Israel, and Professor William Schneider of Harvard University emphasize the key role of Zionist organization:

"The only 'veto group' in the American electorate concerned with the Middle East is composed of those dedicated to the survival of Israel. This group, which includes almost all Jews along with many non-Jews, has been ready to bombard Congressmen and the administration with letters, telegrams, phone calls and personal visits to present their case. Many of them have been willing to contribute generously to the campaign funds of politicians who support Israel. Conversely, they will vote against those who oppose Israel, a fact of which office-holders are well aware."[22]

In *The Nation,* journalist David Caploe writes that the most important element of American public opinion support for Israel is "a widely and deeply held perception of Israel's reasonableness, moderation and desire for peace, contrasted with the extremism, bellicosity and irrational blood lust of the Arabs."[23]

Other observers cite negative reactions by the American public to the sometimes shrill tones of third world critics of the U.S. in general, and to traditional Arab hyperbole in particular, as an important element in U.S. public support for Israel. In an interview in the *Journal of Palestine Studies,* veteran Washington journalist James McCartney cites "differences between the essentially European culture of Israel and Arab culture," noting that in America "for the most part Arabs have not really been understood very well."[24]

Even more succinctly, Rabbi Arnold Jacob Wolf, a prominent Jewish critic of present Israeli policy, notes in the American Jewish newsletter, *Sh'ma*, that "The PLO has also worked hard to make Begin's intransigence credible and legitimate."[25]

It would appear that the authors of these varying assessments, like most persons closely concerned with U.S. Middle Eastern policy, see the strong U.S. military, economic, and political support of Israel directly linked, through domestic political activity, to the strong pro-Israel sentiment that has traditionally dominated U.S. public opinion.

Experts may still disagree whether U.S. policy vis-a-vis the Arab-Israeli dispute is in America's self-interest. The point on which virtually all do agree, however, is that self-interest is not the major factor motivating that American policy. The critical factor, from the creation of Israel to the present day, has been a strong pro-Israel bias in American public opinion. To understand that bias, it is appropriate to review the historical record and the U.S. opinion polls to see how American perceptions of the Arab-Israeli dispute developed, what they are today, and where they may be moving.

NOTES

1. Mondale, Vice President Walter F., in remarks at State Dinner, Israeli Knesset, Jerusalem, July 5, 1978.
2. Atherton, Alfred L., Jr., Assistant Secretary of State for Near Eastern and South Asian Affairs, in address entitled "Examination of U.S. Vital Interests in the Middle East" before the World Affairs Council of Pittsburgh, Pa., April 3, 1979.
3. Ball, George W., former U.S. Under Secretary of State, *Washington Post,* June 15, 1981.
4. Brezhnev, Leonid I., Chairman, Presidium of the Supreme Soviet, USSR, in remarks broadcast from Georgian Soviet Republic, May 22, 1981.
5. Taylor, Alan R., Professor of International Relations at The American University, Washington, D.C., "The Meaning of U.S. Aid to Israel," published by the National Association of Arab Americans.
6. Tucker, Robert W., Professor of International Relations at Johns Hopkins University, "Israel and the United States: From Dependence to Nuclear Weapons?" *Commentary,* November 1975, p. 30.
7. Kraft, Joseph, *Washington Post,* July 14, 1981.
8. Rostow, Eugene V., Former Under Secretary of State, in "The American Stake in Israel," *Commentary,* April 1977, p. 37.
9. Sheehan, Edward, Harvard University Research Fellow, in "Step by Step in the Middle East," *Foreign Policy,* Spring 1976, pp. 8-9.
10. Tucker, Robert W., "Israel and the United States: From Dependence to Nuclear Weapons?" *Commentary,* November 1975, p. 38.

11. Ball, George W., "The Coming Crisis in Israeli-American Relations," *Foreign Affairs,* Winter 1979/80, p. 250.
12. Evans, Rowland and Novak, Robert, *Washington Post,* February 13, 1981.
13. Weinberger, Caspar, U.S. Secretary of Defense, in remarks on "Face the Nation," CBS interview, March 8, 1981.
14. *Washington Post* editorial, June 10, 1981.
15. Kirkpatrick, Jeane, U.S. Ambassador to the United Nations, in remarks on June 21, 1981.
16. Geyelin, Philip, *Washington Post,* July 10, 1981.
17. Kraft, Joseph, *Washington Post,* July 14, 1981.
18. Evans, Rowland and Novak, Robert, *Washington Post,* July 24, 1981.
19. Allen, Richard V., former Assistant to President Reagan for National Security Affairs, "Why the AWACS Sale is Good for Us," *Washington Post,* September 9, 1981.
20. Claiborne, William, "Israel Moves to Smooth Ties with U.S., Others After Golan Action," *Washington Post,* December 16, 1981.
21. Raab, Earl, "Is Israel Losing Popular Support? The Evidence of the Polls," *Commentary,* January 1974, p. 27.
22. Lipset, Seymour Martin, Professor of Political Science and Sociology and Senior Fellow of the Hoover Institution, Stanford University, and Schneider, William, Associate Professor at Harvard University, "Carter vs Israel: What the Polls Reveal," *Commentary,* November 1977, p. 29.
23. Caploe, David, Fellow of the Trans-National Institute, "New Look at Israel," *The Nation,* July 23, 1977, p. 71.
24. Ghareeb, Edmund, excerpts from interview with James McCartney, Knight Newspapers, in "American Media and the Palestine Problem," *Journal of Palestine Studies,* Autumn 1975/Winter 1976, p. 138.
25. Wolf, Rabbi Arnold Jacob, "Israel—The Futility of Dissent," *Sh'ma: A Journal of Jewish Responsibility,* November 30, 1979, p. 9.

President Wilson's Fourteen Points and the Palestine Mandate

> *"His Majesty's Government view with favor the establishment in Palestine of a national home for the Jewish people . . . it being clearly understood that nothing shall be done which may prejudice the civil and religious rights of the existing non-Jewish communities in Palestine, or the rights and political status enjoyed by Jews in any other country."*
> British Foreign Secretary Arthur Balfour in letter
> to Lord Lionel Rothschild, November 2, 1917

> *"The other nationalities which are now under Turkish rule should be assured an undoubted security of life and absolutely unmolested opportunity of autonomous development."*
> Twelfth of President Wilson's Fourteen Points
> promulgated to the U.S. Congress, January 8, 1918

> *"No other problem of our time is so deeply rooted in the past."*
> Report of the Peel Royal Commission to Palestine, 1937

> *"The passions aroused by Palestine have done so much to obscure the truth that the facts have become enveloped in a mist of sentiment, legend and propaganda, which acts as a smokescreen of almost impenetrable density."*
> George Antonius, 1938[1]

"The Mandate failed, essentially, because the British were unable to find a solution that would satisfy the Jews without provoking the Arabs. As soon as it became apparent that there was no common ground between the Arabs and Jews in Palestine, the Mandate was no longer workable."

Evan M. Wilson, 1979[2]

Israelis believe that a Jewish presence remained in Palestine even after the Jewish revolt in 135 A.D. that led to Roman destruction of the Second Temple; throughout the subsequent occupations of Palestine by Christian Byzantines, Muslim Arabs, and Crusaders; and then during a succession of Muslim dynasties that culminated in four centuries of Ottoman Turkish rule. Arabs dispute the continuity of this presence, citing the massacres of both Muslims and Jews by the Crusaders as examples of periods when Jews would have had to vacate Palestine in order to avoid annihilation. Both sides agree, however, that before the late 19th century the Jewish presence in Palestine was minute. There were tiny, impoverished colonies of Orthodox Jews, almost totally dependent upon donations from fellow Jews in the European diaspora, and perhaps a few Sephardic Jews whose ancestors had been expelled from Spain in 1492, found sanctuary under the Ottomans, and established relatively prosperous communities in various parts of the far-flung Ottoman Empire.

A return to the Promised Land has figured prominently in Jewish rituals and prayers through the ages. The modern political Zionist movement that made a large-scale return a reality dates, however, only to 1896, when an Austrian Jewish journalist, Theodor Herzl, made the somewhat obscure Zionist cause his own. Although he was not personally religious and was well integrated into his own society, Herzl was profoundly shocked at the anti-Semitism he saw manifested in France in the course of the infamous Dreyfus affair. He concluded that, if such virulent anti-Semitism could arise in the first European country to grant Jews the full rights of citizenship, there was little hope for Jews anywhere until they obtained a land of their own. His message was not popular with the integrated Jews of Western Europe, and particularly not with the most successful members of Jewish communities in those countries, but Herzl's charismatic leadership caught the imagination of many Jews in Eastern Europe just at a time when Czarist pogroms were driving large numbers of Jews out of their communities in Russia and Poland. The vast majority of these displaced Jews were emigrating to the United States. Small groups went to Palestine, however, supplementing the earlier Jewish religious colonies, where they began heavily subsidized experiments with new agricultural crops and techniques.

Zionism's slogan was "a land without a people for a people without a land." However, the Jews of Zionism's "First Aliyah" who began arriving in the late 19th century found that the slogan was based on a false premise: The land in question was already inhabited by a half million Muslim and Christian Arabs. Although most were living at the subsistence level under administrators who had grown increasingly corrupt and venal as the once-powerful Ottoman Empire decayed, their natural rate of increase vastly exceeded the early trickle of Zionist settlers.

Nevertheless, starting in 1905, the year of Herzl's death, the influx of Jewish immigrants increased as revolutionary movements were put down by the Czarist authorities. Numerous disappointed young idealists, inspired more by political Socialism than by religious Judaism, began arriving in Palestine. This "Second Aliyah" increased the Jewish population of Palestine from 23,000 in 1882 to some 80,000 at the outbreak of World War I in 1914. It also set the political and moral tone in Israel for generations to come. Until the Begin era, virtually all of Israel's incumbent leaders traced their origins to the "Second Aliyah" immigration of young political activists from 1905 to 1914.

Leadership of the World Zionist movement was assumed during World War I by Dr. Chaim Weizmann, a brilliant British chemist of Russian Jewish origin. He was a flexible and effective political tactician whose faith in moderation, and in his own ability to obtain a Jewish homeland in Palestine from the British government, never wavered. He developed many allies in the British establishment, among both Britain's increasingly influential Jewish community and British Christians. Many of the latter, including Winston Churchill, shared the almost mystical belief current in 19th century British literature that Britain was somehow destined to help the Jews find their way to their Promised Land in Palestine. Prominent Britons, Jewish and Christian, who supported Zionist goals for purely religious or philosophical reasons, became adept at offering pragmatic explanations of why attaining those goals would also be in the British national interest. This phenomenon, so familiar in the United States today, is clearly illustrated in the debates which accompanied the Balfour Declaration. This was the pledge in 1917 by British Foreign Secretary Arthur Balfour to a private British Jew, Lord Lionel Walter Rothschild, that the British government "view with favor the establishment in Palestine of a national home for the Jewish people . . . it being clearly understood that nothing shall be done which may prejudice the civil and religious rights of the existing non-Jewish communities in Palestine. . . ."

The Declaration was justified to skeptical members of Parliament (and to strong opponents among Britain's Jewish community who feared it could jeopardize the relatively secure status of Britain's Jewish subjects) by Lord Balfour, an enthusiastic supporter of Zionism, on somewhat different grounds. In earlier, unsuccessful drafts, it had been presented as a shrewd step to ensure support for the Allied war effort not only by the large Jewish communities of Europe, but also by the newly-important Jewish community of the United States. It was argued that American Jews, given their strong antipathy to Czarist Russia, from which so many had recently fled, might oppose America's entry into the war on the Allied side. The promise of a national home for the Jews in Palestine if the Allies won might help neutralize that opposition. However, by the time the Balfour Declaration was formally promulgated in 1917, America had already entered the war on the Allied side, and the proponents of Zionism had smoothly shifted to a new rationale. They said that a strong, European-oriented Jewish community in proximity to the Suez Canal would protect that lifeline of the British Empire from interdiction by volatile and hostile local populations.

Strangely, in the long run, it was only the Arab community that really accepted this tortured "strategic" rationalization for the establishment of a Jewish homeland. In their subsequent efforts to oppose that homeland, alternating between periods of relatively meek submission to British authority and violent outbursts when they felt threatened by additional Jewish immigration, the Arabs always missed the key to the persistent support for Zionism in British political life. They alternately invoked or threatened British national interest in the Middle East, when a direct appeal to Britain's traditional sense of fair play might have been far more effective.

During and immediately after World War I, however, British fair play was little in evidence. The Balfour Declaration was only the last of three conflicting World War I commitments entered into by Britain during its campaign to defeat the Central Powers and their Turkish partner. The first was the secret Sykes-Picot agreement to divide the Ottoman Empire into spheres of influence administered by the European Allies. Russia's withdrawal from the war invalidated much of this agreement, which nevertheless left a residue of confusion concerning what international control had been planned for the various regions of Palestine. More important was the correspondence between Sir Henry McMahon, British High Commissioner in Egypt, and the Sherif Hussein, Guardian of the Muslim Holy Places in the Hejaz province of present-day Saudi Arabia. These letters formally promised British support for Arab independence in return for Arab support of the British war effort against the Turks. The result was the "Arab Revolt," known best to westerners through the accounts of Lawrence of Arabia, who served with the Sherif's sons in the battles against the Turks. The pledges in the three sets of British documents were mutually irreconcilable, and the long story of British vacillation among the conflicting demands (again best known to westerners through the moral dilemma of the conscience-stricken Lawrence, who found himself playing an active role in his country's betrayal of its wartime Arab allies) is outside the scope of this study, except as American perceptions are involved.

In fact, Americans were involved at several stages as the backdrop of this century's Middle Eastern tragedies unfolded. American medical and educational missionaries had come to the Middle East in significant numbers starting in the 1820s. Some stayed only for a tour of duty and returned to the United States or left for other missions. Others spent a lifetime of service in the area. The result was a remarkable network of American schools that laid the foundations for the modern educational systems in several Middle Eastern countries, and the establishment of hospitals that endure to this day as some of the finest medical facilities outside the United States.

During World War I, such institutions in Palestine literally saved many of the indigenous communities from extinction by providing them with food and medicine. These were gathered not only through the sponsoring Christian religious institutions but also by an official U.S. government relief program administered under the direction of the U.S. Ambassador in Istanbul, Henry Morgenthau, Sr., a distinguished non-Zionist American Jew.

By the end of the war, as the irreconcilability of British and French purposes with their own sovereignty became apparent, both Arab and Turkish leaders sensed that President Wilson's Fourteen Points, promulgated to the U.S. Congress on January 8, 1918, held the best promise for the Arabs to achieve their independence, and for the Turks to retain theirs.

His twelfth point read: "The other nationalities which are now under Turkish rule should be assured an undoubted security of life and absolutely unmolested opportunity of autonomous development." Six months later, on July 4, 1918, he added the statement that every question should be settled "upon the basis of the free acceptance of that settlement by the people immediately concerned."

The faith of Middle Eastern leaders in Wilson's words on this score was reinforced by their own first-hand experiences during the preceding century with America's missionary and diplomatic representatives. (It is interesting to note that, during World War I, neither Turkey nor the United States declared war upon one another, despite Ottoman participation in the war on the side of the Central Powers and American participation on the side of the Allies.) These Middle Eastern leaders wanted America to accept League of Nations mandates to administer the area. But by then Wilson, weakened politically at home, was losing his battle to have the United States join the League. As a result, the U.S. retreated into an isolationism that was only ended by the 1941 attack on Pearl Harbor.

Britain's pledge to the Sherif Hussein eventually was redeemed in part by the installation of two of his sons as rulers of Iraq and Jordan. Palestine, however, became a British Mandate. There the British doggedly tried to fulfill the obviously contradictory Balfour pledges to establish "a national home for the Jewish people" without prejudicing "the civil and religious rights of the existing non-Jewish communities in Palestine."

A relic of American involvement in the struggles of the time is the report of Dr. Henry C. King, president of Oberlin College, and Charles Crane, an American businessman. They were sent to the Middle East in 1919 by President Wilson with the approval of the Supreme Council of the Paris Peace Conference.

The King-Crane Commission report made grim reading, not only for Zionists, but also for British and French politicians planning to divide the area. The Americans found that the Arabs of Palestine wanted their homeland to remain part of Syria, with the Sherif Hussein's son Faisal as head of state. The King-Crane report warned against "the extreme Zionist program for Palestine of unlimited immigration of Jews looking finally to making Palestine a Jewish state." It concluded that, although some of the Zionist proposals were praiseworthy, implementing the Zionist plans as a whole would be unfair to the Arab majority and could only be effected by application of military force. The American report was ignored by Europe's "peacemakers," and not even made public until 1922.

The prescience of the King-Crane Commission was amply borne out by events throughout the Mandate period. There were widespread disturbances pitting Arab against Jew in 1920, 1921, and 1929. Finally, in 1936, an Arab strike against the British authorities led to three years of anarchy and Arab guerrilla warfare against the British forces. Of this period, it can be said that there were extremists and moderates in both the Arab and the Jewish camps. Among the Jewish settlers, the moderates, led by David Ben Gurion, followed the course charted by Zionist leader Chaim Weizmann who insisted on obtaining Zionist goals through cooperation with the British. They consistently prevailed over the Revisionists, led by Vladimir Jabotinsky, a brilliant orator who advocated militant methods to obtain a revision of the terms of the British Mandate as a first step toward the establishment of a Jewish state embracing all of Palestine and present-day Jordan. The struggle, though intense, was primarily political and involved only sporadic violence and bloodshed within the Jewish community.

On the Arab side, both the tactics and the results were different. The extremists were led by the Grand Mufti of Jerusalem, Al-Haj Muhammad Amin al-Husayni. Interestingly, the Grand Mufti owed his 1921 appointment, despite his prominent role in the 1920 anti-Jewish riots, to the first British Governor of Palestine, Sir Herbert Samuel, a Jew. The Grand Mufti's rivals were the relative moderates of the Nashashibi clan, and eventually also supporters of the Abd al-Hadi clan.

The result was a long and violent three-cornered struggle within the Arab community of Palestine, characterized by extensive intimidation and assassinations. Each bout generally concluded with victory for the extremist elements and the temporary flight from the country of many of the most responsible Palestinian leaders. After each upsurge of violence, Royal investigative commissions would arrive in Palestine. The Grand Mufti's response was not only a boycott of such commissions, but also intimidation of other Arabs invited to testify before them. He thus ensured that, although the Jewish case received a full hearing, the Arab case was presented only by well-meaning local British officials, not by the Arabs themselves. Despite what by western standards can only be described as perversely inept Arab leadership, the commissions generally returned to London calling for corrections to curb Zionist plans and protect the Arab community. But in London politicians were exposed to a patient and effective Zionist campaign to water down such recommendations, led as always by the brilliant and effective Dr. Weizmann, whose sincere devotion to his adopted British country was ultimately and dramatically demonstrated by the death of his RAF pilot son in World War II.

Israel today honors Theodor Herzl, the charismatic journalist who popularized Zionism; Chaim Weizmann, the patient and persistent scientist and political tactician; and David Ben Gurion, the stubbornly optimistic leader of its fight for independence, as its founding fathers. Yet knowledgeable Israelis should also offer up an occasional secret prayer of thanks to the Grand Mufti, Al-Haj Muhammad Amin al-Husayni, who topped even his own record for pre-war self-destructive leadership of the Palestinian community when World War II began by publicly supporting the losing side. When the United States entered the Palestine political scene after World War II, friends of Israel in the United States could identify the leader of the Palestinian Arabs as the devoted admirer of America's implacable enemy, Adolf Hitler.

But the contributions of Israel's Jewish founders and their Arab opponents aside, the ultimate responsibility for Israel's existence in its present form must be assigned to Hitler himself. At the time he assumed power in Germany, Jewish immigration into Palestine had slowed. Economic stagnation there was not only discouraging prospective immigrants to Israel, but was encouraging an even higher number of Jews to emigrate *from* Israel in search of better economic conditions. They either returned to the European countries from which they had come, or re-emigrated to the United States, where most of their relatives had originally traveled.

Only the sudden flight of Jews, first from Hitler's Germany, then from other European countries conquered or threatened by his legions, turned the immigration tide back in favor of Palestine's Jewish community. The flight from Germany also had another, equally important, effect. It neutralized the rising chorus of Jewish voices in virtually every western country expressing grave reservations about the effect that the establishment of a Jewish state would have on the hard-won status and rights of Jews in their many other homelands in both the Old and New Worlds. Particularly in the United States and England, where second-, third-, and fourth-generation Jews were not only successful in business, but had entered the various professions in numbers exceeding their percentage in the population, leaders within the Jewish community expressed their serious concern. If every Jew were now to have a second country, would he still be accepted as a loyal citizen or subject in the country of his birth? While some non-Zionist Jews opposed the establishment of a Jewish homeland on political grounds, others opposed it on purely religious grounds, believing that the Promised Land was intended to be a religious Kingdom of God, not a political state ruled by man.

Regardless of individual feelings, however, the Hitlerian persecutions followed by the ultimate horror of the Holocaust stilled almost all non-Zionist voices, first for the duration of the war and then, more permanently, as the State of Israel became immutable reality.

Meanwhile, the stream of Jews fleeing Nazi persecution and seeking to enter Palestine had become a flood. The Arab inhabitants remained thoroughly aroused, as they saw the lands and jobs they occupied disappearing at a faster rate than ever. The British, looking toward the war they saw approaching and fearing not only continued resistance by the Arab Palestinians but also the hostility of Muslims throughout the Arab world and Asia, once again set up a Royal Commission to investigate the problem. This time competing Palestinian elements combined forces to testify, and were supported by delegates from five independent Arab states. The results of the investigation were contained in a "White Paper" that did not suffer the usual London political dilution. It guided British policy throughout most of World War II. The "White Paper" laid down a final quota of 75,000 Jewish immigrants over five years, after which the doors to Palestine would be closed, not to be reopened except in the unlikely case of mutual consent by Palestine's Arab and Jewish communities. It also restricted land sales to Jews in some areas, and banned them completely in others. The lines were now drawn.

Inside Palestine the Revisionist movement of Jabotinsky gave rise after his death in 1940 to two secret armed organizations. The smaller of the two was known as Lehi by Israelis and as the Stern Gang by the British. Israel's present foreign minister, Yitzhak Shamir, played a leading role in the organization, which never really stopped fighting the British, even as Rommel's Afrika Korps rolled closer to Palestine. Among its accomplishments were the 1944 assassination in Egypt of Britain's wartime Minister of State, resident in Cairo, Lord Moyne; and, much later, the 1948 murder in Jerusalem of the U.N. mediator, Count Folke Bernadotte. The larger of the two secret Revisionist armies, the Irgun Zvai Leumi, led by Israel's present Prime Minister, Menachem Begin, remained quiescent until well after the Nazi tide had been turned back at Al Alamein. However, it then launched a terrorist war against the British authorities which continued with few interruptions until the British withdrew from Palestine.

Meanwhile the bulk of the Jewish population in Palestine, led by David Ben Gurion, followed the moderate course laid down by Weizmann and supported the British war effort. More than 43,000 Palestinian Jews enrolled for service with British forces by 1944, even before Britain agreed to set up a separate Jewish Brigade. It was in an action by British-trained Jewish soldiers against the Vichy French in Lebanon that the future Israeli General, Moshe Dayan, lost an eye.

On the Arab side there was a similar division. The Palestinian population, still demoralized after its revolt against the British, and stripped of much of its leadership either through death in action, assassination or exile, gave ostensible support to the British. By 1943 some 8,000 Palestinian Arabs were serving with the British forces. But at the same time the Grand Mufti made negative headlines as he moved from one Axis front to another. He started in 1941 with support for a short-lived revolt by Iraqi military officers supported by German aircraft, and continued almost to the end as he lent his moral support to German efforts in the Balkans to recruit Muslims to fight on the Russian front.

NOTES

1. Antonius, George, *The Arab Awakening*, London, 1938.
2. Wilson, Evan M., *Decision on Palestine: How the U.S. Came to Recognize Israel*, Hoover Institution Press, Stanford, California, 1979, p. 155.

CHAPTER III

President Roosevelt and the European Holocaust

"Your Majesty will recall that on previous occasions I communicated to you the attitude of the American Government toward Palestine and made clear our desire that no decision be taken with respect to the basic situation in that country without full consultation with both Arabs and Jews. Your Majesty will also doubtless recall that during our recent conversation I assured you that I would take no action, in my capacity as Chief of the Executive Branch of this Government, which might prove hostile to the Arab people. It gives me pleasure to renew to Your Majesty the assurances which you have received regarding the attitude of my Government and my own, as Chief Executive, with regard to the question of Palestine and to inform you that the policy of this Government in this respect is unchanged."[1]

President Roosevelt in letter to King Abd al-Aziz Ibn Saud
of Saudi Arabia, April 5, 1945

"Give me a chance, dear Manny, to talk with Stalin and Churchill. There are all sorts of schemes, crackpot and otherwise, being advanced. Perhaps some solution will come out of this whole matter. I don't want to see war between the one or two million people in Palestine and the whole Moslem world in that area—70 million."[2]

President Roosevelt in letter
to Representative Emmanuel Celler, 1945

"The Arabs, individually and collectively, regard the future of Palestine as a matter of life and death."[3]

Prince Abd al-Illah, Regent of Iraq,
in letter to President Roosevelt, 1945

21

"You know, Eleanor, I've seen so much now of the Middle East, when we get through here I believe I'd like to go there and live. I feel quite an expert. I believe I could help to straighten out the Near East."[4]

President Roosevelt, 1945

Midway in World War II the Palestine problem began to appear increasingly on the American domestic political scene. As war spread throughout Europe, the center of World Zionism necessarily moved to the United States. In 1942, at a conference of the main Zionist groups in New York, the "Biltmore program," named after the conference site, was adopted. It urged, in terms more militant than had ever been voiced publicly outside revisionist circles, that "the gates of Palestine be opened" and "that Palestine be established as a Jewish commonwealth integrated into the structure of the new democratic world." Ben Gurion adopted the militant American Zionist program, openly aimed at Jewish statehood for Palestine, as his own. The stage was set for Zionist entry into American politics.

It seems remarkable, in view of the importance of the "Jewish vote" in political calculations of that period, that there is so little mention of Palestine in the annals of the early years of President Franklin D. Roosevelt's incumbency. After the Biltmore program was adopted, however, and particularly during the last year of Roosevelt's life, the issue gained significance very rapidly.

As a former New York Democratic Party leader, Roosevelt had always maintained close ties with New York's Jewish community leaders. In a joint effort with one such friend, Morris Ernst, an attorney, he first encountered the increasing divergence between American leaders whose first concern was Zionism and those who were more concerned with the immediate rescue of Europe's endangered Jews. Very early in World War II Ernst went to London on Roosevelt's behalf to see if England and the Commonwealth countries would join the United States in taking a half million Jewish refugees. Ernst returned with the British agreement to match the U.S. in granting up to 150,000 visas each. Along with Canadian, Australian and some South American participation, at least 500,000 Jews could be saved.

According to Ernst, a week after he reported the success of his mission to President Roosevelt, the President informed him that the initiative was off, noting that "the dominant vocal Jewish leadership of America won't stand for it." Convinced that the President was wrong, Ernst then sought in vain to garner support himself among influential Jewish friends. Most declined to support the rescue initiative, he reported, on the grounds that it would undermine the Zionist movement. The story is related in detail by the anti-Zionist author, Alfred Lilienthal, in his 1979 book, *The Zionist Connection: What Price Peace?*[5]

By 1944, sentiment had crystallized sufficiently within the U.S. Jewish community so that pro-Zionist planks were included in both major party platforms. American diplomats sought to assure Arab leaders that these pro-Zionist statements were electoral politics, and not statements of U.S. foreign policy. Most

Arab leaders accepted these assurances at the time. After his re-election, however, President Roosevelt found himself holding off Zionist leaders who sought to nail down the campaign pledges in the form of a Palestine Resolution in Congress. Roosevelt said that such a resolution would undermine the Allied war effort in the Middle East. It was introduced nonetheless and defeated only after a personal appeal by Secretary of State Edward R. Stettinius Jr.

The pressure on President Roosevelt escalated rapidly on both sides. On February 14, 1945, en route home from the meeting at Yalta with Winston Churchill and Josef Stalin, the U.S. President met aboard a U.S. naval ship with Saudi Arabia's King Abd al-Aziz Ibn Saud. The King was an imposing figure, well over six feet tall and already a legend for the military audacity and political genius he had exerted to unify the Arabian peninsula under his banner. King Ibn Saud exacted assurances from the President that he would "do nothing to assist the Jews against the Arabs and would make no move hostile to the Arab people."

By the time he returned to the U.S., President Roosevelt apparently had undergone the conversion so familiar from the earlier days of Royal Commission investigators to Palestine, and subsequently from the reactions of Americans who have lived and worked in the Middle East. He told friends that in a few minutes of conversation with the Saudi monarch he learned more about the Palestine situation than he had learned in all of his previous life.

His new knowledge did not prevent him, however, from authorizing a U.S. Zionist leader to state that the President still favored a Jewish state and unrestricted Jewish immigration into Palestine. Then, as the Arabs reacted with angry questions, he authorized the Department of State to reaffirm his pledge to Ibn Saud and other Arab leaders that there would be prior consultation with the Arabs as well as the Jews before the U.S. took any action related to Palestine. Any maneuvering room between Jews and Arabs on Palestine was narrowing dramatically. His untimely death on April 12, 1945 left unresolved the ultimate stand he might have taken on that too-often-promised land.

The President's widow, Eleanor Roosevelt, later became such an ardent and articulate supporter of Israel that her actions as a U.S. delegate to the United Nations, bordering on intimidation of weak nations needing American support, would have provoked cries of outrage in the present international political climate. However, that was after her husband's death. During Roosevelt's lifetime the White House adviser in charge of Zionist concerns was David Niles. In the State Department the role was assumed by Under Secretary of State Sumner Wells. Wells, an intimate friend and former schoolmate of the President, was a Christian, but he supported the concept of a Jewish homeland for Palestine as ardently as did Niles and other American Jews in key positions at that time. Because there is no clear distinction between the actions that Niles and Wells took on the President's initiative, and on their own, not enough evidence exists to determine clearly how Roosevelt himself felt about the Zionist goals. Niles said in 1962 that had President Roosevelt lived longer, Israel probably would never have come into existence.

Whatever his feelings, Roosevelt was an adroit politician who knew how to keep himself publicly uncommitted. He also was sophisticated enough to know that America's Jewish leaders needed his support as much as he needed theirs.

That was not the case after President Roosevelt's death, less than a month before the May 8, 1945 Allied victory in Europe and four months before the victory over Japan. The hard decisions about Palestine devolved upon a man who was conspicuously ill-prepared for the role in terms both of his knowledge of the Middle East and of his domestic political support.

NOTES

1. Foreign Relations of the United States, 1945, Volume VIII, p. 698.
2. Wilson, Evan M., *Decision on Palestine—How the U.S. Came to Recognize Israel*, Hoover Institution Press, Stanford, 1979, p. 49.
3. *Ibid.*, p. 52.
4. Bishop, Jim, *FDR's Last Year, April 1944-April 1945*, Morrow, New York, 1974, p. 526.
5. Lilienthal, Alfred, *The Zionist Connection—What Price Peace?*, Middle East Perspective, Inc., New York, 1979, pp. 35-36.

CHAPTER IV

President Truman and the Creation of Israel

"The fate of the Jewish victims of Hitlerism was a matter of deep personal concern to me."

President Truman, 1955[1]

"As the pressure mounted, I found it necessary to give instructions that I did not want to be approached by any more spokesmen for the extreme Zionist cause."

President Truman, 1955[2]

"I'm sorry, gentlemen, but I have to answer to hundreds of thousands who are anxious for the success of Zionism: I do not have hundreds of thousands of Arabs among my constituents."

President Truman, Nov. 10, 1945[3]

"The inescapable conclusion of my examination of our Palestinian policy during these six years is that many of our present problems in the Middle East must be attributed to Truman's decisons regarding partition and recognition—decisions that have drastically affected American interests in the area to this day. I began this study with the opinion, which I had held since my days on the Palestine desk, that Truman's principal motivation had been humanitarian, but after examining all the evidence, including data that were not available to us in the State Department at the time, I have been forced reluctantly to the conclusion that on certain key occasions (October 1947 and May 1948) he was more influenced by domestic political considerations than by humanitarian ideals."

Evan M. Wilson, 1979[4]

"I am confident that the American people who spent their blood and their money freely to resist aggression, could not possibly support Zionist aggression against a friendly Arab country which has committed no crime except to believe firmly in those principles of justice and equality, for which the United Nations, including the United States, fought and for which both your predecessor and you exerted great efforts."[5]

King Abd al-Aziz Ibn Saud in Oct. 15, 1946 letter to President Truman

"We do not wish at all to believe that Zionist influence in America can reverse facts so as to make right wrong and wrong right."[6]

Prime Minister Nuri al-Said of Iraq in note to U.S. Charge d'Affaires, Baghdad, 1945

"One injury cannot be removed by another even more harmful... In this case we shall be face to face with the Zionist Nazism against the Arabs instead of a German Nazism against the Jews."[7]

Syrian Ministry of Foreign Affairs note to American Legation, Damascus, 1945

As a freshman Vice President under a President in his fourth term, Harry Truman was not likely to know what his predecessor really thought about the struggle shaping up in Palestine. Yet, when he succeeded to the Presidency, Truman was conscientious about accepting the responsibility that was thrust upon him. He was a stubbornly decisive man, and this quality has enshrined him in the minds of Israelis as perhaps their truest friend among American Presidents. At the same time, probably no American President has ever disregarded expert advice so thoroughly and with such relish. In acting to establish and later to support the Jewish State in Palestine, Truman ignored the objections of his Secretary of Defense, James Forrestal, and three of his Secretaries of State: James Byrnes, General George Marshall, and Dean Acheson.

With the war over, and Jewish terrorism against British forces and in support of illegal Jewish immigration increasing, Truman lent himself to what could only be construed by disgusted British observers as cheap shots aimed at a war-drained great power still trying to maintain some semblance of law and order in a land wracked with communal violence between Jews and Arabs.

He pressed the British hard to allow an additional 100,000 Jews to enter Palestine from Europe. Given America's horror over the Nazi concentration camps, it would be ridiculous to attribute this solely to a desire for Jewish electoral support. A somewhat less charitable view must be taken, however, of the simultaneous actions of various American Zionists. In conversations with the leaders of America's wartime ally, these Americans strongly implied that a failure to raise the immigration quota would greatly lessen Britain's chances of post-war cooperation with the United States. It was, unfortunately, not the last instance when private but influential American citizens used the American treasury as both carrot and stick to convince reluctant foreign nations to support the interests of the Jewish State.

President Truman's next decision was far less understandable from a humanitarian point of view. When Britain set May 15, 1948 as the date for its withdrawal from Palestine, Truman decided to support a United Nations plan to partition it between its 1,300,000 Arab and 650,000 Jewish occupants. The plan was a masterpiece of gerrymandering. It awarded 56.4 per cent of the country to the Jews, who comprised 33 per cent of the population and owned less than 6 percent of the land. The plan to give such a huge portion of Palestine to a minority of its inhabitants made for a strange division of population between the two entities. Even after partition, the Jewish portion would contain a very large number of Arabs, a certain recipe for trouble, while the Arab portion would contain almost none of the Jewish population. Despite virtually unanimous opposition to the plan from State and Defense Department experts on the Middle East, President Truman put United States support behind it. When it appeared that the plan could not obtain the necessary two-thirds vote in the UN General Assembly, even with U.S. support, private Americans lobbied small and weak states, particularly countries from the under-developed world which were heavily dependent upon U.S. investment, aid and good will, to support the partition.

General Carlos Romulo, a staunch supporter of the United States through the dark years of World War II in the Pacific, headed the Philippine delegation to the UN. He spoke out against the plan and finally returned to his country rather than vote for it. But the newly-independent Philippine government, dependent upon U.S. support while it rebuilt its war-destroyed economy, had received a telegram supporting the partition from 26 pro-Zionist U.S. Senators. It ordered its UN delegation to support the plan. The same telegram was reported to have changed four votes to yes and seven votes from no to abstentions. Other countries reported both blackmail and bribery attempts in the campaign that elicited a final vote of 33 to 13 in favor of the resolution.

Shocked by the bloody conflict that broke out in Palestine between the Arab and Jewish communities after UN adoption of the partition plan, President Truman gave closer attention to his foreign affairs experts who had accurately predicted this tragic turn of events. When Britain refused to take any measures to implement the partition and other Security Council members expressed similar opposition, the State Department began searching for an alternative plan. Having obtained President Truman's agreement, the Department now advocated postponing partition in favor of a UN trusteeship over Palestine to commence when the British withdrew.

However, neither Secretary of State Marshall nor the head of the U.S. delegation to the UN, former Senator Warren Austin, were aware of the drama taking place in the White House. In his *Memoirs*, published in 1955, President Truman described the atmosphere at the time:

"The matter had been placed in the United Nations and, true to my conviction that the United Nations had to be made to work, I had confidence that a solution would be found there."[8]

According to Merle Miller, author of *Plain Speaking: An Oral Biography of Harry Truman*, pressure from the various American Zionist groups was intense. Mr. Truman told Miller:

"Well, there had never been anything like it before, and there wasn't after. Not even when I fired MacArthur, there wasn't. And I said, I issued orders that I wasn't going to see anyone who was an extremist for the Zionist cause, and I didn't care who it was . . . I had to keep in mind that much as I favored a homeland for the Jews, there were simply other matters awaiting . . . that I had to worry about."[9]

Then on March 13 the President received a telephone call from Eddie Jacobson, his close friend from World War I army service and from a haberdashery partnership they had once had in Missouri. Mr Jacobson said he was in Washington and wanted to see the President. Mr. Truman has described to Miller what followed:

"I said to him, 'Eddie, I'm always glad to see old friends, but there's one thing you've got to promise me. I don't want you to say a *word* about what's going on over there in the Middle East. Do you promise?' And he did."

But, when Mr. Jacobson was ushered into the Oval Office, Mr. Truman recalled:

"Great tears were running down his cheeks and I took one look at him, and I said, 'Eddie, you son of a bitch, you promised me you wouldn't say a word about what's going on over there.' And he said, 'Mr. President, I haven't said a word, but every time I think of the homeless Jews, homeless for thousands of years, and I think about Dr. Weizmann, I start crying. I can't help it. He's an old man, and he's spent his whole life working for a homeland for the Jews, and now he's sick, and he's in New York and wants to see you. And every time I think about it, I can't help crying.'

"I said, 'Eddie, that's enough. That's the last word.'

"And so we talked about this and that, but every once in a while a big tear would roll down his cheek. At one point he said something about how I felt about old Andy Jackson, and he was crying again. He said he knew he wasn't supposed to, but that's how he felt about Weizmann.

"I said, 'Eddie, you son of a bitch, I ought to have you thrown right out of here for breaking your promise; you knew damn good and well I couldn't stand seeing you cry.'

"And he kind of smiled at me, still crying, though, and he said, 'Thank you, Mr. President,' and he left.

"After he was gone, I picked up the phone and called the State Department, and I told them I was going to see Weizmann. Well, you should have heard the carrying-on."[10]

Five days later, on March 18, Dr. Weizmann came into the White House through the east gate for an unannounced visit during which President Truman apparently assured him that the U.S. was supporting partition. The next day,

Ambassador Austin, proceeding with the policy previously agreed to by the President, read a statement calling for a postponement of the partition resolution and the substitution of a UN trusteeship over Palestine.

President Truman stated in his diary entry for that day:

"The State Department pulled the rug from under me today. . . . In Key West, or en route there from St. Croix, I approved the speech and statement of policy by Senator Austin to the UN meeting. This morning I find that the State Department has reversed my Palestine policy. The first I know about it is what I see in the paper. Isn't that hell? I am now in the position of a liar and a double-crosser. . . ."

There has been a great deal of controversy about this ever since, with partisans of Israel, and of President Truman, claiming that he was the victim of treachery by lower echelon officers at the State Department. However, as the documents agreed to by the President have been declassified over the years, it has become apparent that a postponement of the partition plan and substitution of a UN trusteeship was suggested by the State Department and agreed to by the President. Apparently his concern was over the fact that it contradicted statements he subsequently made during the two private visits to the White House, one by his former haberdashery partner and one by the leader of the World Zionist Organization.

The fact that President Truman could approve a policy, fly into a rage when it was officially announced, and later blame his rage not on the substance of the announcement but on its timing, indicates that he faced the same problem that had begun inexorably closing in on President Roosevelt in the weeks prior to his death. The aspirations of American Zionists, which by the end of World War II had become the aspirations of a great majority of American Jewish voters, simply were not compatible with American interests in the world in general and in the Middle East in particular. Further, and this apparently was understood at the time only by American diplomats, and the soldiers, educators, and other Americans who had lived and worked in the Middle East, these Zionist aspirations were incompatible with the principles for which the United States had stood from the time of the American Revolution. The great humanitarian impulse to settle Europe's surviving Jews in Palestine clashed directly with President Wilson's insistence that every international question should be settled "upon the basis of the free acceptance of that settlement by the people immediately concerned."

President Truman's Secretary of State knew that two thirds of the "immediately concerned" people in Palestine were Arabs. The President's domestic political advisers were only interested in the fact that nearly all of America's Jewish community also felt "immediately concerned," and these Americans could vote, make speeches, write editorials, and provide or withhold campaign contributions.

President Truman was fully aware of both dimensions of the problem. As early as 1945, a group of foreign service officers who headed U.S. missions in the Middle East was brought to Washington to report directly to the President on the problems his policies were creating for the entire U.S. position there. The U.S. Minister to

Saudi Arabia, Colonel William Eddy, recounts that the President listened to their individual reports, then dismissed them with the words:

"I am sorry, gentlemen, but I have to answer to hundreds of thousands who are anxious for the success of Zionism. I do not have hundreds of thousands of Arabs among my constituents."[11]

It was certainly this concern that determined the President's policy after the Weizmann meeting and the blow-up over Ambassador Austin's speech. Weizmann followed up his meeting with a letter to President Truman on April 9, 1948 urging that partition be implemented without delay because "the choice of our people is between statehood and extermination." David Niles, who had been President Roosevelt's White House liaison with Jewish groups and who had remained in that position under President Truman, now found a strong backer in Clark Clifford, who already was mapping out the strategy for the Truman 1948 re-election campaign. Clifford had been shocked at the results of a special Congressional election in the Bronx. In a district where 55 per cent of the voters were Jewish, the Democratic Party candidate had lost. Among the campaigners for the victorious American Labor Party candidate had been Truman's predecessor as Vice President, Henry Wallace, who had declared that "Truman still talks Jewish but acts Arab."

The UN trusteeship plan was foundering, and Clifford sensed that U.S. support for it had cost Truman domestic political support. Clifford's strategy for recouping that domestic electoral support was to have President Truman recognize the new Jewish state even before the partition plan went into effect with the May 15, 1948 withdrawal of the British from Palestine. At a meeting called to discuss the subject on May 12, Secretary of State Marshall vehemently opposed premature recognition of a state that had not even defined its own future boundaries. He not only refused to endorse the idea but added some angry words which are surely unprecedented in a conversation between a President and his Secretary of State. In General Marshall's own memorandum of the conversation, he noted:

"I said bluntly that if the President were to follow Mr. Clifford's advice and if in the elections I were to vote, I would vote against the President."

No decision was made at that meeting, but on May 13 Dr. Weizmann wrote the President a letter asking that the U.S. "promptly recognize the Provisional Government of the new Jewish State." The following day Clifford, not the Secretary of State, informed Eliahu Epstein, the Washington representative of the Jewish Agency for Palestine, that the White House would need a formal request for recognition in order to take the desired action. Epstein, who was shortly to change his name to Eliahu Elath and become Israel's first Ambassador to the U.S., explained that the request could not be made until the new state came into existence at midnight, May 14, in the Middle East, which would be 6 p.m., Washington time. Nevertheless, a draft request was prepared in Washington. Since the Jewish Agency representative did not yet know the name of the state to be, it was referred to simply as "the Jewish State." While an Agency representative was driving to the White House with the request, another Agency employe heard on the radio that the state was to be named "Israel." This second employe sped to the White House and in pen substituted "State of Israel" for "the Jewish State" on the request for recognition.

Secretary Marshall was informed late in the afternoon of the President's decision to recognize Israel; Ambassador Austin was notified at 5:40 p.m. At 6 p.m. the British Mandate expired. At 6:01 Israel came into existence. And at 6:11 the U.S. announced its recognition of the new state.

There are many postscripts to this amazing sequence of events. It has been reported that Secretary of State Marshall had to send his then Under Secretary, Dean Rusk, to New York to talk the U.S. delegation to the UN out of resigning en masse. Ambassador Austin retreated to his hotel room rather than appear with the delegation he headed when it announced U.S. recognition of Israel. Even Eleanor Roosevelt, the Jewish State's most active partisan on the delegation, later wrote to Secretary Marshall to complain that the manner of U.S. recognition had caused "consternation" among the other UN delegations.

Mrs. Roosevelt's concern about "consternation" among other UN delegates in New York illustrates the innocence of many active American partisans of the new state, who had never doubted that they were pushing the United States along a humanitarian course. In the Middle East the realities were clearer. At the time of the UN vote in favor of partition, when Jews were dancing in the streets all over Palestine, David Ben Gurion had written:

"I cannot be among the dancers. I am like someone in mourning at a wedding. I am filled with an awful fear at the sacrifice that awaits our people."[12]

By May 14, 1948, when Ben Gurion arose before the new nation's leaders in a small auditorium in the Tel Aviv Museum of Art to proclaim the birth of the new state, deaths from fighting between Arab and Jewish irregulars were already in the hundreds, and the armies of four Arab states were poised for an invasion aimed at eliminating the new state by force.

The outcome is well known. Jewish settlers, under the leadership of officers trained and seasoned by service with the various Jewish armed groups and with British forces in World War II, fought the multi-pronged but badly coordinated Arab attacks. Using motley but sizable collections of secretly stockpiled arms, they gained more territory than they lost before running short of ammunition.

A truce arranged by the UN on June 11 ended after a month when the Arabs refused to extend it. But it had given the Israelis sufficient time to bring in a large number of new fighters. Some were foreign volunteers with essential military skills, others simply raw manpower hurriedly culled from the refugee camps of Europe. These reinforcements were flown or ferried to Israel in a clandestine air and sea fleet assembled from surplus and "liberated" military equipment from the battlefields of Europe, and manned by demobilized Jewish airmen, sailors and soldiers from virtually every Allied army. Equally important, the Israelis bought arms and ammunition from many countries, particularly Czechoslovakia. The Czech deal was brokered by the Soviet Union, which at the time had suddenly become not only a faithful supporter of the new Jewish state, but also a considerably more effective one than the United States, which was futilely seeking to enforce an arms embargo on all parties to the conflict.

The embargo seemed most effective, however, against the Arabs. They did not use the brief truce period to resupply and regroup their strained armies or to train the Palestinian guerrillas, who at the time functioned more as a mob than an army. When all-out fighting resumed, Israel had between 60,000 and 100,000 fighters armed and ready to face between 35,000 and 45,000 Arab regular troops. The superior Israeli numbers and the intensive preparations during the truce rapidly paid off during the next ten days of fighting.

This time, when the United Nations imposed a ceasefire, the territory controlled by the Israeli fighters had been significantly enlarged beyond the original partition boundaries. Jerusalem, which under the partition resolution was to remain under international control, now was about evenly divided between Israeli and Jordanian forces. Jordan's largely British-officered Arab Legion, which during the fighting had refrained from moving into areas given to Israel under the partition plan, now remained in place after the fighting ended. This gave Jordan *de facto* control over all of what had been planned as the Palestinian portion of the partitioned country, with the exception of the Gaza area which now was controlled by Egypt. Thus both the planned international area and the planned Palestinian portions of the partitioned land remained under Israeli, Jordanian or Egyptian control.

Meanwhile, some 750,000 Palestinians, having fled before or been forced out at gunpoint by Israeli soldiers, were barred from returning to their homes inside the extended Israeli lines. Now, as refugees without homes or a country of their own, most found themselves in camps living under even more primitive conditions than had the post-war Jewish refugees of Europe, to alleviate whose suffering President Truman had helped to create the State of Israel.

NOTES

1. Truman, Harry S, *Memoirs*, Doubleday, Garden City, New York, 1955, vol. II *Years of Trial and Hope*, p. 132.
2. *Ibid*, p. 160.
3. Eddy, William A., *F. D. R. Meets Ibn Saud*, American Friends of the Middle East, New York, 1954.
4. Wilson, Evan M., *Decision on Palestine: How the U.S. Came to Recognize Israel*, Hoover Institution Press, Stanford, 1979, p. 149.
5. *Ibid.*, p. 100.
6. *Ibid.*, p. 65.
7. *Ibid.*, p. 65.
8. Truman, Harry S, *Memoirs*, Doubleday, Garden City, New York, 1955, vol. II *Years of Trial and Hope*, p. 157.

9. Miller, Merle, *Plain Speaking—An Oral Biography of Harry S Truman*, Berkley Books, New York, 1974, p. 234.

10. *Ibid.* (pp. 234-235).

11. Eddy, William A., *F. D. R. Meets Ibn Saud*, American Friends of the Middle East, New York, 1954.

12. Derogy, Jacques and Carmel, Hesi, *The Untold History of Israel*, Grove Press, New York, 1979, pp. 75-76.

CHAPTER V

President Truman's Second Term and Post-Partum Depression

"Perhaps they were wrong in pursuing this aim, perhaps their efforts were bound to create new and intractable problems. However, several decades ago Zionism moved out of the realm of the history of ideas, good, bad or indifferent, into the field of action. It has resulted in the birth of a nation to the joy of some and the distress of others."[1]

Walter Laqueur, 1972

"Every Israeli knows in his heart of hearts what injustice to the Palestinians the establishment of Israel has involved."

Walid Khalidi, American University of Beirut, 1981

"The very real admiration and respect which all Arabs held for America is evaporating rapidly and may soon disappear altogether, along with our many mutual interests and cooperation."

Saudi Arabian Foreign Minister Prince
(and later King) Faisal, 1945

"It is no exaggeration to say that our relations with the entire Arab world have never recovered from the events of 1947-48 when we sided with the Jews against the Arabs and advocated a solution in Palestine which went contrary to self-determination as far as the majority population of the country was concerned."[2]

Evan M. Wilson, 1979

34

It is ironic, but perhaps fitting, that after a victorious 1948 election campaign in which his seminal role in the creation of Israel was a major asset, President Truman spent his second term worrying about the 750,000 Palestinian refugees, who now considerably outnumbered the Jewish refugees who had been in Europe's post-war displaced persons camps. As the Israelis stoutly resisted UN resolutions to withdraw from territory captured in their war of independence, or to repatriate the Palestinian refugees who had fled or been ejected from their homes, President Truman's impatience grew.

In May 1948, he told the Israelis that if they persisted in their refusals, "the U.S. government will regretfully be forced to the conclusion that a revision of its attitude toward Israel has become unavoidable." The State Department advised him to pressure Israel to return to the partition lines by halting U.S. technical, financial and diplomatic assistance and lifting the tax exempt status of Jewish organizations raising funds for Israel. Nevertheless, in a foretaste of what every subsequent American President has at some time experienced, Israel formally rejected the American request. Also anticipating diplomatic experiences to come, the American Ambassador to Israel then explained that the tone of the President's note had "embittered Israeli opinion" and that Israeli concessions on the refugees might only be possible if the request were "not put in the form of a demand." The border adjustments, the Ambassador added, were not possible at all. Truman made no more demands, but no Israeli concessions on refugees followed.

Many of those who worked with, or against, President Truman have eloquently summed up their feelings about his Middle East decisions. In his book *Plain Speaking*, based on President Truman's dictated reminiscences, Merle Miller records a memorable event in 1949:

"The Chief Rabbi of Israel came to see the President and he told him, 'God put you in your mother's womb so that you could be the instrument to bring about the rebirth of Israel after two thousand years.' At that, great tears started rolling down Harry Truman's cheeks."[3]

In his book, *Present at the Creation: My Years at the State Department*, Dean Acheson revealed his own feelings:

"I did not share the President's views on the Palestine solution to the pressing and desperate plight of great numbers of displaced Jews in Eastern Europe. The numbers that could be absorbed by Arab Palestine without creating a grave problem would be inadequate, and to transform the country into a Jewish state capable of receiving a million or more immigrants would vastly exacerbate the political problem and imperil not only American but all Western interests in the Near East. From Justice Brandeis, whom I revered, and Felix Frankfurter, my intimate friend, I had learned to understand, but not to share, the mystical emotion of the Jews to return to Palestine and end the Diaspora. In urging Zionism as an American Government policy, they had allowed, so I thought, their emotion to obscure the totality of American interests."[4]

In a letter to the anti-Zionist author, Alfred Lilienthal, in 1977, former Secretary of State Dean Rusk said of Mr. Truman:

"He, as all Americans, had been deeply shocked by the full exposure of the frightful atrocities of the Hitler regime. Mr. Truman was strongly impelled toward a homeland for the Jews where such things could not be repeated, and this view was politically reinforced by a large, active and dedicated group in this country who were working very hard on behalf of a Jewish State in Palestine. It would be naive to think that these domestic political considerations played no part in Mr. Truman's own thinking and decisions."[5]

In his *Study of History,* British historian Arnold Toynbee also provides a mixed assessment:

"The Missourian politician-philanthropist's eagerness to combine expediency with charity by assisting the wronged and suffering Jews would appear to have been untempered by any sensitive awareness that he was thereby abetting the infliction of wrongs and sufferings on the Arabs."[6]

Britain's post-war Prime Minister, Earl Clement Attlee, was not at all charitable in two recorded comments after he left office. He said that "U.S. policy in Palestine was molded by the Jewish vote and by party contributions of several big Jewish firms," and "there is no Arab vote in America."

Perhaps the best explanation of the era is provided by President Truman himself. In a memorandum to his Jewish affairs adviser, Harry Niles, on May 13, 1947, a year to the day before his decision to recognize Israel against the advice of his foreign and military affairs advisers, he wrote:

"We could have settled this Palestine thing if U.S. politics had been kept out of it. Terror and Silver [U.S. Zionist Leader Rabbi Abba Hillel Silver] are the contributing cause of some, if not all, of our troubles."[7]

NOTES

1. Laqueur, Walter Z., *A History of Zionism,* Holt, Rinehart and Winston, New York, 1972, p. xv.
2. Wilson, Evan M., *Decision on Palestine: How the U.S. Came to Recognize Israel,* Hoover Institution Press, Stanford, 1979, p. 154.
3. Miller, Merle, *Plain Speaking—An Oral Biography of Harry S Truman,* Berkley Books, New York, 1974, p. 236.
4. Acheson, Dean, *Present at the Creation: My Years in the State Department,* Norton, New York, 1969, p. 169.
5. Lilienthal, Alfred M., *The Zionist Connection: What Price Peace?* Middle East Perspective, Inc., New York, 1978, p. 96.
6. Toynbee, Arnold J., *A Study of History,* Oxford University Press, New York, 1956, vol. XIII, p. 308.
7. Lilienthal, Alfred M., *The Zionist Connection: What Price Peace?* Page 95, from Truman to Niles memorandum dated May 13, 1947 in files of Harry S Truman Library, Independence, Missouri.

CHAPTER VI

President Eisenhower
and the Buildup to Suez

*"I just can't figure out what the Israelis think they're up to.
. . . Maybe they're thinking they just can't survive without more land. . . . But I don't
see how they can survive without coming to some honorable and peaceful terms with
the whole Arab World that surrounds them. . . .*[1]

President Dwight D. Eisenhower, 1956

*"During the campaign, some political figures kept talking of our failure to 'back
Israel.' If the administration had been incapable of withstanding that kind of advice in
an election year, could the United Nations thereafter have retained any influence
whatsoever?"*[2]

President Dwight D. Eisenhower, 1965

*"With the exception of the Eisenhower Administration, which virtually compelled
Israel's withdrawal from Sinai after the 1956 war, American Presidents, and to an
even greater degree Senators and Representatives, have been subjected to recurrent
pressures from what has come to be known as the Israel lobby. For the most part they
have been responsive, and for reasons not always related either to personal conviction
or careful reflection on the national interest."*[3]

Senator Charles McC. Mathias, Jr., 1981

The election of General of the Armies Dwight D. Eisenhower to the Presidency
brought more than a change of parties to the White House. After the Allied victory
in World War II, Eisenhower had accepted the Presidency of Columbia University
and returned to civilian life. But as the U.S. and Western Europe grew increasingly
fearful of Soviet intentions, America's hero of World War II returned to Europe to
organize NATO and its defenses. By the time this task was completed, he was so

popular with the American public that he could have had the Presidential nomination of either party. He chose the Republicans, who then passed over their expected nominee, Senator Taft, to hand the General the nomination. He easily defeated the Democratic candidate, Adlai Stevenson. As a result, when he entered the White House, Eisenhower was his own man, with a personal political base so secure he could not seriously be challenged by any single interest group. Eisenhower was also a West Pointer who had come up the peacetime army career ladder. Unlike his predecessor, he preferred to delegate authority, and he listened carefully to those who did the staff work before he made any decision. Strangely, these traits almost brought about a complete change in U.S. Middle Eastern policy, but they eventually resulted in the undoing of Eisenhower's plans for the Middle East.

While Eisenhower was accepting the Presidential nomination in July, 1952, Egypt was undergoing a revolution. Given the predelictions of its playboy King, the revolution probably was inevitable. But Egypt's 1948 debacle in Palestine was, at the very least, the catalyst for a coup by army officers humiliated at the Egyptian defeat, and outraged by the high-level sloth and corruption it had revealed. In 1954 Colonel Gamal Abd al-Nasser, the driving force behind the original coup, deposed its ostensible leader, General Mohammad Naguib, and assumed power himself. To the credit of Arab affairs experts both in the United States and in Israel, they had early on picked the handsome, fiery colonel as the Egyptian to watch. In each country secret chains of events were set in motion, but at least one of the Israeli plans was diametrically opposed to the plan of the United States.

Eisenhower understood the unique potential for flexibility of a charismatic leader with a strong political base. Assured by his Middle East advisers that Nasser was such a leader, he set out to woo the Egyptian leader through Kermit Roosevelt, grandson of President Theodore Roosevelt. To keep the press off the track, U.S. and Egyptian intelligence channels were used. The idea was to make it clear to this Arab reformer that the U.S. was ready to adjust its Middle East policies to Nasser's new politics if the Egyptian leader was willing to make peace with Israel and thus to remove at one stroke both the greatest single strain on Egypt's budget and the only serious irritant in U.S.-Arab relations.

Meanwhile, without the knowledge of the United States, several operations in Israel were initiated at the same time. One of them was eventually destined to become a cancer in the Israeli body politic, considered by some to be "Israel's Dreyfus case." At the time there were two main forces in Israeli politics. The dominant figure was David Ben Gurion, Israel's first Prime Minister, who had originally proclaimed the independence of the Jewish State and whose Old-Testament patriarchal mien was the symbol of Israel's war of independence and the years of defiance that followed. Throughout his career, Ben Gurion had moved steadily away from the moderation and flexibility of Chaim Weizmann toward the hardline stance that had become so familiar to Arab opponents and Western mediators. As Prime Minister, he stubbornly refused to accept or comply with repeated UN resolutions calling on Israel to return the territory it had seized in the 1948 fighting, and repatriate or compensate the Arab refugees who had fled or been expelled. Faced with Palestinian guerrilla activities from Gaza and the West Bank, he backed a policy of strong reprisals.

The other force was Moshe Sharett, Ben Gurion's Foreign Minister in 1953, who then succeeded him as Prime Minister during one of the convulsions that increasingly wracked Israel's ruling coalition of labor and non-communist leftist parties. Sharett believed that a policy of Israeli moderation in the face of Arab guerrilla attacks, Israeli compensation of Arab refugees, and an understanding with Egypt on boundaries could ultimately bring about a peaceful acceptance of Israel by its Arab neighbors.

First Ben Gurion, and later Sharett, attempted to contact the new Egyptian leader. With Ben Gurion's blessing, Israel's military hero, Yigael Allon, then a private citizen, had sought to re-establish communication with Nasser. Allon had first met Nasser after the UN ceasefire in 1948, when Allon's troops surrounded and held in place in the Falluja pocket a large Egyptian force which included Nasser. Subsequently, when Sharett became Prime Minister, he also attempted to make indirect contacts with Nasser, hoping that they might eventually lead, if not to face-to-face negotiations between the two leaders, at least to serious discussions between their representatives.

Unknown to the U.S., however, and apparently unknown to Sharett as well, the Israeli Army Intelligence organization—which at that time operated independently of the Mossad, Israel's equivalent of the CIA—was laying the groundwork for its own secret plan. Both before and since Nasser's time, the greatest concerns of many hardline Israeli leaders have focused not on the radical Arabs, but rather on moderate Arab leaders who have sought to establish or maintain close ties with the West. Obviously, if the West ever reached an agreement with the Arabs at the expense of Israel's territorial ambitions, it would be with just such a moderate Arab leader. Therefore the efforts by the Eisenhower administration to cultivate the charismatic Egyptian colonel had not gone unnoticed in Israeli intelligence circles. Nor had the forthcoming British-Egyptian negotiations on the withdrawal of British forces from the Suez canal, scheduled for July 1954.

Two Israeli journalists, Jacques Derogy and Hesi Carmel,[4] relate that early in 1954 Israeli Army Intelligence conceived a plan to attack British personnel inside Jordan. The purpose was to increase suspicion between Britain and Jordan, or Britain and Egypt (which would have been blamed for the attack), or possibly both. Shortly afterward, the same organization initiated a similar plan in Egypt, activating two networks of resident Egyptian Jews. These young people had been recruited in Egypt, secretly trained in Israel, and then sent back to Cairo and Alexandria to await orders to carry out acts of sabotage in case of war between Egypt and Israel. The networks were instructed to explode small incendiary bombs in American installations in Egypt, presumably to set off a chain of mutual recriminations that might spoil the budding American-Egyptian courtship. After completing the sabotage of American installations, the networks were also to bomb various public places in Cairo and Alexandria in order to exacerbate tensions between Nasser and the Muslim Brotherhood, which had backed the ousted General Naguib, and thus establish a general climate of Egyptian instability during the British-Egyptian Canal Zone negotiations.

The plan was set in motion by an Israeli spymaster sent to Cairo posing as a German businessman. On July 14, while Alexandrian Egyptians were observing Bastille Day as a symbol of the overthrow of Monarchist tyranny, incendiary devices were planted in U.S. Information Service libraries and other U.S. government institutions open to the public in both Cairo and Alexandria. A week later, on July 23, during Egypt's national day celebrations, Israeli agents sought to repeat their success with explosions in the Cairo railway station and in movie theaters in Cairo and Alexandria. In Alexandria, however, an incendiary device went off prematurely in the pocket of one of the young Egyptian Jews, Philippe Nathanson, as he stood in front of a theater and he was seized by the police. Within days the members of both the Cairo and Alexandria sabotage networks, along with one additional unaffiliated Israeli spy, were seized. Only the Israeli spymaster escaped the country.

Though the plan misfired, the denouement was rapid, and it succeeded beyond the wildest dreams of its Israeli planners in extinguishing all hopes of moderation, but in Israel rather than in Egypt. The arrested provocateurs were brought to trial in Cairo on December 11, 1954. They included an attractive Egyptian Jewish girl, Victorine Ninio, who was reported to have twice tried to commit suicide while under interrogation and who was brought, wounded, into the courtroom. The Egyptian press reported that the unaffiliated spy, Max Bennett, had been more successful in avoiding interrogation. He had killed himself with a rusty nail pried from his cell door. As the trial opened, the Israeli press seethed with indignation at what it assumed was an Egyptian show trial on baseless charges intended to terrorize Egypt's remaining Jewish community.

British and French politicians, assuming the same thing, begged Nasser to stop the proceedings, but to no avail. Most indignant of all was the first moderate Prime Minister in Israel's history, Moshe Sharett. This, Israeli journalists maintain, was because when the plan failed, the Israeli Army Intelligence chief, Colonel Benjamin Gibli, had so carefully covered his tracks that Sharett, too, at first believed the accused Egyptian Jews to be innocent. There were others who knew the truth, apparently including General Moshe Dayan, Gibli's immediate superior, who seems to have assisted Gibli to assure that ultimate blame for the operation would fall on Dayan's own direct superior, Defense Minister Pinchas Lavon.

On December 12, 1954, the second day of the Cairo trial, Sharett angrily denounced "these calumnies designed to strike at the Jews of Egypt." Later, when death sentences were handed down, Sharett publicly vowed, "We will not negotiate in the shadow of the gallows." At that moment at least four separate efforts, including one initiated by President Eisenhower, to initiate direct or indirect contacts between Colonel Nasser and Israel's heretofore moderate Prime Minister Sharett started to unravel. By the time the Prime Minister and others who apparently had been ignorant of the plot realized that there was substance to the Egyptian charges, the damage was done. Egyptians, angry at the seeming hypocrisy of the Israeli Prime Minister's scathing denials and never dreaming that he truly was uninformed, had also begun to break off contacts.

By January 20, two of the conspirators had been hanged in Egypt and hopes among moderates for an Israeli-Egyptian rapprochement had died with them. The plot and coverup are known as the "Lavon Affair" to western journalists, who have given it virtually no American press coverage in all the years since; and as the "Haessek Habish" or "Ugly Affair" to Israeli journalists, who have written thousands of words about the coverup, but very few words to reveal that the original act was a secret Israeli provocation against American diplomatic and cultural offices in Egypt.

The affair lingered on for a decade as a running sore in Israeli political life. Pinchas Lavon, the Defense Minister who had been hounded from office with forged documents and perjured testimony, was eventually rehabilitated. His ultimate persecutor, the by-then embittered and irascible David Ben Gurion, retired for the last time from public office in 1964. Four years later, the surviving four Jewish provocateurs, including Victorine Ninio and the luckless Nathanson, were handed over by the Egyptians to the Israelis as part of the general exchange of prisoners which took place after the 1967 Arab-Israeli war. Their arrival in Israel received low-key coverage in the Israeli press, and virtually none in the United States.

Even in the wake of the bitter exchange of recriminations in December 1954 and January 1955, some members of the Eisenhower administration hoped that the situation could be salvaged. However, after the disgrace and resignation of Lavon, on February 17 Ben Gurion himself replaced him as Defense Minister in the government of Ben Gurion's rival, Prime Minister Sharett. Ben Gurion immediately initiated drastic acts of retaliation for guerrilla raids, including a massive Israeli incursion into the Gaza strip and the assassination by letter bomb of an Egyptian military officer in Gaza who was said to be directing the guerrillas. The political fallout from the Lavon Affair had opened the way for Ben Gurion's policy of ten eyes for an eye, and ten teeth for a tooth, which delivered the *coup de grace* to Sharett's dream of Egyptian-Israeli negotiations.

Shaken by the massive Israeli raid into Gaza, which he had been powerless to stop, Nasser turned to the U.S. with a request for $27 million in arms. The State Department, mindful of an agreement by Britain, France, and the United States in 1950 to maintain an arms balance between Israel and the Arabs, and confident that Egypt was short of funds, informed Nasser that he would have to pay for the arms in cash.

"Our attitude," President Eisenhower subsequently wrote, "may, with the advantage of hindsight, appear to have been unrealistic."[5]

It was. The Russians, with astonishing speed, moved into the breach with an offer of their own. They were able to offer arms rapidly, and on barter rather than cash terms, because after the death of Josef Stalin, Moscow had adopted a new political policy. Rather than working through communist parties abroad, the Soviets sought to encourage collaboration with countries which might be pulled out, or kept out, of western alliances. This policy was to be followed regardless of the political system of the collaborating country, or of the status of local communists.

President Nasser did nothing about the Soviet offer for a time. In September 1955, however, when the Israelis jarred him with another strong and successful raid on an Egyptian outpost, he made good his threat of the previous June and accepted the Russian proposal. He struck a deal to accept large quantities of arms, ostensibly from Czechoslovakia (the transaction is reminiscent of the Soviet-brokered airlift of Czech arms to the beleaguered Israelis in 1948), in exchange for Egyptian cotton.

The arms sale had an immediate effect on negotiations then under way for the World Bank, the U.S. and the U.K. to provide the foreign exchange required to construct the Aswan High Dam. These negotiations already seemed to be in the same kind of trouble that had overtaken the request for U.S. arms. Nasser objected to requirements by the World Bank that Egypt tighten its belt economically as a condition for receiving the money to build the dam, saying that such requirements infringed on Egypt's sovereignty. Now, however, an even larger problem arose in the U.S. Hostile questions were raised by hard-core cold warriors unwilling to use U.S. economic aid to help a country that was not clearly an ally; by senators from cotton-producing states, who had their own doubts about the political wisdom of appropriating tax money from their constituents to increase the cotton-growing capacity of Egypt; and by friends of Israel, who also played effectively on both of the other concerns. But, regardless of their motivations, all the American critics asked the same hard question: How was Egypt to meet its share of the High Dam's cost now that its cotton crop was mortgaged for years to come to pay the cost of Soviet arms?

Event followed event to worsen Egyptian relations with Britain, France and the U.S., and once again the Soviets moved adroitly, this time offering to replace western financing of the High Dam with their own. Israel, meanwhile, had expressed alarm at the pace of Egyptian rearmament. It pressed its major supplier, France, for additional weapons and also opened a campaign for U.S. military assistance.

Sensing that things were getting out of hand, the U.S. again tried to initiate high-level secret contacts with Egypt in order to lower the tension. President Eisenhower sent a trusted personal emissary, former Secretary of the Navy Robert Anderson, to speak first with Nasser and then with Ben Gurion. It was the American hope that Anderson, shuttling between Israel and Egypt via third countries such as Greece and Italy (in a secret version of the highly visible Kissinger shuttles eighteen years later) could develop enough common ground between Nasser and Ben Gurion to justify eventual Egyptian-Israeli negotiations.

Vastly complicating the problem was Nasser's insistence that a personal meeting was unthinkable in the current Arab political climate (some of it of his own making), and that communication could therefore continue only through intermediaries. Yet Ben Gurion insisted that only in a face-to-face meeting could he reveal the full extent of the Israeli concessions he was prepared to deliver. The impasse was a paradigm for recurrent failures in the years to follow, with most Arab leaders unwilling to meet their Israeli counterparts in the absence of specific advance Israeli concessions, and the Israelis unwilling to make the concessions except in a face-to-face meeting. By the end of February 1956, the Anderson mission had failed. The Egyptians continued to stockpile Soviet arms and Israel, after the U.S. rejected its arms request on April 3, initiated the arrangements that soon resulted in huge secret deliveries of French planes, tanks and munitions to its ports.

U.S. Secretary of State John Foster Dulles was preoccupied with building bulwarks against communism and seemed insensitive to Nasser's determination to remove all vestiges of foreign domination—including military or economic aid with political or even financial strings attached. Similarly, the quick-tempered Egyptian leader displayed little sensitivity to the political problems of an American administration clearly and openly eager to help him. U.S. politicians and journalists with a pro-Israeli bias found that the best way to undermine American public support for Egypt was simply to draw attention to some of the more extreme statements or contradictory actions of its President, who was seeking to achieve undisputed pan-Arab leadership.

The Aswan High Dam negotiations, therefore, were not helped when Nasser announced his recognition of the Chinese People's Republic without warning even to Egyptian Foreign Ministry professionals, much less to the Nationalist Chinese or to the dean of the Cairo diplomatic corps—who happened to be the U.S. Ambassador. The gesture was tied largely to Egyptian arms procurement efforts. But Americans in general, and perhaps Dulles as well, saw this as a direct slap not only at the Nationalist Chinese but also at the Americans themselves, who had so recently fought the Communist Chinese in Korea. One immediate repercussion was a unique Senate rider to the Mutual Security Act of that year requiring "that none of the funds provided in this Act shall be used for assistance in connection with the construction of the Aswan Dam."

Eisenhower appeared willing to defy Congress, or at least to test the constitutionality of the rider, by continuing the negotiations. But he was ill on July 19 when, only days after the Senate action, the Egyptian Ambassador met with Dulles and brought the Egyptian request to a head. Dulles claimed he had just a few days earlier warned the Egyptians against bringing up the matter, given the Congressional sentiment of the moment. He probably was further incensed when the Egyptian Ambassador mentioned in the same conversation the Soviet offer to finance the dam. Without consulting Eisenhower, Dulles withdrew the American offer on the spot. On the same day, he confirmed what seems to have been an abrupt or, at the very least, a graceless decision with a formal announcement that the U.S. would not participate in Aswan financing.

Nasser interpreted the public American rejection as an invitation to the Egyptian people to bring down his regime. On July 24, 1956 he responded with a harsh speech against the United States. Two days later he announced that he was nationalizing the Suez Canal. Even as he spoke, Egyptian technicians who had quietly entered the Canal area earlier in the day seized its key installations from Canal company employees. The takeover occurred just a month after the last British forces, pushed by Egyptian nationalism and pulled by American anti-colonialism, had been withdrawn from the Canal zone.

Egypt's July 24, 1952 revolution had set in motion several chains of events aimed at mediating the Arab-Israeli dispute. The arrest of a Jewish provocateur in Alexandria on July 24, 1954 ultimately brought those initiatives to a halt. Now, after Dulles' withdrawal of U.S. financing for the Aswan Dam, the Egyptian President's July 24, 1956 verbal attack on the U.S., followed by his nationalization of the Canal, set the stage for a new pattern of violence that would plague the Middle East for at least a generation to come.

President Eisenhower, who seldom criticized his Secretary of State, clearly understated his feelings when he wrote:

> "I have never doubted the wisdom of cancelling our offer, but I was concerned, in view of the events of the following weeks, that we might have been undiplomatic in the way the cancellation was handled."[6]

In retrospect it seems clear that the Israelis abandoned serious attempts to reach agreement with Egypt around the time that Sharett stated in January 1955 that he refused to negotiate "in the shadow of the gallows," and Ben Gurion launched his massive raid of February 1955 into the Gaza Strip. The raid convinced Egypt that it must obtain arms, Western if possible and Russian otherwise. Egypt's success in obtaining Soviet arms in turn provided the rationale for Israel's request to the U.S. and France for arms.

The French Prime Minister, Guy Mollet, faced with a full-scale rebellion in Algeria after November 1954 and growing anti-French movements in Morocco and Tunisia, blamed all three on the Egyptian President's propaganda and material support. As a result he was ready to listen to Israel. French arms began reaching Israel in quantities that clearly violated the 1950 tripartite agreement against weapons shipments that would upset a rough Arab-Israeli arms balance. At one point the French notified Eisenhower of their desire to ship twelve Mystere jet fighters to Israel. He replied that he had no objection. Much later, on the eve of hostilities, American photo reconnaissance flights over Israel revealed that the twelve Mysteres had somehow become sixty, displaying, in Eisenhower's words, "a rabbit-like capacity for multiplication." Some time after the secret weapons shipments had begun, secret French-Israeli military planning began as well.

As Churchill's foreign secretary, Anthony Eden had agreed not to try to bring Jordan into the Baghdad Pact, in return for which President Nasser had suspended propaganda attacks against Britain and Jordan. After he became Prime Minister, however, Eden did attempt to enlist Jordan, and Egypt unleashed a violent and effective propaganda barrage. To defend his reputation, King Hussein did more than abandon any idea of joining the Pact. He also dismissed the British commander of his Arab Legion, Glubb Pasha, despite that distinguished officer's long record of service. The new British Prime Minister was so outraged that, according to British statesman and author Anthony Nutting, Eden vowed "the world was not large enough to hold him and Nasser."

In Anglo-American discussions in Washington in February, 1956, even as the renewed Eisenhower attempt to start Egyptian-Israeli negotiations fizzled out, British and U.S. differences emerged clearly. The British were deeply concerned about preserving what remained of their imperial traditions. The Americans, by contrast, found it natural and even inevitable that the last of the 19th-century colonial structures should decay. They were more concerned about the kinds of nationalist leadership that would arise around the fallen pillars of empire. The British saw Nasser as a mortal danger to western interests, and their concern centered on how best to bring him down. The Americans, on the other hand, were particularly eager to preserve and protect strong and independent leaders like Egypt's charismatic President, and they focused their energies, albeit not always effectively, on keeping him from being drawn into the Russian orbit.

Eisenhower's speechwriter, Emmet John Hughes, records Dulles' comments as they worked together on a speech in 1956, at a time when the gap between the U.S. and its erstwhile western allies was widening. Dulles told Hughes:

> "The concepts and words that matter, in all we say, I think, are simply *peace* and *change*. We live in an age of deep change. You can't stop it. What you can do is to bend every effort to direct it—to see that it is evolutionary rather than revolutionary—and to retain, in the process, all that is good in the past. Most particularly, this is true of the whole Afro-Asian problem. What the Western world is moving toward is a new role with these peoples—a role of partnership rather than rule."[7]

Secretary Dulles' action precipitately withdrawing—without consulting the President—U.S. support for Egypt's Aswan Dam was, therefore, a negation of the whole Eisenhower policy of flexibility. At the same time, Nasser's subsequent retaliatory action in nationalizing the Suez Canal was a confirmation, in British and French minds, of their own more rigid stand.

Both Eden and Mollet wanted to use force to restore international control over the Canal and to humiliate, and if possible destroy, Nasser. President Eisenhower would not condone military action, but Dulles' attempts to bring the Canal under international control may not have made this initially clear to the British and

French. They proceeded with plans to halt Canal traffic by withdrawing European pilots. This, they reasoned, would throw the dispute into the United Nations, where they counted on a Russian veto to prevent UN action. The stage then would be set for their own recourse to force.

Dulles knew that, in a U.S. election year, a UN debate would reawaken all the domestic interests that had plagued Roosevelt's last days and Truman's first term. Whether the U.S. supported its old wartime allies or followed its postwar inclination to accommodate new nationalist leaders, Eisenhower was bound to alienate one or another segment of the voters. Dulles suggested that the Canal be run by an association of the maritime powers that used it. He persuaded Eden to sponsor the idea at a conference of maritime powers in London and the conference adopted it. But meanwhile the European pilots had walked out of the Canal zone on September 14, 1956 and the Egyptians had taken it over. The Canal continued to run smoothly and efficiently, and thus the rationale for the users' association vanished. Therefore, as soon as Dulles left London, Eden and Mollet threw the dispute into the UN Security Council according to their original plan.

President Nasser by now was aware that the British and French were preparing for a showdown. He astonished them both by agreeing at the UN to a set of six British principles to settle the Canal dispute. But by then, France, Israel, and Britain had other plans, which did not include a settlement with Egypt. The British introduced more conditions, precipitating more UN debate, and eventually a Soviet veto.

A French-Israeli plan against Egypt had matured in early October. The Israelis suggested that it begin with a preliminary Israeli diversion against Jordanian forces in the West Bank. King Hussein, seeing what the Israelis were up to, appealed for help to Iraq, ruled by his second cousin, the young Faisal II, and to Britain. Iraq sent troops and Jordan's British allies indicated they were prepared to use their aircraft against any Israeli attempt to seize the West Bank. Only then, it seems, did the French and Israelis inform the British that the Israeli move toward Jordan was a feint, and that the ultimate joint goal was the Suez Canal. British participation in the plan against Egypt was approved by the British cabinet on October 25, 1956.

On October 29, as Dag Hammarskjold, Secretary General of the United Nations, initiated private negotiations on Britain's six principles, Israeli paratroops dropped over Sinai, landing close to the Mitla Pass and only forty miles east of the Suez Canal. At the same moment Israeli armored columns roared westward across the Sinai peninsula to link up with the paratroops and southward into Sinai in the direction of Sharm al-Shaikh on the Straits of Tiran.

Eisenhower, after his long association with the British, became more and more upset as fragmentary clues to the French-British plan began to emerge. "My conviction was that the Western world had gotten into a lot of difficulty by selecting the wrong issue about which to be tough," Eisenhower later wrote. "To choose a situation in which Nasser had legal and sovereign rights, and in which world opinion was largely on his side, was not in my opinion a good one on which to make a stand. Accordingly I drafted a reply to this effect."[8]

He was equally concerned about Israeli intentions:

"Both Foster [Dulles] and I suspected that Ben Gurion might be contemplating military action during these pre-election days in the United States because of his possible overestimate of my desire to avoid offending the many voters who might have either sentimental or blood relations with Israel. I emphatically corrected any misapprehension of this kind he might have."[9]

And to his assistant, Hughes, he had trenchant comments on each of the conspirators, starting with Israel:

"I just can't figure out what the Israelis think they're up to. . . . Maybe they're thinking they just *can't* survive without more land. . . . But I don't see how they can survive without coming to some honorable and peaceful terms with the whole Arab world that surrounds them. . . ."[10]

He was even more critical of France:

"Damn it, the French, they're just egging the Israelis on—hoping somehow to get out of their *own* North African troubles. Damn it, they sat right there in those chairs three years ago, and we tried to tell them they would repeat Indochina all over again in North Africa. And they said, 'Oh, no. That's part of metropolitan France'—and all that damn nonsense."[11]

However, prophetic as he was on Israel and France, his comments on his old friend and ally, Britain, make ironic reading twenty-five years later, now that British and American roles with regard to Israel have reversed:

"I just can't believe it. I can't believe they would be so stupid as to invite on *themselves* all the Arab hostility to Israel. . . . What are they going to do—fight the whole Muslim world?"[12]

Eisenhower has commented that "the Presidency seldom affords the luxury of dealing with one problem at a time." That was amply demonstrated on October 29, 1956, the day Israeli paratroopers dropped into the Sinai passes. The Polish people and government had just faced down the Soviet Union. Since 1949 the Russians had forced Poland to include a Russian Marshal in the Polish Cabinet as Secretary of Defense. On October 19, 1956 the Poles had told Krushchev in Warsaw that Soviet Marshal Konstantin Rokossovsky had to go. Khrushchev reportedly informed the Poles that at that moment a Soviet division was moving toward their borders and, "if you don't obey, we will crush you." But the Poles stood their ground and Khrushchev angrily returned to Moscow. When he got there, however, the Russians called off the invasion.

Unfortunately, in Eisenhower's words, "the fire ignited in Poland brought a holocaust to Hungary." When Hungarians sought to emulate the Polish success against the Russians, street fighting broke out in Budapest between Russian tanks and Hungarian youths wielding Molotov cocktails. By October 29, most of the Hungarian armed forces had gone over to the rebels and had brought huge sections of the country under rebel control. Though casualties were heavy, it appeared that the Hungarians were also succeeding in facing down the Russians.

Eisenhower dealt hourly with the ticklish problem of how to dissuade the Russians from further repressive moves, and the Poles and Hungarians from further violence that would make Russian repression inevitable. Meanwhile, he had a heavy schedule of speeches and appearances around the country in his second bid for the presidency. The election was just seven days away.

Hughes was in almost constant contact with Eisenhower as they put together carefully worded statements on all three of the President's concerns: Hungary, the Middle East, and the election. Hughes recorded his own impressions of the situation a few hours before the Israeli paratroop drop was confirmed:

"The pieces of the picture fit together fairly clearly . . . through all the fog of uncertain information. From the viewpoint of Israel, the timing looks superb: Russia is deep in satellite trouble, Britain and France are straining at the leash for a crack at Nasser, and the U.S. is in the middle of a national election. Thus, the chance looks golden. . . ."[13]

However, Eisenhower was a President who was capable of telling Eden in a telephone conversation: "I don't give a darn about the election."[14] The President immediately called for UN Security Council action. Ignoring the U.S. call, the British and French issued an ultimatum to Egypt and Israel, giving each twelve hours to cease hostilities and withdraw to positions ten miles on either side of the Canal. This meant, of course, that Egypt would have to evacuate its own territory east of the Canal, and give up the Canal as well, while Israel would move forward twenty miles to take up positions within striking distance of the Canal. If anyone still thought the British-French ultimatum was truly designed to protect the Canal, this illusion was dispelled on October 31, when British planes swooped in from Cyprus to bomb the Canal's Ismailia headquarters and its Port Said terminal, along with airfields and other installations in both Cairo and Alexandria. It was a reprise of 19th century gunboat diplomacy.

Egypt reacted by sinking ships in the Canal, blocking further navigation. Syria later responded by sabotaging the pipelines carrying oil across its territory from Iraq to the Mediterranean, interrupting the flow of oil to Western Europe. When the British and French vetoed a ceasefire resolution in the UN Security Council, the United States introduced a resolution in the General Assembly calling for a ceasefire and for the dispatch of UN soldiers to enforce it. Surprisingly, not only Egypt but Israel too accepted it. This pulled the rug out from under the Anglo-French invasion force, still steaming from Malta toward Egypt. The British and French, however, announced that their troops would land to keep order until the UN force could arrive.

By this time the combination of blunt Soviet threats, unyielding U.S. opposition, and strong domestic criticism in Britain had thoroughly shaken Eden. He informed Mollet that Britain was withdrawing from the operation. The word, however, apparently did not get to his military commanders, and twenty hours later British and French paratroops and infantry landed, broke through fierce Egyptian opposition, and assumed positions along the now totally blocked canal.

Israel, having first stunned her fellow conspirators by accepting the UN ceasefire, now abruptly decided to risk new U.S. disapproval in order to fulfill a long-standing national objective. Israel broke the ceasefire and resumed military operations just long enough to seize Sharm al-Shaikh. It then accepted the ceasefire once again. (This tactic had also been used by Israel in the fighting of 1948 to seize vital objectives and surround enemy forces as at the Falluja pocket. It was successfully used again in 1973 when Israeli troops ignored the ceasefire their government had accepted and cut the roads linking Egyptian troops to their sources of supply.)

Eisenhower meanwhile rejected a Soviet plan for joint action as "unthinkable" and warned that the entry of any new troops into the Middle East would oblige all members of the United Nations, including the United States, to take effective countermeasures. Both countries continued to apply pressure separately, however, and the British and French agreed to withdraw. Eden, whose political career was ended by the debacle, as a last act delivered his own scathing denunciation of the hypocrisy of the Soviet Union's entry into the Middle East as a peacemaker while its hands were still stained with Hungarian blood.

On November 8, 1956, after receiving reports that Ben Gurion had rejected the UN order to withdraw his forces, Eisenhower informed the Israeli leader that the U.S. viewed Israel's refusal "with deep concern." Ben Gurion rapidly reconsidered and, after meeting with his cabinet for nine hours, informed Eisenhower that Israeli forces would withdraw after all since "we have never planned to annex the Sinai Desert." When the fighting was over, Britain admitted to sixteen dead, and France to ten. Press reports put the Israeli dead near 200 and the Egyptian dead at 1000.

In Hungary, where the Soviets had feigned withdrawal and then, on November 4, launched a major tank assault across the borders to crush the rebels, 25,000 Hungarians were dead. By the end of the year, another 150,000 Hungarians had fled the country. The Soviets had given Imre Nagy, the Prime Minister of Hungary during its short-lived rebellion, a pledge of safe conduct. They had then seized and executed him after giving him a "secret trial."

Secretary Dulles, already afflicted with the cancer that would soon kill him, realized that the West had fallen into disarray over the Middle East at the very moment he had awaited in Eastern Europe for all the years since World War II. He sadly told the President on November 1:

> "It is nothing less than tragic that at this very time when we are on the point of winning an immense and long-hoped-for victory over Soviet colonialism in Eastern Europe, we should be forced to choose between following in the footsteps of Anglo-French colonialism in Asia and Africa, or splitting our course away from their course."[15]

Eisenhower, writing later, added:

"I still wonder what would have been my recommendation to the Congress and the American people had Hungary been accessible by sea or through the territory of allies who might have agreed to react positively to the tragic fate of the Hungarian people. As it was, however, Britain and France could not possibly have moved with us into Hungary. . . ."[16]

Finally, speaking more boldly on the Middle East than almost any U.S. President since, Eisenhower summed up his thoughts on Suez and the 1956 Presidential campaign:

"During the campaign, some political figures kept talking of our failure to 'back Israel.' If the administration had been incapable of withstanding this kind of advice in an election year, could the United Nations thereafter have retained any influence whatsoever?"[17]

NOTES

1. Hughes, Emmet John, *The Ordeal of Power: A Political Memoir of the Eisenhower Years,* Atheneum, New York, 1963, p. 212.
2. Eisenhower, Dwight D., *The White House Years: Waging Peace 1956-1961,* Doubleday, Garden City, New York, 1965, p. 99.
3. Mathias, Senator Charles McC. Jr., "Ethnic Groups and Foreign Policy," *Foreign Affairs,* Summer, 1981, pp. 992-993.
4. Derogy, Jacques and Carmel, Hesi, *The Untold History of Israel,* Grove Press, New York, 1979, pp. 101-128.
5. Eisenhower, Dwight D., *The White House Years: Waging Peace 1956-1961,* Doubleday, Garden City, New York, 1965, p. 24.
6. *Ibid.,* p. 33.
7. Hughes, Emmet John, *The Ordeal of Power: A Political Memoir of the Eisenhower Years,* Atheneum, New York, 1963, pp. 208-209.
8. Eisenhower, Dwight D., *The White House Years: Waging Peace 1956-1961,* Doubleday, Garden City, New York, 1965, p. 50.
9. *Ibid.,* p. 56.
10. Hughes, Emmet John, *The Ordeal of Power: A Political Memoir of the Eisenhower Years,* Atheneum, New York, 1963, p. 212.
11. *Ibid.,* p. 212.
12. *Ibid.,* pp. 212-213.
13. *Ibid.,* p. 213.
14. Eisenhower, Dwight D., *The White House Years: Waging Peace 1956–1961,* Doubleday, Garden City, New York, 1965, p. 92.
15. *Ibid.,* p. 83.
16. *Ibid.,* p. 88.
17. *Ibid.,* p. 99.

CHAPTER VII

President Eisenhower's Second Term and the Coca Cola Invasion

"Ironically, instead of bringing peace nearer, the Sinai War, by increasing Arab hatred and fear, by giving the Arabs still another reason for wanting revenge, and by further humiliating them, made the Arabs even more adamant in their refusal to come to terms with Israel. Besides by exaggerating the extent of Israel's military victory and of Egypt's defeat in the Sinai, the Israelis became, as the New York Times reported on November 12, 1956, more overconfident and cocky and, therefore, 'more difficult to handle' and less willing to make concessions."[1]

Fred J. Khouri, 1968

"Jewish genius has amply manifested itself on the field of battle. Its impact is yet to be felt at the conference table on the issue of the Palestinians."

Walid Khalidi, Professor of Political Studies, American University of Beirut, 1981

"To prevent an outbreak of hostilities I preferred a resolution which would call on all United Nations members to suspend not only governmental but private assistance to Israel. Such a move would be no hollow gesture."[2]

Dwight D. Eisenhower, 1965

The Suez crisis ended as raggedly as it began. The British and French withdrew in December 1956 and the Egyptians had agreed by the end of the same month to start clearing the Canal. The Israelis, however, still hoped to drive a hard bargain.

51

For a time after the 1948 war, Israeli-chartered ships carrying cargoes for Israel had passed through the Canal flying the flags of their country of registry. After 1950, however, the Egyptians had brought this to a halt. They linked their refusal to allow Israeli cargoes to transit either the Canal or the Straits of Tiran controlling the Gulf of Aqaba with Israel's refusal to comply with UN resolutions concerning withdrawal from territory seized during the 1948 fighting and the repatriation or compensation of Palestinians made homeless at that time.

The Israelis now made it clear that they were not going to complete their withdrawal from Sinai until they secured guaranteed access through the Canal and the Tiran Straits. They also said that they would not permit Egyptian authorities back into the Gaza Strip at all.

The U.S., concerned that Britain and France were now considered allies of Israel, and hoping to position itself as an impartial mediator, did not want the issue to go back to the UN, where the U.S. would have to stand up and be counted on one side or the other. Messages were exchanged between the U.S. and Israel, but Ben Gurion grew increasingly outspoken in his rejection of U.S. requests that he withdraw his forces. When Israel sent the U.S. a refusal in writing, and the U.S. delegate to the UN told Eisenhower there was no further way to delay a UN discussion, the President began a series of meetings with his advisers on February 15. He later wrote about the discussions:

"Secretary Dulles strongly expressed the view that we had gone as far as possible to try to make it easy for the Israelis to withdraw. To go further, he said, would surely jeopardize the entire Western influence in the Middle East, and the nations of that region would conclude that United States policy toward the area was, in the last analysis, controlled by Jewish influence in the United States. In such event the only hope of the Arab countries would be found in a firm association with the Soviet Union."[3]

Like Truman before him, Eisenhower considered stronger action than has ever been threatened since to make Israel withdraw so that he could get on with his program to stabilize the post-Suez situation in the Middle East:

"In considering various possible courses of action, I rejected, from the outset, any more United Nations resolutions designed merely to condemn Israel's conduct. Once more, I rejected also any new resolution like that of October 30, 1956, which had called only for a suspension of governmental support of Israel. Indeed, such a suspension against both Israel and Egypt was already in effect by the United States. To prevent an outbreak of hostilities I preferred a resolution which would call on all United Nations members to suspend not just governmental but private assistance to Israel. Such a move would be no hollow gesture. As we discussed it [Treasury Secretary] George Humphrey put in a call to W. Randolph Burgess, Undersecretary of the Treasury for Monetary Affairs, who gave a rough estimate that American private gifts to Israel were about $40 million a year and sale of Israel's bonds in our country between $50 and $60 million a year."[4]

To gain time, Eisenhower then made public earlier messages he had sent to Israel, predictably unleashing a storm of domestic protest. He writes:

"In a special White House conference with congressional leaders of both parties two days later, politics was in the back of many of the conferees' minds. In 1956 the Republican national ticket had carried New York by more than one and one-half million votes—the largest margin in the history of the Empire State. But faced with the possibility of having to take a stand for strong American action against Israel, some of those present were more than a little nervous."[5]

Congressional leaders at the meeting on February 20 were doubtful. One of them, Senator Lyndon Johnson, argued that in "cracking down" on Israel the U.S. was using a double standard, following one policy for weak countries like Israel and another for strong countries like the Soviet Union, since the Soviets were not complying with a UN resolution on Hungary. Johnson also had reservations about any congressional statement on the matter, unless it was certain that such a statement would cause Israel to withdraw.

As the Eisenhower administration pursued its double confrontation, with Israel on the one hand and with Israel's domestic supporters in the U.S. on the other, the UN moved inexorably toward calling for world-wide sanctions against Israel. Finally, on March 1, 1957, Israeli Foreign Minister Golda Meir went before the UN General Assembly to announce Israeli readiness for a "full and complete withdrawal" of military forces, and Eisenhower was free to pursue his own Middle Eastern plans.

Even before the British and French withdrawals from the Suez Canal, Eisenhower had outlined what later became known as the Eisenhower Doctrine, to fill the vacuum he believed the decline of British and French power had created, "before it is filled by Russia." To the Arabs, however, it looked like the substitution of one kind of western tutelage for another. Harold Macmillan, Britain's new Prime Minister and Eisenhower's old wartime colleague and friend, was also unenthusiastic at a British-American meeting held March 21, 1957 in Bermuda. Afterward, Eisenhower wrote:

"Foster and I at first found it difficult to talk constructively with our British colleagues about Suez because of the blinding bitterness they felt toward Nasser. Prime Minister Harold Macmillan and Foreign Minister Selwyn Lloyd were so obsessed with the possibilities of getting rid of Nasser that they were handicapped in searching, objectively, for any realistic method of operating the Canal."[6]

Prior to the Suez crisis British Prime Minister Eden had concluded that either he or Nasser must go. His prediction was fulfilled with his own resignation. The Egyptian President, on the other hand, had emerged from the affair with enormously enhanced prestige. Some Arab countries were still struggling with colonial rule, and most others with its psychological and economic aftereffects. Therefore, Nasser's success in turning back both of the major colonial powers made him a symbol of the aspirations of Arabs almost everywhere.

It was a time of increasing turbulence in the Arab world, as individual leaders and political parties, appealing alternately to Pan-Arabism and to regional rival-ries or separatist traditions, struggled among themselves. The era is now known as the "Arab Cold War." Nearly all of it lies outside the parameters of a study of U.S. perceptions of the Arab-Israeli dispute. Yet the events of this period reinforced a growing impression among Americans in general that the entire Middle East was an area of shifting, unstable alliances and of emotional, volatile people.

The Eisenhower Doctrine sought to focus U.S. economic and military aid on strengthening those leaders the U.S. considered moderate, while ignoring those the U.S. considered too dependent upon the Soviet Union, or too weak and unpopular within their own countries to rule without eventual Soviet help. Implicit in the doctrine was the possibility of U.S. military action if a country requested armed assistance against an internal or external threat. Liberal critics complained that Eisenhower's administration was becoming too much like the ousted colonial regimes, insensitive to the new nationalist aspirations not only of the Arabs, but of all emerging countries. Conservative critics, on the other hand, attributed increasing turbulence and Soviet infiltration into the Arab countries to Eisenhower's original decision to oppose the French, British, and Israelis at Suez. Nasser became the focus of much of this debate in the U.S. as well as among other Western powers. Critics on either side found it convenient to cite the words and actions of the Egyptian leader to prove their points.

U.S. diplomats and military officers serving in Egypt had fallen under Nasser's charismatic sway even before he emerged as the undisputed leader of the officers who overthrew King Farouk. By now, some of those who supported Nasser and the Arab nationalist tendencies he personified had risen to important second- and third-echelon positions in the U.S. foreign affairs establishment. On the other hand, diplomats whose foreign service assignments had given them a more European orientation saw Nasser as the original wrecker of the Western Alliance, whose influence should be ended as soon as possible.

Friends of Israel, by no means all of them Jewish, were also influential in governmental circles. In addition, Israel had partisans in media and in academic circles. Although journalists and scholars could not make U.S. policy, their words could raise or lower the fortunes of both career and elected government officials, and they were willing to ally themselves with anyone who opposed the Egyptian President. The result was a running series of battles within the foreign affairs establishment and an extraordinary policy in which the U.S. repeatedly prepared for possible military action, as happened in Jordan early in 1957, in Syria later the same year, and then in Lebanon in 1958.

In the first two cases the situation appeared to stabilize before any overt U.S. action was taken. All contenders for influence in the U.S. saw this as a vindication of their own recommendations. Those among the State Department's Middle East hands who had counseled moderation could say that, by not intervening, the U.S. had enabled the Arabs to work things out themselves. Those who had wanted the U.S. to intervene militarily in coordination with conservative Arab states argued from the same events that, if even the threat of force persuaded Egypt's ruler to adopt policies of conciliation, a demonstration of real force might bring him down.

The Israeli influence was most overtly demonstrated during the 1957 events in Syria. U.S. officials, eventually including the President, became convinced that a government of Communists and leftists, with none strong enough to assert mastery, made Syria ripe for Soviet plucking. From Israel, Ben Gurion tossed gasoline on the embers of U.S. doubt and suspicion, cabling Eisenhower that "it is impossible to distinguish between Syria and Russia" and that "the establishment of Syria as a base for international Communism is one of the most dangerous events which has befallen the Free World in our time."

State Department officials and other Americans who counseled moderation were soon reinforced by the clear reluctance of such conservative Arab regimes as Saudi Arabia, Iraq, and Jordan to become directly involved. The latter two countries, along with Lebanon, had raised the alarm in the first place and would be most threatened by the Soviet penetration of Syria. As a result U.S. hawks, who by then had President Eisenhower's ear, could say little that would justify U.S. intervention.

A combination of Syrian army officers and political leaders, some fearing the rise of Soviet influence and some dismayed by Syria's isolation from all other Arab countries, eventually requested a union with Nasser's Egypt. The United Arab Republic came into existence on February 22, 1958, and soon was expanded to include northern Yemen in a confederation known as the United Arab States.

American diplomats who feared that use of U.S. military force would create far more problems in the Arab world than it would solve pointed to this as vindication of their stand. Nasser had without bloodshed closed the hole through which Soviet influence might have entered Syria. Americans who by then had developed a distaste for Nasser reminiscent of Anthony Eden's sentiments on the eve of Suez depicted the Egyptian as a "dictator" brandishing Soviet arms to intimidate Arabs into joining his makeshift empire, one certainly destined to fall under Soviet sway when he had sufficiently overextended himself. The dynamic Egyptian could speak extemporaneously for hours at a time in a simple, highly-personalized style that combined colloquial Egyptian Arabic with the melodic classical Arabic of the Koran, and mesmerized not only his countrymen but also Arabs throughout the Middle East. As a result, in the United States Nasser's supporters and detractors both could generally find something in his speeches to quote in support of their differing viewpoints.

The political confusion in the Middle East, and the divisions in the U.S. over how or whether to deal with it, finally intersected in Lebanon in 1958. When the French created Lebanon as a largely Christian entity out of predominantly Muslim Greater Syria, they unwittingly built in a time bomb. The tiny country is centered on the mountain range where Maronite Christians and Druzes (the followers of a secretive religion which branched off from Islam after the 11th century A.D.) have lived for centuries, aloof from domination by the Muslims who inhabit the coastal and inland plains around them.

The French wanted to make the Christian enclave as economically viable as possible. They therefore attached to the mountain territory not only the port of Beirut, which had many Christian and Druze residents, but also coastal Tripoli, Sidon, and Tyre, which had virtually none. As the years went by a higher birthrate among the Muslims, and extensive emigration to the U.S. and Latin America by the Christians, began to alter the religious balance. The Christian-dominated Lebanese government refused to authorize any further census after 1934. The influx of a predominantly Muslim Palestinian refugee population in 1948 increased the imbalance. The Muslims already were restive with their slightly inferior share of official positions and other governmental benefits. They also were strongly attracted to Nasser's pan-Arabism. When rumors spread that the conservative Maronite President, Camille Chamoun, was going to seek to amend the Lebanese Constitution to permit himself an unprecedented second six-year term, the large Muslim quarters of both Beirut and Tripoli, as well as many all-Muslim towns and villages, began to defy the President's rule. On May 13, 1958, Chamoun appealed to Eisenhower, charging that the arms and ammunition being used by the Muslims were being smuggled over the mountains from Nasser's new Syrian province.

Eisenhower informed Chamoun that U.S. troops invoked under the Eisenhower Doctrine would not come to Lebanon to give him a second presidential term, and would not come at all unless Lebanon's request had the concurrence of a second Arab nation. Eisenhower had managed to remain somewhat detached from his immediate advisers' strongly negative feelings about the Egyptian President. Yet even Eisenhower was surprised when Nasser quickly agreed with an American suggestion to send in UN observers to investigate the infiltration of weapons and men. The Egyptian President went considerably further, suggesting that the U.S. and Egypt jointly sponsor new Lebanese elections that would make it possible for the Army commander, General Fuad Chehab, to assume the Presidency. Lebanon's National Pact specifies that the President must be a Maronite Christian, and by tradition the commander of the Army also is a Maronite. Therefore, Chehab was eligible so far as the Pact and the Christians upholding it were concerned, while his actions in keeping the Lebanese army out of the incipient civil war (and thus avoiding a split between its Muslim and Christian soldiers) had made him readily acceptable to Lebanon's Muslims.

Eisenhower declined Nasser's suggestion of joint action but welcomed what he later described as the "puzzling" favorable Egyptian attitude toward UN intervention. The Lebanese crisis seemed to be simmering down.

Three months earlier—when Egypt and Syria had formed the United Arab Republic—Iraq and Jordan, ruled by second cousins, had reacted by forming a Hashemite Union, uniting the two Kingdoms into one, with the stipulation that the ruler of the considerably larger, richer and more populous Iraq would have specified prior rights. The Union was unpopular among many of the thousands of Palestinian refugees to whom King Hussein had granted full Jordanian citizenship, but who looked to Nasser as the Pan-Arab leader who might some day restore their Palestinian homeland.

The Iraqi Prime Minister, Nuri al-Said, offered to redeploy some of his troops from the Iranian border to the Jordanian border in case Jordan's Arab Legion could not handle the resulting instability. Normally, troop movements in Iraq were carried out via circuitous routes in order to bypass Baghdad completely. When troops had to pass through the Iraqi capital, it was customary for them to unload their guns. This was an emergency deployment, however, and the old Iraqi strongman, whose career had started in the Ottoman army before World War I, had grown blatantly overconfident about his power and luck. For some time he had ignored the public's discontent over his use of oil revenues, deferring immediate benefits—such as rapid expansion of public education—to build an infrastructure of dams, canals and power plants for expanded agricultural production. His program was not widely understood, and neither Nuri al-Said nor the unpopular Regent, Prince Abd al-Illah, had made a serious effort to explain it to the people of Iraq. Now Nuri ignored urgent warnings by his security police about the troop movement. As a result, two ambitious army officers, Brigadier Abd al-Karim Qasim and his popular chief of staff, Colonel Abd al-Salam Arif, found themselves moving their entire motorized force with loaded guns by night through the streets of Baghdad.

By mid-morning of the next day, July 14, 1958, the Regent, the King and their immediate relatives, both male and female, were dead. Brigadier Qasim had taken over the government, jubilant mobs ruled the streets, and Nuri al-Said was in hiding. A few days later, Nuri tried to escape disguised as a veiled, black-robed pious woman. He is said to have been spotted by a small boy who noted a man's shoes under the woman's robe, and to have been killed on the spot. Brigadier Qasim's politics were a mystery—and remained so—to Westerners, but Colonel Arif was known to be a great admirer of Nasser. Arif made this manifestly clear by taking a trip to Cairo immediately after the coup.

Although these events aroused anti-Nasser sentiment among leaders of both Britain and the U.S., Eisenhower continued to insist that a rescue effort for Chamoun would need another Arab country's blessing. Britain immediately consulted with Hussein, who was shocked and angered over the fate of his Iraqi relatives and also of members of a Jordanian delegation visiting Baghdad who were killed by a mob in the first hours of the revolution. Shortly afterward, still on July 14, the British Prime Minister was able to report requests for military assistance from both President Chamoun and King Hussein. In an excited attempt at telephone code, Macmillan shouted to Eisenhower: "We have had a request from the two little chaps."

The day after the Iraqi revolution, the U.S. called for an emergency meeting of the UN, and U.S. Marines went ashore in full battle gear on a long sandy beach south of Beirut bordering the international air field. In view of the Lebanese army's neutrality, Eisenhower was not sure whether his Marines would be welcomed or met with army gunfire. Nevertheless, demonstrating the political caution that characterized all of his military actions, he had decided not to land in a secure Christian area. Instead, the U.S. force would limit itself to securing the capital and its airport adjacent to the landing site. He later explained:

"The decision to occupy only the air field and capital was a political one which I adhered to over the recommendations of some of the military. If the Lebanese army were unable to subdue the rebels when we had secured their capital and protected their government, I felt, we were backing up a government with so little popular support that we probably should not be there."[7]

There was a tense moment, however, as the troops prepared to drive slowly into the city. They were met on the road by an official party composed of Army Commander Chehab, the U.S. Admiral in charge of the operation, who had flown into Lebanon in advance of his troops, and by the U.S. Ambassador. There was a lengthy period of negotiations as the Marines waited all along the landing area.

Lebanon's beaches normally are jammed in July with crowds of bathers, among whom move vendors of soft drinks, ice cream, and various Lebanese foods. There were no bathers on July 15, 1958, but while the U.S. troops waited, vendors who had been watching the invasion from their nearby houses warily approached. By the time the order to drive on into the city was given, the U.S. Marines and the Lebanese soft-drink vendors had had their first mutually satisfactory encounter. Twelve hours later, when the landing craft of the next Marine battalion hit the beach, Marines were mobbed by vendors of soft drinks, ice cream, and spicy foods. The entire three-stage Marine landing has gone down in both U.S. and Lebanese history as "the Coca Cola invasion." It presaged the commercial bonanza enjoyed by the merchants of Beirut for three months until they waved farewell to the last members of the 14,000-man U.S. force on October 21.

In Jordan, just two days after the U.S. Marines had landed in Beirut, British troops were airlifted into Amman in support of King Hussein and found a similar welcome. The main concern throughout their brief stay in Jordan was the awkward fact that the only available supply route for their forces lay through the air space of Jordan's enemy, Israel.

After the U.S. landing in Lebanon, there was no lack of advice from Americans in the area. Some conservative U.S. businessmen resident in Beirut strongly backed Chamoun. Most diplomats were gravely concerned about hostile Arab reactions to direct U.S. intervention. Eisenhower characteristically sent his own emissary, Robert Murphy, a diplomat whose association with Eisenhower went back to World War II and the Allied landings in North Africa. After talking to everyone he could contact, including Nasser in Egypt and Qasim in Iraq, Murphy concluded that only a special Lebanese election giving General Chehab an opportunity to assume the Presidency would restore consensus rule.

The election was held July 31 and General Chehab was elected with the support of both Muslims and Christians in Lebanon. It was exactly the solution Nasser, depicted by many British and American opponents as the chief agent of international Communism in the Arab world, had proposed to the U.S. President three months earlier.

A year after the Lebanon landing Eisenhower was visited in Washington by Rashid Karami, Prime Minister of Lebanon (where under the National Pact the Prime Minister is a Sunni Muslim), and one of the two main "rebel" leaders of 1958. Eisenhower has recorded his impressions of the visit:

"I enjoyed that conversation. In the course of it I happened to mention the landings in Lebanon the year before; Mr. Karami said with a laugh that it would have been better had the United States held off sending troops but had merely sent Mr. Murphy to straighten out the situation. I was highly pleased with the implicit compliment to Bob Murphy . . . who was participating in our talk. But . . . no one man could possibly have composed the differences that were then tearing Lebanon to pieces. . . . However, as our conversation ended, I could not completely smother the thought that if our visitor's statement had been true, every one in my administration could have been saved a lot of anxious hours."[8]

NOTES

1. Khouri, Fred J., *The Arab Israeli Dilemma*, The University Press, Syracuse, N.Y., 1968 and 1976, p. 218.
2. Eisenhower, Dwight D., *The White House Years: Waging Peace 1956-1961*, Doubleday, Garden City, New York, 1965, p. 185.
3. *Ibid.*, p. 185.
4. *Ibid.*, pp. 185-186.
5. *Ibid.*, p.186.
6. *Ibid.*, p. 122.
7. *Ibid.*, p. 175.
8. *Ibid.*, p. 189.

CHAPTER VIII

President Kennedy and Good Intentions Deferred Too Long

"Once countries had gained their independence, Kennedy believed that the sensible thing was to try to live with the new nations and their new leaders. Not domination or preachment, but adjustment and rapprochement seemed to him the fruitful relationship."[1]

Arthur M. Schlessinger, 1965

"Nasser liked Kennedy's Ambassador, John Badeau, and he liked Kennedy's practice of personal correspondence. Kennedy put off, however, an invitation for a Nasser visit until improved relations could enable him to answer the political attacks such a visit would bring from voters more sympathetic to Israel."[2]

Theodore Sorensen, 1965

Since President Eisenhower was not eligible for a third term, the election contest in 1960 was between his vice president, Richard Nixon, and Senator John F. Kennedy. Kennedy, the candidate of the liberal, eastern wing of the Democratic Party, had wrested the nomination from Senator Lyndon Johnson, who was supported by its southern, conservative elements. Kennedy courteously offered the older, more seasoned Johnson the Party's vice presidential nomination, and reportedly was shocked and disappointed when Johnson swallowed his pride and accepted it.

The only remarkable aspect of the campaign itself was the fact that Nixon, already well known, unwisely agreed to a series of televised debates with the relatively unknown Kennedy. Fearing the still-unexplored potential of the new medium, both candidates largely avoided the controversial issues that would have given substance to their debates. Instead they competed with ringing declarations on non-controversial issues. Most of the foreign policy debate concerned the need to get tough with America's favorite enemy, Cuba's Fidel Castro. Israel was praised by both candidates, loudly and often, both on television and in personal appearances before Jewish groups. As always, when the electoral campaign turned to the Middle East, the challenger had the advantage. He could take the previous administration to task for not doing more for the Jewish State. At that time it probably made little real difference what either candidate said on Israel, so long as each made the ritual pledges of support and devotion. For historical reasons, most of the Jewish vote went to the Democratic candidate in any case. In this election, the vote was even less likely to go to Nixon. His outspoken conservatism and his aggressive tactics in the searches during the 1950s for real or fancied Communist influence in the U.S. government had made Jews in all walks of life frankly uneasy.

The television debates introduced a crucial new factor to what clearly was going to be a very close election, and to what the press had been calling a Tweedledum versus Tweedledee campaign. Senator Kennedy was indisputably better looking than Vice President Nixon. Despite the frantic efforts of a series of make-up persons, platitudes delivered with a touch of humor by a fresh-faced Irishman from Massachusetts sounded more promising than similar lines delivered by a somber Californian with five o'clock shadow. Pundits generally agreed that the debates were a draw on substance, but that Kennedy had won them on style. The voters subsequently confirmed that judgment.

It was such a close victory that, had Nixon chosen to follow up serious charges of fraud in the decisive Illinois vote, he might have thrown not only the election results but the country into chaos. Kennedy could not be expected, therefore, to launch his administration with controversial new foreign policy initiatives that could erode his already uncomfortably narrow political base. His first foreign initiative, the Bay of Pigs landing by anti-Castro Cubans, backfired. In that operation each party had good reason to blame the other. Eisenhower, a Republican, had initially approved a military operation that was politically unsound. When Kennedy, a Democrat, took office, he had made it militarily unsound as well by denying it U.S. air cover.

Therefore, it is surprising to realize, with the benefit of hindsight, that from the time Kennedy entered office as the narrowly-elected candidate of a party heavily dependent upon Jewish votes, he was planning to take a whole new look at U.S. Mideast policy. He obviously could not turn the clock back and undo the work of President Truman, his Democratic predecessor, in making the establishment of Israel possible. Nor, perhaps, would he have wanted to. Kennedy was determined, however, to develop good new personal relationships with individual Arab leaders, including those with whom the previous administration's relations had deteriorated. As a result, various leaders of newly independent countries were surprised to find their *pro forma* messages of congratulation upon Kennedy's assumption of office answered with personalized letters from the young American President.

The explanation was simple. As a child in a proudly Irish-American family, Kennedy had listened with fascination to the tales of Ireland's struggle for independence. As the son of a U.S. Ambassador to the Court of St. James, he had seen more of other countries during school vacations than most Americans see in a lifetime. He was also a member of the World War II generation that had personally paid the price for international greed and shortsightedness between the wars. He was an authentic war hero who had come back. His heroic older brother Joseph had not. John Kennedy had been hospitalized repeatedly for back injuries sustained when the torpedo boat he commanded was cut in half by a Japanese destroyer. He had had a lot of time to read and think about the false pride and wishful thinking of the old that has so often sent the young off to war.

His colleague and biographer, Arthur M. Schlesinger, Jr., described the conclusions Kennedy had reached by the time he joined the Senate concerning America's adjustment to the post-war world:

"Once countries had gained their independence, Kennedy believed that the sensible thing was to try to live with the new nations and their new leaders. Not domination or preachment but adjustment and rapprochement seemed to him the fruitful relationship. He saw this as a long-term investment and was ready in the meantime to put up with a certain amount of nonsense."[3]

Kennedy had visited Indochina in 1951. By 1957, as a freshman member of the Senate Foreign Relations Committee, he thought he recognized the same tragedy of colonial inflexibility unfolding in Algeria. Already one of the congressional library's heaviest borrowers, he now spent additional time in conversation with William J. Porter, an Arabist and the director of the State Department's Office of North African Affairs. Porter feared that Washington's uncritical support of its NATO ally, France, in an increasingly brutal repression of the Algerian nationalists, threatened the whole future of the United States in North Africa. Kennedy also talked to members of the Algerian FLN delegation at the United Nations.

In July 1957 he rose on the Senate floor to deliver his first major foreign policy speech. He told his colleagues:

"No amount of mutual politeness, wishful thinking, nostalgia or regret should blind either France or the United States to the fact that, if France and the West at large are to have a continuing influence in North Africa . . . the essential first step is the independence of Algeria."[4]

The speech prompted more mail than any other he ever delivered as a senator. The foreign policy establishment in New York, a bastion of Atlantic solidarity, expressed righteous indignation. The bumptious young senator had publicly criticized America's oldest ally. The French were irritated and Republicans professed shock. (Kennedy's words, however, were akin to Eisenhower's private comments of the same period.) Even the arbiters of his own Democratic Party establishment, Adlai Stevenson, the twice-defeated Presidential nominee, and Dean Acheson, the former Secretary of State, criticized Kennedy's irresponsibility in undermining an ally. Yet, as Chairman of the Africa Subcommittee of the Senate Foreign Relations Committee, the young senator continued to speak in the same vein, warning that "the word is out—and spreading in a thousand languages and dialects—that it is no longer necessary to remain forever poor or forever in bondage."[5]

Not everyone was critical, however. Secretary of State Dulles privately told the young senator from the opposing party that he had used Kennedy's speech in arguing for moderation in Paris. French moderates similarly welcomed the speech as support for their futile attempts to prevent extremists from taking over both camps in the Algerian conflict. Three years later, an American journalist who had visited the rebels in Algeria told the senator that his weary, battle-hardened hosts had astonished him by asking about Kennedy's chances for the Presidency.

Kennedy became President in January 1961, and Algeria achieved its independence on July 3, 1962. That was only five years and one day after Kennedy had given his Senate speech calling for independence. But what tragedies had unfolded in the meantime: Algeria had lost a tenth of its population and it now had a ravaged economy presided over by a radicalized leadership. However, despite their suffering, much of it at the hands of soldiers wielding American-made arms supplied to France under NATO auspices, Algeria's FLN leaders had not forgotten the American senator who had championed their cause and they publicly hailed his election.

Kennedy in turn sent William Porter, the U.S. Foreign Service officer who had explained to him the Algerian cause, as the first U.S. Ambassador to Algeria. Ahmad Ben Bella visited Washington in the same year. Afterward, in the words of Ambassador Porter, Ben Bella "ascribed to Kennedy everything he thought good in the United States." Unfortunately, to Kennedy's baffled disappointment, Ben Bella proceeded directly from his visit with Kennedy in Washington to Havana for a visit to Castro, and then signed his name to a communique calling, among other things, for the U.S. to withdraw from its base in Guantanamo.

In discussing their struggle with Israel, Arabs frequently remind Americans of the Arabic proverb that "the friend of my enemy is my enemy." Kennedy was learning that in practice the Arabs sometimes forget that their proverb cuts both ways.

Kennedy also struck up a warm friendship with Tunisia's Habib Bourguiba, which was reinforced by friendly ties between the Tunisian Ambassador to Washington, Habib Bourguiba, Jr., and many of the young White House advisers.

Kennedy's relationship with Nasser was more tentative. It probably was not helped by the fact that one of the two White House staffers responsible for Middle Eastern matters was also a major White House liaison with the U.S. Jewish community. Nevertheless, the Kennedy White House was preoccupied with the question of whether better relations were possible with the Egyptian leader, whose standing with the Eisenhower White House seemed to have fallen in direct proportion to his rising prestige in the Arab world.

John Badeau, a man who had invested his entire life in educational and charitable work in the Middle East and who had served as President of the American University in Cairo, was sent to Egypt as the new U.S. Ambassador. A long and personalized response by Nasser to a fairly routine message that Kennedy sent to the Arab chiefs of state initiated a serious correspondence between the two leaders.

Kennedy had made strong public commitments to Israel during the election campaign and he was under great pressure to follow through on them. Nevertheless, in 1961, when Kennedy recognized the new government in Syria that had broken away from the union with Egypt; and in 1962, when Kennedy sent Hawk anti-aircraft missiles to Israel, he was careful to inform Nasser in advance of the impending actions and the reasons for taking them.

In 1962 there was a coup in Yemen. The ensuing struggle pitted Egyptian troops and Egyptian-supported Yemeni Republicans against British and Saudi-supplied forces loyal to the Imam Badr and created chaos not only in the Middle East but also in relations between the Middle East and the United States. Kennedy recognized the new Yemeni Republic. In doing so he followed the instincts he had first exhibited on the Senate floor, as well as the advice of those State Department area specialists who had always seen Nasser as the pan-Arab portent of the future in the Arab world. But Kennedy's immediate motive was to secure an Egyptian withdrawal in order to prevent a clash with Saudi Arabia, the traditional U.S. ally in the area. The Saudis, and the British who at that time were still in Aden, considered Nasser's occupation of Yemen a preliminary to direct attacks on their own territory. The ensuing confusion in U.S. Middle Eastern policy interrupted Kennedy's efforts to cultivate the Egyptian leader, although limited U.S. programs of grants and loans to Egypt continued.

In his biography of Kennedy, Theodore Sorensen has written of the incipient Kennedy-Nasser relationship:

"Nasser liked Kennedy's Ambassador, John Badeau, and he liked Kennedy's practice of personal correspondence. Kennedy put off, however, an invitation for a Nasser visit until improved relations could enable him to answer the political attacks such a visit would bring from voters more sympathetic to Israel."[6]

As with most good intentions deferred, the invitation to Nasser for a personal meeting with Kennedy was never issued. On November 22, 1963, President Kennedy was killed in Dallas by Lee Harvey Oswald, an American who had lived for a time in the Soviet Union and then returned to the United States. Americans will never know whether the course of U.S. policies in the Middle East might have been altered by a young President eager to reexamine any problem, and with a demonstrated, clear understanding of colonialism and its psychological aftermath. They were too stunned to ask any such questions as they watched their new President take the oath while at his side stood the young widow of the former President, her clothing still stained with his blood. They watched grief-stricken as Kennedy's young son saluted his father's funeral cortege and the world statesmen who walked behind it.

Only later did Americans learn with amazement about the spontaneous outpouring of grief all over the globe. In Berlin lighted candles were placed in darkened windows. In Poland church bells tolled throughout a funeral half way around the world. And in Ireland, said a distant kinsman of the fallen President, "they cried the rain down that night." In Belgrade Marshal Tito telephoned the American Ambassador and then was too overcome to speak. In Guinea President Sekou Toure said, "I have lost my only true friend in the outside world." And in Algiers Ahmad Ben Bella telephoned Ambassador Porter to express his incredulity, adding: "Believe me, I'd rather it had happened to me than to him."

The mourning stretched across the Arab world, where to this day faded photographs on humble walls depict the young hero who, though grievously wounded in war, had set out again in peacetime to slay the dragons of bigotry, ignorance, poverty and disease and who, at the beginning of his political quest, had risked his future to speak up for Algerian heroes fighting their own lonely battle against crushing odds.

Even in Baghdad, where fighting between Baathist and Nasserist elements in the government and army was putting Nasserist President Abd al-Salam Arif in undisputed control, residents under a nighttime curfew cried before the television sets that brought them the tragic news. Later, by daylight, a young American woman checking on the welfare of isolated American citizens and protected by her diplomatic license plates drove slowly through the deserted Baghdad streets. As she turned into a side street, she found her progress blocked by a huge tank, its guns leveled at a barricaded building across the Tigris River. When she tried to back away, the tank left its station and lumbered over to her car. A turret opened and an Iraqi officer, sweating in oil-spattered coveralls, clambered down to confront the American woman as she nervously gripped her steering wheel.

"Don't be frightened," the officer said gently. "I have only come to tell you how sad we all are about the death of your President." There were tears in his eyes as he clambered back into his tank.

"I started crying too," the woman reported. "He was crying for the young President we'd lost, before any of us really knew what he stood for. But when I looked at that Iraqi soldier who took time out from a battle in which he could have been killed himself to comfort an American, I realized I was crying for all of us. For Arabs and for Americans in the Middle East. Not just for what we'd lost in Dallas that week, but for what we'd been losing in the Middle East for a whole generation."

NOTES

1. Schlesinger, Arthur M., Jr., *A Thousand Days—John F. Kennedy in the White House,* Houghton Mifflin, Boston, 1965, p. 564.
2. Sorensen, Theodore C., *Kennedy,* Harper and Row, New York, 1965, p. 540.
3. Schlesinger, Arthur M., Jr., *A Thousand Days—John F. Kennedy in the White House,* Houghton Mifflin, Boston, 1965, p. 564.
4. *Ibid.,* p. 553.
5. *Ibid.,* p. 554.
6. Sorensen, Theodore C., *Kennedy,* Harper and Row, New York, 1965, p. 540.

CHAPTER IX

President Johnson
and the Six-Day War

"Lyndon, and Sam Rayburn too, were very much opposed to the Eisenhower Doctrine, which was so clearly designed to placate the Arabs early in 1957, and Lyndon in the Senate managed to defuse some of the sanctions John Foster Dulles wanted to impose on Israel."[1]

Merle Miller, 1980

"You have lost a very great friend, but you have found a better one."[2]

President Lyndon Johnson (in comment to Israeli diplomat), 1963

"However tantalizing the initial U.S.-Arab relationship in the early fifties—and the hopes of renewal during the first Kennedy months—Arab nationalism was irritatingly and increasingly cramping the governing American style by the mid-sixties; and for men like President Johnson and his advisers—the Rostows—irritations are dealt with by a 'bold' course of action."[3]

Abdullah Schleifer, 1972

Lyndon Johnson had spent all of his adult life striving toward power, including the Presidency. He filled Washington with "Lyndon's people," parking political aides who could help him at campaign time in "Schedule C" political positions all through the government. Johnson himself was an astute professional politician. Therefore, as he took the oath of office, standing with John Kennedy's widow in the airplane that was about to take his slain predecessor's body back with them to Washington, he was well aware that this was a horrible way to take over the job he had wanted so long.

One of the first things President Johnson did was solicit advice from his two living predecessors, Harry S Truman and Dwight D. Eisenhower, both of whom were generous with their time and thoughts. It is a moving commentary on the strength of U.S. institutions to read Johnson's reminiscences of his interview with former President Eisenhower, whom he had asked to come to Washington. Johnson, as the Democratic Senate Majority Leader, had often helped Republican President Eisenhower to prepare bi-partisan legislation. Now Eisenhower gave Johnson suggestions for quickly pulling a deeply divided Congress behind his efforts, some notes on what to say, and, interestingly, a list of Eisenhower's own three or four most trusted advisers in government. The top name on the list was that of Robert Anderson, the former Secretary of the Navy and later of the Treasury who had so frequently served as a personal emissary from Eisenhower to the rulers of the Middle East and who had conducted the secret U.S. attempt in 1956 to get the Israelis and Egyptians negotiating instead of arming for war.

Johnson, the defeated candidate for his party's presidential nomination only three years earlier, was now deeply resented by the liberal wing of the Democratic party. He faithfully carried out Kennedy's domestic programs, but the Kennedy partisans could never forget that Johnson was not their own fallen leader. The Kennedy mixture of intellectuals, artists and backroom power brokers had in their minds become an American "Camelot." The stocking-feet and suspenders style of the Johnson White House was not an acceptable substitute, and one by one the Kennedy advisers left. Few of their successors appeared to be men of international vision. None exhibited much patience with seemingly unpredictable Arab leaders. It would be charitable to say that Johnson failed to follow up what had seemed to be promising Kennedy initiatives with the new leaders of Arab nationalism because he feared the political opposition would endanger his important domestic programs. It would be charitable, but it would not be true.

In fact, Johnson put Kennedy's domestic programs through Congress far more rapidly than would have been possible if their originator had not been martyred. Also, as time and Vietnam unfortunately proved, Johnson was not afraid of controversial foreign policy initiatives. It appears that he let the initiatives with Nasser, the Algerians and others lapse simply because neither he nor some of his blatantly pro-Israel advisers thought they were a good idea.

In the thirties, the lanky, hard-working congressman from Texas had been unswerving in his commitment to the programs of the New Deal and had become something of a protege of Franklin D. Roosevelt. President Roosevelt, as a former governor of New York, had close ties to what was then called "the New York Jewish community." This was long before the birth of Israel, and even before Adolf Hitler's persecutions of German Jews had had such a searing impact in the U.S. The "community" was a network of wealthy, and in many cases highly influential, persons in New York. What distinguished them from the big rich in many other parts of the country was their strong attraction to the kind of liberal causes personified by President Roosevelt and, in her own right, by his wife Eleanor.

In his informative book, *Lyndon: An Oral Biography,* Merle Miller quotes Edwin Weisl, Jr., the son of one of the influential members of that New York Jewish community of the 1930s:

"Our family relationship with President Johnson arose over thirty years ago through my father's relationship with President Roosevelt's personal adviser and assistant [Harry Hopkins]. Roosevelt, it is well known, took a liking to Johnson and wanted to make sure that he got a broader acquaintance with people throughout the country, and he asked Hopkins to put Johnson in touch with someone in New York who could introduce him around, and Hopkins picked my father.

"Johnson got to know him, used to come up frequently and stay at our house or our apartment in New York, and we involved ourselves in many ways throughout his career, with helping him in his campaigns, helping him get newspaper support in Texas, and became very friendly with Johnson. We worked on his preparedness committee at one point, and in his campaign for the presidency in '60, and then in '64, we of course were very active."[4]

When Eisenhower and Dulles threatened to remove the unique tax-free status of donations to Israel in order to make the Israelis withdraw from the Sinai, Democratic Senator Johnson and Republican Senator William Knowland of California, the most prominent member of the "China lobby," had been two of the most persistent and powerful senators blocking the administration's plan.

It came as no surprise, therefore, that when Johnson assumed the Presidency, he remained strongly sympathetic to Israel. Isaiah "Si" Kenan, Israel's chief American lobbyist of the time, later told Merle Miller:

"One of Johnson's first statements concerning Israel was when he said to an Israeli diplomat shortly after the assassination of Kennedy, 'You have lost a very great friend, but you have found a better one.' And I would say that everything he did as president supported that statement."[5]

The Israeli diplomat probably was Ephraim "Eppy" Evron, then the second man in Israel's embassy in Washington. Evron had been personal assistant to the ill-starred Pinchas Lavon. To Evron's credit, he had remained unswervingly loyal to his chief when Moshe Dayan, Shimon Peres and perhaps others reportedly had sought to enlist him in a campaign to pin the blame on Lavon for the 1954 Israeli order to provocateurs in Egypt to place incendiary devices in American Embassy and Consulate libraries in order to upset relations between Eisenhower and Nasser. Evron would have nothing to do with the forgery of evidence and, when Lavon was forced to resign, Evron went too. He became living proof that in the politics of any country, loyalty to the former boss is a cardinal virtue when applicants are being interviewed for a new job.

In 1963 Evron was in Washington in charge of Israeli intelligence. He was developing, with James Angleton of the CIA, perhaps the closest partnership U.S. intelligence services have ever had with any country other than Britain. In a way it was closer. Starting in the time of the Eisenhower Administration, the U.S. had dispensed with some of its own intelligence resources in Israel. Subsequently, the CIA became increasingly dependent on the Mossad and other Israeli intelligence services for information about both Israel and the countries around it. Most Americans are familiar with some of the harmful side effects of the close intelligence collaboration with Britain, which resulted in many U.S. secrets finding their way to the Soviet Union. They may not be aware of the results of similar collaboration with Israel when, in 1967, the Israelis launched a preemptive war in the Middle East, initiated some secret actions, and then apparently tried to wipe out the evidence, and a lot of Americans with it. But that incident, described in the next chapter, was near the end of the Johnson Administration.

Evron's presence in Washington in 1963 and 1964 was highly visible proof that, if the CIA then had little intelligence capability in Israel, the arrangement was not reciprocal. Evron (who at the beginning of the Reagan administration was the Israeli Ambassador to the U.S.) did not confine himself to his frequent meetings with Angleton to exchange intelligence with the CIA. He also became a close personal friend of President Johnson.

Harry McPherson, Johnson's longtime friend, has described the relationship to Merle Miller:

"Eppy is five foot three with a quintessential Jewish face . . . and one of the most marvelous people I have ever known. I think Eppy felt what I've always felt, that some place in Lyndon Johnson's blood there are a great many Jewish corpuscles. He really reminds me of a six-foot-three-inch slightly corny Texas version of a rabbi. . . . He is just as likely to spill out all of his woes, his vanity, his joy. . . . He is not afraid of making a fool of himself—as Martin Buber describes—the kind of divine foolishness."[6]

Everyone talked to Miller about the warm feeling Lyndon Johnson had for Israel, even Evron himself. Miller quotes him as follows:

"Johnson's feeling about Israel came out very early in the crisis of 1957 when he was a majority leader. When at that time President Eisenhower and Secretary of State Dulles wanted to force us to withdraw from Sinai, they threatened us with economic sanctions. Johnson persuaded Senator William Knowland of California, who was then minority leader, to come with him to the White House and tell the President that it just wouldn't do."[7]

Miller summarized what he heard from Johnson about the President's role in blocking the Eisenhower initiatives as follows:

"Lyndon, and Sam Rayburn too, were very much opposed to the Eisenhower Doctrine, which was clearly designed to placate the Arabs early in 1957, and Lyndon in the Senate managed to defuse some of the sanctions John Foster Dulles wanted to impose on Israel."[8]

All these words reflect the golden first years of the Johnson Administration, when the domestic ideas of the Kennedy "New Frontier" were incorporated in the legislation of the Johnson "Great Society." They characterize the period before a few moves in Southeast Asia to help the South Vietnamese government escalated into Johnson's guns-with-butter war in Vietnam, and they reflect the kind of superficial faith in any self-proclaimed U.S. ally that seemed to guide Johnson's early foreign policy initiatives.

What played well in the U.S. polls could not be all bad. Therefore, a President who carried the latest polls in his jacket pocket did not have to look ahead. If he took an action and it played in Peoria, he could do it again. In the Johnson era, as in the Truman era, Attlee's comments about the U.S. still held true: "There is no Arab vote in America."

For a few days in May and early June of 1967, however, Johnson seemed to wish that he had not so conspicuously depicted himself as Israel's great American friend. To understand the ensuing crisis in U.S.-Israeli relations, it is necessary to sketch in some intervening history.

When Nasser found he no longer had even a tentative suitor in the White House, his relationship with the Soviet Union began to flourish. The Soviets sent him arms, dumped his cotton all over the world at any price they could get for it, used his ports and airfields for secret missions of their own, and undoubtedly gave him more advice than he thought he needed. What he probably did not realize at the time was that Soviet adventurism in the Middle East had become a key issue in a power struggle within the Kremlin. Hardliners, led by Leonid Brezhnev, were determined to retaliate against—or take advantage of—the growing American involvement in Vietnam, which followed the seemingly successful U.S. venture in the Dominican Republic. The U.S. appeared to be becoming progressively more reckless, playing for higher and higher stakes at increasing distances from home. The Brezhnev faction believed it could call the U.S. hand in the Middle East, an area where the Americans now seemed to be doing everything wrong.

For some time the Syrians had been supporting Palestinian guerrilla raids across Israel's borders. The Israelis complained to the Syrians and threatened them. But, true to their policy of retaliating against moderate Arab regimes, the Israeli reprisal raids were against Jordan, and more specifically against the Palestinian West Bank villages under Jordanian rule.

In November 1966, an Al Fatah mine planted on an Israeli road near the Jordanian frontier killed three and wounded six Israeli soldiers. A column of Israeli tanks and armored vehicles, supported by Mirage aircraft, crossed the frontier and destroyed the West Bank village of Sammu. Eighteen Jordanians were killed and 134 wounded in the fighting, which involved both the villagers and lightly-armed Jordanian soldiers who tried to come to their rescue.

At this time King Hussein was the only really effective spokesman for the Arabs before U.S. audiences. His English was excellent and he had become a familiar television personality on his frequent visits to the United States, stating the Palestinian and Arab cause moderately and effectively time and time again. The U.S. had joined in condemnation at the UN of the Israeli raid. President Johnson, however, did not ask the Israelis, why, if they were fed up with Syria, they kept pounding Hussein's subjects on the West Bank. With little U.S. intelligence capability in Israel, perhaps there was no one with easy access to the President to tell him that Israeli planners had calculated that, if Hussein appeared too weak to defend his subjects, those subjects sooner or later would find a way to replace him. Nor was there anyone to warn Johnson that the new ruler probably would be more like Nasser or the rulers of Syria. Then the Israelis would have an excuse to do what they wanted to do in 1956: Move into Jerusalem and the West Bank, expel Jordan's Arab Legion, and hope that as many of Jordan's Palestinian subjects as possible would go with it.

However, exactly what the Israelis were going to do to realize this plan suddenly became immaterial. The power play in the Kremlin momentarily pre-empted all other plans in the Middle East, and in the end accomplished the Israeli purpose far more gracefully than they could have done it for themselves.

The Russians told the Syrians that the Israelis were massing troops on their border for a major strike. It made sense, since the Israelis in April, 1967, had lured the Syrians into an aerial dogfight in an incident that began when Israel sent an armored tractor into a demilitarized zone. By the end of the day six Syrian planes had been shot out of the skies, some over Damascus, others over Jordan. Syrian peasants, believing Syrian radio claims that the planes being shot down were Israeli, had even taken prisoner one of the Syrian pilots as he walked in from the desert where his parachute had taken him. While the Syrians were denying losses of their own, Jordanian television, which can be seen in Syria, showed downed Syrian pilots being treated in an Amman hospital. It all had been very embarrassing for the extremist Syrian government of that time and it was easy for the Syrians in May, 1967, to believe that the Israelis were massing on their borders for the long-threatened ground retaliation. There was only one problem: It was not true. Either the Israelis had fooled the Russians with fake messages or the Russians had simply made it up.

The Syrians, who had long since ostensibly mended their fences with Nasser after their break from the United Arab Republic, now demanded his assistance. By this time taunts against the Egyptian President from many parts of the Arab World had become nearly unbearable. Egyptian troops, separated from the Israelis by a screen of UN forces on Egyptian territory, had done nothing in November, 1966, while a short distance away in Sammu Israeli tanks were leveling Palestinian homes with the occupants still in them. Again in April, 1967, Egyptian forces did nothing as Israeli planes shot down Syrian planes over the Syrian capital. The Syrians now demanded to know whether Egyptian forces would hide behind the UN screen while Israeli tanks ran over Syrian villages as well. Nasser had always vowed that the moment for Egypt to strike at Israel would come, but that it should be at a time and place of his own choosing. Could he stand by, however, watch a major Israeli attack on Syria, and still claim to be a leader of all the Arabs? He asked the Russians if the Syrian reports of Israeli troop concentrations on their borders were true. The Russians confirmed the reports, which of course Nasser did not know the Russians themselves had originated.

Nasser then made one of the theatrical gestures which in the past had helped him capture Arab minds and hearts, and which had also made him increasingly dependent on the Soviet Union. He asked the UN Secretary General to remove the UN forces "from the international frontier between Egypt and Israel." The Israelis are depicted in the U.S. as eternally on the defensive. In fact, however, they had never permitted UN forces to be stationed on Israeli territory. That meant that the only UN forces separating Egypt and Israel were on Egyptian territory. When they were removed, Egyptian forces would be free to strike against Israel's southern borders if Israeli tanks and planes crossed their northern borders against Syria. UN Secretary General U Thant, however, decided to remove UN forces from all Egyptian territory, not just those on the border with Israel. Unfortunately for Nasser, the UN withdrawal meant that his troops were perfectly free to move back into their former position on the Egyptian side of the Straits of Tiran. The position had been occupied in 1956 by the Israelis, who violated the ceasefire they had already accepted just long enough to seize it. Facing Eisenhower's displeasure, and the threat of UN sanctions which the U.S. obviously would not veto, the Israelis reluctantly turned the position over to UN forces when they withdrew from Sinai.

Now, UN forces were gone and Egyptian forces were back on the Straits. It is not clear whether Nasser was trapped by circumstances and by his own rhetoric or whether he really believed he could use political means to win a decisive strategic victory over the Israelis. Whatever the reason, he announced that he would not permit Israeli shipping to enter the Gulf of Aqaba, Israel's only outlet to Asia and the Far East.

It was obvious to the U.S. that the Israelis would not accept this, even though very few Israeli ships actually used the Gulf of Aqaba at that time. President Johnson realized he had to watch while Israel took the Straits back through another Middle East war, or else try to head off the war by organizing an international fleet to steam into the Gulf of Aqaba and break the blockade. President Johnson set about organizing such an action, which became known as "the Red Sea regatta" by White House aides. Meanwhile, the Israelis were organizing their own forces, which had all the necessary strike plans meticulously worked out.

Did the Israelis plan military action all along? Was it only Russian disinformation to the Arabs that made war inevitable? Or was it simply time for another Middle East round? No clear answer emerges from reading memoirs of the Americans involved with the situation. They simply do not jibe. They only demonstrate that in fact there were many forces at work. Not only were different groups working at cross purposes within the Arab camp, but also within the governments of both Israel and the United States.

One such memoir is Louis Heren's book on the Johnson Presidency, *No Hail, No Farewell.* If one believes the Heren version, when the Israelis seemed to be in trouble, Johnson the friend of Israel began to depict himself as Johnson the prisoner of commitments to Israel made by a Republican predecessor. Heren's book omits the fact that, as a Senator, Johnson had fought all U.S. efforts to use a big stick to make Israel withdraw from Sinai in 1956. It depicts Johnson as shocked and surprised that the U.S. had been compelled to offer carrots instead. Heren writes:

"There was a quick flight to Ottawa for discussions with Lester Pearson, the Canadian prime minister, and Harold Wilson flew from London to Washington. The two discussed joint action by the maritime nations to ensure the free passage of the Strait of Tiran, as Anthony Eden and Eisenhower had once discussed joint action for keeping open the Suez Canal. Into this rather uninspired diplomacy, Abba Eban, the Israeli foreign minister, dropped a bombshell. He arrived in May and told a horrified Johnson that there was a secret American commitment guaranteeing free access of shipping through the Strait of Tiran to Aqaba. Eban produced copies of documents so secret that they were not in the State Department's files.

"The first commitment was made by Eisenhower's Secretary of State, the late John Foster Dulles, after the 1956 war in an effort to persuade the Israelis to withdraw from Sinai, and especially Sharm el Sheikh. He had assisted in the writing of Israel's final statement in the United Nations debate in 1957. It said that interference in shipping in the Strait of Tiran would be regarded as an act of war. I understood at the time that Eban produced a copy of the statement with corrections written in Dulles' hand. He also produced a personal letter from Eisenhower to Ben-Gurion, thanking the then Israeli prime minister for agreeing to the arrangement and strongly emphasizing the American commitment. Johnson was naturally appalled, and without corroborative documents in the White House and State Department files fobbed off Eban while a search was made. He knew that presidential papers are not the property of the state but the personal papers of the president concerned. Since FDR, presidents had followed the custom of putting their papers in special libraries, and that Friday night Tom Hughes, of the State Department, was sent to Gettysburg to go through the Eisenhower papers. He returned the following day, exhausted but with the evidence. Without the benefit of a treaty, and senatorial advice and consent, the United States was fully committed to keeping the Strait of Tiran open and morally committed to go to Israel's help in the event of war."[9]

In Heren's version of the situation, Johnson is not hoisted on his own pro-Israel petard, but instead gamely struggled to uphold secret commitments unwisely made by Eisenhower and Dulles, closet pro-Israelis all along. But if Heren is correct and that was the view from the Johnson camp early in May, by the end of the month things apparently looked different to President Johnson. By that time he certainly had been informed by every branch of U.S. intelligence that the Israelis would win any Middle East war, no matter how or where it started. Merle Miller interviewed John P. Roche, Johnson's White House speech writer, about the atmosphere at the time. As Roche tells it:

"Of course his [Johnson's] purpose at the time was to try to keep the Israelis from attacking and try to bring some pressure on Nasser to open the straits, and at the same time make it clear that he was not going to support the Arabs, that we were going to support Israel if it came to a crunch.

"The State Department had prepared a draft for him which was the most incredible document. It was a completely 'on the one hand' and 'on the other hand' thing. It didn't cut any ice at all. It didn't have one declarative sentence in it as to what we were going to do.

"I worked until about two or three o'clock in the morning on May 23, using some quite tough operational language regarding the fact that the closing of the Straits of Tiran had been a violation of international law and norms and so forth. I called Walt Rostow and I read it to him, and Walt said, 'That sounds fine to me but mark it for the president'. . . .

"The next day there was tremendous pressure brought on Johnson to get him to come out for Israel. Jewish pressure groups in this country were lined up all the way from Washington to California, and Johnson engaged in one of his malicious little games. The various Jewish groups would call him and what he did was he'd fish out the State Department draft and read it to them and say, 'Well, how do you feel about that? They think this is the kind of thing I ought to say. How does it sound to you?'

"So boom! The phones are ringing. The Israeli ambassador Avraham Harmon is over in Humphrey's office with Eppy Evron, who is practically in tears. So Humphrey calls me up and he says, 'What do you know about this?' It was very embarrassing, because I happened to know that what I had written the night before had already gone on speech cards, and he was going on television. He'd approved it, signed it, everything else. . . .

"All day Johnson went on doing this. I called Rostow, I said, 'For God's sake, what is he doing?' Walt said, 'Oh, he's just getting a little therapy for all this pressure they put on.' "[10]

President Johnson did read the message that evening, declaring that "the right of free, innocent passage of the international waterway is a vital interest of the international community" and stating his hope that the UN Security Council "can act effectively."

Miller records that, when the Israeli Foreign Minister, Abba Eban, visited him in Washington on May 26, Johnson told Eban, "I want to see that little blue and white Israeli flag sailing down the Strait of Tiran." However, in order to avoid a confrontation with the Soviet Union, Johnson added that the U.S. must remain above it all. Roche recalled for Miller a White House discussion following the same meeting.

"That night I was working and around nine thirty or ten o'clock the phone rang and he said, 'Come on down.' I went down. Walt Rostow was there, and the president had some of that poisonous low-cal Dr. Pepper, and I had a cup of coffee. He told a little bit about his visit with Eban. You know he was a great mimic, Johnson was. He did a takeoff on Eban, and he said, 'What do you think they're going to do?' We sat around and talked about what we thought the Israelis were going to do. . . . I said, 'I think they'll hit them.' He [Johnson] said, 'Yes, they're going to hit. There's nothing we can do about it.' "[11]

In his own book, *The Vantage Point*, Johnson recalls the May 26 meeting with the Israeli Foreign Minister:

"Our conversation was direct and frank. Eban said that according to Israeli intelligence, the United Arab Republic (UAR) was preparing an all-out attack. I asked Secretary McNamara, who was present, to give Mr. Eban a summary of our findings. Three separate intelligence groups had looked into the matter, McNamara said, and it was our best judgment that a UAR attack was not imminent. 'All of our intelligence people are unanimous,' I added, 'that if the UAR attacks, you will whip hell out of them.'

"Eban asked what the United States was willing to do to keep the Gulf of Aqaba open. I reminded him that I had defined our position on May 23. We were hard at work on what to do to assure free access, and when to do it. 'You can assure the Israeli Cabinet,' I said, 'we will pursue vigorously any and all possible measures to keep the strait open.' . . .

"Abba Eban is an intelligent and sensitive man. I wanted him to understand the U.S. position fully and clearly, and to communicate what I said to his government. 'The central point, Mr. Minister,' I told him, 'is that your nation will not be the one to bear the responsibility for any outbreak of war.' Then I said very slowly and very positively: 'Israel will not be alone unless it decides to go alone.' "[12]

After Eban's return to Israel, he cabled Johnson on May 30 that the Israeli Cabinet had decided two days earlier to postpone military action and to "await developments for a further limited period." Eban added, however, that "it is crucial that the international naval escort should move through the Strait within a week or two." On June 2 an Israeli diplomat told the President's aide, Walter Rostow, that nothing would happen before "the week beginning Sunday, June 11."

Johnson was not overwhelmed by nations volunteering their ships to join a U.S.-led flotilla to break the blockade of the Straits of Tiran. He believed, however, that he had lined up the Netherlands and Australia as well as the British. He therefore planned to go to Congress with the plan during the week of June 5. Meanwhile, both Ambassador Charles Yost and President Eisenhower's long-time confidant and occasional secret emissary to the Middle East, Robert Anderson, were in Cairo. Initially they suggested a visit to Cairo by Vice President Hubert Humphrey. Then it was decided that Vice President Zakaria Mohieddin of the UAR would first visit Washington on June 7 to confer on the crisis. Neither of those plans to avert war was to be tested, however. Instead, some American Middle East specialists believe that the scheduled visit to Washington by the Egyptian Vice President caused Israel to move the date of the attack forward by one week.

In yet another interview about the feverish days before June 5, Miller quotes a Democratic political leader, Abe Feinberg:

"Finally, on the night of June 4 we had a Democratic rally in New York, and Johnson was the main speaker. I had gotten word that afternoon and I went up to where he was sitting. I remember Mary Lasker was on one side and Mathilde Krim, who was then a professor at the Weizmann Institute, was on the other. And I whispered to him, on the side where Mrs. Krim was sitting. I said, 'Mr. President, it cannot be held any longer. It's going to be within the next twenty-four hours.' Well, he made a speech that night that absolutely brought the house down, completely extemporaneous. About Israel and about its survival."[13]

The Israeli aerial attack that followed on June 5, 1967 was such a masterpiece of meticulous planning that, given the exigencies of war, any unexpected action from the other side should have spoiled it all. But nothing did. The date was known only to a few senior officers. As a deception, Defense Minister Moshe Dayan sent several thousand Israeli soldiers on leave. They were photographed for the press as they relaxed on the beaches of Tel Aviv over the weekend. The time was carefully fixed, but not at either of the traditional times for a military attack: It was not sunrise, as might have been expected in order to maximize the daylight hours available to the attackers. Nor was it a few hours before sunset, which would permit the attack to be completed just before darkness and eliminate the possibility of rapid retaliation. Instead, the attack was set for 8 a.m. Israeli intelligence had established that the Egyptian armed forces remained on alert all night long. Then, starting at 7:30 a.m., Egyptian watch officers began going to breakfast. Therefore, at 6 a.m. on June 5 Israeli air force planes had engaged in routine maneuvers, landing back at their bases at 7:30. As the Egyptian radar operators who had been watching them land relaxed and headed off to breakfast, wave after wave of Israeli aircraft took off from Israeli bases. Some flew west out to sea, some headed south toward Elath. The last waves to take off streaked straight toward Egypt. All of these Israeli planes, whether they had turned south from the Mediterranean, west from the Negev desert, or were flying directly from Israeli bases, thundered into Egyptian airspace at exactly the same moment. The fastest planes were targeted at the most distant Egyptian airfields; the slowest struck closest to Egypt's borders with Israel.

Within minutes, every major military airfield in Egypt was under simultaneous attack. Waves of planes dove to unleash bombs or rockets on grounded Egyptian aircraft, and then rose to circle and dive again. Only minutes, and sometimes seconds, after each attack ended and the last Israeli planes vanished into the clear skies, a new wave would roar in over the same battered Egyptian fields. The turnaround time on Israeli airfields for rearming and refueling was down to as little as four minutes. The result was that most Egyptian airfields stayed under almost continuous attack all morning, unable to activate their anti-aircraft defenses or to get their own planes airborne before all were destroyed.

Egypt's air force was permanently out of action by 1 p.m. Then it was Syria's turn. Six separate waves of Israeli fighter bombers swooped in to destroy the Damascus international airport in the course of a seemingly endless afternoon, while Damascenes stood on their flat rooftops watching in glum astonishment. Each wave came in high from the east and then one by one the planes dove at top speed through a cloud of black anti-aircraft bursts from batteries ringing the airport. As each wave departed it left behind dense clouds of black smoke from gasoline storage tanks and airport buildings, as well as the planes caught on the ground. The same tactics that had worked so well in Egypt throughout the morning were followed in Syria throughout the afternoon. The planes made pass after pass until every rocket and shell was gone, and then darted back through mountain passes to Israel to make way for the next group of attackers. Syrians on the high mountains above Damascus could see columns of smoke rising far out across the desert, each one marking the site of a destroyed Syrian military airfield. The fastest Israeli planes struck distant bases near Aleppo in the north, and in the eastern desert and along the Euphrates River near the Iraqi border. The older, slower planes meanwhile continued the shorter bombing shuttle between the Syrian capital and Israeli bases less than 100 miles away.

Having achieved total mastery of the air on Monday, the first day of the war, Israel knew that the Egyptian forces in Sinai stood no chance. It became a twice-fought war. Israeli armored columns repeated the 1956 race to Suez as Israeli aircraft carried out disabling attacks against vehicles on the narrow winding roads of the Mitla and Gidi Passes. This stopped reinforcements or supplies from reaching the Egyptians in Sinai, and cut off their retreat. When the race was finished, what might have been at least an Egyptian delaying action became a rout.

There were unexpected occurrences all through the first day of the war, but they seemed to favor only the Israelis. When the first Israeli planes struck Egyptian airfields while many of the radar operators were at breakfast, the top Air Force base commanders were not even at their commands. Nearly all had assembled at one airfield to welcome the Egyptian Air Force Commander back from an inspection trip. In retrospect, it seems incredible that with Israel poised for an attack for days, and with foreign residents being evacuated from virtually every Middle Eastern capital, the officers in charge of Egypt's air defenses would assemble in any one place, no matter what the occasion. The absence of the military commanders was particularly serious because the Egyptian military organization of the time was extremely centralized, with little initiative expected or permitted from below. If, when the attacks began, middle level officers did not defy tradition and take the initiative, there literally was no one at some bases to order the pilots to scramble their planes, or what was left of them after the first attack.

King Hussein of Jordan had flown secretly to Cairo May 30 and in a six-hour visit had patched up things with President Nasser. Jordan's army was placed under a unified Arab command and token Egyptian units were flown to Jordan. It should have been a day of celebration for Israeli military planners. Six days later, on the morning of the Israeli strike at Egypt, Jordanian guns opened up against the Israelis in Jerusalem. They thus gave the Israelis the long-awaited grounds to move against Jordanian-occupied Jerusalem and the West Bank.

A little later on June 5 came the most self-destructive decision of all for the Arabs. President Nasser and King Hussein together accused the U.S. and Britain of participating in the Israeli aerial attacks. This was precisely the moment when the Arabs most needed their viewpoints conveyed to an unreceptive administration in Washington. One of their best means was through the generally sympathetic chiefs of U.S. diplomatic missions in the Arab World. Yet, just when these ambassadors should have been burning up the wires to Washington describing the carefully-planned Israeli attacks they were witnessing and trying to explain to the Johnson administration the catastrophic consequences that might befall U.S. interests in the Middle East if the war continued, each American embassy was coming under attack by hostile Arab mobs. Acting on the false reports of U.S. complicity in the attacks, several Arab governments, including Egypt, Syria, Iraq, Algeria and the Sudan, broke diplomatic relations with the U.S. and ordered the embassies' American employes to depart within 48 hours. Thus ambassadors who might have counseled the U.S. to put pressure on Israel to stop the attacks were engrossed in

time, on the northern Jordanian sector; we had looked for a springboard from which we could join up with the police garrison on Mount Scopus. Now that Hussein had elected to join in the war and had attacked us, the objective had changed: we were thinking suddenly not only of Mount Scopus, but of the liberation of the whole of Jerusalem."[15]

Gur's book implies that the plan for a general attack was hurriedly improvised when events on the first day of the war made such an attack politically possible. Other passages of the same book, however, indicate how long the Israelis had awaited this opportunity and the enormous amount of advance planning and preparation involved:

"The houses in the immediate vicinity of the boundary had been prepared in advance as battle sites. On every roof positions for weapons had been constructed. Now we found that the iron gates to the roofs were locked. The rapidity with which the battle plan had evolved made it impossible to coordinate all necessary details, and the men with the keys couldn't be found."[16]

Even more revealing is this passage by General Gur:

"Suddenly Colonel David came in, brimming over, as always, with energy and smiles. . . Behind us we had years of working together. Long ago he and I had planted charges of explosives to undermine the wall of the Old City, hoping that some day we would have a` chance to set them off."[17]

The Israeli attack began after dark June 5. It was quick and deadly. The Arab Legion resisted, but both Jerusalem and the West Bank, which the Israelis had fought so hard to occupy in 1948, and which they had come so tantalizingly close to obtaining with French cooperation in 1956, finally fell to the Israeli Army. Who can forget the dramatic photos of sweat-stained, powder-blackened Israeli soldiers, who had just broken through the dense cluster of stone houses around Jerusalem's Wailing Wall, weeping with exaltation as they pressed themselves in prayer against the ancient rocks of the most sacred site of Judaism? For them, the time-honored religious vow, "Next year in Jerusalem," had finally been fulfilled.

As Israeli troops on Wednesday mopped up the last defenses of the Suez Canal, and even allowed a few dazed or lightly wounded Egyptian stragglers to swim across to their own lines, attention shifted to Syria. The defenses of the Golan Heights overlooking Israel's Hula Valley seemed impregnable. But the Israeli Air Force, which totally dominated the skies, had already stopped harassing the fleeing Egyptians and had begun softening up the Syrian positions with bombs, rockets, and napalm. An attack scheduled for Thursday was postponed for 24 hours. Finally, at a heavy price in blood, Israeli infantrymen climbed up the hills, fighting from one fortified bunker to the next, while Israeli armored bulldozers scraped a road out of one of the steepest hillsides. After the infantrymen and the bulldozers finally reached the crest, hundreds of Israeli tanks were free to roll across the rocky but level terrain of the Golan Heights. All day Friday, ceasefires with the Egyptians were being violated and reinstated. In Syria, however, the Israelis ignored the UN Secretary General's ceasefire proposals and kept moving forward. It appeared that they might try to drive their tanks down from the heights against Damascus itself, where the Syrians were digging anti-tank ditches across southern approaches to the sprawling, oasis capital.

On the morning of June 10, Soviet Chairman Kosygin asked that Johnson personally come to the hot line. He told Johnson flatly that if the Israelis did not stop their thrust into Syria the Soviets would take "necessary actions, including military."

Incredibly—though perhaps not, in light of what was already going on in Vietnam—Johnson's first reaction was not to call off the Israelis. Instead he ordered the Sixth Fleet, which had been steaming in circles 300 miles west of the Syrian coast, to change course and proceed directly toward Syria. Later in the day, the Israelis agreed to a ceasefire with Syria through the UN negotiators, thus sparing President Johnson and Chairman Kosygin, who had exchanged additional hot line messages throughout the day, from rushing into a decision about whether or not to begin World War III.

NOTES

1. Miller, Merle, *Lyndon: An Oral Biography,* Ballantine, New York, 1980, p. 476.
2. *Ibid.* p.475.
3. Schleifer, Abdullah. *The Fall of Jerusalem,* Monthly Review Press, New York, 1972, p. 94.
4. Miller, Merle, *Lyndon: An Oral Biography,* Ballantine, New York, 1980, p. 475.
5. *Ibid,* p. 475.
6. *Ibid,* pp. 475-476.
7. *Ibid,* p. 476.
8. *Ibid,* p.476.
9. Heren, Louis, *No Hail, No Farewell,* Harper and Row, New York, 1970, pp. 162-163.
10. Miller, Merle, *Lyndon: An Oral Biography,* p.479.
11. *Ibid,* p.480.
12. Johnson, Lyndon B., *The Vantage Point: Perspectives of the Presidency 1963-1969,* Holt, Rinehart and Winston, 1971, p.293.
13. Miller, Merle, *Lyndon: An Oral Biography,* p.480.
14. Johnson, Lyndon B., *The Vantage Point: Perspectives of the Presidency 1963-1969,* Holt, Rinehart and Winston, 1971, pp. 298-299.
15. Gur, Lt. Gen. Mordechai, *The Battle for Jerusalem.* Popular Library, New York, 1974, pp. 18-19.
16. *Ibid,* p. 28.
17. *Ibid,* pp. 31-32.

CHAPTER X

An Awkwardness for President Johnson, the Friend of Israel

"As for the attack on the defenseless Liberty, *the Israeli government claimed that the converted freighter had been mistaken for an Egyptian warship. A U.S. naval board of inquiry found that the daylight attack had been unprovoked and deliberate. Then the U.S. government shrouded the entire* Liberty *matter in secrecy under a cloak of 'national security' considerations, where it remains even now."*[1]

Wilbur Crane Eveland, 1980

"Whatever [Admiral] Kidd or Admiral John McCain or [Commander] McGonagle or the Joint Chiefs of Staff in Washington or every surviving member of the crew of the Liberty *thought—and they all knew damn well they had been attacked in cold blood—they had to accept they had lost the game. Because of political expedience and a frightened presidential administration in Washington, its eye on the next election and the powerful pro-Democratic Jewish vote, absolutely nothing would be done to repair the damaged honor of the U.S. Navy and the personal hardship the killing of 34 American sailors and the maiming of another 171 had brought to so many innocent families."*[2]

Anthony Pearson, 1978

"Not surprisingly, Israel claimed that nearly everything she did was in self-defense. The preemptive strikes of the fifth of June were in self-defense. The capture of El Arish, the naval and paratroop assault on Sharm al-Sheikh, the sweep through Sinai,

82

and the armed penetration of Jordan were all in self-defense. Now, with the war virtually over and with the world crying for peace, could Israel put troops in Syria without being seen as an aggressor? Probably not. Not with the USS Liberty *so close to shore and presumably listening.* Liberty *would have to go."*[3]

James M. Ennes, Jr., 1979

"We in the Department of Defense cannot accept an attack upon a clearly marked noncombatant United States naval ship in international waters as 'plausible' under any circumstances whatever. The implications that the identification markings were in any way inadequate are both unrealistic and innaccurate. The identification markings of U.S. Naval vessels have proven satisfactory for international recognition for nearly 200 years."[4]

U.S. Department of Defense Statement, 1967

The euphoria that gripped the Israelis after the June 1967 war may well stand as a high water mark in the nation's history. It certainly marks the moment when Israel peaked in world esteem. Only a year earlier, in 1966, Israel's economy had slowed to a standstill in the absence of serious external pressures, and the essential foreign subsidies they generated. More Jewish Israelis were leaving Israel than were coming in, an impossible situation for a country whose public image was that of a refuge for all of the world's homeless Jews. In 1966 even Israel's Jews had been heading for the promised lands of Australia and North and South America.

Now again, in 1967, the world rang with deserved praise for the courage of Israeli fighting men and women, the brilliance of Israeli leaders, and the spirit of Israeli reservists abroad who had rushed to book air passage back to their country to join their units at the front.

The Russians had supplied both Syria and Egypt with false information so elaborate that it even included an Israeli military planning document, stolen years earlier by a highly-placed Russian spy in Israel. The date was altered to corroborate Russian reports of Israeli preparations for an imminent attack on Syria. The Russian plan had produced the very Middle East war that the hardline Brezhnev faction had wanted, but the war had produced the wrong results. Instead of pushing the U.S., busy with Vietnam, out of the Middle East and more firmly implanting Soviet influence in the Eastern Arab countries, it had produced a humiliating defeat for Russian arms. Much of the Israeli armament was still French. However, the sophisticated weapons that Israel increasingly had received from the United States, as American concern grew over Soviet arms shipments to Egypt and Syria, had triumphed over the Russian tanks that lay scattered in vast junkpiles from the Mitla Pass to the Golan Heights and the charred Russian planes that marked every airfield in Egypt and Syria.

After the Israeli victory, Johnson expressed regret that the Israelis did not wait (though he seems to have made no serious effort to compel them to do so) for his own actions to open the Straits of Tiran. He wrote:

"I have always had a deep feeling of sympathy for Israel and its people, gallantly building and defending a modern nation against great odds and against the tragic background of Jewish experience, I can understand that men might decide to act on their own when hostile forces gather on their frontiers and cut off a major port, and when antagonistic political leaders fill the air with threats to destroy their nation. Nonetheless, I have never concealed my regret that Israel decided to move when it did. I always made it equally clear, however, to the Russians and to every other nation, that I did not accept the oversimplified charge of Israeli aggression."[5]

Although Johnson regretted the Israelis' moving forward on their own, he was relieved at the way things turned out. In the U.S., only he and his immediate aides fully realized how close the Israeli actions had again brought the world to the brink of a disastrous Soviet-U.S. confrontation. He wrote:

"Aside from the tragic accident involving the *Liberty*, no American died in the Middle East war in 1967. But the peace of the world walked a tightrope between June 5 and June 10, 1967, as it does today."[6]

The "tragic accident involving the *Liberty*," however, merits some attention. At the time, it was dismissed by much of the U.S. press as simply an erroneous attack by Israeli war planes and torpedo boats on a U.S. Navy intelligence-gathering vessel which the Israelis said they had mistaken for Egypt's only military transport ship. Nearly every American aboard was killed or wounded. After considerable prompting by the U.S. government and Israel's friends in the U.S., Israel paid the families of the victims a total of $6.8 million. It also promised at first to pay for the material damages, but then ignored the U.S. government's claim of $7.6 million for the ship. A U.S. Naval Board of Inquiry was convened, but it sought to limit its investigation to any failures in U.S. performance that might have contributed to the disaster.

The whole matter might have rested there except for one awkward detail: The ship had not sunk. As a result there were survivors, more than two hundred of them, all U.S. Navy or National Security Agency personnel. The father of one of the dead American officers was a retired Navy captain who had served in U.S. Naval intelligence. He interviewed many of the survivors, then went back and talked to his old Navy colleagues about the limits imposed on the inquiry. It is one thing to pass on without comment a report that you believe is a whitewash. It is another thing to look an old wartime buddy in the eye, and pretend to him that you believe it, especially when you know the incident it describes cost him his son.

It was difficult, but not completely impossible, to believe that the Israelis could, in the heat of the Six-Day War, have briefly mistaken a U.S. vessel for an Egyptian one. Alternatively, it was not too difficult to believe that the Israelis suddenly found that they had a reason of such national importance that it overrode all moral objections to the sinking of an American Navy ship gathering electronic intelligence on the edges of the most successful war in Israeli history. What still is difficult to believe, however, is that, if the United States subsequently discovered the true nature of the Israeli action, and the reason why it was taken, it would seek to withhold this information.

Among rational Americans, talk of high-level plots and high-level coverups always, and rightly, strains credulity. Therefore, before continuing with the story it is perhaps best to digress with Richard Deacon, a pro-Israel English writer, who was formerly Foreign Manager of the London *Sunday Times*. The British author's book, *The Israeli Secret Service*, gives a brief account of the incident and offers its own explanation for the Israeli action. A passage in Deacon's book also vividly describes the attitude toward Israel in the Washington of the Lyndon Johnson era, sketching in the background against which otherwise responsible Americans might have gone along with a coverup, and why it might have worked—for a while. Deacon writes:

"For a brief period Ephraim Evron was Israel's most powerful figure in Washington, more highly regarded than the Ambassador, and welcomed as a collaborator and Mossad liaison officer to the CIA. For years the tentacles of the Israeli Secret Service had reached out into all walks of American life, not in any sinister way, as was sometimes alleged by her enemies, but in a quietly persistent manner which embraced making friends and influencing people, establishing opinion lobbies and gathering intelligence. This influence extended into the U.S. Congress and the Senate, the Pentagon, the defense and electronic industries, the research laboratories and such Jewish-oriented organizations as the Anti-Defamation League, the Jewish Defense Committee, Bonds for Israel and the Federation of Jewish Philanthropies. Some of these bodies have served as fronts for intelligence-gathering and there are few of the important Congressional Committees which do not possess one member or staff assistant who does not feed the Israeli network material."[7]

That, from a pro-Zionist author, is perhaps the best preparation for what follows. These are the words of the mother of Lt. Stephen Toth, who was killed on the *Liberty*, and whose retired intelligence officer father, Navy Captain Joe Toth, had insisted on pursuing the matter. Reports Mrs. Toth:

"They killed my husband. . . . First my son, then my husband. The harassment took the form of threats and claims that Joe was damaging national security, and there was surveillance and pressure from people like the IRS. It was too much for his bad heart. It took a year to kill him, but it did."[8]

She spoke these words to a British journalist, Anthony Pearson. His book, *Conspiracy of Silence: The Attack on the U.S.S. Liberty* relates the stories of the survivors, and the by now fairly successful efforts of many well-meaning people in and out of the U.S. government to put together a coherent version of what happened, possible reasons for it, and the coverup that followed.

Like most tragedies, it started out routinely. The *Liberty* was a Navy ship used by the U.S. National Security Agency to monitor foreign communications. Such "snooper ships" or "ferrets," flying the flags of the Soviet Union, the U.S., and other countries and laden with antennae and electronic gear, are familiar sights to all sailors and to those who live in the ports used by the world's principal navies.

Their function was relatively unknown to the American public until the North Koreans seized one of the *Liberty*'s sister ships, the *Pueblo,* in 1968. Today, nearly every American recalls the *Pueblo.* Yet very few Americans recall the *Liberty,* despite the fact that nearly every member of its crew was killed or wounded.

On May 24, 1967, 19 days before hostilities broke out on June 5, the National Security Agency ordered its U.S. Navy spy ship, with a complement of 297 men aboard, to leave its normal station off West Africa and start its trip to the Middle East. By the night of June 7, the ship was proceeding cautiously toward the Gaza Strip and the Sinai coast, relaying the findings of its array of sophisticated monitoring equipment. The equipment was operated solely by personnel of the National Security Agency. Even the ship's U.S. Navy commander was not allowed to enter the restricted portions of the hold, where the equipment functioned day and night, pulling in a variety of information that traveled across the area radio waves.

Various authors claim that as early as June 7, the third day of the war, Washington had become aware of a highly disturbing fact. Whatever the Israelis had been doing overtly to keep King Hussein from committing his forces to the war, Israeli intelligence wizards were doing something else entirely. Using highly sophisticated equipment, they reportedly had devised a means to intercept, change, and then relay onward communications between Cairo and Amman. They were "cooking" the messages to lure King Hussein into committing his forces fully to attacks in support of the Egyptian army and draw them away from defense of the West Bank and Syria. This is Deacon's version of the still-murky details:

"Now once war had been launched the Israelis had one tremendous advantage over the Egyptians in that they had broken Egyptian and Jordanian ciphers and codes, while the Arabs had not done the same with the Israeli ciphers. Thus the Israelis, thanks to their superior intelligence, were in a position to exploit this advantage by feeding false information by signals to the enemy. In a relay station in Sinai radio messages from Cairo to Amman were being blocked by the Israelis and, in the jargon of the intelligence world, 'cooked' before being swiftly rerouted to Amman. The Israeli plan was to create the impression that the war was going well for the Egyptians. Throughout the first day of the war the aim was to feed these false signals to the enemy, thereby creating the maximum confusion in their ranks, and to black out and jam messages from Cairo to Amman telling King Hussein that the Israelis were gaining ground. Later Israel falsely informed Jordan by 'cooked' messages that the Egyptians were counter-attacking in Sinai and needed support from Hussein by an attack on Israeli positions in the Hebron area."[9]

That day Eugene Rostow reportedly called the Israeli Ambassador, Avraham Harman, to the Department of State and told him that the U.S. knew about the "cooked" messages, and understood that they were intended to draw King Hussein further into the war and to keep his forces fighting long enough for Israel to seize all of Jerusalem and the West Bank.

It is not clear whether he discussed with the Israelis how the U.S. was able to monitor their messages. It probably did not make any difference. If Ambassador

Harman could not find out, his popular deputy, "Eppi." Evron, almost certainly could.

The morning of June 8 dawned bright and Mediterranean-clear as the *Liberty* steamed off Al Arish. Immediately after sun-up, a French-built "Noralas" transport circled the ship three times and then flew off toward Israel. The Liberty's crew was not concerned, since the ship was showing a huge American flag 100 feet above its flying bridge. The number 5 on both of its bows was twelve feet tall and had been freshly painted a few weeks earlier. Its name was lettered on the stern in English. On such a clear day, and in such calm weather, everything should have been going well, but it was not. According to some reports, the *Liberty*'s receivers were encountering such loud jamming that it prevented the ship from receiving any other radio signals. At first, the chief radioman thought that it was because his own transmitters were malfunctioning, but a check proved otherwise. Significantly, perhaps, the jamming was loud enough to make radio transmission from the ship very difficult.

The *Liberty* had just made a turn on its roughly circular course at 8:50 a.m. when a single unidentified jet circled her, and then flew toward the mainland. There was no attempt at communication either way. At 10:56 the Noralas transport appeared again and circled three or four times, apparently photographing the *Liberty* from a low altitude. It repeated this scrutiny again at 11:26 a.m. and 12:20 p.m. Also during the morning, two unidentified jets circled the ship twice and flew off toward the south.

The ship's captain, Commander William McGonagle, was puzzled and concerned at this almost continuous Israeli aerial surveillance but, in the absence of further orders from his base, he stayed in his own pattern while the NSA technicians continued their monitoring operations. Commander McGonagle did not know that three separate messages had been dispatched from Washington ordering the *Liberty* to leave the area. None of the messages reached him. All had been misrouted somewhere along the chain of communications, even though all had been given the highest priority designation in order to assure instant transmission. Suddenly, shortly before 2 p.m., the ship's radar picked up the tracks of both planes and ships racing toward the *Liberty*. It was just about the time the last message had been sent from Washington. The planes, Israeli Mirage fighters, one by one dove without warning toward the ship in an attack pattern. Their concentrated rocket, cannon, and machine gun fire rapidly swept away virtually everything above deck—sunbathing off-duty crewmen, lookouts, sailors seeking to man the four pedestal-mounted 50 caliber machine guns that would have allowed the ship to protect itself, and the antennae needed to get off a distress signal. For five to six minutes according to Commander McGonagle, and as long as 20 to 30 minutes according to some officers, the Israeli planes made pass after pass. Their armor-piercing shells left more than 800 holes in the hull and superstructure. In the first minutes nearly everyone above deck was down—dead or wounded.

Lieutenant James Ennes, electronic material officer on the *Liberty*, in his book *Assault on the Liberty*, describes the scene:

"Blood flowed, puddled and coagulated everywhere. Men stepped in blood, slipped and fell in it, tracked it about in great crimson footprints."[10]

Lieutenant Stephen Toth was killed as he climbed to the lookout station to identify the attacking planes. Although painfully wounded himself, Commander McGonagle used those first few moments well. At 2:10, while still under the initial attack, he reported that he got off an all-channel distress message: "Mayday! Mayday! Am under attack from jet aircraft." Seconds later the jets silenced his radio and took out his antennae, so that he never heard the response from the Sixth Fleet aircraft carrier *Little Rock* confirming the receipt of his only transmission and reporting that it was dispatching jet aircraft to his assistance. Lieutenant Ennes, whose memory of the duration and details of the attack differs in several respects from Commander McGonagle's, describes it in these words:

"The first airplane had emptied the gun mounts and removed exposed personnel. The second airplane, through extraordinary luck or fantastic marksmanship, disabled nearly every radio antenna on the ship, temporarily preventing our call for help. Soon the high-performance Mirage fighter bombers that initiated the attack were joined by smaller swept-wing Dassault Mystere jets, carrying dreaded napalm—jelled gasoline. The Mysteres, slower and more maneuverable than the Mirages, directed rockets and napalm against the bridge and the few remaining topside targets. In a technique probably designed for desert warfare but fiendish against a ship at sea, the Mystere pilots launched rockets from a distance, then dropped huge silvery metallic napalm canisters as they passed overhead. The jellied slop burst into furious flame on impact, coating everything, then surged through the fresh rocket holes to burn frantically among the men inside."[11]

As is the case with most dramatic events, many discrepancies exist among the recollections of eyewitnesses to the attack concerning the number of planes participating, the duration of the attack, and even how many distress messages the *Liberty* was able to get to Sixth Fleet units, and whether or not the *Liberty* heard responses to its messages. Whether or not Commander McGonagle heard the responses to his SOS, a lot of other people probably did, and that may have saved his ship from going to the bottom with all hands.

As armed Sixth Fleet jets streaked eastward toward the *Liberty* (and the war zone), Johnson informed Kosygin on the hot line that they were on a reconnaissance mission to investigate the distress call, and were not planning any hostile activity against the Arab forces. The point was to keep the Russians, fearing an attack, from mounting a counterstrike. The U.S. Embassy in Moscow later reported that Johnson's precautionary measure had convinced the Russians more than anything else that he really was trying to keep the Arab-Israeli war from developing into a general holocaust. At the same time, however, Americans have reported that impromptu preparations were being made for a punitive strike at Egypt if it turned out that Egyptian planes were attacking the U.S. ship. It simply

never occurred to U.S. planners in those first reactive moments that the attack on an American ship off Al Arish was being made by Israelis.

While all of this was happening around the globe, and the surviving crew members of the *Liberty* were battling fires all over the ship, three Israeli motor torpedo boats were bearing down upon her to open an all-out attack. While 20 and 40-millimeter guns riddled the ship, at least two torpedoes were launched, one of which struck the communications room dead center in the number 3 hold. The entire communications center was destroyed, and its commander and most of his staff were killed by the explosion or trapped by the rush of water that filled the hold.

Here again, recollections differ as to what happened next. It would be immaterial except that some of the recollections of Commander McGonagle, as related to the Naval Board of Inquiry, were subsequently published in unclassified, summary form. Shortly afterward, "eyewitness" accounts by Israeli military personnel appeared in the Israeli press which closely matched the published recollections of the ship's commander and which attributed the attack to mistaken identification. It was only later, when detailed recollections by other ship's officers began to leak out, that the wide discrepancies between the Israeli version of events and those of some of the American eyewitnesses became glaringly obvious.

McGonagle recalled that as he awaited another salvo from the torpedo boats, the firing stopped and one of the torpedo boats blinked out the question, "Do you need assistance?" Torn between astonishment and fury, McGonagle declined assistance.

However, Ennes recalls the attack by the torpedo boats as continuing for a protracted period after the torpedo struck. He writes:

"Petty Officer John Randall was knocked off his feet by the impact of the torpedo . . . Randall burst out of his shop and onto the main deck in time to see torpedo boat *Tahmass* drift slowly down the ship's starboard side, her guns trained on *Liberty*'s bridge. Randall extended the middle finger of his right hand in a universal gesture of contempt—and then watched the 40 mm cannon swing around until it came to bear squarely on his chest. But Randall was too angry to be frightened and too proud to move; he stared defiantly at the gunner while the boat drifted past. Luckily for him, that gunner had no stomach for firing at such an easy target. Moments later all three boats commenced circling *Liberty* at high speed while firing at the waterline and at any men they could see moving. . . . An engineman brought the news the bullets were whistling over the ship's boilers: 'The boats are firing at the waterline. They're trying to explode the boilers!' he yelled. But most of the bullets were passing harmlessly through the ship. . . .

"Thomas Smith, the ship's laundry operator . . . waited for the sound of the machine guns to stop. When the torpedo boats finally pulled back, he raced to his abandon-ship station where he was alarmed to see sticky rubber sealant leaking from the life rafts. . . Finally, at a life-raft rack on the ship's port quarter, Smith found several apparently sound rubber rafts. When he pulled cords on the CO_2 cylinders, only three rafts held air. These he secured with heavy line and dropped over the side, where they would be ready if the abandon-ship order came. Lurking lazily a few hundred yards away, patiently waiting for

Liberty to sink, the men on the torpedo boats watched the orange rafts drop into the water. Smith saw someone move on the center boat as her engine growled and her stern settled lower in the water. The boat moved closer to *Liberty*. When within good machine-gun range she opened fire on the empty life rafts, deflating two and cutting the line on the third, which floated away like a child's balloon on the surface of the water. Smith cursed helplessly as a torpedo boat stopped to take the raft aboard. Then the boats added speed, taking the raft with them, and turned toward their base at Ashdod, sixty-five miles away."[12]

Whether the sea attack continued long after the torpedo hit as recalled by Ennes or stopped almost immediately afterward as recalled by McGonagle, there is little disagreement about other events occurring after the torpedo hit and before the boats left the area. Two large Hornet helicopters embellished with the Star of David insignia began circling the ship at a distance of only 100 yards. They made no offer of rescue, nor did they attack. The American crew could see, however, that they contained armed Israeli troops in battle dress. The torpedo boats then closed in again and at the same moment the surviving *Liberty* crew members braced themselves as two jets swept toward the ship in attack formation. But nothing happened. The aircraft departed without firing, the helicopters left without trying to put their soldiers aboard and, according to Ennes, it was at this time that the *Tahmass*, one of the torpedo boats, blinked out a message which the *Liberty*'s crew could not understand. The *Tahmass* came still closer, according to Ennes, and the Israeli commander inquired with a bullhorn, "Do you need any help?" Captain McGonagle declined the offer and after an hour the torpedo boats departed as well.

The attack was over although the ship was approached once more, as it limped away, by an Israeli helicopter apparently offering to assist with casualties, some of whom were still lying dead on the shattered decks. Having lost its radio, the ship could not establish communication and, recalling the armed troops on the previous helicopters, Captain McGonagle refused to let this one land. By this time Washington officials had established voice contact with the *Liberty*, knew that Israeli planes and ships were responsible for the attack and had dropped the idea of a retaliatory attack against Egypt.

Many mysteries and some inconsistencies still exist concerning the *Liberty*. It seems likely that the Israeli Defense Minister, Moshe Dayan, personally ordered the attack. A charitable interpretation of what followed is that, once the area containing the electronic monitoring equipment and its crew had been wiped out by the first torpedo, the attackers saw no reason to continue. The *Liberty* obviously would discover nothing more. However, given the jamming of the *Liberty*'s radio frequencies and the violence and coordination of the combined air-sea attack, which was aimed at knocking out all of the ship's communications in the first few seconds, and followed up with a torpedo at the water line, it seems likely that the object was to sink the ship without a trace. One can only speculate on why the attack stopped so suddenly, just short of completion. It is hard to imagine that

Dayan, who 13 years earlier at the time of the "Lavon affair" had not balked at the order to carry out provocations against American installations in Cairo, would have missed this chance to kill two birds with one stone. If he had already decided that the communications monitoring must be stopped, even at the cost of the lives of the American crew, why not send the ship to the bottom? That way, Egypt would be blamed and the U.S. might be provoked into a move that would accomplish Israel's (and the USSR's) long-standing aim of once and for all alienating the Egyptians and Americans.

There are various possible explanations why the attack stopped. One, of course, is that the Israelis really had just discovered for the first time that they were sinking an American ship. This is the official Israeli explanation, but it seems not to have been accepted by most of the Americans involved in the attack or in the naval inquiry that followed.

A second explanation is that, at some point after the attack began, an Israeli officer rebelled against the order to sink the ship and refused to allow it to continue. That is at least consistent with the evidence. It is also supported by a CIA information report which, with the informant's name deleted, was declassified and released into the public domain under the Freedom of Information Act. (In fairness it should be noted that by preparing such reports the U.S. government agency involved does not necessarily authenticate the information they contain. It simply transmits the report, rumor or theory which has been presented to the drafting officer by an informant.) The CIA message read:

"(Sources deleted) commented on the sinking of the US Communications ship *Liberty.* They said that Dayan personally ordered the attack on the ship and that one of his generals adamantly opposed the action and said, 'This is pure murder.' One of the admirals who was present also disapproved the action, and it was he who ordered it stopped."[13]

Still a third explanation is simply that the Israelis suddenly realized, or were told, that they had been caught. Whether they were aware that the initial distress message had not identified the attackers is not clear. Nor is it clear whether they thought they could have finished the job before the arrival of American jets at the scene. What does seem certain is that an American submarine, the *Andrew Jackson,* was in the immediate vicinity and closely coordinating its movements with those of the *Liberty.* (Some authors report that although the submarine could not participate in the fight, it actually filmed the attack on the *Liberty* through its periscope.) If at some point in the action the Israelis became aware of this, they would know that the game was up. In any case, they had already destroyed electronic evidence of their actions at the beginning of the war, and any capability of the *Liberty* to monitor those actions further.

Another possibly relevant factor was the fact that pilots of two of the attacking Israeli aircraft were in fact dual-nationality American-Israelis. In a conversation in Israel with British journalist Anthony Pearson, one of those pilots, who learned to fly in the U.S. Air Force, stated that when he and his comrade, a former U.S. Navy flyer, first saw the U.S. Navy markings on the *Liberty,* they twice asked for reconfirmation of the attack orders. The orders were reconfirmed and the attack began. The pilot told Pearson that his father, who had emigrated from the U.S. to Israel, had denounced him for "carrying out orders" to kill his own former countrymen just as had members of the Nazi S.S.

Whatever the reasons for the Israeli orders to start and to stop the attack, it is the attitude of the U.S. government in impeding investigation into the matter that most puzzles subsequent investigators.

In his book, Lieutenant Ennes articulates this concern:

"There *were* a number of perfectly legitimate security issues that had to be reckoned with: the mission and capabilities of the ship; the reaction time of the fleet; the deployment and control of nuclear weapons; the deployment of submarines. All of these things are sensitive and could provide useful information for a potential enemy. However, the coverup went far beyond that."[14]

Former CIA agent Wilbur Crane Eveland advances his own explanations both for the motive behind the attack, and for government reluctance to investigate it. He reports in his book:

"Message intercepts by the *Liberty* made it clear that Israel had never intended to limit its attack to Egypt. Furthermore, we learned that the Israelis were themselves intercepting communications among the Arab leaders. The Israelis then retransmitted "doctored" texts to encourage Jordan and Syria to commit their armies in the erroneous belief that Nasser's army had repelled the Israeli invaders. To destroy this incriminating evidence, Moshe Dayan ordered his jets and torpedo boats to destroy the *Liberty* immediately. . . . The Israeli government claimed that the converted freighter had been mistaken for an Egyptian warship. A U.S. naval board of inquiry found that the daylight attack had been unprovoked and deliberate. Then the U.S. government shrouded the entire *Liberty* matter in secrecy under a cloak of 'national security' considerations, where it remains even now. Individual claims of compensation for the ship's dead and wounded were paid by the U.S. government, supposedly on behalf of Israel. Even moves by Congress to stop all aid to Israel until $7 million in compensation for the *Liberty* was paid succumbed to White House and Department of State pressure. Why? Defense Minister Dayan had stated his government's position bluntly: Unless the United States wished the Russians and Arabs to learn of joint CIA-Mossad covert operations in the Middle East and of Angleton's discussions before the 1967 fighting started, the questions of the lost American ship and how the war originated should be dropped. That ended the U.S. protestations."[15]

The U.S. government's motivation for continuing to withhold information about the attack continues to bother well-intentioned Americans. If their own government does not tell the truth about the transgressions of its allies, what about its own sins of omission or commission? How can decent and respected Americans, sworn to protect and preserve the Constitution of the United States, act in a manner so inconsistent with both its letter and its spirit? Is it not better to admit the truth, no matter how damaging to the U.S. relationship with Israel, than go on telling new lies to cover it up?

The significance of the Dreyfus affair was not the fact that an innocent Jewish army officer was convicted on trumped-up charges of treason against the France he served and loved. What shocked the world (and launched Zionism as a serious movement) was the fact that, when his innocence was proved, the authorities tried to disregard the truth in order to protect the French institutions under which he had been convicted.

In Israel's Lavon affair, it was not the stupidity or immorality of the plan to incite the U.S. against Egypt that ultimately shocked Israelis. It was the fact that, years later, when it was revealed that Pinchas Lavon had been blamed on the basis of forged documents, Ben Gurion not only refused to accept the evidence but intensified his persecution of Lavon in order to protect the institutions of Israel, which, in his mind, seemed to be identical with the political fortunes of his Labor party proteges such as Dayan and Peres.

After the Gulf of Tonkin incident, and the Watergate coverup, Americans reluctantly realized that the leaders of both U.S. political parties in recent decades have persuaded themselves that, under certain circumstances, fabricated evidence or outright lies are justified. Many well-intentioned Americans would say that withholding facts or even lying is permissible if it is demonstrably in the national interest. Others, equally well-intentioned, would disagree, saying that the lie becomes a spreading cancer in the body of mutual trust upon which all democratic societies must rest, and that, in the end, the cancer is far more destructive than the evil the lie originally was devised to counter.

Whatever the answers to those abstract questions, in the case of the *Liberty* it appears that any withholding of facts or lying that may still be taking place is in the national interest of Israel. It does not appear to be in the national interest of the United States, and it certainly is not in the interest of international morality.

In the prologue to his book about the attack, Ennes summarizes the entire case nicely:

"Even before the wounded were evacuated, a news lid went down over the entire episode. This story was not to be told. The Navy's own failures were never exposed or acknowledged, and Israel's fragile alibi was nurtured and protected. Israel claimed that the ship was at fault for being near the coast, for 'trying to escape' after being fired upon by jets, and for not informing the Israeli government of her location; and our government tolerantly kept those assertions from public knowledge. Israel claimed that the attack resulted from mistaken identity, and our government quietly accepted that excuse."[16]

Some have called this a whitewash, but that is not entirely true. When pressed, various government departments eventually released documents pointing to Israeli guilt, as for example the CIA document quoted previously. Nor has there been a permanent total news blackout, as the number of books already published concerning the attack on the *Liberty* indicates. But the reluctance of any department of the government to look squarely and objectively at the evidence, and offer its own opinion as to whether the attack was deliberate and as to probable motives for the attack has been very effective in making the incident gradually recede from public consciousness. For anyone who doubts the all-pervasive effect of this information "brown-out," it may be instructive to complete this chapter with President Johnson's own account of the attack on the *Liberty,* written long after the facts had been studied and published, at least in classified form. His description of the *Liberty* affair in his own book, *The Vantage Point,* reads:

"Thursday, June 8, began on a note of tragedy. A morning news bulletin reported that a U.S. Navy communications ship, the *Liberty,* had been torpedoed in international waters off the Sinai coast. For seventy tense minutes we had no idea who was responsible, but at eleven o'clock we learned that the ship had been attacked in error by Israeli gunboats and planes. Ten men of the *Liberty* crew were killed and a hundred were wounded. This heartbreaking episode grieved the Israelis deeply, as it did us."[17]

The true toll of the attack on the *Liberty,* as President Johnson already seemed to have forgotten, was 34 men killed and another 171 men wounded.

NOTES

1. Eveland, Wilbur Crane, *Ropes of Sand: America's Failure in the Middle East,* Norton, New York, 1980, p. 325.
2. Pearson, Anthony, *Conspiracy of Silence: The Attack on the U.S.S. Liberty,* Quartet Books, London, 1978, p. 61.
3. Ennes, James M., Jr., *Assault on the Liberty. The True Story of the Israeli Attack on an American Intelligence Ship,* Random House, New York, 1979, p. 212.
4. Goulding, Phil G., *Confirm or Deny—Informing the People on National Security,* Harper & Row, New York, 1970, p. 124.
5. Johnson, Lyndon B., *The Vantage Point: Perspectives of the Presidency, 1963–1969,* Holt, Rinehart and Winston, 1971, p. 297.
6. *Ibid,* p. 304.
7. Deacon, Richard, *The Israeli Secret Service,* Taplinger, New York, 1980, pp. 169-170.
8. Pearson, Anthony, *Conspiracy of Silence: The Attack on the U.S.S. Liberty,* Quartet Books, London, 1978, p. 132.
9. Deacon, Richard, *The Israeli Secret Service,* Taplinger, New York, 1980, p. 180.
10. Ennes, James M., Jr., *Assault on the Liberty.* Random House, New York, 1979, p. 62.
11. *Ibid,* p. 67.
12. *Ibid,* pp. 91-92, 95-96.
13. *Ibid,* p. 214.
14. *Ibid,* pp. 203-204.
15. Eveland, Wilbur Crane, *Ropes of Sand: America's Failure in the Middle East,* Norton, New York, 1980, p.325.
16. Ennes, James M., Jr., *Assault on the Liberty.,* Random House, New York, 1979, pp. 3-4.
17. Johnson, Lyndon B., *The Vantage Point: Perspectives of the Presidency, 1963–1969,* Holt, Rinehart and Winston, 1971, pp. 300-301.

CHAPTER XI

President Nixon
and the October War

"In effect, the October war made it possible for Secretary Kissinger to pose as the savior of both sides. When the Israelis were in trouble, the American resupply effort made it possible for them to continue the battle on a scale commensurate with their needs. When the Egyptians were in trouble, American pressure on Israel enabled them to avert a defeat which would have fractured the Egyptian army and shaken the Sadat regime. Throughout the Nixon years, the administration had been straining to achieve 'even-handedness': By force of circumstances, that blessed state was reached in practice in October 1973."[1]

Theodore Draper, April 1975

"Ironically enough, the Israelis' failure to win the Yom Kippur War in the convincing style of 1967 may actually have made it easier for them to achieve the goal they failed to achieve after their crushing six-day victory. For some time ahead they will probably feel beleaguered, but they will also probably find it easier to talk to their opponents—and their opponents to them. If the superpowers can bring them together there are at least prospects of a lasting peace—a peace that guarantees the state of Israel as well as respecting Arab rights."[2]

Colonel A. L. Barker, November 1974

The Arab defeat in 1948 could be blamed on corrupt rulers. The defeat of 1956 had resulted from a combined sneak attack by Israel, France, and Britain. But in 1967 there was no one to blame. President Gamal Abd al-Nasser accepted the consequences and resigned, but in a truly spontaneous outpouring, Egyptians insisted that he remain in power.

National pride had been grievously wounded throughout the Arab World. Leaders of the Arab states met in Khartoum and vowed no peace and no recogni-

95

tion of Israel. At the same time, however, King Faisal of Saudi Arabia and President Nasser of Egypt both accepted a Sudanese compromise proposal to settle the Yemeni dispute that had tied down Egyptian forces and polarized inter-Arab relationships. Behind the facade of intransigent slogans emerging from Khartoum, there eventually emerged a new current of moderation. The June war had awakened some of those Arabs who, until that moment of truth, had accepted all of the political slogans that for so long had been a substitute for rational thought, careful planning, and hard work.

In Israel, too, new positions were taking shape. Those who had always accepted the Revisionist philosophy that made Jerusalem and the West Bank (and the East Bank as well) a part of Israel, were determined that not an inch would go back to the Arabs, ever. Moderates spoke of giving areas of the barren hills and the populous West Bank towns back to the Arabs, while keeping a network of strategic settlements in the Jordan valley and on the heights above to act as a tripwire against future invasions.

Neither extremists nor moderates talked about giving back any part of Jerusalem. Instead, they began a high-speed campaign to restore a Jewish population to the former Jewish quarter of the old city, to construct huge new apartment buildings for Jews on the hillsides all around the former Arab areas, and to extend Jerusalem's municipal limits toward the boundaries of other West Bank towns. Once-barren intervening tracts, one by one, were incorporated into Jerusalem proper.

The Arabs took their case to the United Nations, but this time Israel declined to withdraw from territory taken from any of the three Arab belligerents in the absence of direct negotiations for a permanent peace. For their part, all of the Arabs adamantly refused to negotiate from their self-perceived position of weakness.

As a result of the impasse, the western powers, the Soviet Union, and eventually the Israeli government of Prime Minister Golda Meir and the Arab confrontation states finally agreed to UN Security Council Resolution 242 of November 22, 1967. In slightly ambiguous language, it set out as the basis for a final settlement Israeli withdrawals from conquered lands in return for Arab acquiescence in Israel's right to exist within secure and recognized boundaries.

The ambiguity was created by a difference in the French and English language phrasing of one provision of the resolution. The English language version specifies "withdrawal of Israeli armed forces from territories occupied in the recent conflict." The French version specifies "retrait des forces armées Israéliennes des territoires occupés lors du récent conflit." Arab signatories point to the French text's specification of withdrawal from "*the* territories occupied" while Israel cites the English phrase "territories occupied" for their conflicting contentions. The Arabs say Resolution 242 specifies that Israel must withdraw from *all* of the territories occupied while the Israelis say it specifies only that they withdraw from some of the territories, with the extent of the withdrawals still to be negotiated. The ambiguity of the two versions is not accidental. Framers of the resolution were aware that this was the only way to secure the agreement of all parties to Resolution 242 as a framework for settlement.

This was the situation that confronted Richard Nixon after his defeat of Hubert Humphrey, Johnson's Vice President, in the 1968 election campaign. In the campaign both had made all the requisite pledges of support for Israel, Nixon rising to special fervor because of Humphrey's lengthy, vocal, and apparently sincere support of Israel over many years in the Senate. Nixon, on the other hand, had drawn special criticism from Jewish friends of Israel as early as the 1954 campaign, when, as Vice President, he had accused them of misrepresenting American Middle Eastern policies abroad. His enthusiastic support of the Eisenhower policies at Suez and after, and his reputation for implying that certain Democrats had at times been sympathetic to Communism, which went back to his first Senatorial campaign in California in the late 1940s, made him difficult for many liberal Jewish voters to accept.

Nixon entered the Presidency, however, with better-formulated foreign policy goals than any successor to date. He had a general philosophy and all he had to do was find good men to carry it out. He picked William Rogers as his Secretary of State. Rogers had little foreign affairs experience, but he and Nixon had developed a friendly relationship in the Eisenhower administration. For his White House foreign policy adviser, Nixon picked Harvard professor Henry Kissinger, a protege of Nelson Rockefeller, Nixon's first-term Vice President. Since the first job of the Nixon administration was to end the disastrous war in Vietnam "with honor," Kissinger concentrated on that while Rogers concentrated on the Middle East.

From the first, Nixon's Middle East policy appeared to run on two tracks. One was to build up some confidence in Israel (and, perhaps, support among its American friends) by giving Israel more sophisticated weapons, and in greater quantities, than ever before. The White House official in charge of these efforts was Leonard Garment, a former Nixon law partner and former Democrat, who was Nixon's liaison with the Jewish community and a low-key, moderate man who got along with almost everyone. At the same time, however, Rogers was steadily pursuing an image of "even-handedness" that became an increasing annoyance to the Israeli lobby in the U.S. as it gradually warmed U.S. relationships with the Arab World that had been cool or non-existent since the 1967 war.

After 1967, during a period marked not only by guerrilla activities but also the bloody Egyptian-Israeli "War of Attrition," two new elements had emerged in the Arab World. One was an armed Palestinian national movement, which, if not independent of the competing Arab countries that sponsored it, was at least strong enough and wily enough to play one Arab country against another for its own benefit. The major elements of this Palestinian armed movement, although still individually sponsored by separate Arab countries or by the Soviet Union, are now contained within the Palestine Liberation Organization, which has never accepted Resolution 242.

The other notable development after 1967 was the evolution of more moderate public positions among the Arab confrontation states. Their internal as well as external statements began to reflect the understanding that, in accepting Resolution 242, they were in fact limiting Arab land claims from Israel to those areas occupied in 1967, and not those awarded to or seized by Israel in the period before 1967.

Rogers' actions also became increasingly successful. He developed a strategy, known as the "Rogers Plan," to base a Middle East peace on Israeli withdrawals and Arab renunciation of force against Israel. This was at first rejected, and then reexamined, by Nasser. Rogers also negotiated a stand-still agreement that ended the bloody aerial combat along the Suez Canal between Egyptians and Israelis. When the Egyptians violated it by continuing to move up anti-aircraft rockets for the first few hours, and were caught by aerial photography, Nixon and Rogers calmed the Israelis instead of denouncing the Egyptians.

The death of Nasser and Anwar Sadat's efforts to consolidate power in Egypt by neutralizing any threats to his orderly succession, gave everyone in the Middle East a breathing space, and ruptured U.S. relations with individual Arab countries were gradually improved. But in Israel, the lines were hardening, not softening.

By the beginning of Nixon's second term in 1973, and with Kissinger now Secretary of State as well as White House National Security Adviser, the stage seemed set for the U.S. to put some pressure on each side to meet the other side halfway. For some time, Sadat had been threatening to take matters in his own hands and try to push the Israelis off Arab territory by force if the U.S. could not do it by peaceful persuasion. Until he carried out his threat with a coordinated attack by Egyptian and Syrian forces on the Israelis in the fall of 1973, however, the Americans did not take his threats very seriously.

Israelis speak of the Yom Kippur War, Arabs of the Ramadan War, and westerners call it the October War. But all can agree that it was a turning point in the long struggle between Jew and Arab. After demonstrating the near-total lethality of modern tank, aerial, and missile warfare, the fighting subsided into a stalemate, with Egyptian forces in former Israeli positions and Israeli forces in former Egyptian positions on both sides of the Suez Canal. The Golan Heights between Damascus and northern Israel became a vast junkyard of burned-out Syrian and Israeli tanks and missiles marking the advances and retreats of both armies. In fact, none of the armies had been able to continue for more than a few days without an airborne resupply effort by their superpower sponsors, and those Soviet and U.S. rescue efforts came closer to touching off World War III than any events since the Berlin blockade of 1948 and the Cuban missile crisis of 1962. Meanwhile, the Arab oil producing countries had imposed an oil embargo to protest the U.S. resupply of Israel.

The end of the October War, and the continuation of the oil embargo, inaugurated one of the most active years of U.S. diplomacy in the Middle East. Secretary of State Henry Kissinger had flown to Moscow during the war to negotiate terms, eventually incorporated in UN Security Council Resolution 338, which called for the implementation of Resolution 242 in all its aspects through negotiations between the parties.

From the moment the ceasefire finally went into effect, the negotiation of the disengagement agreements became the first U.S. priority. By November 3, the leaders of Egypt, Israel, and Syria had visited Washington, and on November 5, Secretary Kissinger departed for visits to five Arab countries, with members of his party breaking off to visit Israel. Egypt and the U.S. agreed to resume diplomatic relations, broken in 1967. The Secretary visited more Arab countries, and on December 21, 1973, the U.S. and the USSR hosted a peace conference, which only Syria declined to attend, in Geneva.

The Geneva conference adjourned after three days and has not reconvened since. However, in January, 1974, Secretary Kissinger began the first of his famous shuttles, which brought about an Egyptian-Israeli disengagement the same month. There followed an interval in which the Golda Meir government fell in Israel, and Israel publicly expressed suspicion of the new U.S. "even-handedness," including the Nixon administration's condemnation of Israeli raids on southern Lebanon and its efforts to arrange large-scale economic assistance for Egypt.

Most important for Americans, the Arab oil ministers announced on March 18 the lifting of the oil embargo against the U.S. In April Kissinger began a new shuttle between President Asad of Syria and a Golda Meir caretaker cabinet. At the end of May, President Nixon was able to announce the disengagement of Syrian and Israeli forces in the Golan Heights, ending the seven months of bloody skirmishing that had followed the official ceasefire.

In June President Nixon visited Egypt, Saudi Arabia, Syria, Israel, and Jordan, in that order, and announced the restoration of U.S.-Syrian diplomatic relations in the course of his visit to Damascus. He received warm welcomes in each of those countries, particularly in Egypt, where literally millions of spectators turned out to cheer a triumphal procession of two Presidents whose countries had not even had diplomatic relations only seven months earlier. However, the extensive U.S. television coverage of Arabs and Israelis cheering him in their streets did not save the U.S. President from the consequences of the Watergate investigation. Within weeks of his return from the Middle East, he had resigned.

NOTES

1. Draper, Theodore. "The United States and Israel: Tilt in the Middle East?" *Commentary,* April 1975, p. 31.
2. Barker, Colonel A. I. *The Yom Kippur War*, Ballantine, New York, 1974, p. 159.

CHAPTER XII

President Ford
and Sinai II

"An agreement to separate military forces has been implemented on the Egyptian-Israeli front and now a similar accord has been negotiated between Israel and Syria. For the first time in a generation we are witnessing the beginning of a dialogue between the Arab states and Israel."

Richard Nixon, June 5, 1974

"To the nations of the Middle East I pledge continuity in our vigorous efforts to advance the process which has brought hopes of peace to that region after 25 long years as a hot-bed of war."

Gerald Ford, August 12, 1974

As a congressman, Gerald Ford had generally voted a straight pro-Israeli line. As Richard Nixon's second term vice president, Ford may or may not have seen how such knee-jerk support of Israel by congressmen complicated administration efforts to project an image of fairness and impartiality as well as to examine each Middle Eastern issue on the basis of its effect on long-term Middle East stability rather than on its short-run effects on Israel. In any case, President Ford had to hit the ground running when it came to U.S. Middle East policies.

The transition from a Nixon to a Ford administration took place during what Washington diplomats later called "Middle East month." Between July 28 and September 10, 1974, King Hussein of Jordan and two Prime Ministers and four Foreign Ministers representing Israel, Egypt, Syria, and Saudi Arabia trooped into Washington. However, the visit of new Israeli Prime Minister Rabin with new U.S. President Ford broke no new ground. Instead, although the U.S. hoped to follow up Israel's initial disengagement agreements with Egypt and with Syria with a Jordan agreement, Israel made it clear that it was not ready for disengagement negotiations with King Hussein. The outlines of a hardline Israeli policy, including no withdrawal from the West Bank and Jerusalem, began to show clearly through increasingly intransigent Israeli statements. Nevertheless, Israel clearly preferred the continuation of Kissinger-aided step-by-step negotiations to a return to Geneva. The Secretary accordingly undertook two lengthy visits to Middle Eastern countries in the fall of 1974.

Meanwhile, events in the Arab World complicated his task. On October 28, at a meeting of Arab heads of state in Rabat, Morocco, the PLO was designated as spokesman for the Palestinians. It was a major triumph for Yassir Arafat and a major setback for King Hussein, who had not been able to enter negotiations with Israel over a West Bank disengagement. At the same time, it began to lift from Israel the public responsibility for obstructing Kissinger's disengagement timetable. On November 13, PLO Chairman Arafat made a much-heralded first appearance before the UN General Assembly and described his dream of "one democratic state where Christian, Jew and Muslim live in justice, equality and fraternity." Whatever his intention, his statement dashed the hopes of any who expected that he might at least hint at some future recognition of the state of Israel.

Kissinger was encouraged, however, that President Sadat seemed willing to risk the suspension of Soviet arms shipments to Egypt rather than abandon step-by-step negotiations in favor of an immediate return to Geneva. As a result, Kissinger launched an "exploratory" trip to the Middle East in February 1975, reportedly extracting a promise from the Shah of Iran to supply oil to Israel in compensation for the Sinai oil fields that Israel would lose in a withdrawal.

On March 8, 1975, the Secretary began a shuttle that took him eight times to Israel and five times to Egypt, with side visits to Turkey, Syria, and Saudi Arabia. Egypt wanted Israel to withdraw from the Sinai oil fields and both mountain passes, and Israel insisted that Egypt issue a statement of non-belligerency in return. Sadat protested that he could not renounce belligerency while Israel still occupied other Egyptian lands. Proposals for lesser withdrawals in exchange for lesser normalization actions foundered. Finally, on March 23, 1975, the shuttle broke down.

"This is a sad day for America, which has invested much hope and faith," Kissinger said as he left Israel, "and it is a sad day also for Israel, which needs and wants peace so badly." The administration did not officially place the blame for the breakdown on Israel. Yet President Ford announced a reassessment of the administration's policy in the Middle East which another government official described as "one part an effort to bring about more Israeli negotiating flexibility and three parts a serious look at our objectives and options."

It was also announced that, although arms in the pipeline for Israel would go forward, the U.S. would be "reluctant" to enter into new arms procurement contracts. Clearly, the administration was giving Israel time to consider the disadvantages of a decreased arms supply and a probable return to Geneva, where Israel, and the U.S., might face all of the Arab countries simultaneously rather than one by one under Kissinger's auspices. It was a reminder of efforts by both Eisenhower and Truman to substitute the stick when the carrot no longer worked in U.S. dealings with Israel.

While arms shipments to Israel were frozen, the battle for U.S. public opinion heated up. Israel was stung by news stories from Washington blaming Israeli intransigence for the new Middle East impasse. Over a two-month period, Israel sent nine high-level officials to the U.S. for separate speaking engagements blaming Cairo for the shuttle breakdown. In return, Egypt sent a parliamentary delegation to the U.S. to tell Egypt's side of the story. In April, 1975, Clovis Maksoud, an editor from Beirut, started a three-month speaking tour of the U.S. under the sponsorship of the Arab League to explain the Palestinian viewpoint, while in May and June Saudi Arabia launched speaking tours of the U.S. by a six-member "truth squad."

Although major American Jewish organizations provided audiences and produced the media for Israeli speakers, they officially refrained from direct criticism of President Ford or Secretary Kissinger. "Generally the leadership of the Jewish community has been trying to act as responsibly as it can under the circumstances," Bertram Gold, executive vice president of the American Jewish Committee, told *Time* magazine. He continued:

"It has been trying not to make the Administration the enemy. On the other hand, there is an apprehensive feeling that the Administration's reassessment is being used as a form of pressure on Israel. If 1975 turns out to be the year of intense pressure on Israel, there will be a very serious reaction among American Jews. We will go directly to Congress, and 1976 is not that far away."

Local organizations were more outspoken. The New York United Jewish Appeal took advertisements in the *New York Times* and *New York Post* warning: "The price of silence was the Warsaw ghetto. Bergen-Belsen. Auschwitz. Dachau. Buchenwald." An ad hoc group called American Jews Against Ford proclaimed in newspaper advertisements that "American Jewry is called upon to work tirelessly to change the Administration and the kind of thinking that leads to sellouts. . . . Learn what you can do to oust Kissinger and Ford by joining A.J.A.F."

However, the most significant event of the propaganda battle occurred in May, 1975. It followed a visit to Washington by King Hussein and preceded a trip by President Ford to Geneva for a meeting with President Sadat and a trip to Washington by Prime Minister Rabin. Right at that point, 76 U.S. Senators signed a letter to President Ford urging him not to let the military balance shift against Israel, "to be responsive to Israel's urgent military and economic needs," and to seek a settlement "on the basis of secure and recognized boundaries that are defensible."

The letter, signed by three-fourths of the members of the Senate, effectively cut the ground out from under the President at the worst possible moment for U.S. diplomacy. On the one hand, he was engaged in a battle of wills with Israel. And on the other, he was trying to persuade Arab leaders that he could deliver meaningful Israeli concessions in exchange for meaningful concessions of their own.

In retrospect, it may have been the high water mark for the pro-Israeli lobby in the United States. Some of the Senators who had signed the letter told journalists privately that they had been pressured to vote against their own best judgment, and expressed admiration for the few Senators who had resisted. Others were indignant at charges that, with one stroke of the pen, they had cracked, if not completely shattered, a carefully orchestrated Middle East peace initiative that had concerned much of the U.S. foreign policy establishment for most of the first year of the Ford administration.

By mid-1975, however, there were some positive developments in the Middle East. Israel announced on June 2 that it was thinning its forces in the Suez Canal area. On June 5, the eighth anniversary of the outbreak of the war that closed it, Egypt reopened the Suez Canal. But in Washington, the June, 1975, meeting between Ford and Rabin was described as cool and reserved. Later that month, after an Israeli version of its latest negotiating offer had leaked to the *New York Times,* the State Department branded the accompanying maps "inaccurate and highly misleading" and denounced "competitive leaks of confidential diplomatic exchanges."

On June 27, President Ford and Secretary Kissinger met with Israeli Ambassador Dinitz to present what the Israeli press called an "ultimatum" that Israel reconsider its negotiating position. On July 5, Kissinger suggested in an interview on ABC that the degree of U.S. support for Israel would be linked to Israel's response to Egypt's negotiating position. Egypt added to the pressure by announcing that it would not extend the mandate of the UN Expeditionary Force separating its troops from Israel's beyond July 24, 1975 in the absence of progress toward agreement.

Under the growing pressure, contacts were intensifying. On August 21, Secretary Kissinger resumed a shuttle which, despite hostile demonstrations in Israel, took him seven times each to Egypt and Israel, with side trips to Syria, Saudi Arabia, and Jordan. This time an agreement was reached. The "Sinai II" agreement was initialed on the same day, September 1, in both Alexandria and Jerusalem. Kissinger was present for both ceremonies, dramatizing the proximity of the two cities. On September 4 it was signed in Geneva by representatives of both Egypt and Israel.

It is axiomatic that U.S. initiatives on the Middle East grind to a halt in an election year. If an incumbent President undertakes anything more than a courtesy-level communication with Arab countries, his opponent may depict him as selling out Israel. Compliments from Arab countries can be especially damaging at such a time, and most Arab leaders are aware of this. For Israel, U.S. election years are opportunities to carry out with minimum risk actions that in other years might seriously jeopardize Israel's relations with the United States.

Election years also bring Israel unsolicited commitments from American candidates. Israeli leaders have learned to garner these side benefits by making low-key, courteous comments about the incumbent administration. They refrain from heavy-handed statements that could be interpreted as overt interference in U.S. domestic affairs, or could discourage other candidates from pursuing Jewish votes through ardent, if generalized, promises of support to Israel.

The 1976 national election campaign followed the script. However, Egypt's preference for the Ford administration was obvious. Israel's distrust of both the Ford-Kissinger team, based on experience, and the born-again-Christian candidate, Jimmy Carter, based on uncertainty, was also obvious. As in past elections, American Jews tended to vote the Democratic ticket and their support in key states certainly was an important element in the close Carter victory.

Meanwhile, in the Middle East, all initiatives toward a peaceful solution were halted by the civil war in Lebanon. The traditional division of power there, which slightly favored the Christians over Muslims, had become increasingly unstable as more Muslims than Christians were born, and as more Christians than Muslims emigrated from the country. The presence of some 400,000 Palestinians, now heavily armed, was the straw that broke the Lebanese camel's back. This time, unlike 1958, what started as a series of battles between conservative Lebanese Maronite militias and leftist Palestinian armed groups gradually became a full-fledged civil war. It pitted a loose and shifting alliance of Christians and a very few conservative Muslims against an equally unstable alliance of Palestinians, Muslims, and "Progressive" leftist party contingents of mixed Muslim and Christian membership. Virtually every major country in the Middle East, even non-Arab Iran, backed one or more of the contending militias with money, arms, and even manpower. However, Israeli involvement on the Maronite side became increasingly deep and obvious throughout 1976, a destabilizing situation that might have been far more vigorously denounced by the U.S. in a non-election year.

U.S. Middle Eastern diplomacy was fully occupied with attempts to halt the fighting in Lebanon. Because of its duration, this fighting has been far more costly in human lives than any of the earlier fierce but brief Arab-Israeli encounters. The country-wide phase of the Lebanese civil war finally was frozen when the Syrian regular army entered Lebanon, pushed aside advancing Palestinian forces, and took over policing the divided country. By that time all progress toward settling the basic Arab-Israeli dispute, in the U.S., the United Nations, and the Middle East itself, had come to a halt.

CHAPTER XIII

President Carter and the Camp David Agreement

"The Clinton pronouncement indicated that an American administration had finally focused on the core of the Middle East problem and had begun to approach it clearly and publicly, in a manner consistent with the concept of openness which Mr. Carter promised during his campaign.... The President of the United States called for an idea which, after all, is based on the same United Nations resolution which established a state for the Israelis."

Sabah Kabbani, Syrian Ambassador to the U.S., March 17, 1978

"The Middle East is the most crucial foreign-policy problem that faces the Carter Administration. It directly affects the economic fortunes of every American. If we fail to seize the diplomatic opportunity that presents itself now, a fifth war will surely erupt in the Middle East. The Israelis will almost certainly win.... The Arabs, in turn, will retaliate against us as Israel's only ally by shutting off our supply of oil once again."[2]

William E. Griffith, April 1977

The year 1977 was, like 1973, a watershed year in the Arab-Israel dispute. It was not one event like the October War that completely reshuffled the cards, but three in a row which, if not unrelated, seemed at least highly contradictory. The newly-elected Democratic President, Jimmy Carter, seized the initiative almost from his first day in the White House. He believed that the Kissinger step-by-step approach had run its course. He wanted to test the prospects for a comprehensive settlement. He envisioned a solution along the lines outlined in a report entitled "Toward Peace in the Middle East," issued by a study group convened at the Brookings Institution in late 1975. The group included the new White House National Security Adviser, Zbigniew Brzezinski, and his National Security Council Middle

East specialist, William Quandt. One month after the new administration took office, Secretary of State Cyrus Vance traveled to the Middle East to issue a series of invitations. By the end of that spring, they had brought President Carter face to face with (in chronological order) Prime Minister Rabin of Israel, President Sadat of Egypt, King Hussein of Jordan, President Asad of Syria, and Crown Prince Fahd of Saudi Arabia.

In March, 1977, at Clinton, Massachusetts, President Carter had declared that the Palestinians were entitled to a homeland, and that Israel eventually must return captured Arab territory. The reaction in Israel may well have been a major factor in that country's May elections. They brought to power for the first time Menachem Begin, the leader of the terrorist Irgun Zvai Leumi during the British Mandate, who had spent the 29 years since Israel's creation in unyielding opposition to any signs of territorial compromise by successive Labor governments. He was the direct, legitimate heir to Jabotinsky's Revisionist leadership, which had always stood for an Israel that included not only all of Palestine but also the lands east of the Jordan River comprising present-day Jordan. Withdrawal from the West Bank or Jerusalem would be, for Begin, a denial of his entire life's work.

The immediate cause of the first Labor coalition defeat in Israel's history was the defection of a significant number of voters to the Democratic Movement for Change, which had campaigned against alleged Labor Coalition corruption and economic mismanagement as well as against the hawkish views of Labor Candidate Shimon Peres. However, aside from these internal matters, it is possible that many other voters may have seen Mr. Begin as even less susceptible than Mr. Peres to U.S. pressures for Israeli flexibility on Arab territorial claims.

Leaders of major American Jewish organizations greeted the Begin victory with perceptible apprehension. They knew his vociferous support of West Bank settlements for religious rather than security reasons would be hard to explain to an American public anxious for peace in the Middle East. The already aroused American Jewish community flooded the White House with telegrams, however. Their message was that the new Prime Minister deserved a chance not only to speak for himself in Washington, but also to negotiate directly with the Arabs rather than be confronted with a take-it-or-leave-it imposed American solution.

Vice President Walter Mondale was becoming the administration's point man to both Israel and the American Jewish community on the basis of his long record of pro-Israeli statements and votes in Congress. He made what was supposed to be a conciliatory speech in San Francisco, but partisans of Israel seemed to note only that he reiterated administration support for a Palestinian homeland and Israeli territorial withdrawals. Mondale also publicly expressed a new administration confidence that the current moderate Arab leadership sincerely wanted peace.

July was a turning point in two ways. In Washington the initial meeting between Carter and Begin went well, at least publicly, as a President eager for an early settlement and a Prime Minister seeking to reduce U.S. involvement cautiously assessed one another.

In the same month, according to subsequent Israeli newspaper accounts, Begin was informed by his intelligence service of a Libyan-inspired plot to assassinate President Sadat. Begin did not simply sit on the information or turn it over to U.S. intelligence for relay to Egypt, as might have been done in the past. Instead, Begin had one of his intelligence officers pass the information directly to the Egyptians at a secret meeting in Morocco.

According to Israeli press accounts, the initially skeptical Egyptians caught the plotters red-handed. When Egypt retaliated against Colonel Qaddafi by launching a brief border war against Libyan troop concentrations and communications, Begin announced that Israel would do nothing to disturb the Egyptians in Sinai so long as they were preoccupied in Libya.

Meanwhile, the Carter administration was proceeding down its chosen track toward a comprehensive solution. It supported Palestinian participation in the negotiations, a statement that even PLO Chairman Arafat hailed as a "turning point" and a "positive step." On October 1, 1977, the road to Geneva was further prepared with a joint Soviet-American statement. It set out a basis for a peaceful settlement and supported the "legitimate rights" of the Palestinians. These administration steps stirred up opposition both in Israel, which ruled out the U.S.-Soviet statement as a basis for negotiations, and in Congress, where 150 members signed a letter criticizing the joint statement with the Soviets.

World attention was focused on the new U.S.-Soviet initiative, and the firestorm of Israeli opposition it ignited. But in the Middle East, events began moving rapidly down an entirely different track. The July contact between Israel and Egypt reportedly had been followed by a September meeting in Morocco, this time between Foreign Minister Dayan and one of President Sadat's most trusted aides.

On November 9, President Sadat told his Parliament, "I am ready to go to the Israeli Parliament itself to discuss peace." Egyptian Foreign Minister Ismail Fahmy promptly resigned. The Israelis quickly issued an invitation, and on November 19, 1977, President Sadat landed at Ben Gurion International airport. His meetings with Israel's leaders, his magnanimous address in the Knesset and Begin's cautious reply, and the Egyptian President's return to a tumultuous welcome at home were televised to a fascinated world, and are now part of Middle East history.

Whatever the private reservations of the U.S. government, which had risked considerable domestic opposition to develop momentum for a comprehensive settlement, there was little question of opposing the direct Egyptian-Israeli initiative. There was intense continued U.S. popular interest in the follow-up meeting on December 20 between the defense ministers of Israel and Egypt and in the climactic visit, on Christmas Day 1977, by Prime Minister Begin to President Sadat in Egypt.

Events in the Middle East continued to move rapidly. In an effort to seize the peace-making initiative, or at least control the direction in which President Sadat seemed to be taking it, Prime Minister Begin had brought to Washington in December his own plan for the West Bank. Carter's reaction was cool but correct. He characterized Begin's plan as a "good beginning." The comment was intended to prompt an Israeli reexamination of the plan. Instead, in a move reminiscent of the manner in which Israel's supporters had sometimes forced the hand of President Roosevelt and of subsequent American presidents, the Israeli Prime Minister pretended to believe that he had a U.S. endorsement. The U.S. press also insisted on interpreting a year-end statement by Carter that he opposed the creation of a Palestinian state as an endorsement of the Begin plan. Questioned by newsmen before he had seen the full Carter statement, Sadat commented that he was "embarrassed." A chill seemed about to envelop U.S.-Arab relations.

However, since President Carter was in Saudi Arabia at the time the issue was raised in the American media, he made an unscheduled stop in Egypt on his return flight to set matters straight. Two months later, in February 1978, President Sadat spent six triumphal days in the U.S., meeting with Carter and members of Congress, participating in U.S. network television interviews, and giving a televised speech at the National Press Club. On that visit President Carter described Sadat as the "world's foremost peacemaker."

On March 6, 1978, exactly one month after President Sadat's televised speech at the National Press Club, Mark Siegel, a White House deputy political adviser, resigned his position as administration spokesman to the Jewish community. It was a protest at what he saw as a tilt away from Israel. Two weeks later Prime Minister Begin arrived in Washington for meetings on March 21 and 22 with President Carter and members of Congress. The *New York Times* quoted an anonymous administration official on that visit as follows:

"It was a turning point for us. When Begin left, everyone was frustrated, not just in the White House but on Capitol Hill. He left behind heavy footprints and a lot of frustration. That's the first time I saw a break in the solid support base for Begin on the Hill."

What followed may or may not have resulted from the Begin visit. In any case, it too was a turning point in Israel's influence in the Congress. For the first time in history, the pro-Israeli forces took a strong stand on a bill, and then lost in the Congressional voting.

U.S. Middle East specialists had for some time been concerned that the Sadat initiative had derailed their own efforts to get all of the moderate Arabs behind a settlement initiative. Now it also seemed to be driving a wedge between the U.S. and Egypt on the one hand and the rest of the Arabs on the other. Officials at the Department of State and the Pentagon wanted to demonstrate both to Sadat and to the other Arabs that moderation could pay off, quickly and tangibly. Therefore, the Carter administration proposed on February 18, 1978 the sale of 60 F-15 long range fighters to Saudi Arabia and an additional 15 to Israel; 50 F-5E fighter bombers to Egypt; and 75 F-16 fighter-bombers to Israel.

There was a probability that, if left to its own devices, the Senate would approve only the sales to Israel. To forestall that, the administration made it clear to Congress that the sales were firmly linked in an all-or-nothing package. In his visit to Washington, Begin had not discussed the package and the Israeli government reacted slowly. It apparently hoped it could obtain its own portion while American pro-Israeli lobbyists, by now engaged in an all-out effort, prevented the Saudi and Egyptian sales. Belatedly, Israel took a clear position against the entire package and officials at the Israeli Embassy began to contact Senators personally. They were too late, however, to kill the proposal in committee. Instead, an eight-to-eight vote tie in the Senate Foreign Relations Committee allowed the proposal to reach the Senate floor.

The Democratic administration, meanwhile, had received strong assistance from two Republicans. Senate Minority Leader Howard Baker and former Secretary of State Henry Kissinger offered to support the package on two conditions: that it include 20 more F-15 fighters for Israel and that the bomb racks be removed from the Saudi planes to limit their offensive, but not their defensive, capability.

When the Senate finally approved the sale, however, the decisive support came from Democratic Senator Abraham A. Ribicoff. He was the only one of five Jewish members of the Senate to vote for the package. During a ten-hour closed debate on the bill, he and Senator Jacob Javits were reported to have exchanged angry words, both citing their Jewish heritage. In the end there was little doubt that the Ribicoff vote for the package probably had swung enough others with it to carry the day.

Senator Ribicoff, for years one of Israel's staunchest supporters in Washington, had reached a new position after visits earlier in 1978 to Saudi Arabia and Syria. He said that the visit to Saudi Arabia, where his delegation met knowledgeable and efficient American-trained Saudi ministers clearly anxious to maintain their American ties, completely changed his image of that country. The visit to Syria he described as "a shocker." Whatever his earlier thoughts about Egypt, he found himself defending President Sadat's initiative against Syrian charges of betrayal and Syrian predictions that, in any case, Israeli intransigence would make the Sadat initiative fail. He returned, he said, with a whole new perception of what the United States must do in the Middle East.

"It was a tough position to take," he said. Lifelong friends were now "very critical of me." However, after the vote, he told the *Washington Post:*

"There's nothing I have ever done in the Senate that has ever met such an overwhelming approval . . . not only from people who voted on my side, but by people who voted on the other side. . . . I had a lot of senators tell me 'Abe . . . we're ashamed. We agree with you and we know what it means for you to do this and the pressure you must have been under. We've been under pressure and we have voted the opposite way.' It was very interesting to me to get that reaction."

In the spring of 1978, there was other bad news from the United States for the Begin government. Led by Professor Leonard Fein, editor of the Boston Jewish monthly, *Moment,* 36 distinguished American Jews sent a letter of solidarity to Israel's "Peace Now" movement, which had turned out an estimated 300,000 demonstrators to protest the Begin hard line. The signatories included such articulate supporters of Israel as sociologists Daniel Bell and Seymour Martin Lipset, authors Saul Bellow and Irving Howe, historian Walter Laqueur and editors Martin Peretz and Jesse Lurie. In Israel, the *Jerusalem Post* commented on the letter:

> "Fear of showing division and dissent to a hostile Gentile World is deeply etched into Jewish history. What was perhaps acceptable for unobtrusive internal debate was considered dangerous and illegitimate if displayed to general view.... That now a group of such responsible American Jewish personalities has broken through the constraint of public unity testifies to the depth of their concern."

In September, President Carter, President Sadat, Prime Minister Begin, and the principal advisers to all three spent 13 days in near isolation at Camp David, Maryland. World hopes for a peace agreement rose and then slowly sank as leaks from the mountain-top summit described inflexibility and impasse. However, when they emerged for a dramatic late Sunday night appearance before television cameras at the White House, the three leaders announced not defeat but two agreements. One was "A Framework for Peace in the Middle East," and the other, "A Framework for the Conclusion of a Peace Treaty Between Egypt and Israel."

The latter agreement called for an Israeli-Egyptian peace treaty to be signed within three months, major Israeli withdrawals within three to nine months after that, the normalization of all relationships between the two countries within a year, and a complete Israeli withdrawal from Egyptian territory within three years.

In the case of the former agreement, the "Framework for Peace in the Middle East," disputes of interpretation arose almost immediately. They concerned the effect of the agreement on Jewish settlements on the West Bank, the arrangements for Palestinian "autonomy," and the linkage between the two framework agreements. On December 17, 1979, Secretary Vance wearily ended a six-day shuttle with the news that, although the specified three months had passed since the Camp David agreements were signed, no peace treaty was in sight. The Egyptians complained of excessively legalistic maneuvers by Israel, while the Israelis charged "zigzagging" by Sadat.

Perhaps the sharpest complaint was by Menachem Begin himself, who angrily told Vance that the U.S. had abandoned the role of honest broker and was siding with the Egyptian position. His complaint once again brought Israel's U.S. supporters into action. Of the 36 American Jewish intellectuals who only eight months earlier had shocked the Begin government by supporting the peace movement, 33 now stated in a message to President Carter that the U.S. position was "unacceptable" and that Israeli objections to "the proposed Egyptian revisions are reasonable."

A three-way impasse, first between Egypt and Israel, then between Israel and the U.S., and finally between pro-Israel Americans and the Carter administration, continued for three more months. In March, 1979, Carter himself set out on a six-day mission to Cairo and Jerusalem. Few thought he could bridge the gulf between Egypt and Israel concerning the Palestinians. American editorial writers complained that U.S. Presidents are expected to preside over signing ceremonies for treaties already negotiated, and not to expend their efforts and prestige in trying to reconcile the irreconcilable. Once again, the world prepared for a letdown. Then word was flashed jubilantly from the President's homeward-bound plane that at the last moment agreement had been reached. On March 26, the Israeli-Egyptian peace treaty was signed by President Sadat and Prime Minister Begin in televised ceremonies before a huge audience on the White House lawn. Just across the street Palestinians protested noisily from Washington's Lafayette Square.

It will be some time before it is clear whether that moment was a milestone, or another detour, on the long road toward Middle East peace. For the Palestinians, the bitterness they felt in Washington that day was a foretaste of what was to come. While inviting the Palestinians (but not their PLO representatives) to discuss "autonomy" for the people of the West Bank, the Begin government continued to exhibit every sign of preparing for a long, perhaps permanent, occupation of their land. West Bank demonstrations were broken up with escalating Israeli military brutality. The endless war with the Palestinian guerrillas across the Lebanese border was fought with increased ferocity, and with blatant use by Israel of American weapons supplied on the condition that they be used solely for Israel's defense.

Israeli withdrawals from Sinai continued in accordance with the Israeli-Egyptian agreement, although sometimes it appeared that Israel deliberately sought to provoke Sadat into renouncing the agreement before all of the Sinai was gone. As for Sadat, he seemed grimly determined to keep his own people quiet, and to ignore the increasingly vocal criticism from much of the Arab World. Clearly, his objective was to get the Israelis off every last inch of Egyptian soil before he took up the Palestinian cause too vociferously. But after that, who could say how the Israeli-Egyptian peace would turn out?

In the U.S. there was increasing sympathy for the Palestinians, and some understanding of the rejection by the other Arab countries of the Camp David agreement, but there was perplexity too. If the Arabs were so sure that Begin would not give back the West Bank and Israeli-occupied Jerusalem, why did they not let some Palestinians go to the peace table and prove Israeli intransigence before the world? There lingered in American minds a suspicion that the Arab refusal to test the Camp David plan was based not on the certainty that it would not work, but on the fear that it might.

In any case, the PLO could not, and Hussein would not, join the autonomy talks, and therefore Begin was never really tested. The situation smacked of the easy Jewish victories of the Mandate era, when Jewish settlers would testify eloquently before Royal Commissions of inquiry, but the absent Palestinians were represented only by well-meaning but ineffectual friends.

By anyone's reckoning, the Palestinians, as usual, were the losers. But so was Jimmy Carter. From the first, his had been an ill-starred Presidency. He had made an astonishing number of initial bad appointments. When the inevitable wave of criticism began, he reacted by firing some of the strongest appointees and leaving some of the weakest ones in place. He badly needed a triumph before the 1980 election campaign. Each time before, the Middle East had come through for him, but this time it did not.

Carter's attention throughout his last year in office was focused on non-Arab Iran, but the Arab-Israel dispute still caused him a series of small problems. It cost him his old political comrade-in-arms, the U.S. ambassador to the UN, Andrew Young. Young was forced to resign after the Israeli government made an issue of a secret meeting between Young and the PLO observer to the UN. It was not Young's first breach of discipline, but the U.S. black community saw it as a clear decision by Carter that Jewish support was more important to him than black support. Blacks set out to disprove this in the election to come. Just before the 1980 New York Democratic primary, Carter reversed a U.S. vote in the UN condemning Israeli settlements on the West Bank. He lost the Jewish vote in New York to Senator Kennedy anyway, and at the same time unnecessarily embarrassed his Secretary of State, Cyrus Vance, who took the blame for a "failure of communication" leading to the bizarre U.S. reversal of position. Vance resigned a short time later over Carter's attempt to rescue American hostages in Iran by force.

There were no more triumphs to be wrung out of the Middle East, and in fact the confusion over the UN vote only solidified growing voter perception that Carter had become a weak and irresolute leader, especially around election time.

As it turned out, given the strong victory by Ronald Reagan, Carter probably never had a chance short of simultaneously turning the U.S. economy around and getting the hostages safely out of Iran. However, he almost went down in history as the only U.S. President to turn the Arab-Israeli dispute to his own political advantage. With all of the others, it had been largely a matter of containing the damage.

The new President-elect gave little sign that he was deterred by any of this. In fact, prior to actually assuming office he gave little sign that he might need to reexamine the hardline pro-Israeli views he had been enunciating for years in Southern California film circles, where they were extremely popular. The next four years promised to be a chapter of a whole new kind in the delicate U.S. relationship to the Arab-Israeli dispute.

NOTES

1. Kabbani, Ambassador Sabah, "Carter, the Palestinians and Israel," *New York Times*, March 17, 1978.
2. Griffith, William E, "Let's Resolve the Middle East Crisis—Now," *Reader's Digest*, April 1977.

CHAPTER XIV

A Word About Lobbies and Their Supporters

"For this generation of Americans, the news from the Middle East, and indeed from most of the Muslim world, has tended more and more to merge with the sociology of what happens at home—the results of oil embargoes, energy crises, and the impassioned efforts of Jewish-Americans, Arab-Americans, Greek-Americans, Armenian-Americans and others to make ethnocentric views prevail in a willing, hostile or more often than not, simply indifferent public opinion and Congress."[1]

John Cooley, 1981

"The ability of pro-Israel groups to marshall and maintain the support of the mass media, mass public opinion, and broad cross-sections of associational life in this country such as organized labor and non-Jewish interest groups have enabled them to amplify and disseminate their policy preferences far beyond the limits of their own organizational structures."[2]

Robert H. Trice, 1977

Since the creation of Israel, the popular American perception of the resulting conflict has been that of a Jewish David repeatedly vanquishing an Arab Goliath. In describing the relative size of the informational and educational efforts supporting the Middle Eastern antagonists in America, it is tempting to skew the image. In the battle of the pro-Israel and pro-Arab lobbies in the United States, Goliath wears the Star of David and, until recently, no one had ever laid a glove on him.

In the Middle East, however, the tables finally turned and the Israeli David had to settle for a draw with the Arab Goliath in the war of 1973. Similarly, in the United States the pro-Israeli Goliath finally lost his first battle in the spring of 1978 over the Carter administration plan to tie the sale of F-15 fighters to Saudi Arabia and F-5Es to Egypt to sales of F-15s and F-16s to Israel. Senate approval for the package came despite strenuous, though tardy, Israeli objections. Then, in case anyone thought the Israeli defeat was a one-time exception, the Israel lobby was defeated again in the 1981 Senate vote on AWACS for Saudi Arabia. This time the lobby had started its campaign long before the administration had begun its own spade work.

Just as the 1973 military standoff in the Middle East completely altered the attitudes of many of the Arabs and Israelis there, there are indications that the defeats of the Israel lobby on its own favorite turf, the U.S. Senate floor, have altered the tactics of both lobbies, the messages they advocate, and even their relative access to their audiences.

Pro-Arab and pro-Israeli groups in Washington, and to only a slightly lesser extent elsewhere in the U.S., have one thing in common that strikes a visitor to their offices immediately: tight security. Getting past the closed-circuit television cameras and electronically controlled doors to enter the Washington offices of AIPAC (rhymes with hay-pack), the American Israel Public Affairs Committee, is only slightly less awesome than being admitted to an Israeli or Arab embassy in Washington. Security at the pro-Arab groups is not as tight, but most have some sort of device which can be activated in case of need to keep a visitor outside the door until he identifies himself.

Fortunately, however, the Arab and Israeli assassination squads that in the past have stalked each other across the Middle East, and spilled over into European cities and towns, have at this writing not yet set up large-scale operations in the United States. There are in the U.S. nevertheless some disturbed and dangerous people on both sides. Young storm troopers of Rabbi Meir Kahane's Jewish Defense League bomb automobiles, break up campus meetings with bicycle chains, and telephone death threats to Arab as well as Russian diplomats in the United States. In the case of the Soviet mission to the UN in New York, terrorists claiming to represent the Jewish Defense League actually have fired into houses and apartments occupied by diplomatic families, missing two sleeping children by inches in one case. One JDL member arrested by Israeli authorities in Israel was planning a free-lance assassination mission against an Arab speaker then touring U.S. universities. As a result, service in the U.S., particularly New York, is a nightmare for many Arab diplomats and in the past some have chosen to send their families home.

On the Arab side, international terrorists of Dr. George Habash's Marxist-line Popular Front for the Liberation of Palestine have carried out successful recruiting activities among Arab students at American universities. Libyan "Cultural Attaches"—and in the past diplomats representing other extremist Arab regimes—have incited or at least discussed madcap acts of violence, such as the serious wounding in Colorado of a Libyan student leader opposed to the regime of Colonel Muammar Qaddafi. These actions are intended primarily to terrorize or discipline students or opposition figures from their own countries. But they are potentially also a threat to Israeli diplomats or their U.S. supporters.

Such lunatic fringe organizations or actions are so far outside the acceptable boundaries of American political tradition that they can only have extremely negative repercussions on U.S. public opinion. They are reminiscent of the era in which Dr. Habash and his PFLP "Director of Operations," the late Wadi'a Hadad, mindlessly killed innocent bystanders in aircraft and air terminals in Europe, and left an extremely negative world opinion concerning their cause as well as their tactics, which persists strongly in the United States to this day.

Madmen and fanatics aside, after the visitor has penetrated the closed circuit television monitors and combination door locks designed to protect the legitimate pro-Israel and pro-Arab organizations, there is much similarity in the perceptions of both sides on how they can most effectively go about their work, what their strengths and weaknesses are, and how the battle for American public opinion is going.

Ronald Koven, then a foreign editor of the *Washington Post*, summarized it nicely in an interview in 1975:

"I think there is a cultural factor involved. The Israelis are of European origin and they have an advanced public relations sense. They know how to speak our language. They understand how we reason, and they are able to use that to their advantage. The Arabs as a group have not even really played the public relations game.

"Moreover, there is a cultural barrier. People of European origin and Arabs think differently. The Israelis, for example, have been able to use to very good effect statements by Arabs which are intemperate. It has taken a long time for the American and European press to realize that in Arab culture rhetoric is often just rhetoric, something which exists by itself and does not necessarily imply actions.

"Now I think things are changing, both because the American press is finally beginning to pay better attention to the Arab world and because the Arab world is beginning to understand public relations. Of course, if you are looking at the pro-Arab and pro-Israel forces within the U.S., you have to take into account the fact that while there are two million people of Arab origin in the U.S., for the most part they tend to be low on the economic scale—the workers of Detroit and not the opinion leaders.

"The Jewish population in the United States, on the other hand, is three times as large and probably twice as rich for all sorts of historical reasons. Having worked with the political system, they know how it functions and are in positions of influence out of proportion to their number, especially on the Democratic side."[3]

NOTES

1. Cooley, John K., "The News from the Mideast: A Working Approach," *The Middle East Journal*, Autumn, 1981, pp. 465-466.
2. Trice, Robert H., "Congress and the Arab-Israeli Conflict: Support for Israel in the U.S. Senate, 1970–1973," *Political Science Quarterly*, Fall, 1977, p. 463.
3. Ghareeb, Edmund. Quotation from interview with Ronald Koven, Middle East editor for the *Washington Post*, in "The American Media and the Palestine Problem," *Journal of Palestine Studies*, Autumn 1975/Winter 1976, pp. 132-133.

CHAPTER XV

The Israeli Lobby: Where Goliath Works for Little David

"You can conjure a situation where there is another oil embargo and people in this country are not only inconvenienced and uncomfortable, but suffer. They get tough-minded enough to set down the Jewish influence in this country and break that lobby. . . . It's so strong you wouldn't believe now. We have the Israelis coming to us for equipment. We say we can't possibly get the Congress to support that. They say, 'Don't worry about the Congress.' Now this is somebody from another country, but they can do it."[1]

General George S. Brown, Former Chairman,
Joint Chiefs of Staff, October 10, 1974

"Whatever resentment many congressmen may inwardly entertain about the pressures of the lobby, the American system itself predestines them to yield. Israel possesses a powerful American constituency, the Arabs do not, and despite their wealth, the oil companies as well are unequal to the impact of ethnic politics."[2]

Edward Sheehan, 1976

"At home the key to preventing Israel's abandonment remains the vigilance and vitality of Israel's advocates."[3]

Steven L. Spiegel, 1977

General Brown's words surfaced in press reports of a supposedly off-the-record question and answer session at Duke University which earned him a reprimand from President Ford. His comments were also the subject of indignant editorials across the nation which concentrated on a demonstrably inaccurate reference to Jewish ownership of banks, and a debatable reference to newspapers. The editorial writers generally ignored General Brown's references to Congress and "that lobby," and thus saved themselves possible embarrassment on both counts only seven months later when 76 U.S. Senators, at the urging of "that lobby," signed a letter to President Ford aimed at torpedoing his administration's "reassessment" of its policy toward Israel.

Jewish fund-raising organizations in the U.S. go back at least to the 19th century and more than 235 autonomous central Jewish community organizations cover 800 communities in North America. Their United Jewish Appeal annual drives are designed to fund charitable activities in Israel, the U.S., and elsewhere in the world, in about that order, since far more than half of the total funds raised are passed to the United Israel Appeal for charitable, educational, and development work in Israel. The remarkable success in fund-raising also means that effective pro-Israeli organizations in the U.S. need not be under-financed. Because the flow of money is from American citizens, and the boards of directors are made up of American citizens, even organizations that frankly back all policies of the Israeli government across the board are not required to register as "foreign agents."

Thus, although Israeli Embassy personnel are extremely good at their jobs and very well attuned both to the U.S. media and to individual members of Congress, their efforts largely duplicate those of the various American organizations. A spokesman for the New York-based Conference of Presidents of Major American Jewish Organizations, an umbrella group representing 34 separate Jewish organizations in the United States, made no apologies in stating to the author that "it is our policy to support any democratically-elected government of Israel, and we feel that what is good for Israel is good for the United States."

Among the many constituent organizations with their own separate Washington and New York offices are the B'Nai B'Rith, with some half million members world-wide, and the 40,000-member American Jewish Committee, which publishes *Commentary* magazine. Both organizations are also extremely active in mobilizing support for Israel. Of all the Jewish organizations separately engaged in one or more activities in support of Israel, the only one actually registered to lobby in Congress on Israel's behalf is the American Israel Public Affairs Committee. Founded in 1954 as an outgrowth of the American Zionist Council, AIPAC was expanded to include representatives of the other Jewish organizations on its board, and to utilize their grassroots resources for its lobbying activities. Administered by a small, highly professional, and dedicated staff, it provides an extensive library and research service heavily utilized by the Washington media and Congressional staffers.

AIPAC purchases and distributes to large numbers of opinion makers copies of any book that is favorable to Israel. It turns out, rapidly and in large quantities, reports on current Israel-related questions for distribution to members of Congress, its own membership of some 11,000 persons, and others on its mailing list.

Most important, perhaps, is its computerized listing of supporters of Israel in every state and congressional district. As a result, a member of Congress who is undecided or hostile on a matter of great concern to Israel can routinely expect to receive letters and telegrams not merely from a scattering of leading citizens in his own constituency, but perhaps also from past and potential campaign contributors. Legend has it that one New York representative who told pro-Israeli lobbyists in 1977 that he would have to hear from taxpayers at home before he voted to bring the U.S. aid appropriation to Israel up to the $1.7 billion level received 3,000 letters supporting the bill from his constituents in only two days.

AIPAC has "power of attorney" from many of the supporters in its computerized files. When a pending matter is urgent, a congressman may see telegrams from his constituents, billed to their home telephone numbers, even before some of the constituents themselves know the telegrams or mailgrams have been sent over their names.

AIPAC was for years synonymous with Isaiah "Si" Kenen, a well-connected, genial lobbyist of a back-slapping era when Americans were less knowledgeable about the Middle East. Its second Executive Director was Morris Amitay, a foreign service officer for seven years and a legislative assistant on Capitol Hill for five more. Under his active stewardship, AIPAC still was able to keep Congress in line until the 1978 aircraft package vote. The geniality had gone out of its approach, however. Instead of using the carrots of generous speaking honoraria and campaign contributions, it now resorted to the stick. Congressmen and their assistants knew that AIPAC would try to turn off the contributions, and the voters, if they did not shape up. However, in his effort to corral votes to defeat the 1978 bill on the floor, Amitay apparently overextended himself and lost credits that could not easily be recouped. After his former Capitol Hill employer, Senator Abraham Ribicoff of Connecticut, who was not standing for reelection, voted for the package, the Senator criticized the pressure tactics of the AIPAC lobbyists, saying "they do a great disservice to the U.S., to Israel, and to the Jewish community." Amitay resigned in 1980.

Thomas Dine, the new AIPAC Executive Director, also a long-time Capitol Hill legislative assistant, is a low-key manager. In fact, until he accepted the position, he was not particularly identified by his colleagues with Israeli issues. He seems to rely as much on providing timely information to congressmen and the media as on putting pressure on them. Even the rare pro-Arab legislative aides and lobbyists express little or no resentment of him personally or of his tactics.

Perhaps the most remarkable thing about the vast congeries of pro-Israeli organizations is not the money they have raised, nor even the political support they have rallied for Israel, but rather the manner in which they have maintained a public unity of purpose in supporting Israel within the American Jewish community, despite the factionalization and fluidity that now characterize Israeli domestic politics. The chairmanship of the Conference of Presidents rotates automatically from one constituent organization to the next. It was an ironic coincidence that, just prior to the election that made Menachem Begin the first right-wing Prime Minister of Israel, the chairmanship should have devolved upon Reform Rabbi Alexander Schindler, an outspoken liberal who was an early opponent of the Vietnam War and who, prior to assuming the position, had expressed dovish views on the Palestinians and the occupied territories.

The drama that followed demonstrates the determination of mainstream American supporters of Israel, and particularly Rabbi Schindler as the then "leader of organized American Jewry," to sweep dissension within the American organizations supporting Israel, or between American Jewish leaders and Israeli leaders, behind a screen of public unity. According to reports that preceded their first meeting after Begin's election, Rabbi Schindler strongly disapproved of the Gush Emunim West Bank settlements, which were avowedly not based upon security concerns but rather "on the right of Jews to settle anywhere in the land of Eretz Israel." Yet the official Israeli government statements following that first meeting implied that the American Jewish leader had endorsed such settlements.

"I pretty well knew what I was going to say before I went," Rabbi Schindler reported subsequently. "I knew he was the only Prime Minister Israel had; that there was a danger of fragmentation within the American Jewish community; that I had at least the obligation to keep the community united in order to give this man a chance to form a government." Since then the annual report of the Conference of Presidents of Major American Jewish Organizations has added:

"Dissent ought not and should not be made public . . . when Jewish dissent is made public in the daily press or in the halls of government, the result is to give aid and comfort to the enemy and to weaken that Jewish unity which is essential for the security of Israel."

A subsequent president, Howard Squadron, regularly rallied behind Menachem Begin's actions publicly. But he made no secret of his concern that, even if a majority of American Jews remain doggedly supportive of Begin's Israel, non-Jewish support for Israel has suffered a dramatic erosion. After the 1981 Israeli bombing of a residential area of west (Muslim) Beirut which cost 300 civilian lives, Squadron flew off for a conference with Begin in Israel.

At the same time a pro-Arab lobbyist, who admitted that the American Arab community will never reach the cohesion or effectiveness of American Jews, added his own assessment of the current situation. "It's the first time in the history of the Israeli lobby that their people over there are burning bridges faster than their friends here can build them."

NOTES

1. *Time,* November 25, 1974, report on extemporaneous comments by General George S. Brown, Chairman, Joint Chiefs of Staff, at Duke University question and answer session October 10, 1974.
2. Sheehan, Edward. "Step by Step in the Middle East," *Foreign Policy,* Spring, 1976, p. 58.
3. Spiegel, Steven L., University of California at Los Angeles, letter to *Commentary,* September, 1977, p. 31.

CHAPTER XVI

Jewish Dissenters

"How sad it would be if Israel used its privileged position merely to ward off pressure and postpone a settlement to an indefinite date. When that settlement comes, not only will its terms have worsened for Israel, but Israel's influence within the U.S. will have decreased as that of others grows."[1]

Guido Goldman, May, 1978

"[Rabbi Moshe] Levinger is the tail that wags the Israeli dog that in turn wags the United States. He is the personification of the settlement controversy, a zealot who takes orders from the Bible, certainly not from Menachem Begin or Jimmy Carter or Anwar Sadat. . . . What the Rabbi Levingers of Israel would do is turn their country into a permanent occupying power, squandering Israel's moral mandate in the process."[2]

Richard Cohen, *Washington Post*, April, 1980

Not all American Jewish supporters of Israel accept the philosophy that dissent must stay within the community. Nor do they accept the accompanying maxim that, although American supporters are the lifeline of Israel, they have no business advising Israelis on matters of diplomacy or security, because "Israeli lives, not ours, are on the line." A new panorama of pro-Israel but also dovish sentiment has surfaced within a small but articulate and influential segment of the Jewish community. It is centered primarily on the campuses of major U.S. universities and among young Jewish professionals, many of them veterans of the campus-based "new left" movements of the 60s and 70s. Although these trends may be increasing in reaction to policies of Israeli Prime Minister Begin, they were already evident under the previous Israeli Labor governments, and there is a long history of American Jewish dissent toward Israel.

Support for beleaguered Jewish communities abroad has been characteristic of American Jews almost since they themselves became firmly established in the

United States. Yet a large and highly influential segment of Jewish opinion in the United States, as in Western Europe, has traditionally viewed the Zionist movement with great reserve. In the U.S., support of political Zionism originally was most likely to be found among the newer American Jewish communities of Eastern European origin. The descendants of earlier waves of immigrants, many of German origin, were more likely to be concerned with their assimilation into American life. Representatives of this earlier group had achieved great distinction in American public life. Like their counterparts in France and Britain, they saw the creation of a specific Jewish "nationality," as distinct from Jewish religious adherence, anywhere in the world as a serious threat to the increasingly secure status of Jews in the United States and the western democracies.

During World War I, the U.S. Ambassador to the Ottoman Empire, Henry Morgenthau, Sr., gave great assistance to the hard-pressed Jewish community in Palestine, just as he did to other religious and national and minority groups impoverished and threatened by drawn-out fighting in the area between Arab-assisted British forces and the Ottoman Turkish armies. By saving the tiny Jewish community from starvation and possible extinction in Palestine, he preserved it for the ultimate statehood which he came to believe was a "stupendous fallacy" and "blackest error." Ambassador Morgenthau remained a lifelong opponent of a separate political homeland for the Jews in Palestine. Similarly, members of the Sulzberger family were reluctant to put the support of the *New York Times* squarely behind a movement they had long opposed, even for some time after Israel had become a *fait accompli.*

However, American support for a Jewish state in Palestine grew steadily during World War II. The *coup de grace* was administered to the once significant anti-Zionist sentiment in the American Jewish community by the dramatic, successful moves to transport the survivors of Nazi death camps, legally or illegally, to Palestine, and the even more dramatic defense by Jewish settlers of their newly-created state against the combined armies of Egypt, Jordan, Iraq, and Syria, as well as the indigenous Palestinians who were being displaced.

Today, although she writes movingly and sympathetically of Ambassador Morgenthau, her grandfather, historian Barbara Tuchmann is a convinced Zionist. And although the *New York Times*, through its columns and editorials, may severely criticize specific Israeli government policies, one would look in vain for any doubt as to the wisdom or validity of the existence of Israel as a nation. Nevertheless, there are still vestiges of that original Jewish dissent from the establishment of Israel. The American Council for Judaism for many years sent groups of prominent American Jews to the White House and, as the welcome there wore thinner, to the Department of State to protest new manifestations of U.S. support for Israel. Finally, in the wake of the Six-Day War of 1967, the Council dropped its active opposition to Israel and its long-time executive director, Rabbi Elmer Berger, set up a new organization in New York, American Jewish Alternatives to Zionism Inc., where he issues regular newsletters and speaks to interested groups.

Rabbi Berger's colleague in the early days of the anti-Israel movement, Dr. Alfred M. Lilienthal, also maintains a New York office. He travels extensively and has done a great deal of historical research not only into all aspects of the Zionist movement but also into modern Arab history and the tangled history of U.S. support for Israel. The result has been, over 30 years, a stream of articles in his own publications and national magazines. He also has written four books: *What Price Israel?*, *There Goes the Middle East*, *The Other Side of the Coin*, and, in 1979, *The Zionist Connection: What Price Peace?* Nearly 900 pages long, it is the most comprehensive report on Zionist activities in the U.S.

These veteran Jewish anti-Zionists have a growing number of American followers in many walks of life, but probably limited following within the organized Jewish community. The final verdict certainly is not in. It may well be, however, that since both Rabbi Berger and Dr. Lilienthal have traveled and lectured frequently in Arab countries, their most lasting contribution in the battle of public opinion has been to demonstrate conclusively to the Arabs that one can be Jewish and yet not support Israel. The beneficiaries of their example have been the remaining members of Jewish communities in such Arab countries as Egypt, Syria and Morocco and of course the many American Jews who travel or work in Arab countries.

Although there is an ideological gulf between Jewish anti-Zionists and the apparently growing number of American Jewish intellectuals who criticize Israeli policies rather than the state itself, many of those under forty have one thing in common. They have been identified with, or at least exposed to, the campus activism of the 1960s and 1970s. After early immersion in idealistic social programs, the anti-Vietnam war movement, and environmental causes, it is difficult for many politically-aware young Jewish professionals to accept everything they see (and many have visited Israel in person as summer Kibbutzniks, students, tourists, or all three) happening today in Israel. They see the tiny country now almost submerged by the economic burdens of maintaining both a large modern army and a long-term military occupation. The latter they find particularly paradoxical not only because of the brutalities that occur, but also because it keeps within Israel's current extended frontiers a captive Arab population that, together with the Arabs living inside Israel's pre-1967 boundaries, someday may outnumber the Jewish inhabitants of Israel.

Because of the precept that American Jews do not advise Israelis on how best to defend themselves, such currents of dissent within the American Jewish community seem to coalesce around movements, or visitors, from Israel itself. The Breira (Hebrew for "Alternative") movement, which emerged after the October 1973 war, brought Israeli doves, many with impeccable military records, to the U.S. to meet with Jewish groups on and off campus. Its speakers called for Israel to make peace with the Palestinians before a fifth war, and perhaps a shift in the relative strength of the combatants, made such a peace impossible. Breira did not last even until the end of the decade, however, and the circumstances of its demise created much bitterness. Members of the Jewish mainstream might say that the Breira leaders were drawn from the campus counterculture and that their goals were those of the New Left; that their fatal mistake was to put too much emphasis upon the supposed moderation of the PLO; and that predictably the reaffirmation of hardline statements by PLO leaders pulled the rug out from under them. They might or might not add that Breira's final, unpardonable sin was to take the argument outside the Jewish community through invitations to non-Jews to hear their speakers and through paid advertisements in non-Jewish publications.

Breira sympathizers might counter with charges of McCarthyism by such hawkish American writers as Jean Rael Isaac of "Americans for a Safe Israel" and by The American Jewish Committee's popular monthly *Commentary*, which commissioned its own article on Breira to reiterate the Isaac charges and to add some of its own. They also speak of the reprimands or threats of dismissal received by young rabbis who provided a forum for Breira speakers, thus eventually closing off Breira from such natural constituencies as campus Hillel groups. History aside, the problem remains and the Shalom Achshav (Peace Now) movement in Israel provides a new nucleus for American Jews concerned about the consequences of uncritical support for present Israeli policies.

Veterans of the campus activist movements of the 60s and early 70s are now older, and many have "dropped out" of dissenting activities under the pressure of jobs, family opposition, and increasing uncertainty as to what is the best course for Israel as the Arab world grows perceptibly stronger. Though some still predict a significant new wave of dissent from inside rather than outside American Zionist ranks, only time will determine whether such movements will also follow the path of diminishing public impact already taken by their anti-Zionist Jewish predecessors.

There is one major difference between the two movements, however. The anti-Zionist assimilationists still represented by Dr. Lilienthal and Rabbi Berger were concerned about the effect of support for Israel on the American Jewish community. If every Jew, they asked, were automatically accepted as a citizen of Israel, would any Jew still be accepted by other Americans as a citizen whose primary loyalty was to the United States? The current American Zionist dissenters describe an entirely different concern. It is not so much what Zionism might do to their own seemingly secure status in the U.S. that worries them, but what militarism and occupation duty is doing to Israel, the Israelis, and the Zionist ideal.

The dualism of deep misgivings about the new Israeli reality, combined with profound devotion to the Zionist ideal, was eloquently expressed by Professor Leonard Fein in an article describing his experiences as an outspoken American visitor to Israel in 1979.[3] Fein describes the plight of Israeli doves concerned about their government's support of West Bank settlements; the problems of Theodore Mann, then chairman of the Conference of Presidents of Major American Jewish

Organizations, who had come to tell the Prime Minister American Jews find it "difficult to explain the government's timing for the settlement in Eilon Moreh"; and Prime Minister Begin's angry question about a prominent American Jew who had devoted much of his life to raising funds for Israel: "Does he think that his subsidies and donations entitle him to influence our policies and actions?" Fein is one of the American Jewish intellectuals who publicly protested Begin's policies in the spring of 1978, and then with equal vehemence protested "unacceptable" U.S. stands in dealing with Begin that December. In his eloquent way, he typifies the dilemma of young U.S. Zionist intellectuals today: alternately of critical of current Israeli policies, and then critical of non-Jewish Americans who say essentially the same things.

NOTES

1. Goldman, Guido. *New York Review of Books,* May, 1978.
2. Cohen, Richard. Column entitled "An Unseeing Course for a Man of Vision," *Washington Post*, April, 1980.
3. Fein, Leonard. "Israel, Summer 1979: A Visitor's Journal," *Moment,* January, 1980, pp. 27-28.

The Arab Lobby—Their Own Worst Enemies or An Idea Whose Time Has Come?

"Numerous stories have appeared recently about some sort of powerful 'Arab Lobby,' under whose auspices a massive grand propaganda plan has supposedly been designed to brainwash the American public. A recent rundown also appeared in newspapers identifying several lawyers who were lobbying for the Arabs, listing their salaries. I asked the reporter why no corresponding story appeared about the Israeli lobby and his response was that he had written the piece based upon who was registered as a foreign agent. He could not respond to my statement that nearly every Jewish organization in the U.S. lobbied directly for Israel without registering as foreign agents."[1]

Senator James Abourezk, 1976

"You may put it down as a matter of fact that any criticism of Israel will be met with a cry of anti-Semitism."[2]

James Reston, 1975

"In the U.S., all opposition to or breaking rank from the official Israeli government policies . . . is painted with the 'terrorist PLO' or 'Arab petro-dollar' brush."[3]

James J. Zogby, Director, American-Arab
Anti-Discrimination Committee, 1981

"It's easy to sloganize by saying oil profits are being put ahead of America's honor in the world. We're not above doing that from time to time."[4]

Hyman Bookbinder, American Jewish Committee, 1981

"The Saudis are a foreign lobby. They hire foreign agents to do their bidding. Their support is not rooted in American soil."[5]

Thomas A. Dine, Director,
American Israel Public Affairs Committee, 1981

Between 100,000 and 200,000 Lebanese and Syrians have immigrated to the United States over the past century, more than half of them between 1890 and 1920. The early immigrants had little formal education and were primarily interested in making enough money to alleviate the poverty of their families in the Middle East. However, they brought with them large measures of optimism, energy, thrift, and business acumen. They soon brought up a first American-born generation with considerably more formal education and professional and technical skills than they had themselves. Assimilation was the goal of this group of immigrants, and their children achieved it far more rapidly than the children of some earlier and larger immigrant groups. Thus, when Arab-Americans attained political or community leadership, it generally was on the basis of local achievement and local issues, not ethnic identity or support. Whatever ethnic identity remained coalesced largely around their churches or family social activities rather than politics or occupations.

In 1932 a number of regional groups formed the "National Association of Syrian and Lebanese-American Organizations." Some regional federations grew large enough to permit the formation of a National Association of Federations, which in the early 1950s sponsored a convention in Lebanon and Syria, but subsequently declined and disappeared. Even though some vestiges of regional federation leadership remained, particularly in the Midwest, conditions were changing. New groups of immigrants were coming to the U.S. from many parts of the Middle East. Their social composition ranged from unskilled workers from the Yemen to members of the entrepreneurial classes of Egypt, Iraq, and Syria, all of which were experimenting with socialist measures. Muslims made up a much higher percentage of this new wave of immigrants. Students, mostly Muslim, came from virtually every Arab country to study in American universities. Some married Americans and remained in the U.S. Others eventually returned to the U.S. after finding little market for their specialized technical skills in certain Arab countries with still underdeveloped economies or unstable governments.

As the new Arab-Americans, more diverse in terms of national origin and religion, joined the children of the older Lebanese-Syrian immigrants, a split developed between some of the less Americanized newcomers and the totally assimilated children and grandchildren of the first-comers. This dichotomy persists in the political activities of the Arab-American community.

Raised with strong assimilationist goals and suspicious of changeable and sometimes radical Arab regimes, the American-born Arab-Americans, and some of the newer Christian Arab immigrants as well, are frankly uneasy in political organizations without strong and obvious American identity, flagged by the "American" in organizational titles. They also seem to welcome a certain nonethnic leavening in their groups. This is an inevitable development in all portions of the Arab-American community, because virtually all of its members adhere to religions that cross ethnic lines. Whether they are Muslims, Catholics, or Orthodox or Evangelical Protestants, most Arab-American families, through marriage of some members outside the Arab community, begin the process of ethnic assimilation within a generation.

Membership in virtually every organization that could be considered part of a general "Arab lobby," except for those essentially social groups built around a very specific regional or religious affiliation, reflects the tendency among non-Arab Americans who have lived and worked in the Arab countries, whether as educators, business people, diplomats, or missionaries, to become personally, often zealously, involved in making the Arab world better known in the U.S., and Arab political viewpoints better understood.

The best known of such organizations in Washington is the National Association of Arab Americans (called "N triple A"). Its membership includes some whose ties with the Middle East are largely sentimental, based on friendships or past residence there, rather than on actual bloodlines. The NAAA, whose President is Peter Tanous and Executive Director is David Sadd, is a registered lobby. Although it operates with about a quarter of the staff and a vastly smaller membership, it clearly was inspired by the success of AIPAC, its pro-Israel counterpart. The NAAA concentrates mainly on Congress, though it has always enjoyed a sympathetic rapport with some personnel from the Department of State, the Pentagon, and other government agencies who have served in the Middle East and who probably long for the day when the NAAA and other components of the Arab lobby can act as a serious counterweight to the Israeli lobby on Capitol Hill.

Although the NAAA lobbyists joke that they must use "the back door" when they visit congressmen with active pro-Israeli constituents, there is little doubt that, operating without large data banks of pro-Arab names from each Congressional constituency, their low-key approach has developed a friendly, if not particularly effective, audience on Capitol Hill. They do not have the power to bring about even the most innocuous Congressional action in opposition to an incumbent administration. But when marching in tandem with the administration, as in the case of arms sales to moderate Arab countries, they can now make a perceptible contribution.

Several other organizations in Washington are also engaged in activities sufficiently political to be described as part of the miniscule, but growing, Arab lobby. A new but growing membership organization is the American Arab Anti-Discrimination Committee. It was founded by former Senator James Abourezk, perhaps the single most influential leader among Arab-Americans nationwide. The fulltime director of the organization (called "Ad-see") is James Zogby, a young veteran of Arab-American activities with a proven talent for grass-roots organization.

Also Washington-based is the Foundation for Middle East Peace. Merle Thorpe, Jr., a prominent Washington attorney, is its president. A new organization, the Center for U.S.-European Middle East Cooperation, has as its president John Richardson, one of the best-known Washington advocates of Arab causes, who previously served as Executive Director of the NAAA. Even newer in Washington are two organizations founded by recently-retired U.S. diplomats. One is the American Arab Affairs Council, which publishes a quarterly journal.Its President is Isa Khalil Sabbagh and its Executive Director is George Naifeh. Both are retired U.S. Foreign Service officers and the Council's various advisory boards are made up of Americans who have lived and worked in the Middle East as diplomats, educators, journalists, or businessmen. The other is the American Educational Trust, which maintains a Middle East speakers referral service and publishes a fortnightly newsletter, *The Washington Report on Middle East Affairs*. Retired British Ambassador Edward Henderson, former director of the Council for the Advancement of Arab-British Understanding, is its chairman. Its president is retired U. S. Ambassador Andrew I. Killgore. The Middle East Resource Center is a Washington office for Search for Justice and Equality in Palestine, an organization based in Waverly, Massachusetts, which publishes the *Palestine/Israel Bulletin*. The operation concentrates on the Arab-Israel dispute and brings together persons identified both with anti-Zionist Jewish affairs and with Palestinian rights activities.

There are other Washington groups which superficially seem to be part of the Arab Lobby. However, since most are heavily dependent upon U.S. government money received for educational services, training contracts, and programming Middle Eastern visitors to the United States, their political activities have been reduced almost to the vanishing point in order not to jeopardize their federal grants. One such organization is the Middle East Institute, with membership made up largely of retired and active diplomats, educators, and businessmen in the Washington area who have served in the Middle East. Its president is retired U.S. Ambassador Dean Brown and the editor of its prestigious quarterly magazine, *The Middle East Journal,* is retired U.S. Ambassador Richard Parker. It maintains a large library and provides a forum for political as well as cultural programs from Middle Eastern countries. It also conducts a book publishing program and sponsors language classes in Arabic, Hebrew and Persian.

AMIDEAST, formerly known as The American Friends of the Middle East, now is totally apolitical and provides overseas educational counseling and placement services for Middle Eastern students planning to study at U.S. universities. It also conducts training programs both overseas and in the U.S. on contract to the U.S. and Middle Eastern governments and companies. AMIDEAST conducts a limited publications program with a focus on educational and manpower training subjects.

Also non-political, but particularly active on cultural and historical projects is the National Committee to Honor the Fourteenth Centennial of Islam, headed by retired U.S. Ambassador William Crawford. Another newly established but ambitious and active cultural organization is the American Arab Cultural Foundation established by Hisham Sharabi, a professor at Georgetown University and a former NAAA president. American Near East Refugee Aid (ANERA) is another such non-political group, active with self-help projects in the Middle East.

Pro-Arab groups are active in some other major cities throughout the U.S. Just as the Washington-based groups have much of their impact in the national capital, the impact of the others tends to be concentrated in their own geographical areas. In New York, Americans for Middle East Understanding Inc. has, like the Middle East Institute in Washington, a prestigious board of directors.It takes strong political positions and distributes an informative monthly bulletin, *The Link,* to a mailing list of 50,000. Arab-American Chambers of Commerce in New York, Washington, Houston and Dallas provide information on U.S. suppliers and Middle Eastern markets to U.S. businessmen and Middle Eastern customers.

An active relief organization in the Middle East, and probably the most politicized of any organization not based on ethnic Arab membership, is the American Friends Service Committee. The AFSC, whose social service work in the occupied West Bank has brought it into frequent conflict with Israeli military occupation authorities, is actively supported throughout the United States and has sponsored several U.S. speaking engagements by the nearest thing the West Bank has to indigenous political leadership, the West Bank mayors. That too has brought the AFSC into conflict with the Israeli military government, which now seems to have resolved that source of conflict by denying further exit visas or access by the press to the mayors involved.

Another organization is the Association of Arab American University Graduates (AAUG), established in Detroit and now headquartered in the Boston area. Founded in 1968, largely as a social and mutual assistance society by young Arab-born professionals who had taken U.S. citizenship and settled for good in the United States, it has taken on more and more political activity in the course of its annual national meetings and an extensive publishing program.

Though both are membership organizations, the NAAA and AAUG have distinct aims and methods. As a registered lobbying group, the NAAA concentrates its work on specific, realizable, political goals. It makes no attempt to embrace all causes just because they are Arab. It undoubtedly would be very careful not to be drawn into a defense, for example, of the present governments of Libya or South Yemen. Even the NAAA's stand on the Palestine problem is distinctly American and coincides only with that of the more moderate Arab regimes. It essentially supports UN Resolution 242, which calls for Israeli withdrawal from lands occupied in the 1967 war in exchange for Arab recognition of Israel's right to exist within secure and recognized borders. Since this has also been the U.S. position since 1967, the NAAA's program to enforce it in all its particulars and without further delay is potentially salable in all quarters of the U.S. government, including Congress. In addition to its support for Resolution 242, the NAAA supports self-determination for the Palestinians and U.S. negotiations with the PLO as their political representative.

The AAUG, on the other hand, supports the single "democratic secular state" for both the Jews of Israel and the Arabs of Palestine which is still the official program of the PLO and most of the Arab regimes supporting it. Though this program is orthodox in most Arab countries, including some the U.S. considers moderate, it would not be acceptable to the U.S. government nor the American public in the foreseeable future. Even Yassir Arafat's wing of relative moderates within the PLO has been rumored for some time to have at least debated giving up this last "bargaining chip" by recognizing a modified version of Resolution 242, which would include a more specific recognition of Palestinian rights while also recognizing Israel's existence within its pre-1967 war boundaries. Therefore, the position of the AAUG within the Arab camp is reasonably analogous to the position of the mainstream American Jewish groups in supporting Israel's position without any apparent overt attempt to modify it or to reconcile it with that of the U.S. government.

Although large American firms generally eschew direct contributions to organizations providing support to political rather than charitable Middle Eastern activities, more money is reaching partisans of the Arabs in the U.S., as the increase in pro-Arab organizations attests. Most of the major contributors seem to be individuals, both American and Arab, in international business. Since the dollar volume of business between the U.S. and the oil-exporting countries has grown so rapidly in the past decade, it is likely that these individual contributions will continue to rise. If at this point they are still insignificant compared to the funds available to the Israeli lobby, in the future this may not always be so. For years, members of the Arab lobby, fractious and disorganized, have joked that they are their own worst enemies. Now with some increase in funding, the adoption of more moderate positions by individual Arab countries, and a perceptible boost from the policies of Prime Minister Begin, they may find that theirs is an idea whose time has come.

NOTES

1. Abourezk, Senator James, in a talk delivered to the "Arab and American Cultures Conference" of the Middle East Institute, Washington, D.C., September, 1976.
2. Reston, James, quoted by Edmund Ghareeb in "The American Media and the Palestine Problem," *Journal of Palestine Studies,* Autumn 1975/Winter 1976, p. 130.
3. Zogby, James J., Director of the American-Arab Anti-Discrimination Committee, quoted in "Lobbying and the Middle East," *Congressional Quarterly Weekly Report,* August 22, 1981, p. 7.
4. Bookbinder, Hyman, Washington Representative of the American Jewish Committee, quoted in "Lobbying and the Middle East," *Congressional Quarterly Weekly Report,* August 22, 1981, p. 7.
5. Dine, Thomas A., Director, American Israel Public Affairs Committee, quoted in "Lobbying and the Middle East," *Congressional Quarterly Weekly Report,* August 22, 1981, p. 7.

American Business and the Arab Lobby

"A curious thing is that the archives contain little or no evidence of the oil company pressure which is so often alleged by the Zionists to have taken place. It was to be expected that the companies having an interest in petroleum concessions in the Arab countries, particularly Saudi Arabia, would be opposed to the creation of a Jewish state in Palestine. They undoubtedly were, but I recall no instances where the representatives of ARAMCO or any other oil company came into the Department and urged that our government follow a particular line regarding Palestine, nor could I find any letters to that effect in the files. Those of my colleagues whom I have consulted on this point, notably Loy Henderson, Gordon Merriam, and Fraser Wilkins, likewise can recall no pressure on the part of the oil companies. It is of course possible that the oil companies made oral representations at a higher level, but if they did so we were not aware of it. In any event, if there was oil company pressure, it failed of its objective."[1]

Evan M. Wilson, 1979

"We can no longer doltishly ignore the prime political reality of the Palestinian issue. So far we have persistently approached the Middle Eastern problem from the wrong side, spending enormous political capital to settle the Israeli-Egyptian quarrel, which has little to do with oil, while in the process inflaming the Israeli-Palestinian dispute, which critically affects our relations with oil-producing countries. . . . Let there be no mistake about it. So long as we delay a frontal attack on the Palestinian issue, we are alienating the whole Muslim world, as our shattered embassies have demonstrated."[2]

George Ball, 1980

Looking for the relationship between political activities of the Arab lobby and the U.S. oil companies and other large American corporations doing business in the Middle East is a little like the country bumpkin looking for the pea in the carnival shell game. Even a bumpkin realizes, after turning the shells over often enough, that the pea probably is not there at all.

U.S. corporations have provided little financial assistance for pro-Arab political causes. This is obvious to anyone who visits the various pro-Arab organizations. The visitor walks up to the fourth floor (no elevator) to visit the AAADC and to the third floor (also no elevator) to visit the Center for U.S.-European Middle East Cooperation. As the president of the latter organization remarks to visitors who come panting up his stairway, "It's a young man's game." It is a stark contrast with the large, new, multi-windowed buildings occupied by various components of the "Israel Lobby," such as AIPAC, which has its headquarters almost in the shadow of the Capitol dome.

This is not to say that the big companies have no interest in impressing the Arabs, or in international economic issues such as income tax allowances for overseas Americans or U.S. regulations concerning the Arab boycott of Israel. These same U.S. companies, however, have no interest whatsoever in providing domestic critics with excuses to call them anti-Israel, anti-Semitic, or anti-anything that can be avoided. They are well aware that there are vigilant friends of Israel in all walks of American life, including positions on their own boards of directors, who would rapidly alert a host of federal regulatory agencies to any pro-Arab activities that have even the appearance of conspiracy, illegality, or irregularity of any sort.

Whatever the desires of the Arab countries in which they operate, the oil companies simply are not going to use up their Congressional credits on the Arab-Israeli dispute. They have legitimate, and to them more immediately important, battles to fight in such areas as oil depletion allowances and windfall profits taxes.

By saving their credibility, the oil companies and other U.S. concerns in the Middle East were able to move fairly effectively in the case of U.S. anti-boycott legislation, which threatened to cripple American companies in their competition with European and Japanese firms for Middle Eastern markets. Working through the Business Roundtable, U.S. businessmen with interests in the Middle East reached an agreement with Israel's American partisans, represented by B'Nai B'Rith, on what legal measures were appropriate to prohibit "secondary" and "tertiary" boycott measures as distinguished from the internationally acceptable "primary" Arab boycott of Israel. The results were incorporated into the administration's bill before it became the subject of Congressional debate. The bill has made it considerably more difficult for American companies to do business in the Middle East, costing the U.S. at least $1 billion per year. But at least the bill worked out by the Business Roundtable and the B'Nai B'Rith has not totally shut U.S. contractors and exporters out of profitable Arab markets.

Similarly, businessmen have been influential in lobbying against some federal income tax levies on allowances that would, for all practical purposes, make it impossible for American contracting firms in the Middle East to employ Americans rather than foreigners for work ranging from engineering positions through clerical and blue-collar jobs. Here again, a modicum of reason has ultimately prevailed. A potential balance of payments loss in the billions, and a U.S. employment loss in the many thousands, has been partially averted. This took place, however, only after extensive lobbying by "big business" against federal tax measures so destructive to long-range American economic interests that it was hard to envision what purpose the drafters could have had other than to drive all U.S. firms and workers completely from the Middle East. It is to keep their powder dry for such challenges, however, that large American companies have stayed as far as possible from the Arab-Israeli dispute.

As tokens of esteem for their Middle Eastern hosts, businessmen find it far more prudent to subsidize the publication of books on Arab art, literature, and culture, or to underwrite traveling cultural exhibitions or performances from the Middle East. The recent public television showing of the controversial film on Saudi Arabia, "Death of a Princess," provided an opportunity for Mobil Oil to purchase advertisements opposing the showing. But the dispute had nothing directly to do with Israel. Mobil subsequently has taken other public positions on controversial Middle East matters, but to date it is almost the only U. S. oil company to do so.

American companies also give funds to American and non-American organizations for use in refugee relief, education, and vocational training programs. Even such actions on behalf of Palestinian refugees, however, are subject to criticism by some pro-Israel partisans. A $2.2 million gift to American Near East Refugee Aid (ANERA) by Gulf Oil immediately after the war of October 1973 reportedly resulted in a virtual boycott of Gulf by some U.S. Jewish groups.

In the case of the Middle East, even the time-honored idea of grants for academic projects is not totally free of risk for large companies. As discussed elsewhere in this study, the University of Southern California recently returned to American companies all initial contributions aimed at supporting a Middle East Studies Center after a local press campaign alleged possible Saudi control and after the contributors were subjected to careful SEC scrutiny concerning the conditions under which contributions had been solicited from U.S. firms doing business in Saudi Arabia.

The lengths to which even small businessmen go to avoid U.S. domestic problems while seeking to impress favorably the countries of the Middle East is described by veteran anti-Zionist author Alfred Lilienthal, who in 1979 published *The Zionist Connection: What Price Peace in the Middle East?* An American businessman purchased 20 copies of the book. Instead of distributing them to American opinion-makers who might be in a position to do something about Zionist activities, however, he then prudently shipped all 20 copies to the Middle Eastern country in which his firm was working. There the books were distributed to local government officials, a classic case of preaching to the converted and offending no one.

One might expect U.S. companies doing business in the Middle East to purchase large and expensive advertisements in the publications of pro-Arab U.S. lobbying organizations, such as those described above, or to purchase and distribute to interested parties in the media or academia books that reflect favorably on the Arab cause, just as AIPAC does in the case of pro-Israeli books. Apparently, however, most feel the risks of criticism from within the U.S. far outweigh whatever vague or intangible public relations advantages might accrue to them in the Middle East. Subsidizing non-political charitable, cultural, or educational activity is less controversial and just as impressive.

The October 1981 Congressional battle over approval of the sale of AWACS to Saudi Arabia, however, provided a conspicuous exception to the timidity usually shown by American industry and business on such questions. Led by representatives of the companies which would benefit directly from the sale, proponents mustered a potent coalition of private corporations and political conservatives to contact individual senators who seemed to be wavering over the vote.

Richard M. Hunt, director of government for NL Industries, a manufacturer of petroleum equipment, assembled an *ad hoc* group of Washington representatives of some 40 companies with Middle East interests to support the sale. Leading members were the Boeing Company, which faced the closure of its AWACS production line if the sale were not approved, and Pratt and Whitney, maker of the engines for AWACS. Others included Exxon and Mobil from the petroleum industry and Brown and Root and Bechtel representing major U.S. construction firms. Some of the *ad hoc* group's meetings were held in the Washington offices of the Business Roundtable, although that business lobbying group did not take a formal stand on the sale.

A similar *ad hoc* coalition of 34 conservative organizations was coordinated by Richard Sellers, Washington director for the Coalition for Peace Through Strength and director of congressional relations for the American Security Council. Supporting groups included the Veterans of Foreign Wars, the American Military Retirees Association, Catholics for Christian Political Action, Young Americans for Freedom, the Conservative Victory Fund and the National Christian Action Committee.

Representatives of groups in both the political and industrial catagories worked on individual senators, stressing both the national security aspects and the economic advantages of the sale. The president of Boeing sent telegrams to 1600 of his firm's sub-contractors urging their support through their own representatives. Brown and Root supplied position papers to senators from states in which the firm and its affiliates are located. The president of Pratt and Whitney sent telegrams predicting that a Senate veto of the President's plan would only force the Saudis to turn to non-American aircraft producers and "would cost the U.S. both exports and jobs."

Summing up the effort, which may well have been crucial to the close Senate vote which made the sale possible, a businessman explained it had "created the environment" which enabled key senators to drop their uncommitted positions and support President Reagan.

NOTES

1. Wilson, Evan M., *Decision on Palestine: How the U.S. Came to Recognize Israel*, Hoover Institution Press, Stanford, 1979, p. 152.
2. Ball, George, "Our Threatened Lifeline," *Washington Post* Outlook section, January 20, 1980.

CHAPTER XIX

Christian Churches on Both Sides of the Arab-Israeli Dispute

"Jerry has said that as a pastor he believes God deals with nations in direct proportion to how those nations deal with Israel and its people, because the Jews are God's chosen people."[1]

Cal Thomas, Moral Majority
Vice President for Communications, 1981

"The Christian has a major responsibility to stand by Israel, to defend her divine right, to vote with her . . . Christians cannot stand by and witness the PLO, the Communists, and Islam doing again to the Jews what was done to their land in the first century."[2]

From advertisement in the *New York Times* by
"Twentieth Century Reformation Hour Broadcast," 1977

"I've been to Israel and Egypt. I went to Lebanon for a couple of weeks and met with Yassir Arafat. I also talked to our ambassador, John Gunther Dean, and to church-men and leaders on both sides of the issue. Arafat challenged me to go back to Los Angeles and find a bookstore where there's even one book about the Palestinians. I went to Pickwick, Vroman's and everywhere and found not one book, not even a pamphlet. But there were literally hundreds of titles on the Israelis. This is the greatest country in the world for information flow, yet we have almost no information at all about the problem which most plagues us."[3]

Mel White, Christian educator and filmmaker, 1981

"The continuing interest of the Jew is in exactly the kind of society that makes Mr. Falwell uncomfortable."[4]

Rabbi Arthur Hertzberg, 1981

Many Americans—especially, perhaps, liberal American Jews—expressed surprise at the public courtship between Prime Minister Begin and the Reverend Jerry Falwell of Lynchburg, Virginia, founder and leader of the Moral Majority. Falwell's support for Begin was so absolute that he split openly with at least one Moral Majority local chapter leader in the Washington, D.C. area who would not go along with it. Even Falwell's most loyal followers must have been concerned when, after Begin's American-furnished warplanes killed 300 civilians in one afternoon raid in Beirut in July 1981, the fundamentalist clergyman telephoned the Israeli Prime Minister "to cheer his spirits." Various informal media polls indicated that few American Jews felt like cheering the Israeli Prime Minister that day. Instead, American Jews seemed intent on reminding non-Jews that "Begin isn't Israel."

The whole Falwell-Begin episode was the subject of controversy inside as well as outside Jewish circles, as Rabbi Arthur Hertzberg's comment above indicates. Howard Squadron, chairman of the Conference of Presidents of Major American Jewish Organizations, apparently found the Reverend Jerry Falwell one more inconvenience in a long hot summer that had already included Begin's June bombing of the Iraqi nuclear reactor and the July bombing of Beirut. In the August 22, 1981, issue of the *Congressional Quarterly,* he was quoted as saying of the Moral Majority:

"They strongly support a lot of things I think are dreadful for the country. But I'm not going to turn away their support of Israel for that."[5]

For Americans who had followed closely the long shadows cast in the U.S. by the Arab-Israeli dispute, the warm relationship between Falwell and Begin came as no surprise. For as long as Israel has existed, and before, many fundamentalist Christian clergymen could be counted upon for support by pro-Israel lobbying groups or Jewish religious leaders. Some of these Christian fundamentalists had visited the Holy Land many times, often with some degree of Israeli sponsorship or support; others simply considered the creation of Israel as the fulfillment of Biblical prophecy. There is no question that Falwell and certain other fundamentalist U.S. clergymen are just as emotional, if not always so subtle, on Israel's place in the Middle East as are Israeli religious leaders themselves.

It is difficult to estimate whether most members of fundamentalist churches are as passionate about Israel as some of their clergymen. It is certain, however, that large numbers of Americans who believe that the Old Testament is the literal word of God find much Biblical justification not only for the establishment of Israel, but for all of its territorial expansion to date. When poll responses concerning the Middle East are broken down by religion, Protestants are slightly more likely to be positive about Israel than are Catholics. Similarly, there is evidence indicating higher favor for Israel in areas where fundamentalist churches are strong.

Mr. Falwell believes, according to a Moral Majority spokesman, that "God deals with nations in direct proportion to how those nations deal with Israel." It is not a totally new slant. Lyndon Johnson had an aunt in Texas whose advice to him was essentially the same. She is said to have sent a message to her nephew pointing out that from the moment President Truman helped in the creation of Israel, he was certain to win the 1948 election. The point of her advice to President Johnson was that he should be on the lookout for similar opportunities to pile up future credits.

Over the years other self-proclaimed Christian fundamentalists have not hesi-tated to issue blatantly political appeals for support of Israel against the Arabs. At the time of President Sadat's journey to Jerusalem readers of the *New York Times* were confronted with a full-page advertisement headlined "Fundamentalists Vote with Israel" and paid for by "The 20th Century Reformation Hour Broadcast" of Collingswood, New Jersey. It read, in part:

"The Old Testament belongs to Jews and Christians alike. Here we learn that the Holy Land is the 'Land of Promise' for Israel and the Messiah. We are called fundamentalists because we believe the Bible to be the very word of God and that it is to be taken literally on its every representation. The covenants made with Abraham, Isaac and Jacob and their descendants by Almighty God are not myth or legend. These are clear and from God a land grant and divine deed. . . . Just before the Six-Day War, the radios from the Arab lands were announcing that on Saturday the Jews would be driven into the sea, the Mediterranean, and on Sunday the Christians would also be dealt with. . . . The fear of the loss of Arab oil cannot replace the fear of God. Nor can it be used against the prophecies and purposes of God. . . . Israel's immediate adversary today is . . . the descendants of Esau, the Palestinians, and the Arabs. The world is back again to Jacob and Esau. Esau is claiming Jacob's land. . . . The Christian has a major responsibility to stand by Israel, to defend her divine right, to vote with her. . . . Christians cannot stand by and witness the PLO, the Communists and Islam doing again to the Jews what was done to their land in the first century."[6]

On October 26, 1981, two days before the Senate AWACS vote, a group calling itself "Christians United for American Security" and chaired by a longtime friend of Israel, Dr. Franklin H. Littell, published a full-page advertisement in the *Washington Post* headlined "U.S. Secrets in Saudi Hands Threaten American Security." The advertisement charged the Saudi regime is "anti-American," "vulnerable to subversion from within" and has "provided massive funding for PLO terrorism . . . reviled President Sadat . . . and sworn jihad (holy war) against Israel." The advertisement described Israel as "our one democratic friend and reliable ally in the region" and urged "the U.S. Senate to reject the plan to feed the Saudi appetite for more military hardware." It was signed by 29 "responsible Christian leaders" including such diverse public figures as Dr. Jerry Falwell and the Reverend Father Robert Drinan, former Congressman and president of Americans for Democratic Action.

There is an apocryphal story that a newly-arrived UN negotiator once appealed to his Israeli and Arab colleagues to "sit down and settle your differences like good Christians." Presumably that particular UN official was not familiar with the message of "The 20th Century Reformation Hour Broadcast" of Collingswood, New Jersey or "Christians United for American Security."

What is new about the relationship between Begin and Falwell therefore has little to do with the United States, where fundamentalism has always been strong. The change is in Israel, which, until Menachem Begin came to power, had never had a Prime Minister who would display such enthusiasm for Falwell's friendship.

More significant, perhaps, are actions of various Christian church groups in providing a hearing for Arab speakers, or even sponsorship as is the case with the American Friends Service Committee. It is ironic that the more liberal Protestant churches, which in the past have often allied themselves with Jewish groups in defense of separation of church and state in the United States, now frequently find themselves at odds with the same Jewish groups because of their stand on Palestinian questions. There have been frequent difficulties between Jewish organizations and the National Council of Churches, and some Protestant denominations—generally but not always of liberal persuasion—continue to provide both the hall and the audience for Palestinian speakers. This has also been true of the Roman Catholic Church in the U.S., and of course of the church groups with which Christian Arab-Americans are affiliated. The Lebanese civil war has further complicated the picture. Some Lebanese Americans of Maronite Catholic background no longer support Palestinian causes.

On balance, one might say that within the liberal Protestant denominations, sympathy for the newly-perceived Palestinian underdog is to some extent offset by traditional concern for good relations and dialogue with neighboring Jewish congregations. Within the fundamentalist denominations support for Israel as the fulfillment of Biblical prophecy is similarly offset to some extent by accompanying conservative reservations against unnecessary foreign political involvement. Within both the Catholic and Orthodox Christian churches in the U.S., the concern of local parishioners with ethnic ties to Arab countries and clergy who have become partisans of the Arabs through service in the Middle East is somewhat offset by ties between Christian and Jewish leadership at the national level, and also by concern for the church institutions now operating with Israeli sufferance both in Israel proper and in the militarily-occupied areas.

All of these pluses and minuses do not quite add up to zero, however. Given the relative strength of the two camps in the United States, any support in the form of audiences provided for Arab spokesmen by Christian organizations may be a significant part of the total of such activity in the United States. By contrast, Christian support for Israel, though probably equal or perhaps even greater in terms of total sympathetic audiences, resolutions, paid advertisements, and so on, is nevertheless an almost insignificant portion of the total pro-Israel political and religious activity in the United States.

NOTES

1. Thomas, Cal, Vice President for Communications, Moral Majority, quoted in "Lobbying and the Middle East," *Congressional Quarterly Weekly Report,* August 22, 1981, p. 4.
2. Quoted from text of full-page advertisement in *New York Times* of November 15, 1977 signed by 15 churchmen and paid for by "The 20th Century Reformation Hour Broadcast" of Collingswood, N.J.
3. White, Mel, "Please, Church, Look at This One," *World Vision,* October, 1981, pp. 12–13.
4. Hertzberg, Rabbi Arthur, quoted in "Lobbying and the Middle East," *Congressional Quarterly Weekly Report,* p. 4.
5. Squadron, Howard M., Chairman of the Conference of Presidents of Major American Jewish Organizations quoted in "Lobbying and the Middle East," *Congressional Quarterly Weekly Report,* August 22, 1981 p. 4.
6. Quoted from advertisement in *New York Times* of November 15, 1977 by "The 20th Century Reformation Hour Broadcast" of Collingswood, N.J.

CHAPTER XX

Arab Diplomatic Activities

"The Arabs have been their own worst enemies when trying to reach the American media and the American people with their arguments about Middle East questions. The Israelis, on the other hand, have been the most effective spokesmen for a foreign nation I have dealt with."[1]

Lee Eggerstrom, Rider Newspapers, 1975

"Although a good deal of attention and publicity are periodically attracted by the activities of foreign lobbyists or agents, a close examination of their activities shows that those lacking strong indigenous support acquire only limited or transient influence on American foreign policy."[2]

Senator Charles McC. Mathias, Jr., 1981

"The disparity between American and Arab culture lends support to Americans' impression of the Arab world, an impression, I must say, that is helped very little by Arab attitudes toward what we call public relations. I once told a Kuwaiti Cabinet Minister that the Arabs ought to try to explain their position to the American people. Indignantly, he said, 'Why should we tell the Americans anything, because we have the truth.'"[3]

Senator James Abourezk, September 24, 1976

Some twenty Arab League members are represented in the United States. However, only a few conduct active information programs, and not all of those are deeply concerned with the Arab-Israeli dispute. Among those that are, the most active is the Arab League Information Program.

After many years of essentially negative initiatives, simplistically depicting U.S. support for Israel as an imperialist plot rather than trying to explain the Palestinian case to Americans, the Arab League Information Center has modified its message somewhat and in some cases employed American-educated Arab personnel well attuned to the American mentality. Its leadership is of mixed quality, however, and some of its spokesmen are still as eager for confrontation as for understanding.

Palestinians once met even constructive American criticism with statements to the effect that "our cause is just, and if you cannot understand that, it's your problem, not ours." Some now assume more responsibility for U.S. perceptions. Many still publicly defend the necessity of a stage of violence as a means of bringing their cause to world attention. Yet most probably realize that the years of international violence and terrorism, presumably now past, were lost years concerning promotion of their cause in the U.S. While some may still cite "Jewish control of the media" as justification for their inaction in the U.S., others do not hesitate to reprint and distribute favorable articles about their cause from the U.S. and western press and, led by Arab League Special Ambassador Clovis Maksoud, travel the U.S. lecture circuit to compete with their opponents. It is too soon to assess the new PLO information offices in New York and Washington, but their relations are close with Arab League and other Arab diplomats. From the initial evidence, they have learned from the mistakes of past years. Their more experienced spokesmen, too, seek to project an image of reasonableness and moderation.

Saudi Arabia has contracted, on a case-by-case basis, with Americans such as Washington attorney Frederick G. Dutton for legal and public relations assistance, particularly on economic initiatives. It has also dispatched some very effective Saudi spokesmen on speaking tours of the U.S., selecting highly intelligent government officials, generally American-educated, and briefing them carefully on current American sensitivities. Their messages focus on the benefits to Americans of the economic relationship between Saudi Arabia and the United States. They seek to allay popular American fears that the Saudis use their investments to control any sector of the U.S. economy. Their well-briefed spokesmen have been particularly cautious not to link Saudi economic power with Saudi political concerns in their public statements, having learned how easily such linkage brings charges of "economic blackmail." In general, these speaking programs have been efficiently conducted to counteract a strong long-range effort openly directed by the Israeli Embassy in Washington to arouse hostility toward Saudi Arabia among Americans.

Libya and Iraq have both taken American groups, composed primarily but not exclusively of Arab-Americans, to their countries to see and hear for themselves about current economic and political developments. Whatever impressions the Americans may bring back of the prevailing political leadership or systems, there is little doubt that they return impressed by the economic potential of both of those oil-producing nations.

Though very small, the Jordanian and Syrian embassies have had skilled personnel in the U.S. However, both are presently limited in what they can accomplish because their governments' opposition to the Camp David agreements has made it difficult for them to find any positive common ground on which to build an active information program in the U.S.

For many years prior to the Camp David agreements, however, Jordan's King Hussein seemed uniquely successful in his ability to reach American public opinion. He had become to Americans such a well-known and respected international figure that, despite differences over Camp David, his positive image in the U.S. was undiminished.

After President Sadat's journey to Jerusalem and his regular U.S. press and television interviews, he became so personally popular in the U.S. that President Carter could get an appreciative laugh from American audiences by saying how grateful he was that he did not have to run for re-election against Anwar Sadat.

Each of these Arab leaders, King Hussein in the 1960s and 1970s and President Sadat from the early 1970s until his death in 1981, clearly understood the power of American television and the American press. Each used those media with great effect to send his message directly to the American public. The ultimate persuader, however, was not the medium, but the message: Moderation, reasonableness, and a willingness to compromise on small matters in order to get on with important concerns. In short, each leader seemed to tell Americans that he wanted to do just what Americans hoped he would do: Go at least fifty per cent of the way towards peace with each of his neighbors in the Middle East.

Their successes, in their own times and without the blessing of the bulk of the "Arab Lobby" in the U.S., illustrate that lobby's basic problem. No matter how skilled they may eventually become, Arab spokesmen in the U.S. will not make politically significant inroads into uncommitted American public opinion until the Arab countries themselves can agree on a unified policy. In terms of population, Libya may be one of the smallest and least significant Arab countries. But so long as the suspicion remains that it supports international terrorism as an instrument of national policy, the entire Arab image is severely tarnished. When Saudi Arabia, Egypt, Syria, and Jordan briefly seemed to move in tandem after the 1973 war, and American friends of the Arabs could speak confidently of a "moderate Arab camp," American perceptions of the Arabs began to change. Later, when those four countries seemingly embarked on separate courses, old American stereotypes quietly resumed their places.

After all has been said about the relative strengths of the Israeli and Arab lobbies, the accessibility of the media, and east-west cultural differences, the overriding importance of Arab leadership and Arab policies is still evident. When PLO Chairman Yassir Arafat first went before the United Nations, every American turned on his television set to see the "terrorist" in the flesh. Had he chosen to address popular American concerns rather than the concerns of the Third World and radicals within his own Palestinian constituency, the U.S. would almost certainly be engaged in a constructive dialogue with the PLO today.

If the PLO chairman had been able to extricate the American hostages in Iran in 1979, or even if he had visibly persisted in such efforts without success, he would have struck directly at the heart of the American people in their moment of maximum vulnerability. Such an action would have revised in a season literally years of negative perceptions.

Had the Saudi principles for a Middle East settlement been accepted at the Arab summit conference in Fez in late 1981, the Arab information effort would suddenly have had a "salable" program for U.S. audiences, and would again have been able to move effectively to revise American perceptions. (It is interesting to note that prior to the Fez meeting Israel described the Saudi principles as a "plan for the liquidation of Israel." Immediately after the plan was rejected, and Israel had "annexed" the Golan Heights taken from Syria in 1967, the Israelis used Syrian rejection of the plan as one of the justifications for the Israeli annexation action).

It is no fault of the Arab information programs in the U.S. that, despite the changes recorded in recent years, American perceptions of the Arab-Israeli dispute are still basically one-sided. For all practical purposes, only twice since World War II has an Arab chief of state set out to influence American public opinion, regardless of the consequences in his country or elsewhere in the Arab world, and the polls in each case recorded almost immediate success. By contrast, prior to the incumbency of Menachem Begin, Israel's leaders never lost sight of the crucial importance of U.S. public opinion for their cause.

NOTES

1.   Eggerstrom, Lee, of Rider Newspapers, quoted by Edmund Ghareeb in "The American Media and the Palestine Problem," *Journal of Palestine Studies*, Autumn 1975/Winter 1976, p. 144.
2.   Mathias, Senator Charles McC. Jr., "Ethnic Groups and Foreign Policy," *Foreign Affairs*, Summer, 1981.
3.   Abourezk, Senator James, in a talk delivered to the "Arab and American Cultural Conference" of the Middle East Institute, Washington, D.C., September, 1976.

CHAPTER XXI

The Media

"Let me warn here that I am not one of those who believes that Jews own all the newspapers. That statement is both racist and inaccurate. What I do believe is that a great sympathy for Israel exists in the American media, among both Jews and non-Jews. I also believe that journalists like to write what is fashionable."[1]

Senator James Abourezk, 1976

"It is my personal belief that if the media as a whole in the Western world had done an adequate job in reporting from the Middle East, it would not have been necessary for the Palestinians to resort to violence to draw attention to their case."[2]

James McCartney, 1975

James McCartney's comment is not the assessment of a Palestinian spokesman, but that of the Washington correspondent for Knight newspapers. It typifies a consensus that, whatever the failings of the world media, the U.S. media for a long time did a woefully inadequate job of informing the American public on the Middle East. That said, most American observers would also agree that the situation has improved steadily throughout the 70s. Many still question, however, whether the improvement is sufficient to enable even the better-informed members of the American public to reach informed conclusions on Middle Eastern matters. Those who believe that U. S. Middle Eastern coverage has been inadequate describe deficiencies ranging from insufficient or incomplete coverage of events to biased reporting and commentary. Is this dismal past record the result of a conspiracy or a "gentlemen's agreement?" Or is it the result of benign or ignorant neglect? In short, if the media have inadequately or unfairly covered an area now generally agreed to be of vital importance to the western world in general and to Americans in particular, was it a sin of commission or of omission? Since the media now have their own ombudsmen and academic watchdogs, and since members of the media are often their own severest critics, perhaps it is best to let them speak mostly for themselves, medium by medium.

NEWSPAPER EDITORIAL POSITIONS

"The duty of the mass media, the duty of journalism, is to educate—to tell the truth. But your American mass media are not telling the truth. You are covering up."[3]

Yassir Arafat, Beirut, 1981

"You see it time and time again. The image of Palestinians as Russian agents, as terrorists, versus the image of Israelis as a people who make the desert bloom. Believe me, if I had all the money in foreign aid Israel had from the U.S., and all the European technicians who emigrated there, I could make trees grow out of cement. But while they create and reinforce a good image we sit back and complain that the Western media is biased. The fault is ours."[4]

Rami Khouri, Amman, 1981

The print media are still the primary sources of information for American leaders and opinion makers. In considering both newspapers and news magazines, a distinction must be made between the editorial pages and political columns, which are of great importance to decision makers, and the news pages, which may have a greater influence on the informed general public.

Since newspaper editorials take distinct positions, the bias of each newspaper's editorial pages can be measured over a period to provide a general portrait of American press attitudes toward the Arab-Israeli dispute. This was done for an eight-year period from 1966 to 1974 by Robert Trice, subsequently director of arms transfer policy of the Department of Defense, while he was on the Ohio State University faculty. Trice coded a total of 2,924 editorials from eleven dailies which he described as "the American elite press." They were the *New York Times, Washington Post, Chicago Tribune, Los Angeles Times, Denver Post, Atlanta Constitution, Christian Science Monitor, St. Louis Post-Dispatch, Wall Street Journal, Louisville Courier Journal,* and the *Dallas Morning News.* Among his conclusions:

"As American involvement in Indochina wound down, the Arab-Israeli conflict emerged to join U.S.-Soviet relations and Sino-American relations as one of the few foreign policy topics to garner the sustained interest of the press. . . . In terms of the possible roles played by the opinion makers of the prestige press, the evidence . . . provides hints that American editors may have been predisposed to follow the lead of the American government to adopt an open-minded, cautiously supportive stance toward Israel, and to approach the actions of all others with a jaundiced outlook that ran the gamut from skepticism (in the case of the UN) to open antipathy (in the case of the Palestinians). . . . It is significant that through all these periods of crisis between successive Administrations and virtually every other relevant party—Arab governments, Israel, the Soviet Union and American pro-Israel groups—the press provided steady support for the actions of the U.S. government. . . . The unwavering if qualified editorial support shown toward the United States stands in sharp contrast to press opinion concerning other major actors. Support for Israel was greatest in 1970 during the War of Attrition and was particularly strong during the final third of that year in the wake of Egyptian-Soviet violations of the cease-fire agreement. However, the elite press was critical of a number of Israeli actions over the years, particularly those concerning the annexation of Jerusalem, policies toward the occupied territories and the Israeli retaliatory raid policy. The Arab governments were never able to elicit much sympathy from American newspapers. . . . However . . . after the end of the War of Attrition the press was less critical of the Arabs than in preceding years. The Soviet Union was consistently treated as the major villain in the Middle East. With the exception of 1969, when hopes ran high that a solution could be hammered out in the Big Four and Big Two talks, the Soviets always received more criticism from the American press than any other government actor. . . .

"Editorial opinions on most foreign policy issues are a function of the persuasiveness of the arguments presented by the U.S. government as well as other governments; the cultural, religious and political belief systems of the editorial staffs, and their perceptions of the opinions of significant individuals and groups in the domestic and international political environments. . . . Israel received moderately favorable editorial treatment on most issues over the nine-year period. Two of the most important issues on which it enjoyed the support of the American elite press concerned preconditions for a negotiated peace, and demands for recognized and secure national boundaries. . . . The Arab states did not fare as well as Israel in the competition for American editorial support. In particular, perceived Arab aggression, support for Palestinian military activities, policies toward Arab Jews (particularly in Iraq), and the 1973-74 oil price rise and embargo aroused strong criticism from U.S. newspapers. . . . The United States government was able to rally editorial support for its position on most issues. However, the degree of enthusiasm shown by the elite press varied considerably from issue to issue. Successive Administrations found strong backing for almost any peace initiative, cautious support for U.S. aid policy to Israel (whether generous or stingy), and general skepticism about the wisdom of providing economic and military aid to the front-line Arab states. . . . The dominant themes running through the editorials on American Middle East policy were the need for the government to defend U.S. "national interests," to act in an "even-handed" manner, to avoid being dragged into a confrontation with the Soviet Union, and, interestingly, the need for Soviet-American cooperation. . . . It is possible to cast editorial coverage of Palestinian-related issues in two different lights. On the one hand, it is quite accurate to say that the irregular military activities of Palestinian groups received almost universal condemnation from prestige American newspapers. Palestinians were the target of more criticism on the issue of their commando and terrorist attacks than any other single party or any other issue that arose during the 1966-1974 period. On the other hand, American editors would also frequently refer to Palestinian demands for the right of self determination. And, more often than not, they would at least grudgingly admit that Palestinian demands, however intolerable their methods, were legitimate, and that a resolution of the 'Palestinian problem' was a prerequisite to a lasting Middle East settlement. . . .

". . . As a group, America's prestige newspapers were more supportive of most Israeli policies and actions than those of the Arab states. However, we were a bit surprised to find that both support for Israel and criticism of the Arab states were considerably weaker than we had anticipated. The Palestinians and the French rivaled the Soviets as consistent targets of strong editorial attacks on most issues.

"There were also some variations in the orientation of different elite newspapers toward the Middle East conflict. The *Christian Science Monitor* and the *St. Louis Post-Dispatch* were the only newspapers that were 'net critics' of Israel, and the *Monitor* was alone as a 'net supporter' of the Arab states. Although there were substantial differences in their enthusiasm, all 11 papers showed overall support for the policies and actions of the U.S. government. . . . The clear message sent to policy makers by the opinion shapers and transmitters of the elite press was that they would support any reasonable U.S. initiative to bring about an equitable and permanent settlement as long as it avoided the prospect of direct U.S. military involvement. We suspect that the general trends established during the 1966–1974 period have changed only slightly since then. If the time frame of the analysis was extended through 1978 the data would probably show increasingly similar general levels of support for Israel and the Arab governments (particularly Egypt, Jordan and Saudi Arabia), increased recognition of the importance of Palestinian self-determination as an element in any stable peace, and continued condemnation of Palestinian commando and terrorist activities. . . ."[5]

NEWSPAPER NEWS COVERAGE

"Daily we have air raids; daily we have sea raids; daily we have shelling. If this were happening in Maalot it would make headlines. . . .

"Why don't you see both sides of the coin? Why do you cover the news only from the Israeli angle?"[6]

Yassir Arafat, 1981

"I call it the audience factor—in this case a tremendous interest in and sympathy for Israel. It's a factor in how editorial judgments are made."[7]

Steve Bell, American Broadcasting Company, 1981

So much for the official editorial positions of America's elite newspapers. What about the impressions conveyed in the news columns of those papers, read by a far greater audience and subject to almost imperceptible manipulation by reporters, copy readers, headline writers, and editors? In the absence of a scholarly critique, it is useful to rely on some comments by those in the best position to keep score, the media personnel themselves. In 1975, Edmund Ghareeb interviewed prominent U.S. news personnel for the *Journal of Palestine Studies* about American media coverage of the Palestine problem and the Arab-Israeli conflict. The individuals offered sometimes conflicting but generally forthright comments:

LEE EGGERSTROM: RIDER NEWSPAPERS

"It is correct that the U.S. news media have been generally pro-Israeli and anti-Arab. Until the October 1973 War and the resultant Arab oil embargo, the U.S. citizen and the media paid little attention to the Arab states. The Middle East was an area where the creation of Israel was watched with great interest, fostered by an effective interest group within the U.S. . . . The Arab oil embargo made many changes in the U.S. One significant result was a 'new discovery' of the Arab nations by the American news media. I have no way of citing statistics, but I believe it is a safe assumption to say that the news media stories about the Arab nations and datelined from Arab states since the October War equal the total news coverage out of those countries since 1948 . . .

"The treatment of Palestinian commandos, or guerrillas, represents in my opinion the best example of the American news media's lack of understanding about what is really happening in the Middle East. Good reporters . . . can write provocative and informative articles about Middle East altercations and developments. The headline over their stories, however, will end up stating something like 'Arab Terrorists Strike Again.' It is unfortunate that desk editors and newsroom personnel do not know the difference between the various Arab ethnic and national groups. It is unfortunate for the American people, who must rely on the news media to inform them of wars of liberation for homelands abroad and what the issues are."[8]

JAMES MCCARTNEY, KNIGHT NEWSPAPERS

"It is my belief that because of the large Jewish populations in major cities, where there is a kind of built-in audience for what's happening in Israel, the automatic reaction of some of our editors was to view the situation in terms of what those readers would want to know. And what they would want to know was: How was Israel doing? . . . There is an immensely large Jewish community in New York City, and there is no doubt that the *New York Times* is owned by a Jewish family. But I am not willing to make the possible inference that this leads to slanted reports on the Middle East, which would impugn the integrity of the *New York Times*. I believe that they believe they are objective within their intellectual frame of reference. But I think that there are certain questions any newspaper should ask itself in the reporting of any controversial situation in which there are known divergent views. I think the *Times* should perhaps increase its own credibility by not assigning Jews to play a major role in covering Middle East issues. And I think in many newspapers with Jewish staff who have a great interest in Israel, there is sometimes a certain degree of bias."[9]

RONALD KOVEN, *WASHINGTON POST*

"Historically, the American press has been a reflection of its society. The press has been a way for immigrant groups to be upwardly mobile. Up until about 1950 or earlier, newsrooms of major metropolitan newspapers on the East Coast had large numbers of people of Irish origin in dominant positions. About that period the Irish were accepted into our society in a different way, so journalism didn't seem to be so desirable as a profession. They went on to places where they made more money and had more prestige. In the same way the next wave in American journalism was the Jews. For that reason there were and are disproportionate numbers of Jews in the American media, relative to the population. . . . I think the next wave after the Jews—you can just see the thin edge of the wedge—are blacks. . . . I want to put the question of the presence of Jews in the media in its historical perspective; it's not a Zionist plot."[10]

TELEVISION NEWS

"Television is now the first and most dramatic shaper of public information on the Middle East. Where television coverage of the region is now skewed, technological and time constraints and especially the lack of access granted by countries in the region can most often be blamed."[11]

Robert Hershman (PBS) and Henry Griggs, Jr. (NBC), 1981

"We have a terrible problem of balance. The network has a very good bureau in Tel Aviv, and the ability to satellite news directly out of Israel. But there is a continuing problem of access in Arab nations."[12]

Steve Bell, ABC, 1981

"The Arabs just don't give us access. And they pay the price for that—and they have never seemed to figure out that they'd have a lot more people in this country sympathetic to them if they'd opened up to us over the years. . . . The Israelis know how to feed the press."[13]

Sanford Socolow, CBS, 1981

"In television there is a control room, there is a policy. Sometimes we find the TV studios open for us. Then when we want to expose something, the lines go dead. As if somebody upstairs just pushed a button. You talk to us about changing our image. It is not our image that should be changed, but your American mentality."[14]

Shafiq al-Hout, Palestine Liberation Organization, 1981

As with the press, there are two significant dimensions to television coverage of the Arab-Israeli dispute. The first is the formal coverage in news and documentary shows. According to Robert Trice, "studies have shown that there are virtually no differences in foreign policy news coverage among the three national television networks that dominate the electronic media."[15]

If this is the case, comments by two prominent network reporters to Edmund Ghareeb may be representative of foreign correspondents and "anchor persons" in general. One, former ABC Middle East correspondent Peter Jennings, said:

"I spent five years off and on in the Middle East, and I probably did more reporting in the Arab world than any other television correspondent. I was never 'politically' edited by ABC no matter what kind of story I covered, or what I had to say. At present, on the broadcast 'A.M. America' that I am engaged in, I've seen no sign whatever that anyone has resisted me presenting an Arab point of view when it was justifiable, just as nobody has prevented me from presenting an Israeli point of view when it was justifiable."[16]

However, asked to comment on a statement by political columnist James Reston that, "you may put it down as a matter of fact that any criticism of Israel will be met with a cry of anti-Semitism," Jennings agreed:

"That's quite true. The editor of an article in *Commentary* magazine labelled me, along with Reston and others, as being notably pro-Arab or notably anti-Semitic. I think it is extremely unfortunate and misguided to suggest that because someone happens to disagree with . . the politics of Israel, he should be regarded as anti-Semitic."[17]

Marilyn Robinson, then an NBC Washington reporter, had similarly mixed comments:

"I think there is a great deal of anti-Arab bias, especially in the magazines, where you have caricatures. They have to be a little bit more careful on television. . . . I used to do 'cut-ins' on the *Today* show. . . . At 7:25 and 8:25 every morning, the local stations cut in and do their own local news for 5 minutes and then go back to the *Today* show in New York. Well, I was the girl in charge of the local cut-ins for Washington during the time when Yassir Arafat was supposed to come over here to the United States . . . and I led with Arafat every day. When I began to introduce my copy about Arafat, I would never refer to the Palestinians as Palestinian terrorists. I'd even up the copy. Now, when Arafat went to the United Nations I was evening up the copy and I was using a lot of tape on Arafat, letting him have a chance to talk. But when we cut back to New York at 7:35, the guy who did the national news was doing the same story and he didn't even up the copy. He would repeat the same story that I had read locally, using words like 'terrorists,' which means that everybody who was listening to the local cut-in and listening to the national news right after heard me even up the copy and heard him leave the copy as it came straight over the wire. . . . I got a lot of phone calls from Jewish people saying that I had no business reading national news on a local cut-in. That is, they knew that I was supposed to be doing local news but I was doing national news. But they also knew I was evening up the copy, and they didn't like it. And they wrote to the news director. Within a week I was told never to do national news in the local cut-ins again. Not one Arab between here and the Mississippi River called in to say 'Thank you, Miss Robinson, for being fair.' Not objective, but just fair. Now nobody can do national news on the local cut-ins. . . .

"The Jewish people know, instinctively, how to manage the press. . . . They're at home with media and communications, and are very good. The Arabs, on the other hand, are not at home with communications. They are afraid when a reporter comes up to them. They don't know that if there is something anti-Arab on the air and enough Arabs call and say, 'We're not going to take this,' it will stop."[18]

Five years after the *Journal of Palestine Studies* article on "The American Media and the Palestine Problem" was written, *TV Guide* commissioned author John Weisman to conduct a series of interviews and prepare an article concerning treatment of the Arab-Israel dispute by American television.

PLO Chairman Yassir Arafat told Weisman that "the duty of the mass media, the duty of journalism, is to educate—to tell the truth. But your American mass media are not telling the truth. You are covering up."

The *TV Guide* investigation "seems to confirm Arafat's opinion," Weisman reported. In his article, "Why the Palestinians Are Losing the Propaganda War: An on the Scene Report," he reported:

"There is, of course, the unshakable fact that some Palestinians have engaged regularly in acts of terrorism, trying to slaughter Israeli civilians as a way to draw attention to their cause. Yet, without discussing the merits of that cause, it is undeniable that, in covering the conflict between Palestinians and Israelis, the U.S. networks are much more likely to give the Israeli perspective than they are to voice Palestinian concerns.

"*TV Guide* reviewed 10 months of coverage on the nightly news shows from logs and tapes supplied by the Vanderbilt University Television News Archive—from July 1980 through April 1981. There were 38 reports of raids and retaliations by both sides; 24 of the 38 were Israeli raids on Palestinian targets in South Lebanon. Only three of these reports—for a total of one minute, 10 seconds—showed pictures of the effects of the Israeli attacks. None showed any Palestinian victims. On the other hand, of the 14 reports of

Palestinian raids and attacks on Israel during the period, 11 included pictures of Israeli victims, and the filmed reports totaled some 17 minutes.

"Not that the Israelis have been exempt from criticism. Coverage of military actions on the West Bank has caused them embarrassment. And our survey using the Vanderbilt Archive does not encompass the events of this past summer: Israel's bombing of Iraq's nuclear reactor in June and the intensified fighting between Israeli and Palestinian forces that reached its height when the Israelis bombed Beirut on July 17, killing, some say, more than 300.

"During the pre-July 17 crescendo, American networks all showed pictures of Israeli victims. What Americans did not see until the bombings in Lebanon became too serious to ignore were the Palestinian and Lebanese civilians who had borne the brunt of attacks on settlement camps and the Lebanese cities. It took an event of the magnitude of the Beirut bombing—with its resultant Lebanese civilian dead—to bring extensive coverage to American TV.

"There were other imbalances. In the first five days of fighting, all three U.S. networks elicited the opinions of Israeli Prime Minister Menachem Begin, who appeared more than a dozen times on network news shows. Arafat was not heard from directly until July 20."[19]

John Cooley, long-time *Christian Science Monitor* correspondent in the Middle East and now in London with ABC, is highly respected by his American foreign correspondent colleagues and also by the leaders of Middle Eastern countries whom he has interviewed over the years. In his article, "The News from the Mideast: A Working Approach," published in the Autumn 1981 issue of the *Middle East Journal,* Cooley cites lack of access to the Arab side as a major factor in the unbalanced television coverage depicted in all of the studies quoted. So do Henry L. Griggs, Jr., foreign producer of "NBC Nightly News," and Robert Hershman, former Middle East correspondent for the MacNeil/Lehrer Report on the Public Broadcasting System and associate producer of "CBS Reports," in their article "American Television News and the Middle East," also published in the Autumn, 1981 issue of the *Middle East Journal.*

If the Arab explanation for lack of balance in U.S. television coverage of the Arab-Israeli dispute were narrowed down to one word, it would be "conspiracy." If the explanation by most American professional television reporters were also boiled down to one word, it would have to be "access." The truth, perhaps, lies somewhere in between.

All, however, agree with Hershman and Griggs that in the United States "television now is the first and most dramatic shaper of public information on the Middle East." They also seem unanimous in declaring that for many years U.S. television, for whatever reason, has not provided Americans with balanced information on the Middle East in general, and the Israeli-Palestinian dispute in particular.

It is the duty of the U.S. government to formulate foreign policies which support U.S. interests and which take into consideration traditional American concerns for human rights, self-determination, and political and social justice.

However, such policies can neither be adopted nor carried out without strong and continuing public support. How can such essential support be engendered, however, if the principal medium of American public information about the Middle East has over a period of many years consistently presented an unbalanced picture of events there?

It is a question all concerned Americans must ponder.

TELEVISION ENTERTAINMENT

"To be an Arab in America today is to be an object of contempt and ridicule by television under the guise of entertainment. To me this anti-Arab image on entertainment manifests itself in the politics of America."[20]

Jack Shaheen, 1978

"No other ethnic group in America would willingly submit to what Arabs and Muslims in general have faced in the United States media."[21]

John Cooley, 1981

"No religious, national and cultural group . . . has been so massively and consistently vilified."[22]

Nicholas Von Hoffman, 1981

"We must remember that if one group is under attack we all are under attack. If Jews are not safe, then Arabs are not safe. If Blacks are not safe, then neither are Chicanos, or Poles, or Irish or whatever ethnic group you can think of."[23]

Former Senator James Abourezk, 1980

Entertainment programs are the other side of the television coin. Here, until very recently, Arab-Americans have been surprisingly quiescent in the face of racial slurs and jokes that would have drawn torrents of protest had they been directed at any other ethnic minority in the U.S. Professor Jack Shaheen of Southern Illinois University, who has carefully followed the treatment of Arabs on U.S. television programs for several years, writes:

"Because Arabs and Arab civilizations are held in contempt by many in Hollywood, many Americans and their political representatives have few if any positive feelings about Arabs. Their impressions are based in part on the clouded image of the TV screen. . . . Stereotyping tends to be self-perpetuating, providing not only information but, as Walter Lippmann wrote, 'pictures in our heads.' These pictures of Arabs reinforce and sharpen viewer prejudices. Television shows are entertainment, but they are also symbols."[24]

"As any television fan knows, a villain is needed in conflicts that pit good against evil. Today's villain is the Arab, simplistically and unfairly portrayed. . . . Depicted as the murderous white-slaver, the dope dealer, the fanatic or, more sympathetically, as the spoiled rich kid who thinks money can buy love, the television Arab, as seen on entertainment programs, is about as close to being a real Arab as Rudolph Valentino was. . . . To make matters worse, programs stereotyping the Arab are sold in syndication to foreign countries. Thus America's TV image of the Arab is marketed throughout the world. . . ."[25]

This picture may change with the founding of the American Arab Anti-Discrimination Committee, described elsewhere in this study, and with Dr. Shaheen's work. The former is sensitizing Arab-American viewers, and showing them how to protest specific ethnic slurs directly to the television networks. Dr. Shaheen is sensitizing the networks themselves, through his interviews and correspondence with them and a forthcoming book on the subject.

CARTOONS

"Mark Twain described Palestine as a bleak, barren land, where even the sky and the landscape are dreary, a country peopled by rather greasy, hook-nosed Arabs, pronounced of course Ay-rabs by Twain's enlightened traveller. . . . In some of the characters of *Innocents Abroad* you can almost recognize the ill-intentioned Ay-rabs of today's cartoons of a Bill Mauldin or a Herbert Block."[26]

John Cooley, 1981

"There is a dehumanizing, circular process at work here. The caricature dehumanizes. But it is inspired and made acceptable by an earlier dehumanizing influence, namely, an absence of feeling for who the Arabs are and where they have been."[27]

Meg Greenfield, 1977

Most American political cartoonists have demonstrated, perhaps even more obviously than the editorial writers of their newspapers, a new readiness to see the Arab side of Middle Eastern problems, particularly since President Sadat's Jerusalem initiative. Nevertheless, the leering, hand-rubbing Arab oil sheikh, with a line of fat veiled wives trailing behind his dirty robes, has become a familiar fixture to American newspaper readers. This is especially true in the nation's capital where, since the creation of Israel, the *Washington Post's* Pulitzer prize-winning cartoonist, Herbert Block, has waged an almost continuous one-man war against the Arabs. His targets included the late Egyptian President Anwar Sadat, even after the latter's journey to Jerusalem. It is perhaps an indication of the true editorial freedom enjoyed in the U.S. that in the current era of relative Arab moderation, Block's anti-Arab cartoons are sometimes totally at variance with adjacent *Post* editorials lauding specific positive actions by Arab countries such as the eight principles of a Middle East settlement advanced in 1981 by Saudi Arabia.

A thoughtful lobbyist for Israel in Washington has described the style of portraying a hook-nosed Arab, either armed to his jagged teeth or fondling the gas pump to which his camel is tethered, as a manifestation of anti-Semitism just as vicious as anything ever directed against the Jews in the U.S. in earlier eras. A prominent Harvard University educator has demonstrated close parallels in technique between recent depictions of Arabs by American cartoonists and anti-Jewish newspaper cartoons from the Nazi era in Germany.

Meg Greenfield, columnist for *Newsweek* and editorial page editor for the *Washington Post,* describes the "two pillars of our misunderstanding" of the Arab:

"One is our own cultural insularity. The other is the general willingness of Arab leaders to let their purposes be defined by the aberrant and extreme." The result, she says, has been "an Arab caricature in our culture." She continues:

"That caricature, incidently, is one of the very few 'ethnic jokes' still indulged in by our cartoonists and stand-up comics. It is somehow considered permissible where comparable jokes are not, and I do not think this is wholly owing to the absence of a big enough Arab-American political constituency to raise hell. There is a dehumanizing, circular process at work here. The caricature dehumanizes. But it is inspired and made acceptable by an earlier dehumanizing influence, namely, an absence of feeling for who the Arabs are and where they have been."[28]

In a country as vast as the United States, and a field as diverse as its media, it is impossible to draw clear-cut conclusions as to why the media seem not, at least until recently, to have served the public adequately in the case of the Middle East. If one can generalize from the particular, however, perhaps a look at a specific western American city is instructive. What is atypical about that city, which here must remain unnamed, is the fact that the handful of local partisans of the Arabs have few complaints about media bias. They feel that pro-Arab speakers usually receive adequate press coverage. When pro-Palestinian speakers sponsored by the American Friends Service Committee gave a talk in that city, Arab partisans noted that even the local Jewish community newspaper provided an objective account of the talk, though the newspaper noted that unfortunately informed partisans of Israel had not made a point of being present to refute some of the allegations made.

There is an obvious explanation for the unusual situation in that western city. For many years, a daily newspaper reporter of partial Lebanese descent had developed an informed and sympathetic interest in Middle Eastern matters entirely outside the scope of that reporter's normal journalistic training or responsibilities. For a long period the same reporter was a daily newspaper TV editor and columnist. However, if the sponsors of a talk on the Middle East asked for coverage, the reporter would personally cover the event even if it meant giving up an evening with the reporter's family. As long as the event itself was newsworthy and the time spent covering it did not detract from the reporter's regular responsibilities, the coverage of pro-Arab speakers was generally accepted and printed by the newspaper's editors.

This heartening example of journalistic freedom and media accessibility to all points of view gives rise to one obvious question. If, in that western city, there is one skilled and experienced reporter who, by an accident of birth, is personally committed to the proposition that visiting pro-Arab spokesmen should receive fair and accurate coverage in the reporter's newspaper, how many similarly skilled and experienced reporters (or editors, or copy-readers) are there in the same city who are equally committed to the full and fair presentation of each pro-Israel program in that city? And what of all the other American cities, where there may be not a single friend of the Arabs, but many friends of Israel, on the local newspaper city desks?

The odds against equal time for the Arab viewpoint are further illustrated by the perfectly logical methods used by one daily newspaper in the same western city for selecting the letters to the editor to print on its editorial pages. To avoid even an appearance of bias, the newspaper prints letters in strict arithmetical proportion to the number received on each side of any given subject. Thus, on a specific issue, if 100 letters supporting Israel's position and 10 letters criticizing it are received, the paper might print the ten most logical, or literate, or interesting pro-Israel letters, and the best one of the anti-Israel letters. The methods are fair to those who write in to the newspaper. In a sense, they also reward industry and keep readers informed of opinion trends in their community. But is it really fair to the uninformed reader who may simply want to hear all of the arguments on both sides and then make up his own mind? Given this overwhelming flood of opinion on one side, and only token representation of the other, can the general reader judge U.S. Middle Eastern policies intelligently and constructively? And what happens when not even ten, or not even one, letter presenting the Arab viewpoint is received?

When a delegation of Arab journalists visited the National Association of Arab Americans a few years ago, one Arab journalist asked how the NAAA could work effectively in the face of "an American media conspiracy to exclude Arab viewpoints." His NAAA host assured him that there is no conspiracy blocking access to the American media. "The levers are there to be used by anyone who knows how to pull them," the NAAA representative explained. The problem, perhaps, is that there are far too many skilled hands willing to pull those levers for one side, and far too few for the other.

NOTES

1. Abourezk, Senator James, from address at the "Arab and American Cultures Conference" of the Middle East Institute, Washington, D.C., September 24, 1976.
2. Ghareeb, Edmund. Excerpted from interview with James McCartney, Knight Newspapers, quoted in "The American Media and the Palestine Problem," *Journal of Palestine Studies*, Autumn 1975/Winter 1976, p. 140.
3. Weisman, John. Excerpted from interview with PLO Chairman Yassir Arafat quoted in "Why the Palestinians Are Losing the Propaganda War: An-on-the Scene Report," *TV Guide*, October 24–30 and October 31–November 6, 1981, Part 2, p. 8.
4. Weisman, John. Excerpted from interview with Amman Editor Rami Khouri quoted in "Why the Palestinians Are Losing the Propaganda War: An-on-the Scene Report," *TV Guide*, October 24–30 and October 31–November 6, 1981, Part 2, p. 12.
5. Trice, Robert H., "The American Elite Press and the Arab-Israeli Conflict," *Middle East Journal*, Summer 1979, pp. 310-325.
6. Weisman, John. Excerpted from interview with PLO Chairmn Yassir Arafat quoted in "Why the Palestinians Are Losing the Propaganda War: An-on-the Scene Report," *TV Guide*, October 24–30 and October 31–November 6, 1981, Part 1, pp. 7, 10.

7. Weisman, John. Excerpted from interview with Steve Bell, American Broadcasting Company, quoted in "Why the Palestinians Are Losing the Propaganda War: An on the Scene Report," *TV Guide*, October 24–30 and October 31–November 6, 1981, Part 1, p. 12.

8. Ghareeb, Edmund. Excerpted from interview with Lee Eggerstrom, Rider Newspapers, quoted in "The American Media and the Palestine Problem," *Journal of Palestine Studies*, Autumn 1975/Winter 1976, pp. 142-143.

9. Ghareeb, Edmund. Excerpted from interview with James McCartney, Knight Newspapers, quoted in "The American Media and the Palestine Problem," *Journal of Palestine Studies*, Autumn 1975/Winter 1976, pp. 138-140.

10. Ghareeb, Edmund. Excerpted from interview with Ronald Koven, Foreign Editor, *Washington Post*, quoted in "The American Media and the Palestine Problem," *Journal of Palestine Studies*, Autumn 1975/Winter 1976, pp. 136-137.

11. Hershman, Robert and Griggs, Henry L., Jr., "American Television News and the Middle East," *Middle East Journal*, Autumn, 1981, p. 471.

12. Weisman, John. Excerpted from interview with Steve Bell of the American Broadcasting Corporation quoted in "Why the Palestinians Are Losing the Propaganda War: An-on-the Scene Report," *TV Guide*, October 24–30 and October 31–November 6, 1981, Part 1, p. 8.

13. Weisman, John. Excerpted from interview with Sanford Socolow of the Columbia Broadcasting System quoted in "Why the Palestinians Are Losing the Propaganda War: An on-the-Scene Report," *TV Guide*, October 24–30 and October 31–November 6, 1981, Part 1, p. 14; Part 2, p. 14.

14. Weisman, John. Excerpted from interview with Shafiq al-Hout of the Palestine Liberation Organization quoted in "Why the Palestinians Are Losing the Propaganda War: An-on-the Scene Report," *TV Guide*, October 24–30 and October 31–November 6, 1981, Part 2, p. 14.

15. Trice, Robert, "The American Elite Press and the Arab-Israeli Conflict," *Middle East Journal*, Summer 1979, p. 306.

16. Ghareeb, Edmund. Excerpted from interview with Peter Jennings of the American Broadcasting Corporation in "The American Media and the Palestine Problem," *Journal of Palestine Studies*, Autumn 1975/Winter 1976, p. 129.

17. *Ibid*, p. 130.

18. Ghareeb, Edmund. Excerpted from interview with Marilyn Robinson of the National Broadcasting Corporation in "The American Media and the Palestine Problem," *Journal of Palestine Studies*, Autumn 1975/Winter 1976, pp. 146-147.

19. Weisman, John, "Why the Arabs Are Losing the Propaganda War: An on-the-Scene Report," *TV Guide*, October 24–30 and October 31–November 6, 1981, Part 1, p. 8.

20. Shaheen, Jack, Professor of Mass Communications, Southern Illinois University, in "The Arab: TV's Most Popular Villain," *Christian Century*, December 13, 1978.

21. Cooley, John, "The News from the Mideast: A Working Approach," *The Middle East Journal*, Autumn 1981, p. 468.

22. Abourezk, James, former U.S. Senator, in remarks at the founding meeting of the American Arab Anti-Discrimination Committee, May 3, 1980.

23. Von Hoffman, Nicholas, in publication of the American Arab Anti-Discrimination Committee, May 3, 1980.
24. Shaheen, Jack, "The Arab: TV's Most Popular Villain," *Christian Century*, December 13, 1978.
25. Shaheen, Jack, "Do Television Programs Stereotype the Arabs?" *The Wall Street Journal*, October 12, 1979.
26. Cooley, John, "The News from the Mideast: A Working Approach," *The Middle East Journal*, Autumn 1981, p. 468.
27. Greenfield, Meg, "Our Ugly-Arab Complex," *Newsweek*, December 5, 1977, p. 110.
28. *Ibid*, p. 110.

CHAPTER XXII

The Universities

"To bring about a settlement of the Middle East conflict, my judgment is that the perceptions of the Arab world will have to change in this country. And I know of no one else who can effect such a change, other than the Arabs themselves. It would involve nothing more than simply telling the truth about themselves—good or bad—so that the American people can better understand what they're all about."[1]

Senator James Abourezk, 1976

"Israel is creating a kind of moral schizophrenia in world Jewry. In the outside world, the welfare of Jewry depends on the maintenance of secular, non-racial pluralistic societies. In Israel, Jewry finds itself defending a society in which the ideal is racial and exclusionist. Jews must fight everywhere for their very security and existence against principles and practices they find themselves defending in Israel."[2]

I. F. Stone, 1975

Nowhere are the partisans of Israel and the Arabs forced into closer proximity than in American universities, where those who teach Middle Eastern history or political science or Semitic languages must deal with both of these closely-related peoples. In a series of off-the-record discussions on the subject with educators of widely divergent views, all of whom were involved in teaching some aspect of modern Middle Eastern history, politics or economics, it came as no surprise to hear each declare vehemently that he or she had not compromised personal academic or intellectual integrity, "despite what others may have done." For those who were Jewish, or who were sympathetic to Israel, or both, the subject usually ended there. For those who were none of those, however, it continued along disturbing lines. Many, perhaps most, declared flatly that they seldom lose the feeling that they are being watched—by students, faculty colleagues, university administrators, and the community at large, including the state legislators or private donors upon whom their universities depend.

Those faculty members who did not have university tenure found the situation highly threatening or inhibiting. They worried that their statements would be reported out of context to their superiors, perhaps via influential members of the community. Those with tenure were less concerned, and dismissed the possibility that they could be intimidated by such happenings. Nevertheless, some stated that expressing their beliefs on Middle Eastern affairs ultimately could affect, or in some cases had affected, their positions or influence within their university departments.

It is difficult for an outsider to evaluate these comments. Just as a scholar is unlikely to declare that he got ahead by intellectual dishonesty, neither is he likely to attribute not rising higher in his field to personal limitations if there are other possible factors involved. Therefore, it seems best to refer to a cautious and thorough report prepared in mid-1979 by a distinguished scholar in Middle Eastern affairs, Dr. Richard H. Nolte. Dr. Nolte was commissioned by Esso Middle East to visit and assess 18 Middle East study centers, to many of which the company, a division of Exxon, had made support grants.

The centers, all established after 1946, are generally interdisciplinary committees of professors from various departments rather than separate faculties. Only a few give separate degrees. As a rule, their function is to encourage or improve the teaching of Middle Eastern languages and to interest history, political science, or related departments in hiring Middle East specialists. The centers use whatever funds are available to them to assume part or all of the costs of such experts. They also organize lectures and conferences around foreign specialists. Such Middle East centers, Dr. Nolte reported, include some 500 full and part-time faculty members teaching some 16,000 undergraduates, including more than 1,000 majoring in Middle East studies, and about 1,300 graduate students in fields related to the Middle East.

Federal money for such foreign language and area centers has steadily diminished since it reached a peak in the 1969–70 academic year. The Ford Foundation, which devoted millions of dollars in seed money to the creation of study programs and centers for various areas, also considers its role ended. Thus, in a period of academic belt-tightening, and given a tradition of "last in, first out" when the academic environment faces financial stress, Middle East centers are now particularly concerned with finding new sources of funds. They therefore seem unusually vulnerable, via the purse strings, to anyone who seeks to limit or channel their activities. It is against this background that Dr. Nolte wrote the portion of his report concerning the Arab-Israeli dispute. It is quoted in full below:

"Foreign disputes often have echoes on U.S. campuses, sometimes of considerable though temporary vehemence. None has generated as much intensity of feeling over so long a period, however, as the Arab-Israel issue. One might think that the Middle East centers, precisely the focus of those most involved with the Middle East, would be vulnerable to partisan disruptions and that instruction would be impaired. Not so. In every center without exception, the director, faculty and students of every faith and ethnic background were unanimous that in their program, academic objectivity was scrupulously observed, political feelings were excluded from the classroom, relationships were open and friendly, and instruction was in no way impaired.

"Underlying this unexpected unanimity one sensed an almost urgent awareness that the self-interest of each demanded that the scholarly canon be maintained by all. On a few campuses (Arizona, Utah, Texas) the unanimity was there but the sense of necessity was missing; the Arab-Israel issue seemed remote, the protagonists of Israel were relatively few, other causes appeared more important.

"The apolitical virtue of one's own center, however, was not the whole story. It was freely acknowledged at some universities that center-connected professors exercising their citizen's right outside the academic programs to express extreme views or engage in political activity, had on occasion created difficulties for center directors.

"Again it was not unknown for student and even faculty members unconnected with the Middle East Program (who were better informed) to indulge in invective and noisy discourtesies of one kind or another—shouting down a guest speaker for example.

"Another curiosity: the commonly held view that while the home program was 'clean,' other centers had been politicized, 'Center X has been taken over by the Zionists' or 'Center Y is 100 per cent pro-PLO.' Both untrue, but such views, which have a certain wishful quality about them, seem to have inordinate staying power."[3]

It is with some trepidation that one from outside the academic world takes issue with a report by a scholar on an academic subject. Yet, this writer's own observations after conversations at nine of the same centers visited by Dr. Nolte differ in one major respect. Comments indeed centered on the suppression of dissent and takeovers by partisan groups at *other* university centers. Nevertheless, many of the persons with whom I spoke were not so sanguine about the situation at their *own* centers or universities. It may be that, in talking to a member of their own profession, they were weighing their words carefully, and that, in talking to me, they were simply blowing off steam. Or it may have been naive of Dr. Nolte to expect his respondents to criticize the situation at their own centers. Such criticism could reflect upon the personal integrity of the respondent himself who, after all, is employed there. It certainly also reflects upon the integrity of his own department superiors in an era when confidences are sometimes lightly taken. Criticism might also jeopardize future funding prospects for the respondent's institution, since Dr. Nolte was compiling information for one potential sponsoring organization and writing a report that very likely would serve as a guide to many others. Perhaps, as a complete outsider conducting totally off-the-record interviews, it was natural that I would hear enough about each interviewee's own institution and colleagues to convince me that a majority of Middle East center faculty members believe that complete freedom of expression on the Arab-Israeli dispute exists at few such centers on American campuses today.

At one of America's largest state universities, a Jewish graduate student reported that his non-Jewish faculty adviser warned him away from a Palestine-oriented and toward an Egypt-oriented dissertation topic so that he would not jeopardize his chances of future university employment by acquiring the reputation of being anti-Israel. At another of America's most prestigious universities, an outspokenly pro-Arab professor asserted that "only my tenure and the conspiracy laws protect me in an institution where more than half of my colleagues are Jewish and where almost no one else, Jew or Gentile, dares to speak frankly about Israel."

Some center directors and faculty members maintain vehemently that they and their colleagues enjoy total freedom of expression on the Arab-Israeli dispute, and that their publications conclusively demonstrate this. I can only report that of the strong partisans of the Israeli cause and the Arab cause with whom I spoke, nearly all of the former report that they are satisfied with the academic environment in which they work, and a majority of the latter report they are not.

A French scholar, Dr. Irine Errera-Hoechstetter, who visited American Middle East study centers in 1970, reported afterward that "political cleavages in the Middle East" have "strong partisan echoes in the U.S." which "put the canon of inter-disciplinarity in jeopardy" and "could result for some of the centers in actual dissolution."[4]

Her prediction seems to have been fulfilled, at least for the present, at the University of Southern California. This second-largest private university in the United States has graduated large numbers of students from Middle Eastern countries. Members of the leading Saudi Arabian families began going to USC shortly after World War II, and by now there is hardly a government ministry in Riyadh that could not organize a USC alumni association chapter. Some years ago, the university received a $1 million endowment from the late King Faisal of Saudi Arabia for a chair in Middle Eastern studies. The gift was generous, but not inordinately so for a private university that played a pioneering role in educating many of the most prominent leaders of Saudi Arabia.

In 1978, however, after a vote by the University Board of Trustees approving the organization of a Middle East Studies Center, in which two members of the Board abstained and one voted negatively, a firestorm of criticism broke out over the university. Leaders of the large Los Angeles Jewish community, and the *Los Angeles Times,* focused their criticism on the center director, who had held the King Faisal chair since its founding. They charged that his dual role as Center Director and chairman of its fund-raising arm, the Middle East Center Foundation, in effect gave him—and possibly through him, the Saudis—undue influence over university programs. Members of the university faculty charged that the Center would usurp faculty prerogatives and compromise academic integrity. The Securities and Exchange Commission launched an investigation to determine under what circumstances funds for the foundation had been solicited from American companies, and whether the donors had received the impression that the size of their donations might influence the degree of cooperation their representatives received in Saudi Arabia. The university subsequently dissolved the fund-raising Middle East Center Foundation and returned all the contributions it had received to the donor companies. The Center still exists on paper, but no longer in fact.

Whatever the merits of the various allegations, one fact impresses even the uninformed. The Center and its fundraising foundation were structured almost identically with other similar semi-autonomous organizations at private universities in the United States. The agreement of the heavily endowed Annenberg School of Communications with USC was the model for the Middle East Center's agreement with the university. But the Annenberg School continues its existence on the same campus without community, faculty, or media concern about its funding, programs, or effect on academic integrity.

Similar disputes have brought controversy to other universities. An article entitled "Arab Money and the Universities," published in the American Jewish Committee periodical *Commentary* in April, 1979, cited Middle East programs that had fallen through at Swarthmore, MIT, the University of Alabama, and the University of Pennsylvania. The magazine did not offer specific criticism of a Duke University program in Islamic and Arabian Development Studies, which received a $20,000 grant from Saudi Arabia, but it pointedly equated the program at Duke with the one discontinued at USC.

Commentary and other national publications saved their severest criticism for Georgetown University, which in 1977 accepted a gift of $750,000 from Libya to endow a chair at Georgetown's Center for Contemporary Arab Studies, a grant of $50,000 from Iraq, and other donations from Saudi Arabia, Egypt, Qatar, Jordan, the United Arab Emirates, and the Sultanate of Oman. Columnist Art Buchwald publicly accused the university of accepting "blood money from one of the most notorious regimes in the world today." In a subsequent exchange, he wrote: "I don't see why the PLO has to have a PR organization when Georgetown is doing all their work for them." After sustained public criticism, Father Timothy Healy, president of the university, eventually returned both the Iraqi and Libyan contributions. At no time were there serious allegations that the funds from either country came with strings attached.

Demonstrating that no issue is too mundane or routine to ignite the glowing coals of campus Middle East partisanship, a dispute on a faculty appointment at the University of Texas was catapulted into the pages of the *Wall Street Journal* even before the local Texas newspapers had heard of it. The university's Middle East Studies Center had offered to pay half the costs of a jointly-approved appointment to the history department, so that the department could offer courses in modern Arab history. When the Middle East Center did not approve on academic grounds an Israeli-born candidate who did not have a Ph.D., what seemed a routine exercise of the Center's prerogative was suddenly escalated into a confrontation. Charges of discrimination were leveled against the Center's acting director. The ultimate decision was to hire two persons, one at history department and one at Middle East Center expense, to handle what administrators from both the department and the Center agree is less than a normal teaching load for even one instructor.

Given the cultural differences between the Arab countries and the U.S., and the sensitivities of the American Jewish community, it is obvious that no American university should accept Middle Eastern gifts casually. If they are from American companies doing business in the Middle East, it is appropriate to look into the circumstances under which the donation was solicited. If the gift comes directly from a Middle Eastern country, the expectations and conditions of the donor should be carefully examined, frankly dealt with, and fully explained to the university community. That done, however, there should be no further stigma attached to a university faculty honestly striving to familiarize American students with a critically important and little-understood part of the world.

There are many more students of Hebrew in the United States than there are students of Arabic. There are many more students enrolled in courses on various aspects of modern Israel than there are in courses on the Arab countries. And for every donation to an American university by a country or an individual who may support an Arab cause, there are surely many sizable donations from Jewish institutions or wealthy Americans who enthusiastically support Israel. Yet there is no record of public protest or university refusal of any such gift for Hebrew, Judaic, or similar studies. Equal treatment for gifts to strengthen scholarship and knowledge about both parties to the Middle Eastern dispute would be the best evidence that true freedom of inquiry and expression about that dispute exists on American campuses.

NOTES

1. Abourezk, Senator James, from address at the "Arab and American Cultures Conference" of the Middle East Institute, Washington, D.C., September 24, 1976.
2. Stone, I.F., quoted by Alfred Lilienthal in *The Zionist Connection: What Price Peace?*, 1979, p. 136.
3. Nolte, Richard H., Report for Esso Middle East on "Middle East Centers at U.S. Universities," May, 1979.
4. *Ibid.*, pages 22 and 23.

CHAPTER XXIII

The Congress

> *"There is a moderate positive association . . . between the amount of money received by Senators for speaking to Jewish groups and their voting records on Israel-related issues."*[1]
>
> Robert Trice, 1977

> *"Congress' foreign affairs role is typically marginal, but American-Israeli relations are an exception. Historically Congress' role has been large in this issue-area, and Congress is consistently more supportive of Israel than is the executive branch."*[2]
>
> David Garnham, 1977

No one would quarrel with the statement above by David Garnham from the *Jerusalem Journal of International Relations*. Nevertheless, as the Arab-Israeli dispute has evolved, so has the manner in which the U.S. government deals with it. The early struggles by Israel's partisans for American government support are thoroughly, if not consistently, documented. At the time when U.S. support was crucial for UN approval of the plan to partition Palestine, the struggle was waged to some extent between State Department officials who had worked in the Middle East on the one hand, and offiical and unofficial White House advisers close to the American Jewish community on the other.

The State Department officials saw no peaceful way to carry out the plan in the face of armed opposition from the majority Arab population. They also feared the ultimate consequences for U.S. interests in an area where educational and medical ties had long been close, and where promising postwar economic ties were developing rapidly.

The White House advisers were equally adamant that the European Jews who had survived Hitler's extermination camps should find a refuge and national home in Palestine. President Truman expressed impatience alternately with the persistent pressures applied to him by proponents of the Jewish state, and with the efforts of the State Department "lower echelons" to steer the U.S. away from supporting creation of such a state. Truman felt buffeted between his awe at the determination of Dr. Chaim Weizman, who almost seemed to be presiding over the birth of the new state from his deathbed, and the equally firm disapproval of the partition plan by General George Marshall, then Secretary of State. As a result, the President followed such a tortuous course that proponents of both sides felt they were prevailing throughout much of the struggle. The partition plan was ultimately carried, due to U.S. as well as Soviet support; attempts to delay its implementation were beaten down after a change of signals by the U.S.; and the U.S. became the first nation to recognize the new state minutes after its birth, followed almost immediately by the Soviet Union. In each case, President Truman made the ultimate choice among the sharply opposed alternatives submitted by his advisers, and historians will be able to argue for all time whether he was pulled by compassion for the homeless death camp survivors or pushed by the passionate dedication to their cause of a large portion of America's Jewish leadership.

Since that time the locus of the American battleground has shifted somewhat. Support for Israel has coalesced in the Congress, while concern for Arab positions and reactions is still voiced most clearly in the Department of State. The White House staff itself can go either way, given the presence there of both domestic liaison officers to the U.S. Jewish community, and National Security Council advisers who are Middle East specialists. Recent U.S. Presidents have found themselves frequently under attack domestically for supporting Arab positions and almost continuously under attack in the Middle East for their support of Israel. Increasingly, they have let Congress follow its own historic tendencies to favor Israel with both military and economic aid on extremely generous terms.

Given the great domestic interest in the Middle Eastern conflict, the votes of individual Congressmen on pro-Israel issues have been tracked exhaustively. Scholars have then analyzed the characteristics shared by those Congressmen who consistently support Israel, regardless of the administration's position. The results of these studies are so consistent, from Congress to Congress, and from scholar to scholar, that they are simply recorded on the following pages in the words of their authors. Appropriate credits go to Robert H. Trice, for his analysis of support for Israel in the U.S. Senate from 1970 to 1973, published in the *Political Science Quarterly*; David Garnham, for his analysis of the 93rd Congress, published in the *Jerusalem Journal of International Relations*; and David Logan, for his analysis of the 95th Congress, published by the National Association of Arab Americans.

The historical bias of Congress on issues related to Israel was demonstrated anew by all of these studies. Support for Israel does not seem to be based on party politics. Roughly equal percentages of Republican and Democratic members have supported Israel in the key votes that have been analyzed. Support did correlate quite closely, however, to liberal voting records. Congressional liberals support Israel more consistently than do Congressional conservatives. Regional differences have also had some importance in determining how a Congressman will vote on the Middle East. In the words of Dr. Trice:

"The bases of pro-Israel support are strongest in the heavily industrialized, urbanized states of the Northeast, and weaker in the South and the less populous heartland of the country. Particularly striking is the weak support for Israel shown by senators from the Rocky Mountain states relative to all other regions."[3]

Trice's study finds some evidence supporting three popular explanations for the pro-Israeli bias in Congressional voting patterns. One of these is the impact of the "Jewish vote." He writes:

"According to the standard argument, Jews offset their numerical weakness as a voting group because they, more than other ethnic minority, tend to vote as a bloc. It is contended that legislation that in any way affects Israel is of high salience to American Jews, and they are quick to articulate their policy preferences to their representatives in Congress. Because Congressmen seek to garner and maintain the support of their Jewish constituents, they will tend to vote in accordance with the policy demands of Jewish community leaders. Over time, Congressmen come to anticipate the reactions of organized Jewry to their position on relevant legislation. . . . Direct pressures by Jewish voters become less necessary, and the support of Congressmen from states with sizable Jewish populations for pro-Israeli legislation becomes more automatic."[4]

Trice notes also that other studies of Jewish voting patterns in Presidential elections confirm that Jews do tend to vote as a bloc, but that party differences rather than the policies of the individual candidates seem to be the most important factor in capturing the Jewish vote. On the national level, a Democratic candidate generally does better than a Republican with Jewish voters. This held true even during President Nixon's 1972 landslide victory over Senator George McGovern, despite Nixon's first-term record of extremely generous military and economic support for Israel. Even if the popular perception of how Jewish votes are cast is incorrect, however, it apparently is shared by Congressmen. Trice reports:

"Senators who come from states with relatively larger percentages of Jewish voters are, on the whole, more likely to vote in favor of Israel's interests than are those with smaller Jewish constituencies. . . . The implication is that very small Jewish populations—in some cases as small as two percent or less of a state's total population—were capable of generating and maintaining consistent support for their policy preferences from their respective Senators."[5]

Turning to a second popular explanation for the pro-Israel bias in Congress, Trice writes:

"Critics of pro-Israel interest group activities frequently charge that American Jews extend their political leverage well beyond the limits of their voting strength by means of their willingness to give generous financial assistance to Congressmen who are sympathetic to their policy preferences. There is some evidence to support the contention that Jews as a group do contribute heavily to Congressional and Presidential campaigns. However, it is not possible to determine accurately the size or the recipients of these campaign contributions. There is, however, another common form of financial assistance that is measurable, and that may serve as a surrogate for campaign contributions. It is an accepted practice of domestic interest groups to assist supporters in Congress by inviting the Congressman to speak to their conventions or working groups, and to pay these speakers honoraria for their remarks.

. . . The question is whether such financial assistance affects the voting behavior of the recipients. There is, of course, a 'chicken and egg' problem. . . . Critics of the pro-Israel lobby may argue that giving Senators honoraria amounts to little more than an attempt to buy support for Israel. Supporters of pro-Israel group efforts, however, may argue that the honoraria represent a perfectly legitimate and widely used means of giving financial backing to those incumbents who have already demonstrated their willingness to vote in favor of Israel's interest. Our purpose here is not to resolve the broader, more important issue of why particular Senators receive honoraria, but rather to examine the following proposition. . . . There will be a positive association between the total amount of honoraria received by a given Senator and his support for Israel score. . . . The proposition is supported by the evidence. There is a moderate positive association . . . between the amount of money received by Senators for speaking to Jewish groups and their voting records on Israel-related issues."[6]

Trice also states that even the combined positive correlations between pro-Israeli voting and all three of these factors—higher percentages of Jewish constituents, financial support from Jewish groups, and liberal voting records—are not sufficient to explain the variations in Senatorial voting records. He therefore lists some additional factors which probably influence the Congressional bias for Israel significantly even if they are not measurable.

"One important factor is the direct lobbying efforts of domestic interest groups. While it is not possible to measure precisely the relative influence of pro-Israel and pro-Arab groups, there is little doubt that the greater organizational strength and activity level of domestic pro-Israel groups has resulted in considerable political payoffs in terms of Congressional receptivity and willingness to make public statements in support of Israeli positions. . . . Some analysts argue that a major source of strength for the pro-Israel movement is the network of Congressional aides who are openly supportive of Israel's interests and who work hard to convince their bosses and their bosses'colleagues to support Israel. In the absence of any strong countervailing pressure from pro-Arab groups we might expect those Senators with only marginal interest in the dispute to follow the path of least political resistance and vote as their staffs and colleagues suggest. . . .

"For some Senators, however, the Arab-Israel conflict is likely to be a very salient issue. Congressmen with Presidential aspirations are likely to be sensitive to the fact that as they become more nationally prominent their voting records on Israel-relevant issues will be closely and publicly scrutinized by pro-Israel groups. A mixed record of support for Israel in the past may be sufficient for some Jewish groups to question a Congressman's willingness to support Israel if elected President. Such doubts could result in the withholding of Jewish financial and electoral support.

"The actual strength of domestic pro-Israel forces is not nearly as relevant as the political constraints that potential Presidential candidates may perceive. Few men with either immediate or long term visions of national office are likely to run the risks associated with openly challenging the political muscle of pro-Israel groups. The lack of any readily-observable political benefits for assuming an anti-Israel stance, coupled with the prospect that such a position would be likely to alienate an identifiable bloc of American voters, may explain the support for Israel displayed by some Senators.

"Beyond these identifiable and separable sources of support looms the entire domestic political environment that surrounds the governmental policy-making system. The ability of pro-Israel groups to marshall and maintain the support of the mass media, mass public opinion, and broad cross-sections of associational life in this country such as organized labor and non-Jewish interest groups have enabled them to amplify and disseminate their policy preferences far beyond the limits of their own organizational structures. Overlaying the specific sources of support that we have examined here is the general factor that for whatever reasons a particular Congressman supports Israel, he is likely to be well in the mainstream of opinion in his home district or state. For many Americans, congressional backing for Israel has come to be generally expected, irrespective of the ethnic or religious makeup of the district. The pro-Israel sentiments of major, non-Jewish segments of the articulate public are probably at least as important in determining Congressional support as the electoral and financial strength of the Jewish community in the United States."[7]

The Garnham study was based on seven Senate votes between December 20, 1973 and October 1, 1974, and two House votes on December 11, 1973. It produced generally similar conclusions. Garnham found that 75 per cent of the representatives had voted in favor of Israel and only eight per cent had voted against Israel on both bills. In the Senate, 38 per cent of the Senators had voted in favor of Israel on all seven issues, while only two Senators had opposed Israel on all seven votes. Some of Garnham's conclusions are excerpted below:

"Future Congressional support for Israel is likely to remain high, but it may decline somewhat from past levels. Since the Yom Kippur War, many U.S. officials and scholars have concluded that the heterogeneous Middle Eastern interests of the United States are served best by a policy which continues close ties with Israel but seeks to improve relations with the Arabs. . . . Congressional support may decline also because of negative reaction to Israel's intrusions into domestic U.S. politics."[8]

Garnham stated that Senators were more likely to adopt pro-Israeli stances regardless of the percentage of Jewish constituents in their states, while the stances of Representatives correlated more closely with the percentage in their districts. He explained:

"It is more probable that a Senator will have Jewish constituents, and given the high level of Jewish political activity, Senators are more likely to be exposed to articulate pro-Israel arguments. This point has been made by Morris Amitay, the executive director of the American Israel Public Affairs Committee. . . . 'You look about at who the Jewish constituents are from sparsely inhabited states. They're teachers, they're doctors, they've invariably been involved some way in politics. They're usually respected people in the community, so you don't have to pitch it at the level of I contributed $10,000 to your campaign— unless you do this you'll make me unhappy and I'll contribute to your opponent next time. At most it's implicit, and it's not even implicit a large percentage of the time.' "[9]

Like Trice, Garnham notes that:

"Potential Presidential candidates appear to support Israel more ardently than other Senators. This would partially explain why Jewish population is a less powerful explanation of Senate voting. Given the more national orientation of Senators, and the much larger number of potential aspirants, more Senators are inclined to support Israel regardless of the size of their own State's Jewish population."[10]

Garnham concludes his study as follows:

"The perspectives of the Congress and the executive branch are significantly different. The Congress is much more supportive of assistance to Israel while the executive branch is more concerned with offering inducements to Arab governments. This situation is largely unrelated to the fact that during the 93rd and 94th Congresses the Republican Party controlled the Presidency and the Democratic Party controlled the Congress. The executive branch has been consistently less supportive of Israel and relatively more concerned with Arab-American relations. At least in part this reflects the perspective of career officers of the Departments of State and Defense."[11]

In his study of the 95th Congress, Logan found no significant contradictions with the previous studies cited above. However, his conclusions point to an evolution in the role of Congress with regard to the Middle East. He writes:

"First, Middle East policy is becoming increasingly complex. It is no longer valid to look at American Middle East policy solely through eyeglasses oriented towards the Arab-Israeli conflict. There are now many other issues involved. These include oil, strategic concerns and worry about Soviet influence, Arab-to-Arab relations, and Arab conflicts with other Arab states. The votes of the 95th Congress reflected this growing complexity; the range of issues was wider and the voting patterns less consistent than in previous Congresses. . . .

"Second, the influence of the Administration on Middle East policy is increasing. Although it is a commonly heard current generalization that Congress is more assertive than it used to be and more willing to play an independent role in foreign policy, this is simply not true of Middle East policy. Whereas past Congresses frequently ran into confrontations with the Administration, the 95th Congress followed the lead of the Administration on virtually every Middle East issue. That this finding runs counter to the general trend of increased Congressional assertiveness only increases its significance.

"Finally, it was found that there has been no real decrease in support for Israel, but that there has been an increase in support for other factors in the Middle East. The 95th Congress continued to give Israel most of what it wanted, but the 95th Congress also gave Arab states, particularly Egypt and Saudi Arabia, more than any Congress had before. As one Senate staff aide put it, 'People now realize that what is good for the Arabs doesn't have to be bad for Israel.' "[12]

NOTES

1. Trice, Robert H., "Congress and the Arab-Israeli Conflict: Support for Israel in the U.S. Senate, 1970–1973," *Political Science Quarterly,* Fall 1977, p. 460.
2. Garnham, David, "Factors Influencing Congressional Support for Israel During the 93rd Congress," *The Jerusalem Journal of International Relations,* Spring 1977, p.25.
3. Trice, Robert H., "Congress and the Arab-Israeli Conflict: Support for Israel in the U.S. Senate, 1970–1973," *Political Science Quarterly,* Fall 1977, pp. 452-453.
4. *Ibid,* p.456.
5. *Ibid,* pp. 457-458.
6. *Ibid,* pp. 458-460.
7. *Ibid,* pp. 462-463.

8. Garnham, David, "Factors Influencing Congressional Support for Israel During the 93rd Congress," *The Jerusalem Journal of International Relations,* Spring 1977, p. 27.

9. *Ibid,* p. 34.

10. *Ibid,* p. 35.

11. *Ibid,* pp. 40-41.

12. Logan, David, "The 95th Congress and Middle East Policy: Voting Patterns and Trends," study prepared for and published by the National Association of Arab Americans, April 23, 1979, pp. 4-5.

CHAPTER XXIV

President Reagan and the Future

"The administration acted prudently in fulfilling the commitments of its predecessors on the AWACS sale. The damage of a negative vote to our position in the Middle East, to a moderate evolution of the area and to a constructive peace process would be grave, perhaps irretrievable. The Congress must not undermine the President's authority in international affairs by a rejection of the sale; the consequences would haunt us for many years in many fields. We cannot afford this—especially after a decade and a half of domestic division."[1]

Former Secretary of State Henry Kissinger, October, 1981

"Defeat on AWACS would be a serious embarrassment to Reagan, both at home and abroad. Israel's friends should not be under any illusion that they help Israel's cause by embarrassing and undermining the authority of their indispensable friend in the White House. . . . Those who worry about the deal ought to trust the President, the Secretary of State and the Secretary of Defense."[2]

Former President Richard Nixon, October, 1981

"I would not want to pick the date today, but in a realistic way, that (U.S.-PLO) dialogue has to take place. . . . There are some responsible preconditions and it may need some negotiations as to their (the PLO) attitude vis-a-vis Israel . . . and it may take some actions by Israel vis-a-vis the PLO. But as you go down the road at some point that dialogue has to take place and I think that (it) will happen."[3]

Former President Gerald R. Ford, October, 1981

"There is no way for Israel ever to have an assured permanent peace without resolving the Palestinian issue. . . . So I think Jerry is certainly right in saying these discussions have to be done. The problem is the recognition of the PLO as a political entity by the

172

United States before the Palestinians were willing to acknowledge that Israel is a nation that has a right to exist. So any mechanism that can be found to resolve that difficulty would be a very successful step forward."[4]

Former President Jimmy Carter, October, 1981

Each U.S. President since World War II has spoken and written frequently about the Middle East. It is fairly simple, therefore, for partisans of either side, by selective quotation, posthumously to recruit each deceased President to their cause. If partisans of Israel have the edge in claiming Truman and Johnson, and partisans of the Arabs have at least a prior claim on Eisenhower, partisans of both sides can make an equally valid claim for Roosevelt and Kennedy. This is irrelevant to the contemporary scene, however. Each U.S. President reacts to events as they unfold, and the Arab-Israeli problem has evolved considerably since the time of any of the Presidents named.

Americans basically sympathetic to Israel have excused what they almost certainly would call racism in any other country on grounds that it is a reaction to the searing impact of the European Holocaust on the world's surviving Jews. Now, belatedly, many of the same Americans have become aware of the enormity of the injustices suffered by the Palestinians, not just in 1947 and 1948, but throughout all the years since. If the Arabs have seemed to react violently, or irresponsibly, to that injustice, Americans must ask themselves honestly whether that reaction is any different or more extreme than that condoned by the United States in the case of Israel.

It is important that all Americans, not just American Jewish partisans of Israel or American "old Middle East hand" partisans of the Arabs, begin to listen and think carefully about Middle Eastern matters. In the decades between World War II and the 1967 Arab-Israeli war, Americans were in fact deeply involved in the progress and the outcome of the Arab-Israeli dispute. They were not, however, aware of the extent of their own involvement. Now, as American interests inextricably intertwine with those of all of the peoples of the Middle East, we can no longer shrug off our own responsibility for much of what is happening there. We cannot dismiss it with journalistic cliches such as "crescent of crisis" or "arc of instability." The area will remain unstable, and a grave threat to world peace, until Americans assume a major share of the responsibility for bringing about a settlement of the genuine grievances that underlie the instability. If we continue to guarantee one side military superiority, but do not at the same time make that guarantee conditional upon good faith efforts toward a just settlement, we ensure continued tension and warfare. How can moderate elements in Israel nudge their government toward making the compromises necessary for peace with their neighbors, if unlimited U.S. backing is assured to any elected Israeli government, regardless of whether its moves lead to peace or to renewed warfare?

The same considerations apply to the Arabs. The U.S. must direct its efforts toward encouraging moderate leaders within the Arab camp to stand up and be counted. This will never be attained by insisting upon humiliating conditions or limitations on every U.S. transaction involving Arabs, such as some Congressmen have sought to impose repeatedly, not only on arms sales but even on purely commercial transactions. These restrictions may appeal to voter sentiment in the home districts of individual members of Congress, but they in no way serve U.S. foreign policy goals.

There was a time when building public support for subtleties in our own Middle Eastern policies seemed impossible. The area seemed to Americans to be one where leaders were unpredictable or intractable, and where Arab public opinion seemed to respond positively only to leaders who proclaimed hostility to all things American or Western, regardless of changes in American leadership or policies. Even in the case of the Eisenhower administration, which chose to support Egypt over traditional American allies in 1956, few if any Arab leaders expressed their appreciation in public. Rather, in the Jordanian parliament deputies voted to break diplomatic relations with the United States, a resolution King Hussein ignored. In 1969, when the newly-installed Nixon administration announced its "Rogers Plan," encompassing points that the Arabs have unsuccessfully pressed for ever since, the first reaction from Egypt was widespread public denunciation. By the time President Nasser had studied the plan and began sending private signals that he was favorably disposed, the damage had been done. In the United States, from the moment the plan was proposed, supporters of Israel had invoked the shades of dead Presidents and railed against "sell-outs," "betrayals," and "fuzzy thinking."

Much, though not all, of this has changed. President Reagan, in the words of former President Nixon, is "probably the strongest supporter of Israel to occupy the White House since Harry Truman." It would be difficult to depict him as "anti-Semitic" or ready to sell out Israeli interests for Arab oil. The record, past and present, simply wouldn't sustain such charges.

Equally important, there are at this writing three living American ex-Presidents representing both U.S. political parties. Whatever their domestic political strengths and weaknesses, they cannot be accused singly or collectively of lack of foreign policy sophistication. Nor can they be accused collectively of partisanship for either Israel or the Arabs. When they stand together to support the incumbent President on an important Middle Eastern question, as they did in the case of the sale of AWACS to Saudi Arabia, Americans who are interested in the survival of their country as a responsible world power must listen, and ponder carefully what they hear.

If the situation in the United States now is more favorable for a settlement, so is the situation in the Middle East. For a long period responsible Middle East experts could truthfully say that the minimum demands of the Israelis and of the Palestinians were mutually irreconcilable. Since Israel seemingly had unlimited backing from the United States and other Western powers on the one hand, and the Palestinians had seemingly unlimited backing from both the Arab nations and the Soviet Union on the other, the dispute was truly insoluble.

In the wake of the 1967 war, however, all that was changed. Out of the United Nations deliberations came an agreement on the principles of a Middle East peace. It is United Nations Resolution 242 of November 22, 1967. This resolution, originally drafted by Lord Caradon of the United Kingdom, calls for "withdrawal of Israeli armed forces from territories occupied in the recent conflict" and "termination of all claims or states of belligerency and respect for and acknowledgement of the sovereignty, territorial integrity and political independence of every State in the area and their right to live in peace within secure and recognized boundaries free from threats or acts of force." In short, the return of Arab land occupied in 1967 by the Israelis in exchange for Arab guarantees of peace for Israel.

The resolution eventually was approved not only by the U.S., U.K., France and the Soviet Union, but also by the Israeli Government of Prime Minister Golda Meir, all of the Arab confrontation states bordering Israel (Lebanon, Syria, Jordan and Egypt), and Saudi Arabia. It was the first time all the concerned parties had agreed on the essentials of a Middle East peace. For a time the Arab-Israeli dispute narrowed essentially to technicalities, though important ones. Did Resolution 242 apply to "territories occupied in the recent conflict," as stated in the English language text, or "*the* territories occupied in the recent conflict" as specified in the French text? The ambiguity resulting from the slightly different wording in the two versions was not accidental. Lord Caradon reported that it had been the only way the resolution draft could be written and still receive the unanimous approval it eventually obtained. In any case, no final agreement was reached on withdrawals and the result was another war.

In the wake of the 1973 war other agreements followed. Sinai I and Sinai II disengaged Israeli forces from those of Egypt and Syria. The Israeli-Egyptian treaty took the process a long step further. Although all meetings between Arab and Israeli leaders had been clandestine or through intermediaries before, from the time of President Sadat's journey to Jerusalem both populations became accustomed to seeing Egyptian and Israeli leaders discussing their differences face to face. They also saw the beginnings of public "normalization" of Arab-Israeli relations. For many years the proximity of Jordan and Israel had led to *de facto* arrangements to ease passage of people and goods from the territory controlled by one country to that controlled by the other. Now, however, aircraft began to fly directly between Egypt and Israel. Egyptian and Israeli tourists, as well as journalists and diplomats, began tentatively exploring each other's countries, even as Egyptian-Israeli negotiations concerning the future of the Palestinians dragged on uncertainly in the absence of representatives of the Palestinians themselves.

The rest, sooner or later, will follow. The West, the Arab confrontation states, and Israel all have more to lose than to gain from continuing the dangerous, and frequently tragic, status quo.

Whatever the original injustices done to the Palestinians—and these can no more be ignored by the world than could the earlier injustices suffered by Jews in Europe—an exchange of population has taken place. Within Israel's pre-1967 boundaries the displaced Palestinians have been replaced by almost as many Jews displaced from Arab countries. Partisans may argue that some of the Arab inhabitants of Palestine or some of the Jewish inhabitants of the Arab countries were not forced to leave. Such arguments are irrelevant. Few left their original homes willingly. All feared for their lives and the lives of their children. Middle Eastern Jews and Arabs have crossed the borders in roughly equal numbers, and the *de facto* exchange of population has been completed. It can be said that even together the West Bank and Gaza, to which so many of the Palestinian refugees fled, are not economically viable. By the same standards, however, neither is Israel. Any independent Palestinian state, whether confined to the West Bank and Gaza or united with Jordan, would depend on the assistance of other Arab States for the foreseeable future. Israel is similarly dependent upon help from the world Jewish community. On both sides of the lines outside supporters have paid the bills for 35 years of intermittent warfare. They will have to continue paying for at least the first years of peace, and perhaps indefinitely. The area has always been under-endowed in terms of resources. The 1947 separation of population by religion only exacerbated the long-standing problems of an overpopulated region.

Costs on both sides for such projects as establishing labor-intensive industries, building water distillation plants and digging deeper wells, and building more schools to provide vocational training will be considerably less than the cost of procuring vast quantities of aircraft and tanks and training personnel to operate them.

While the dimensions of the Middle East dispute have changed, so also have the situations of the participants. The Arabs have evolved since World War II from have-not to have status. What they need now is time and, most of all, stability to spread the benefits of their newly-developed natural resources more equitably among all segments of the population, and among the different regions of the Arab World. Israel, by making itself acceptable to its neighbors through peace and normalization agreements freely entered into by both sides, can do more than share in the benefits of this wealth. It can make its own lasting contribution to the tempo of regional development through the participation of its skilled and highly educated population.

Just as economic circumstances have improved dramatically in the Middle East, political tactics also are evolving. In the past, in times of domestic or international tension, Arab leaders traditionally garnered personal support by outbidding each other in terms of defiance, hostility and threats not only toward Israel, but toward the West as well.

Now voices of moderation are increasingly raised in many areas of the Arab World. If moderate Arab leaders can demonstrate conclusively that their way works best for the Arabs as a whole, others may also be prepared to follow Senator Abourezk's advice by "simply telling the truth about themselves—good or bad—so that the American people can better understand what they're all about."[5]

If and when that happens, it should soon become apparent that there now are fewer domestic constraints on American policy in the Middle East than in the past.

Within the U.S. government the partisans of either side increasingly have tempered passion with reason. Many members of the American foreign affairs community now frankly describe themselves as followers of the "a plague on both your houses" school. The implication is that they are willing to judge each new proposal solely on its merits, and not on the side from which it originates. On the one hand such knowledgeable Americans have been turned off by the legalistic maneuvers of an Israeli government which, after 35 years of intermittent warfare which has cost it the best of two generations of Israel's youth, seems ready and even determined to pass up its first real chance for peace solely to keep a few more barren hilltops, and a number of urban areas inhabited, not by Jews, but by another million Arabs.

At the same time, at the beginning of the Reagan administration American officials were equally turned off by some Arab leaders who, during the administrations of three previous American presidents, all clearly striving for a genuine even-handedness, were unwilling or unable to put forward an agreed peace plan of their own. At that time Israel could hardly be asked to negotiate a lasting agreement with Arab leaders who could not even reach agreement among themselves. It had escaped no American Middle East specialist's attention, either, that some of the Arab leaders who most fastidiously deplored the terrorist pasts of Israel's current Prime Minister and Foreign Minister, had made no visible effort to isolate or draw away from spoilers, fanatics and international terrorists whose continued acceptance within the Arab camp brought opprobrium upon them all.

If the foreign affairs establishment of the United States is now prepared to be more "even-handed" than in the past, what of Congress? In the Kissinger era it frankly opposed and eventually stalemated new administration initiatives in the Middle East. In the Carter era Congressional reluctance to support his desire to work toward a comprehensive settlement certainly was a factor in Carter's decision to settle for the half-way house of the Camp David agreements. In the Reagan era it appeared to many that Congress would strangle his first important Middle East initiative, the AWACS sale, in the cradle. However, it did not, and the reasons were accurately foreseen in the 1979 David Logan study of the 95th Congress cited earlier. That report concluded:

"The role of the administration in Middle East policy is important and increasing. Every bill that we have looked at in the 95th Congress followed the lead of the administration. The administration wanted to sell the jet fighter package; the Congress did not disapprove the sale. The President wanted to grant aid to Syria, and the full amount of his aid request was reinstated. The foreign aid bills were passed largely in line with Presidential requests. 'Aid to the Middle East is basically on a don't tamper basis,' was the way one aide described it. Finally, it should be noted that there were no major independent Congressional initiatives on Middle East policy in the entire 95th Congress. Clearly the administration is pre-eminent in this area.... As the Middle East becomes more crucial for the nation, the President begins to take a personal interest in the substance of policy. . . . Thus, as U.S. involvement has increased, the administration has dealt with the Middle East as a central issue rather than a peripheral matter. When this happens the influence and independent initiative of Congress are bound to decrease."[6]

The 1981 administration victory, despite an all-out Israeli campaign which began well before the administration formally proposed the sale of AWACS to Saudi Arabia, underlines Logan's point. Not only Congress but also the American public seem more willing to let the administration lead, rather than be driven, in matters concerning the Middle East. It is now widely perceived that U.S. concerns in the Middle East are not limited simply to the traditional support of Israel, but also embrace continued Middle Eastern oil production, availability of that oil to the United States, Japan and Western Europe, Soviet influence and physical penetration, and U.S. transit rights and commercial and strategic access. In short, a few years ago the public was easily aroused to support an Israel that it perceived as fighting for survival with its back to the sea, or to oppose an administration that appeared insufficiently generous with a nation of Holocaust survivors, but perceptions have changed. Israel is no longer an underdog nation, and many of the Arabs have demonstrated that they are more interested in cooperation than confrontation with the West. The complexities of the Middle East are at least acknowledged, if not yet fully understood, by the American public.

Polls bear this out. In 1947, before the creation of Israel, few Americans had taken sides in the Palestinian dispute. Among those who did take sides, however, supporters of the region's Jews outnumbered supporters of its Arabs by two to one. By the time of the June war of 1967, many more Americans had taken sides and among them supporters of the Israelis outnumbered supporters of the Arabs by an overwhelming 15 to 1. Those earlier polls also showed higher support for Israel among the university-educated, the affluent, and the executive-professional class than among the public as a whole.

As an occupying power, Israel's image began to change. At the time of the October 1973 war, however, American supporters of Israel still outnumbered supporters of the Arabs by approximately eight to one. The 1973 Arab oil embargo increased the number of Americans who claimed to be following events in the Middle East, and the number of partisans for both sides. Percentage gains were greater for the Arabs but numerical gains still were greater for Israel. Interestingly, the elite groups were even less susceptible to "oil weapon" pressure than was the public as a whole.

A year later, after the Ford administration had blamed Israel for the breakdown of the Kissinger shuttle, support for Israel had dropped significantly and support for the Arabs began to climb. The ratio in favor of Israel was now down to 4½ to 1, although it tended to drift back toward Israel when peace momentum resumed. It was in late 1977 and early in 1978, however, after Menachem Begin's election victory and the late President Anwar Sadat's journey to Jerusalem, that American public opinion changed rapidly. Support for the Arabs had doubled by then to approximately 13 per cent and support for Israel had declined to a low of 33 per cent. Among the 50 per cent of Americans who favored one side over the other, the ratio was thus down to 2½ to 1 in favor of Israel over the Arabs—a proportion that probably has changed little since then if volunteered statements of support for Egypt are included with responses favoring the Arabs in general. When Sadat's and Begin's efforts for peace were compared, Americans for the first time rated an Arab leader higher than the leader of Israel. They also rated Egypt's desire for peace slightly higher than Israel's.

Most significant, however, was the clear reversal in attitude by American elite groups. According to one CBS poll in which the same questions were asked six months apart, university-educated respondents literally were turned around between October 1977—just prior to the Sadat journey when 49 per cent said the U.S. should "support Israel" and 35 per cent said the U.S. should "pay more attention to the Arabs"—and April 1978 by which time they supported the Arabs over Israel by 40 to 36 per cent. If the opinions of such leader groups eventually become the opinions of the general public, this reversal of American elite attitudes is the most significant American public opinion development recorded by the polls.

American media now are reporting Middle Eastern events more carefully and thoughtfully. They seem less prone to pursue private enthusiasms or to present complex issues emotionally. The American "elite press" already has demonstrated that it is ready consistently to support thoughtful and carefully-prepared administration initiatives in the Middle East, even when initially they seem to run against popular prejudice. The corps of U.S. Middle Eastern correspondents has increased in quality, if not in quantity, and some of the editors to whom they now report have previously served their own tours of duty in the Middle East. As a result, when access is granted, stories that seem controversial and unpleasant to American audiences may be covered almost as thoroughly as the easy and pleasant ones. U.S. Jewish journalists in the Middle East, once suspected by their colleagues of allowing their own private feelings to color their approach to the area, have reported U.S. Middle Eastern diplomatic shuttle missions just as supportively, have cross-questioned Menachem Begin just as searchingly, have brought out the late Anwar Sadat's viewpoints just as assiduously, and have sought out Palestinian and Syrian leaders for interviews just as energetically as their non-Jewish colleagues. As a result the comments, even among the most skeptical Arab leaders, about Israeli influence in the American media are less bitter and certain today than only a decade ago. For every journalistic George Will, Herbert Block or William Safire, eager to impute immorality, imbecility or both to any U.S. administration that does not set its entire Middle Eastern policy by the compass of Israeli interest, there is an Anthony Lewis ready to describe Israel's transformation from Middle Eastern underdog to West Bank overlord, an Evans and Novak to chronicle each move by Israel's potent lobby to discourage or divert U.S. foreign affairs specialists from taking Middle East initiatives, and a George Ball ready to charge with irresponsibility or indecisiveness any administration that does not consistently and actively attack the entire spectrum of Middle Eastern problems. In addition, whatever the case in the past, editorial pages of the *Washington Post,* the *New York Times,* the *Christian Science Monitor* and other establishment media now are open to both sides, or rather all sides, of the Middle Eastern arguments, as some of the quotations scattered throughout this book demonstrate.

Once administration navigators seeking to chart an even-handed course through troubled Middle Eastern waters were forced to reckon with frequently adverse media winds, and strong and unvarying currents of public opinion. These inhibitions are weakening as the media and the public look increasingly to any incumbent administration for guidance and a strong lead in an increasingly complex and critical situation. In the post-1973 era Presidents Nixon, Ford and Carter all faced at one time or another extremely adverse reaction both from the Arabs and from Israel and its U.S. supporters toward their individual Middle East initiatives. Success in each case quieted much of the international criticism, and resulted eventually in praise and heightened domestic political prestige.

Middle East successes, in fact, were among the major foreign policy accomplishments of all three of those Presidents. It is a safe bet, however, that in each case they launched their Middle East initiatives solely because their foreign affairs experts insisted that the international situation demanded American action, and against the strong misgivings of their domestic political advisers. With the Middle East increasingly the center of world attention, a U.S. President is under pressure from the very beginning of his term to take an active role in settling disputes that, by dividing and inflaming this vital area, open it further to outside penetration. The Arab-Israeli dispute is certainly the most persistent and divisive of these disputes. It may now, however, also be one of the disputes most susceptible to solution, to the short- and long-run benefit of the contending parties, the other countries of the region, and the United States and Western Europe as well.

Resolution 242 outlined the political bases of the eventual peace settlement. President Sadat's journey to Jerusalem laid the psychological foundations. For a time it seemed that the next breakthrough might come from Israel, via the Breira (Alternative) or Shalom Achshav (Peace Now) activists in Israel, who actively supported the concept of Israeli withdrawal from the West Bank and Gaza Strip in exchange for Arab and international guarantees of Israel's sovereignty and territorial integrity. After that moderate Israeli groundswell had subsided, PLO Chairman Yassir Arafat seemed sometimes on the verge of agreeing to recognize Israel within its pre-1967 boundaries in exchange for Israeli withdrawal from the West Bank, Gaza, and the eastern portion of Jerusalem taken from the Arabs in 1967. However, whenever he was called upon to say publicly what he reputedly had told Westerners privately, he demurred, asking "Why should we give away our last bargaining chip?"

In the fall of 1981 hopes were raised once more when Saudi Arabia advanced its eight principles for a peaceful settlement. Those principles were in fact the principles of Resolution 242, with two additional features tailored specifically to meet often-reiterated Palestinian objections to the UN plan. Resolution 242 calls only "for achieving a just settlement of the refugee problem." In their principles the Saudis spelled out such a "just settlement" in terms they believed would be acceptable both to the Palestinians and to the United States and other western powers. The Saudi plan specified, first, that after a UN trusteeship period, the Palestinians must have their own independent state in the West Bank. Second, it called for repatriation or compensation for all Palestinians who had lost their homes. Despite Menachem Begin's comment that the Saudi plan is a model of "how to liquidate Israel in stages," U.S. and European officials found nothing to criticize in it. Instead President Reagan called the plan a "hopeful sign." He pointed out that the Arab recognition of Israel implicit in the Saudi plan was in fact a major breakthrough toward eventual peace. Secretary of State Alexander Haig, until then considered closer to the Israeli point of view than most of the State Department's career officers, said "There are aspects in the eight-point proposal made by Crown Prince Fahd by which we are encouraged." Israel's response was to use Knesset members to campaign against the Saudi plan and Saudi Arabia itself in the U.S. The rhetoric was becoming harsher.

For one week in November 1981 it seemed possible that Western perceptions of the respective roles of the Arabs and the Israelis would have to be reversed. As Arab heads of state, including PLO Chairman Yassir Arafat, assembled in Fez to discuss whether to unite behind the Saudi plan, the Israelis were threatening to veto British, French, Italian and Dutch participation in the international force being assembled by the United States to supervise the final Israeli withdrawal from Egyptian territory in the Sinai. It seemed that just as the Arabs finally united behind a concrete peace proposal conforming to Resolution 242, and thus to European and American positions on a settlement, the Israelis were laying the groundwork for a renunciation not only of any Western European support, but possibly even a renunciation of the Camp David commitments Israel had made to Egypt under U.S. auspices. However, the role reversals did not come to pass at that time.

At Fez the scenario changed. Although Arafat had earlier indicated he could support the Saudi plan, his own PLO executive committee, consisting of representatives not only of Arafat's majority Al Fatah but also of other more radical Palestinian groups, would not back him in this bold move. When he arrived in Fez he resumed his familiar zig-zag tactics, refusing to confirm in public what he was reported to have said in private in support of the Saudi plan. President Hafiz al-Asad of Syria cancelled his attendance at the conference so suddenly that a Moroccan delegation actually was on hand at the airport to meet him when it received the news that he would not be aboard the plane. After five hours of debate, with the usual Arab extremists in opposition and neither Syria nor the PLO offering the hoped-for support for the Saudi plan, King Hassan of Morocco abruptly adjourned the Arab summit meeting. It was a tactical move to keep the plan alive and viable for reconsideration at a subsequent Arab summit meeting, rather than letting it go down to defeat in Fez.

Meanwhile, the U.S. and Israel, in the words of columnist Philip Geyelin of the *Washington Post,* "apparently agreed on at least a tentative trade-off of a new 'strategic' military relationship between the two countries in return for Israeli acceptance of Europeans in a Sinai peace-keeping force."[7]

It had been a difficult negotiation, however, with Israeli Defense Minister Ariel

Sharon seeking placement of U.S. bases, troops or military supplies in Israel, and the U.S. seeking to limit the agreement to vaguely defined consultation, coordination, and joint military maneuvers. After it was signed Begin made it clear to the Americans that it contained far less than he had wanted, while at the same time he seemed to be trying through Radio Israel's broadcasts in Arabic to make the Arabs believe that it contained far more than it did.

As early as the summer of 1981, *Washington Post* columnist William Raspberry suggested that in repeatedly seeking to settle Israel's foreign policy problems with his U.S.-supplied warplanes, Menachem Begin was demonstrating that "America has a madman for an ally." What followed the signing of the U.S.-Israeli memorandum on strategic cooperation seemed only to underline this. On Saturday, December 13, 1981, the Polish Army suddenly declared a state of martial law and arrested the entire leadership of the Solidarity free trade union movement in that country. The following morning, Sunday, December 14, Prime Minister Begin suddenly checked out of the hospital where he had been recovering from a broken hip joint. He proceeded directly to an emergency cabinet meeting he had convened in his home. Within 90 minutes the Cabinet had approved annexation of the Golan Heights regions seized from Syria in the 1967 war and lost and then recaptured in 1973. A marathon emergency session of the Knesset ratified the annexation on the same day.

Although world attention was fixed on Poland, there was angry global reaction to Israel's flagrant violation of international law. To the chagrin of Israel, the U.S. joined in a 15-to-0 UN Security Council vote that declared the Golan annexation null and void. The U.S. press reported that President Reagan's anger had been incurred by the obvious Israeli attempt to repeat its 1956 success, when it had invaded Egypt while the rest of the world was preoccupied with the bloody Russian repression in Hungary. Begin's precipitate move on December 14, 1981 seemed timed solely to take advantage of world distraction over the surprise "coup" by Poland's Communist Party and army. Unfortunately, it also gave the Russians an opportunity to distract Third World attention from Poland by conspicuously coming to the support of Syria, and it heightened the tension in a developing Soviet-U.S. confrontation.

Only later did American newsmen realize that Begin's actions had been even more Machiavellian than the press had realized. Secretary Haig had been in Europe and was scheduled to visit Israel over the weekend on which the annexation was announced. Haig had cancelled his trip to Israel at the last moment and returned directly to the United States only because of the declaration of martial law in Poland. Had Haig not suddenly cut short the trip, Begin would have been able to carry out his surprise move while Haig was in the country or just after he had departed. It was the same ploy Begin had used earlier in the year when he traveled to Egypt to meet with President Sadat and then, later in the week, ordered the bombing of the Iraqi nuclear reactor. This had falsely signaled the world that Egypt had acquiesced in advance in the bombing of another Arab country, and further exacerbated Egypt's estrangement from other Arab countries. The same tactics in regard to the Golan annexation might have estranged the Arab world from the United States, perhaps even bringing about a denunciation of the U.S. by Saudi Arabia, clearly Israel's top foreign policy goal throughout 1981.

The American reaction to such transparent deceit by Israel was slow in coming, but strong on arrival. The U.S. suspended the recently-concluded U.S.-Israeli memorandum of understanding on strategic cooperation. It also suspended further discussion of three U.S. military assistance "sweeteners" for Israel for 1982. These would have authorized the Defense Department to make purchases of up to $200 million a year from Israel; permitted Israel to spend part of its U.S. military financing credits on purchases from Israeli domestic defense industries rather than from American industries; and would have permitted other countries receiving U.S. military aid also to use part of that aid to buy equipment and services from Israel instead of from the United States. Such unique and vitally important concessions to Israel have always been over and above the high levels of direct U.S. military and economic aid to that country. The Reagan administration's determination to suspend such hidden benefits, as well as the overt benefits watched by the public in both countries, seemed to signal its intention this time to make the U.S. punishment fit the Israeli crime.

The Begin reaction, if not that of a madman, at least made plain what Middle Eastern specialists had long known. He was not as interested in courting American support as in playing to the Israeli man in the street, who loved the spectacle of the tiny country's feisty Prime Minister telling off the world in general and the United States in particular.

Begin simultaneously summoned American Ambassador Samuel Lewis to his residence, and journalists to the Israeli Foreign Ministry. Lewis for years had followed the time-honored approach of American ambassadors in Tel Aviv. Over and over he had counseled Washington to moderate its language, cautioning that strong U.S. admonitions to Israel only make Israelis "circle the wagons" and rally around whoever is leading their government at the time. The Carter administration generally had followed Lewis' advice, and had found itself the target of escalating Begin abuse. The Reagan administration had, for 10 months, sought to do likewise, with identical results.

Now even Lewis' monumental patience seemed almost at an end. He had been kept completely in the dark about Israel's annexation move and the U.S. government had been severely embarrassed by, and in the eyes of the world almost implicated in, the illegal Israeli action. Now Lewis found himself listening impassively to a tirade against his government which, though it may have sounded like the ravings of a maniac, in fact was being read from carefully prepared notes.

Lewis, who told an aide "I've seen better political theater before, but never to a smaller audience," was wrong about the size of the audience. By the time he got back to his embassy to report the tirade to Washington, Lewis found that his own report was unnecessary. The newsmen summoned to the Foreign Ministry already had received the Ministry's press release describing Begin's statement to the American ambassador. It was summarized by *Time* magazine as follows:

"You declared that you are 'punishing' Israel. What kind of talk is that, 'punishing' Israel? Are we a vassal state? A banana republic? Are we 14-year-old boys that if they don't behave they have their knuckles smacked?

"You have no moral right to lecture us on civilian casualties. We have read the history of [World War II], and we know what happened to civilians when you carried out military operations against the enemy. We also read the history of the Vietnam war and your term 'body counts.'

"You cannot and will not frighten us with 'punishments and threats.' Threats will fall on deaf ears.

"You are trying to make Israel hostage to the memorandum of understanding. No sword of Damocles will be hanging over our heads. The people of Israel have lived for 3700 years without a memorandum of understanding with America and will continue to live without it for another 3700 years.

"You have imposed upon us pecuniary sanctions, and in the process you have broken the word of the President. What do you want to do? Hit us in the pocket?

"Nobody will succeed in intimidating [American Jews] by anti-Semitic propaganda. They will stand by us. This is the land of their forefathers—they have the right and duty to support us.

"The word rescind is a concept from the time of the Inquisition. Our forefathers went to 'the stake' rather than rescind their faith. We are not going to the stake."[8]

This time the images truly had reversed. Israel's Prime Minister was playing to the xenophobic mob, reviling both the U.S. and all its Western allies, making it virtually impossible for Israel's American partisans to support him without incurring charges of turning on their own country, and publicly upbraiding an American ambassador who for years had worked patiently for understanding between Israel and the United States.

The performance was reminiscent of President Nasser in his most self-destructive years, or of the contemporary Colonel Qaddafi. Although leaders of virtually every national Jewish organization eventually spoke out dutifully in Begin's defense, the statements were cautious and half-hearted. The press had already reported that when Senator Claiborne Pell denounced Israel's annexation of the Golan, he received a standing ovation from a B'Nai B'Rith audience in Rhode Island. Even Israel's redoubtable Ambassador Evron, the same Israeli diplomat who long ago had carefully developed ready access not only to President Johnson, but also to top CIA leadership of that time, sounded tired and dispirited as he repeatedly defended his government's actions on U.S. television and in press interviews. He was only two months short of retirement and his scheduled replacement was Philadelphia-raised Moshe Arens, one of the most outspoken hardliners in the Israeli Knesset and normally a staunch Begin supporter, whose most notable difference with Begin had been in March, 1979 when Arens voted *against* the Camp David agreements.

The Evidence of the Polls: American Public Opinion and the Arab-Israeli Dispute

Those who are skeptical of polls in general have expressed particular suspicion of polls pertaining to the Arab-Israeli dispute. They reason that American polls on the Middle East may have been tainted either by partisanship among those who prepare the questions or among the polltakers themselves. It seems likely, however, that major polling organizations would take all reasonable precautions against such problems, simply to protect their own credibility. This is borne out by Department of State analysts who for several years have examined the results obtained by the media and commercial polling organizations on all foreign policy questions. On Middle East affairs they have recorded a high degree of consistency among the various major polling organizations, both in the public attitudes recorded, and in the evolution of those attitudes over 35 years. It would be foolish, therefore, to ignore the polls. They reveal a great deal not only about current American attitudes, but also about the factors that influence those attitudes positively and negatively. A brief summary of such poll results was presented in Chapter 24 of this book. Some of the specific polls upon which those conclusions are based are examined in greater detail in this appendix, adapted from the author's 1980 case study for the Department of State's Foreign Service Institute: *Too Often Promised Land—American Public Opinion and the Arab-Israeli Dispute.*

After more than 35 years in the American public consciousness, and more than two years without a major breakthrough in the public positions proclaimed either by Palestinians or Israelis, the Arab-Israel dispute has become a "mature issue." In the absence of major new developments, there have been no major opinion swings. In fact, through all the years that polls have been taken, only one event has ever caused a sudden, major swing in American public opinion. That was President Anwar Sadat's journey to Jerusalem.

If it was the end of an era in U.S.-Israeli relations, it seemed also to be beginning of an era in the Arab World. Yassir Arafat had not been able to thr his support to the Saudi peace proposals at Fez. After his return to Beirut, howev he had indicated not only his continued personal endorsement of them, but also h belief that they still were viable as a potential unified peace proposal which coul be supported by the major Arab countries.

This Arab near-breakthrough after 35 years of impasse may yet go down in history as simply another hopeful Middle Eastern initiative that never quite got off the ground. It may, however, re-emerge in a few months as the first unified Arab peace proposal totally compatible with Resolution 242, the policy supported by the United States for 14 years.

Whether it is the Saudi or another proposal, some reasonable initiative must eventually emerge from one side or the other. When a moderate proposal emerges from one party to the conflict, the U.S. and its European allies, with or without the Soviet Union, must move firmly and in concert to insure that each party to the dispute goes the necessary 50 per cent of the way toward a peaceful resolution.

That moment may well come during the administration of President Reagan. If it does, and he seizes the opportunity firmly, fairly, and persistently, he almost certainly will find that the Congress, the media, and the American people are ready to support him, no matter how much partisans, lobbyists, or interest groups may object. A successful result would prevent the waste of still a third generation of young Arabs and Israelis. It would also remove once and for all the flashpoint that three times, in 1956, 1967, and 1973, has threatened to ignite World War III, and which remains the single issue most likely to precipitate such an unprecedented human calamity.

NOTES

1. Kissinger, Henry A., former Secretary of State, "Don't Make the AWACS Sale a Test of Strength," *Washington Post,* October 6, 1981, page A-21.
2. Nixon, former President Richard M., in statement released October 4, 1981 and reported in the *New York Times* of the same date, page 1.
3. Ford, former President Gerald, in interview October 10, 1981 aboard U.S. Air Force plane returning from the funeral of President Anwar Sadat in Cairo, Egypt.
4. Carter, former President James E., in interview October 10, 1981 aboard U.S. Air Force plane returning from the funeral of President Anwar Sadat in Cairo, Egypt.
5. Abourezk, Senator James, excerpted from a talk at the Arab and American Cultures Conference of the Middle East Institute, September 24, 1976. Washington, D.C.
6. Logan, David, "The 95th Congress and Middle East Policy: Voting Patterns and Trends," published by the National Association of Arab Americans, April 23, 1979, pp. 25-27.
7. Geyelin, Phillip, "The Failure at Fez Was No Disaster," *Washington Post,* December 9, 1981, page A-21.
8. Begin, Menachem, as summarized in "Begin's Blast," *Time,* January 4, 1982, p. 58.

That event more than doubled American support for the Arabs, and resulted in a still further increase of support for Egypt beyond support for the other Arabs. Over the long run, however, the swing toward the Arabs was not enough to offset the declining, but still overriding popular support for Israel.

There have, however, been other significant changes within American public opinion. When American polls on the Arab-Israeli dispute began in the late 1940s, better-educated Americans were more favorably inclined toward Israel than were other Americans. Today the reverse is true. While shifts toward support for the Arabs are small in terms of overall American opinion, they are significant if one assumes that opinions of better-educated Americans "trickle down" to the less educated or less informed Americans over time. University-educated Americans have shifted from basic sympathy toward Israel to basic sympathy toward the Arabs in remarkable numbers, particularly after the Sadat journey. It is in such responsiveness among the better-educated Americans (and also among the more affluent and those in executive and professional positions) toward more conciliatory positions taken by Arab leaders that hope for eventual American even-handedness lies. It should be the subject of careful attention not only by leaders of Israel and the Arab countries, but also by U.S. leaders responsible for putting into effect an American foreign policy which can enhance the prospects for a Middle Eastern peace.

Before the creation of Israel, three Gallup polls provided the first insights into American opinion on Palestinian events. In the first two, respondents were asked if they had been following specific Palestinian developments. Only those who answered affirmatively were asked to give their opinion. The results: In January 1945 the 55 per cent who said they had "followed the discussion on permitting Jews to settle in Palestine" gave these opinions:

Favor the idea	76%
Favor if Jews do	4
Against the idea	7
Favor leaving it up to the British	1
Favor leaving it up to the Arabs	1
Miscellaneous	3
Don't know	8

In May 1946, the 50 per cent who said they had "heard or read about the Jewish migration into Palestine" were asked: "Do you think it is a good idea or a poor idea to admit 100,000 Jews to settle in Palestine?" The answers:

Good idea	78%
Poor idea	14
No opinion	8

The last of the three pre-Israel Gallup polls made no effort to weed out those who had not been following events. The results therefore cannot be compared with those above. But the differing results for two differently posed questions during this October 1947 poll are worth considering. They illustrate not only the manner in which wording can influence answers, but also how flexible U.S. opinion on the subject was at the time.

> "Question: The UN has recommended that Palestine be divided into two states—one for the Arabs and one for the Jews—and that 150,000 Jews be permitted now to enter the Jewish state. Do you favor or oppose this idea?"
>
> | | |
> |---|---|
> | Favor | 65% |
> | Oppose | 10 |
> | No opinion | 25 |
>
> "Question: If war breaks out between the Arabs and the Jews in Palestine, with which side would you sympathize?"
>
> | | |
> |---|---|
> | Jews | 24% |
> | Arabs | 12 |
> | Neither | 38 |
> | No Opinion | 26 |

The significance of these early polls is that, although Americans overwhelmingly favored allowing large numbers of Jewish survivors of the World War II European Holocaust to settle in Palestine, apparently most of those same Americans had not yet taken sides between the region's Arabs and Jews. Pioneer Jewish settlers, attracted by the Zionist slogan of "a land without a people for a people without a land," reported their surprise upon arriving in Palestine to find it heavily populated by Arabs. From the polls above, it seems likely that in the 1945-1947 period few Americans realized that the Jewish immigration into Palestine they supported might result in a forced Arab emigration. In any case, clearly in 1947 only one in four Americans identified with the Jewish side, half that number identified with the Arab side, and the remaining 64 per cent had no opinion or said they were neutral.

There were no more comparable Gallup polls until the six-day war of June 1967. Strangely, those who said they had been following developments in the Middle East had risen by that time only a few points to 59 per cent. Among those who said they had followed developments, however, sympathy for the Israelis had more than doubled to 59 per cent and sympathy for the Arabs had dropped to an almost insignificant 4 per cent. Something important had happened to American public opinion in the 21 years between 1947 and 1967. Many more Americans had taken sides in the Middle East dispute, and although in 1947 American supporters of Israel outnumbered supporters of the Arabs by two to one, in 1967 Americans supported Israel over the Arabs by fifteen to one.

Through the following years, with Israel an occupying power rather than a nation of refugees apparently in danger of being pushed into the sea, support for

Israel gradually dropped to figures of 50 and 44 per cent in 1969 and 1970 respectively. But U.S. public support for the Arab camp, still led by mercurial President Nasser and still perceived as under the influence of such abrasive personalities as Ahmad Shukairy, the PLO spokesman-leader who was forced to resign after the 1967 debacle, remained insignificant at five per cent in 1969 and three per cent in 1970. Regardless of sympathies, however, most Americans did not want the U.S. to become involved with either side if war should break out. In 1967, 41 per cent of respondents said the U.S. should "stay out" of the conflict and by 1970 this percentage had risen to 58. Perhaps the most significant change in American public opinion recorded by Gallup during the six years between the June 1967 war and the October 1973 war was in the percentage of Americans who said they were following events in the Middle East. From the 59 per cent of 1967 it had risen to 85 and 86 per cent in the 1969 and 1970 polls.

The first Gallup poll in 1973 was taken from October 5 to 8, encompassing the day before and the first three days of the three-week October war. Americans following events in the Middle East had increased still further, to 90 per cent. Of those, 47 per cent, a three per cent increase over 1970, supported Israel while six per cent supported the Arabs, double the 1970 figure.

Two months later in December, 1973, just six weeks after many Arab nations had imposed an embargo on oil shipments to the United States, another Gallup poll found that Americans following events in the Middle East had climbed to an all-time high—before or since—of 97 per cent. This perhaps bore out the Arab adage of the time that Americans sitting in gas lines at last had sufficient time to think about the Middle East.

However, the thoughts of Americans during the oil embargo did not follow predictable patterns. Support for Israel had climbed seven per cent in two months to 54 per cent, only one per cent below the high point reached during the June war of 1967. Support for the Arabs had also climbed from six to eight per cent—a 25 per cent increase. However, although militant Arabs sought to credit this increase in support for the Arabs to the oil embargo, there were other significant factors at work at the time on American perceptions of the Arabs. Americans were impressed by the new military prowess demonstrated by the Egyptian and Syrian armies. They were aware that Egyptian military communiques had been accurate, in startling contrast to Israel's. And, in contrast to 1970 when Nasser's Egypt had openly cheated on ceasefire terms by moving ground to air missiles into the Suez Canal area for many hours after the stand-still deadline, this time, as in 1948 and 1956, it was Israel which continued movement for days after the armies had been pledged to halt. This flagrant Israeli cheating nearly triggered direct Russian intervention to rescue the Egyptian Third Army which was cut off from Egypt by Israeli troops under General Sharon advancing long after the ceasefire deadline.

Thus there were several simultaneous reasons for the increased level of interest by the American public, and the resulting tendency of more individual Americans to side with both the Israeli and Arab causes. The following years, with more frequent polls and with fewer events occurring in between polls, provide clearer indications of what makes American public opinion change, and what does not.

The first half of 1974 saw the fall of the Golda Meir government in Israel, the shuttle negotiations by U.S. Secretary of State Henry Kissinger that eventually led to the Sinai I agreement, the lifting of the Arab oil embargo against the U.S. on March 18, visits by President Nixon to Arab countries and to Israel, restoration of diplomatic relations between the U.S. and Syria, and finally the resignation of President Nixon.

Surprisingly, there were few public polls to record the effects that these momentous events had on American public opinion. The American Jewish Committee commissioned the Daniel Yankelovich organization to carry out three polls in April, July and October of 1974, each containing a different question designed to elicit readiness by the American public to blame Jews for (1) the gasoline shortage; (2) "this whole movement to get rid of Mr. Nixon" and (3) the state of the economy. Two fixed questions, asked in each poll, concerned readiness to vote for a Jew for President, and perceptions of the relative closeness of American Jews to Israel and to the United States.

For purposes of this study, the only question comparable with the Gallup questions previously asked was included in the October 1974 poll, just one year after the outbreak of the 1973 war and the resulting oil embargo. Asked with whom they would identify if war should break out in the Middle East, respondents answered:

Israel	55%
Arabs	9
Both	5
Neither	17
Don't know	14

Support figures, therefore, were just one percentage point higher for both Israel and the Arabs than the figures recorded by Gallup 10 months earlier. Other conclusions of the 1974 surveys were summarized in an American Jewish Committee report as follows:

"While things are not so bad as one had feared, they are not so good as one might hope. Three quarters of the American public see Israel as a viable and necessary state. Although there is no enthusiasm for military aid, this can be seen as an aspect of a reserve about foreign aid in general, rather than as anti-Israel in particular, since there is even less enthusiasm for aid to most other countries. When blame is placed for trouble in the Middle East, Israel and the Jews are low on the list, with the Arabs and Russia high. What seems to warrant concern is that almost a third of the American people would not want a Jewish President and see Jews as being closer to Israel than to the United States. When those who express uncertainty about these matters are added to the antis, the total becomes uncomfortably large."[1]

In the second half of 1974, with President Nixon replaced by his vice president, Gerald Ford, U.S. attention stayed focused on the Middle East as leaders of Israel, Egypt, Syria and Saudi Arabia visited Washington, and Secretary Kissinger continued his shuttle negotiations. At a meeting in Rabat, Arab heads of state designated the PLO, not King Hussein, as spokesman for the Palestinians, and on November 13 PLO Chairman Arafat made his first appearance before the UN General Assembly. The shuttle finally broke down in March 1975, with President Ford and Secretary Kissinger seeming to place the blame on Israel. Arms shipments to Israel were suspended during an administration "reassessment."

Public opinion support for Israel took a precipitous tumble as measured in two Gallup polls for the period. It had crested at 54 per cent in the Gallup poll taken in December 1973, immediately after the October War and during the oil embargo. By January 1975 it had slipped to 44 per cent. In April, immediately after the administration had scarcely concealed its displeasure with Israel over the shuttle failure, it bottomed out at 37 per cent. Support for the Arabs, by contrast, neither rose nor fell, holding at 8 per cent in all three polls of December 1973 and January and April, 1975.

Although basic sympathy for the Arabs neither rose nor fell, American feelings about the Arab oil boycott were negative, even belligerent, in the January 1975 poll taken 10 months after the embargo was lifted. The Gallup question, and answers totalling 129 per cent because of multiple responses, were:

> "If the Arab nations impose another oil boycott on the United States, what policy do you think the United States should follow?"

Try to become self-sufficient	35%
(Develop new energy resources . . . . 15)	
(Conserve energy, don't waste . . . . 12)	
(Ration gasoline . . . . 5)	
(Use other forms of fuel, coal, etc . . . . 3)	
Economic Sanctions: Put embargo on Arab nations, don't send food, other items	24
Military intervention	10
Seek oil from other nations	3
Negotiate/have international conference with Arab nations	4
Meet Arab demands/meet terms	2
Other responses (including those who oppose military intervention)	18
No opinion	33

In the second half of 1975 the Kissinger shuttle resumed and resulted in the signing of the Sinai II agreement in September.

No more Gallup polls record U.S. public opinion reaction in the period of U.S.-Israel tension that preceded and the era of improved relations that followed the signing of the agreement. However, the privately commissioned Yankelovich polls to elicit public attitudes on Israel, U.S. Jews, and the Middle East continued. One was taken in January 1975 and another in January 1976. Conclusions reflected a great deal of confusion about the Middle East in American minds, but they were not out of line with previous Gallup poll results. In a memorandum the sponsoring American Jewish Committee summarized the findings as follows:

"If war should break out between the Arabs and Israel, more than half of those questioned would still identify with Israel and three-quarters would still see Israelis as people they can get along with. Almost as many (73 per cent) described the Palestine Liberation Organization as terrorist and undemocratic. But, as in last year's survey, only a little under one third (31 per cent) support Israel's refusal to negotiate with the PLO. As many (31 per cent) think it is wrong of Israel to refuse, and 38 per cent say they do not know.

"The one conspicuous shift in attitude appears in the question about too much influence over United States Middle East policy. Whereas in April 1974 those seeing American Jews as having too much influence were 29 per cent of the total, in January 1976 their percentage was 49. But respondents selecting organized labor as having too much influence over U.S. Middle East policy rose in the same period from 24 to 45 per cent. The public seems to have become more aware of interest groups in general.

"By contrast, the question asking about too much power in the United States shows a drop of 11 per cent among those who believe Jews have too much power (34 per cent in January 1975, 26 per cent in January 1976). This may indicate that the question is inter-preted as relating to domestic policy which concerns most Americans more than foreign policy. In domestic matters Jews are not perceived as being a special-interest group, while in foreign affairs Jews are perceived—if only because of the media—as vigorous partisans of Israel.

"The one question that was asked in all five surveys is, 'Do you feel most of the Jewish people in the country feel closer to Israel or to the United States?' In the latest poll just under half think them closer to Israel, and a quarter are not sure. These percentages have been essentially stable since 1974."[2]

U.S. initiatives in the Middle East traditionally come to a halt in an election year and 1976 was no exception. As Carter was defeating Ford in the U.S., in the Middle East the Lebanese civil war also had stopped all progress. There were no Gallup polls during 1976 relevant to the Arab-Israeli dispute. However, after the U.S. election, a Louis Harris survey asked whether respondents expected "the new Carter Administration will do a better job, not as good a job, or about the same kind of job in helping to negotiate a settlement in the Middle East?" The answers could not have been more neutral. They were: Better, 22 per cent; not as good, 20 per cent; about the same, 40 per cent; and not sure, 17 per cent. Based on its surveys the Harris organization reported, "it is possible that the country is witnessing a profound change in attitudes toward foreign policy. The public seems increasingly convinced that foreign policy will become an area of essentially bi-partisan effort, and that a new Administration, even of the opposite party, will be fully capable of carrying on as well as the predecessor."

President Carter seized the Middle East initiative almost from his first day in the White House at the beginning of 1977. He declared that the Palestinians were entitled to a homeland; that Israel must eventually return captured Arab territory; and he set out to meet with all the concerned Arab and Israeli leaders. When the election of Menachem Begin in Israel seemed to set back peace prospects, Egyptian President Sadat's dramatic journey to Jerusalem set them forward again. In such a year it is difficult, but not impossible, to relate U.S. public opinion shifts to specific events. Gallup polls in June and October 1977 drew a clear picture of U.S. public opinion prior to the Sadat initiative. In June those who said they had been following events had climbed back up from 1975 levels to 86 per cent, and support for Israel had risen from the all-time low of 37 per cent, recorded after the Ford administration blamed Israel for the shuttle breakdown two years earlier, to 44 per cent. Support for the Arabs, for the fourth time in nearly four years, had been measured at 8 per cent. In October 1977, with the U.S. apparently moving the parties toward Geneva negotiations, 79 per cent of those asked said they were following events. Among those support for Israel had climbed two more points to 46 per cent, and support for the Arabs had made its first rise in four years, from 8 to 11 per cent.

Other 1977 surveys pinpointed specific U.S. attitudes. A February Roper survey reporting American sympathy for Israel at 47 per cent versus sympathy for the Arabs at 6 per cent found a clear majority of 55 per cent favoring a compromise in which Israel would give up conquered territory for a peace settlement. A Harris poll of the same period found 68 per cent in favor of the U.S. "keeping the lead in trying to get negotiations going" toward a peaceful settlement, with only 15 per cent opposed and 17 per cent not sure. Of Jews polled on that question, an even higher 87 per cent favored the U.S. initiative. More than half of elite informed respondents to a Foreign Policy Association poll opposed the idea of "tilting" toward either side and recommended instead that the U.S. follow an evenly-balanced approach.

A July Roper poll found that while 50 per cent of the public disclaimed knowledge of or an opinion on a Palestinian homeland, among the remainder 20 per cent favored it and 20 per cent opposed it. However, even among those who favored a Palestinian homeland, one third volunteered concern over PLO methods. The same poll indicated that if the PLO took a stance that appeared compromising and peaceable regarding Israel, 42 per cent thought Israel should agree to a homeland, 19 per cent thought not, and 39 per cent had no opinion. That was the situation on the eve of the Sadat visit to Jerusalem, which not only broke the old rules of play but also changed American perceptions of the players.

The first polls showing altered American perceptions of the Middle East players were taken even as the drama was unfolding. The Harris organization asked in early December 1977 for an evaluation of Middle East protagonists. The results are juxtaposed below with answers in parentheses to the same questions posed by Harris interviews in October, just before the Sadat visit to Jerusalem:

	Wants a Just Peace		Reluctantly Wants Peace		Doesn't Want Peace		Not Sure	
	Dec.	(Oct.)	Dec.	(Oct.)	Dec.	(Oct.)	Dec.	(Oct.)
Israel	47	(55)	30	(20)	11	(6)	12	(19)
Egypt	52	(37)	26	(27)	10	(9)	12	(27)
Jordan	23	(34)	30	(23)	17	(7)	30	(36)
Saudi Arabia	24	(29)	27	(23)	19	(11)	30	(37)
Syria	15	(22)	26	(25)	27	(11)	32	(42)
Libya	14	(21)	24	(20)	25	(13)	37	(46)
PLO	11	(13)	15	(15)	47	(35)	27	(37)

After the Sadat initiative 52 per cent of Americans believed Egypt wanted a "just peace," a 15 point increase in two months. Israel's rating on the same question dropped eight points to 47 per cent, putting it behind Egypt for the first time since Israel was created. Based possibly on their negative reactions to the Sadat initiative, ratings for all other Arab countries also dropped, but in the case of every Arab country there was a partially offsetting increase in the "reluctantly wants peace" column. Only the PLO, already lower in the ratings than any Arab country, showed little loss in the "wants a just peace" column and none in the "reluctantly wants peace" category, possibly because both already were so low relative to any of the others named.

The Harris poll also documented a rise in positive ratings for President Carter's effort to achieve peace from 34 per cent to 62 per cent and a belief by 85 per cent of the public that direct Arab-Israel talks would be more effective for achieving peace than use of third countries such as the U.S. In short, whatever its original plans or the misgivings of its Middle East experts, the Carter administration was firmly compelled by public opinion to climb on the Sadat initiative bandwagon. Those, like Israel, who showed misgivings suffered a slight drop in U.S. public esteem. Those who actively opposed the initiative, like the other Arab countries, suffered a much sharper drop.

In an effort to seize the peace-making initiative from President Sadat, Prime Minister Begin had brought to Washington his own plan for the West Bank in December, 1977. Carter's reserved comment that it was "a good beginning" was mistakenly seized upon by both Begin and the U.S. media as an endorsement. A chill in U.S.-Egyptian relations seemed inevitable. However, on a return flight from Saudi Arabia President Carter made an unscheduled stop in Cairo and successfully set the record straight. In February, President Sadat spent six days in the U.S., not only meeting with Carter and members of Congress, but also participating in U.S. television interviews and giving a televised speech at the National Press Club in Washington. He was hailed by President Carter as "the world's foremost peacemaker."

The results of these activities were reflected in the February 1978 Gallup poll. Among the 79 per cent who said they were following events, support for Israel had tumbled 13 per cent in four months to an all-time low, before or since, of 33 per cent. Given no chance to single out Egypt for a separate rating, respondents gave the Arabs as a whole an unprecedented 14 per cent rating. This was a six point (75 per cent) climb in eight months, half of it achieved before and half after the Sadat initiative.

The impact of the Sadat initiative on more specific points was revealed by other polls. A January 1978 Harris poll contrasted American opinions of the Egyptian and Israeli leaders as well as opinions about their two countries. The question and answers:

"If it came down to it and there was a difference between (1) Egypt and Israel or (2) President Sadat of Egypt and Prime Minister Begin of Israel, on a peace settlement in the Middle East, whom would you trust more?"

(1) Israel vs. Egypt		(2) Sadat vs. Begin	
Israel	43%	Sadat	32%
Egypt	20	Begin	32
Not Sure	37	Not Sure	36

In a January 1978 NBC poll on their performances "in handling peace negotiations in the Middle East" respondents rated the Egyptian leader considerably higher than the Israeli leader. The results:

Sadat		Begin	
Excellent	30%	Excellent	16%
Good	35	Good	33
(Subtotal)	(65)	(Subtotal)	(48)
Only Fair	21	Only Fair	31
Poor	3	Poor	5
Not Sure	11	Not Sure	15

For the first time in more than 30 years of U.S. public opinion polling, an Arab leader had decisively outscored an Israeli leader. The American public jumped ahead of negotiations to render its verdict on their causes as well. A January 1978 Gallup poll asked the two-thirds of respondents who said they had been following Middle Eastern developments, "Do you think Israel should or should not withdraw its military forces and civilian settlements from the Sinai Peninsula?" A 40 to 29 per cent plurality said Israel should withdraw, while 31 per cent said they had no opinion on the settlement issue, a high level of indecision for a group claiming to be attentive.

At this stage it appeared that the change in U.S. opinion was not at the expense of the Palestinian parties to the dispute. A December 1977 NBC poll asked: "Do you agree or disagree that the Palestinian Arabs should have their own country?" The answers: Agree, 55 per cent; disagree, 25 per cent; not sure, 20 per cent.

Some additional polls of the period further document the contrasting impressions left by the Egyptian President's February visit and the Israeli Prime Minister's visit in March. During the first week in April, 1978, CBS repeated questions it had asked in October 1977, just prior to the Sadat initiative. The question and answers:

> "Some people think the United States should pay more attention to the demands of the Arabs, even if it means antagonizing Israel, while other people think the U.S. should give its strongest support to Israel, even if it means risking an Arab oil boycott. If these were the only two choices, what should the U.S. do—pay more attention to the Arabs, or give our strongest support to Israel?"

	April 1978	October 1977
Support Israel	43%	54%
More Attention to Arabs	29	27
Neither/Both (volunteered responses)	12	8
No Opinion	16	11

Complex wording of the question and mention of an oil boycott may have influenced some, but since it was asked in exactly the same manner before and after President Sadat's journey to Jerusalem and his subsequent, widely publicized statements, it does have value in measuring changes for the period.

Opinions held by the educated elite are generally believed to be precursors of opinions of the general public. Therefore possibly the most significant development of the period was a dramatic reversal in the perceptions of the Middle East protagonists by university-educated Americans, who in earlier years were stronger supporters of Israel than the public at large. In the October 1977 CBS poll above, they still backed Israel over the Arabs 49 to 34 per cent. By April 1978 the tables had turned. University graduates supported the Arabs over Israel by 40 to 36 per cent. Answers to two other CBS questions, in mid-March and in April, brought out a similar shift in opinions by university graduates in favor of Sadat and Egypt and away from Begin and Israel:

"In general do you approve or disapprove of Egyptian President Anwar Sadat's/Israeli Prime Minister Menachem Begin's handling of Arab-Israeli relations?"

| | General Public | | College Graduates | |
March 1978	Sadat	Begin	Sadat	Begin
Approve	57%	34%	80%	33%
Disapprove	27	46	12	55
No Opinion	16	20	8	12

"Israel and Egypt are trying to negotiate a peace settlement. Do you think Israel/Egypt has made too many concessions, not enough concessions, or the right amount of concessions?"

| | General Public | | College Graduates | |
April 1978	Israel	Egypt	Israel	Egypt
Too many	12%	6%	7%	4%
Not enough	50	43	63	34
Right number	19	40	19	51
No Opinion	19	11	11	11

The polls did not indicate how much the Sadat initiative, while clearly diminishing support for Israel and enhancing support for Egypt, affected American opinion about the Arabs as a whole. Already the American public, and college graduates in particular, seemed well aware of the growing divergence of opinion in the Arab camp, as revealed by this April 1978 CBS question:

"Do you think the other Arab states feel as Sadat does, or do you think that Sadat speaks only for Egypt?"

	Total Public	College Graduates
Sadat speaks only for Egypt	65%	73%
Others feel as Sadat	16	12
No Opinion	19	15

The period of intense effort and frequent disagreements between negotiation of the Camp David agreements in September 1978 and the treaty signing on the White House lawn in March 1979 provided several impressions of what the American public thought of the activist American role. In late December, 1978, a Harris poll found that most Americans, specifically including American Jews, wanted the U.S. to remain even-handed, at least when the question indicated the President was tilting toward Egypt:

"President Carter took the side of Egypt in this latest Middle East disagreement. Do you think he was right to back Egypt or should he have backed Israel, or should he not have backed either side?"

	Shouldn't Back Either	Right to Back Egypt	Should Back Israel	Not Sure
Total Public	59%	22%	6%	13%
Jews	68	14	12	6
Catholics	61	24	5	10
Protestants	56	23	7	14

A January 1979 Gallup question found strong majorities of the total public, Israel sympathizers, and Arab sympathizers in agreement that U.S. policy toward Israel and Egypt was even-handed: "Do you think President Carter is leaning too much in favor of Israel, too much in favor of Egypt, or do you feel he is treating both sides equally fairly?"

	Total Public	Pro-Israel Public	Pro-Arab Public
Treating both fairly	62%	61%	68%
Favoring Israel	11	10	18
Favoring Egypt	10	17	5
No Opinion	17	12	9

Another January 1979 Gallup poll demonstrated that even pro-Israel sympathy did not preclude criticism of Israeli policies. A majority 54 per cent of those who expressed sympathy for Israel said Israel was "not doing all it should" to achieve peace, while 36 per cent of Israel's sympathizers disagreed. The same Israel sympathizers were only slightly more critical of Egypt than they were of Israel, with 62 per cent saying Egypt was not doing all it should.

Those polls, at a time of maximum U.S. involvement in the Egyptian-Israeli negotiations, indicated that although many Americans were not abandoning old loyalties, they were nevertheless willing to criticize specific actions of either side and were supportive of an activist U.S. policy to achieve a peace treaty, so long as they perceived it to be even-handed and fair.

During 1979, U.S. public opinion movements became almost too minor and subtle to track. Though implementation of each new normalization step between Egypt and Israel was adequately reported in the United States, Americans who were aware of the Camp David agreement provisions had simply assumed from the beginning that all of the agreements would be carried out. Therefore photographs of a Star of David flag flying over the Israeli Embassy in Cairo, or an Egyptian airliner landing in Israel, made little further impression.

Continuing acts of violence in Israel and Lebanon were reported in the U.S. media, but through sheer repetition they had lost some of their former impact in arousing American public opinion against the perpetrators. Disturbances in the West Bank, and the killing of Palestinian demonstrators, showed Americans an unfamiliar, ugly side of Israel, and perhaps eroded some of the still-considerable public support for Israel. They may have been a significant factor in the already-visible shifts among better educated and better informed Americans. However, negative images from these events were no doubt offset to varying degrees by other Middle East events.

The taking of American diplomatic hostages in Iran was depicted by partisans of the Arabs at the time as the "latest disaster" for U.S. public opinion. They noted that in the immediate aftermath of the Tehran Embassy seizure, angry American demonstrators made no ethnic distinctions, apparently confusing Iranians with "Arab oil sheikhs" in their signs and slogans. If the role of Algeria in retrieving the hostages again helped popular U.S. perceptions of the Arabs, the actions of Colonel Qaddafi did not.

Developments within the U.S. also had little apparent effect on opinion, except within the American Black community. There the resignation of President Carter's representative to the United Nations, Ambassador Andrew Young, had a visible effect on perceptions of the Arab-Israeli dispute. Among Americans in general it was regarded more in terms of a breach of State Department discipline than in terms of dissent—in the national interest—from the Carter administration's inherited policy of no substantive contacts with the PLO until the latter recognized Israel's right to exist. Blacks however felt that only Israel's insistence turned a relatively routine matter into a cause for Young's resignation. Among American Jews with the same perception, there were some private bitter comments at Israel's apparent heedlessness, in pressing for short-term political advantage over the Carter administration, of the ultimate cost to U.S. Jews in terms of their relations with American Blacks.

The issue had considerable repercussions as Black delegations visited both sides in the Middle East. Some, like the Reverend Jesse Jackson and the Southern Christian Leadership Conference, focused their attention on West Bank Palestinians and the PLO. Others, like Vernon Jordan's Urban League, concentrated on fence-mending visits with Israeli leaders. There were angry words in the wake of these trips, with individual Jewish financial backers of Black and civil rights organizations vowing "never again," and Blacks depicting the fracas as still another manifestation of Black-Jewish tensions which crystallized over affirmative action and ethnic quotas. These were perceived by Blacks as a tool to pull themselves up, and were perceived by Jews as a threat that could hold them down in the fluid American social structure.

Black delegations to the Middle East, no matter whether they seemed to favor the Palestinians or the Israelis, all espoused similar messages of non-violence. It remained to be seen, therefore, whether those who visited PLO Chairman Arafat, and who reported to fellow Americans his moderate remarks, would be disappointed at the PLO's subsequent failure to follow up or support Arafat's statements that he would ultimately be willing to settle for less than a democratic secular state embracing the whole of pre-partition Palestine. So long as the PLO refused to play its "last bargaining chip," recognition of Israel's right to exist, there was little chance that American public perceptions of the PLO, as distinct from the Palestinians, would change radically. There was also little evidence that the PLO, engrossed as it was in Third-World, inter-Arab and intra-Palestinian politics, really thought a change in American public opinion very important to it at that time.

For that period the Gallup polls are the most instructive, since they were directly comparable to all the preceding years. Israeli support had plunged to an all-time low of 33 per cent in February 1978, after direct Egyptian-Israeli talks were broken off and President Sadat was so successfully carrying his side of the story directly to the American people. Arab support, by contrast, had reached an all-time high, up to then, of 14 per cent. In May 1978 Israeli support had recovered to 44 per cent, in August this slipped to 42 per cent, and in November, after the Camp David framework agreements had been reached but differences in interpretation seemed about to destroy them, Israel had slipped back to 39 per cent. Support for the Arabs slipped from 14 per cent in February back to 10 per cent in May 1978, but from then on the trend was again upward, with 11 per cent in August and 13 per cent in October, 1978.

In January 1979 Israeli support had returned again to 42 and in August 1981 to 44, about the median for all the gyrations since the October War. The Arab support meanwhile reached an all-time high of 15 per cent in 1979 and 11 per cent in 1981, still far below support for Israel but significantly higher than at any time before late 1977. The number of Americans who told Gallup interviewers they had been following Middle Eastern events reached 93 per cent in November 1978, 92 per cent in January 1979, and slid back to 81 per cent in 1981.

There has been no comparable Gallup poll since August 1981. However, a number of other polls have indicated both the relative stability of U.S. opinion since the Egypt-Israel treaty was signed, and some of the subtleties that have entered into this body of opinion as Americans have become increasingly aware of Middle Eastern issues.

An October 1979 Harris poll demonstrated that although American support for Israel has dropped significantly since 1974, a majority still oppose reducing political or military support for Israel to ensure adequate Arab oil. Following are the two relevant Harris questions and answers:

> (1) "Tell me if you tend to agree or disagree. We need Arab oil for our gasoline shortage here at home, so we had better find ways to get along with the Arabs, even if that means supporting Israel less."

	Oct. 1979	March 1979	Jan. 1976	March 1975	Dec. 1974
Agree	33	39	23	26	20
Disagree	60	55	65	61	68
Not Sure	7	6	12	13	12

(2) "If it came down to it and the only way we could get Arab oil in enough quantity would be to stop supporting Israel with military aid, would you favor or oppose such a move by this country?"

	Oct. 1979	March 1979	Jan. 1976	March 1975	Dec. 1974
Favor	29	31	20	23	18
Oppose	60	57	61	55	64
Not Sure	11	12	19	22	18

Most opposed to cutting military aid to Israel to secure Arab oil were the university-educated, professionals, and those earning more than $25,000 annually, of whom about 25 per cent favored and 65 per cent opposed the proposition. Even more interesting is the fact that although the issue is oil, not peace, the significant movement toward the Arabs on the issue was not recorded until after the Sadat journey to Jerusalem. It seems fair to deduce that American public opinion reacts negatively to any implication of bullying or blackmail on Middle Eastern issues. It will only change or be persuaded if given a relatively altruistic rationale for supporting a step, even if that step is also in America's own self-interest.

Particularly noteworthy is the fact that the better-educated, the more affluent, and the professional-managerial categories—those who presently are most supportive of the Arabs—are those least amenable to "oil weapon" pressure. This is the lesson that American friends of the Arabs emphasize in advising moderate Arabs on how best to make their case to the American public.

Perhaps related to the results above, U.S. public concern about an oil shortage has begun to diminish from its peak in May 1977, based on a question asked by the Roper organization twice a year since the end of the oil embargo. The question and answers:

"Here is a list of statements about the gasoline and oil shortage. Which one of these statements comes closest to expressing your opinion?"

	Sept. 79	May 79	Nov. 78	May 78	Nov. 77	May 77	Nov. 76	May 74
There is a very real oil shortage and the problem will get worse during the next 5 to 10 years.	28	25	31	32	33	40	26	21
There is a real oil shortage but it will be solved in the next year or two.	9	12	10	8	14	15	11	12
There was a short term problem, but it has been largely solved and there is no real problem any longer.	7	6	9	9	9	6	8	8
There never was any real oil shortage—it was contrived for economic and political reasons.	52	51	41	45	39	33	46	53
None of the above, don't know, no answer.	4	6	7	6	5	6	9	6

The university-educated, the executives and professionals, and those earning $25,000 or more were most convinced that oil supplies would tighten during the next 10 years. But even among those, belief in a worsening oil shortage declined from about 55 per cent in May 1977 to 45 per cent in May 1978, compared to a decline from 40 to 32 per cent for the public as a whole.

A February 1979 Roper poll reflects American awareness of Saudi Arabia's key role in world oil production. Respondents were asked to rate Saudi Arabia, Egypt and Israel in terms of importance to the U.S. The question and answers:

"Here is a list of different countries. Would you read that list and for each one tell me how important you think it is to the well-being of the United States that we have good relations with it?"

	Saudi Arabia	Israel	Egypt
Very Important	59%	57%	53%
Fairly important	24	27	29
Sub-total	(83)	(84)	(82)
Not very important	7	8	9
Not at all important	3	3	2
Sub-total	(10)	(11)	(11)
Don't know	7	5	7

A March 1979 Harris poll asked respondents to rate the same three countries in terms of friendliness to the United States. The answers, when compared to the same Harris question and answers for 1974, show a remarkable increase for Egypt and a substantial one for Saudi Arabia although Israel retains its lead.

"As far as you are concerned, do you feel that (Israel, Egypt, Saudi Arabia) is a close ally of the U.S., is friendly but not a close ally, is not friendly but not an enemy, or is an enemy of the U.S.?"

	Israel		Egypt		Saudi Arabia	
	Mar. 1979	Dec. 1974	Mar. 1979	Dec. 1974	Mar. 1979	Dec. 1974
Close ally	30%	26%	16%	1%	6%	1%
Friendly	49	49	51	25	36	21
Sub-total	(79)	(75)	(67)	(26)	(42)	(22)
Not friendly	12	10	20	44	31	41
Enemy	2	1	3	9	6	8
Sub-total	(14)	(11)	(23)	(53)	(37)	(49)
Not sure	7	14	10	21	21	29

Of significance for the next steps in Middle East peacemaking efforts was a Harris poll assessing desire for peace which showed that in less than two years Americans had moved Egypt from well behind to slightly ahead of Israel and in the same period significantly increased their positive assessment of the PLO's desire for peace.

The question and results:

"Do you feel that (Israel, Egypt, the PLO) really wants a just peace in the Middle East, only reluctantly wants a just peace, or really does not want peace?"

	Israel			Egypt			PLO		
	Aug. 79	Jan. 78	Oct. 77	Aug. 79	Jan. 78	Oct. 77	Aug. 79	Jan. 78	Oct. 77
Really wants peace	59	51	55	63	52	37	18	13	13
Reluctantly wants peace	23	27	20	21	25	27	23	18	15
Sub-total	(82)	(78)	(75)	(84)	(77)	(64)	(41)	(31)	(28)
Doesn't want peace	11	8	6	8	7	9	45	44	35
Not sure	7	14	19	8	16	27	14	25	37

American Jewish respondents gave far higher ratings to both Egypt and Israel than did the population as a whole, with some 90 per cent believing that both countries "really want" peace. By contrast, among the same Jewish respondents, only 14 per cent think the PLO "really wants" peace, 22 per cent think it "reluctantly wants" peace, and 62 per cent believe the PLO "doesn't want" peace. Blacks were the only group of which a plurality (33 per cent) believed the PLO "really wants" peace, with 22 per cent saying it "reluctantly wants" peace, 26 per cent saying it "doesn't want" peace, and 19 per cent not sure.

A July 1979 Roper poll found an overwhelming majority of Americans opposed the use of troops to increase the oil output from OPEC countries. The question and responses:

> "Most of our imported oil comes from the OPEC countries—Libya, Iran, Venezuela, Saudi Arabia and other Arab nations. The OPEC countries have recently cut back on the amount of oil they produce and have announced they do not intend to increase their production now or any time soon. Do you think the United States should try to force the OPEC countries to produce more oil, using U.S. military forces if necessary, to accomplish that?"
>
> | | |
> |---|---|
> | U.S. should not use force | 73% |
> | U.S. should use force | 17% |
> | Don't know | 10% |

There are records of 11 different questions asked nationally by polling organizations between 1967 and 1978 on the public's willingness to help defend Israel in case that country were attacked, with some of the questions asked two or three times. The answers vary widely, depending upon wording of the questions and sometimes, apparently, the polling organization itself. In November 1978 a Department of State public affairs opinion analyst summarized these findings as follows:

"Our main conclusion from studying the responses to these questions is that public expressions of willingness to help defend Israel with U.S. troops depend largely on two factors: (1) The seriousness of the threat said to be facing Israel, and (2) the range of possible U.S. responses to this offered in the question. Only about 10 per cent of the public expresses willingness to defend Israel with American troops when the question contains these conditions: (1) Israel is being attacked (but there is no indication it is being beaten); and (2) the choice of how the U.S. should respond to that attack includes sending either military supplies *or* American troops to help defend Israel. .. . . Support for defending Israel with American troops doubles to about 20 per cent when the question omits the military supply option and simply asks whether the U.S. should or should not send troops to help defend Israel against attack. Those respondents who would prefer the less risky course of sending military supplies rather than American troops are 'forced' by this type of question to say 'yes' or 'no' to the proposal to send troops, and some of them respond 'yes.' Thus, it provides a better gauge . . . of the upper limits of public support for sending U.S. troops in case of attack. Finally, when the threat confronting Israel is posed in terms of saving that country from defeat (not just helping it repulse an attack), an additional 10 per cent of the public favors sending U.S. troops to Israel's defense. Thus, given this very high level of threat and the troops/no troops option, about 10 per cent say they are willing to send American troops to prevent Israel's defeat."[3]

With the end of the Carter administration and the beginning of the Reagan administration, events in the Middle East tended to strengthen three growing public perceptions. Although in Israel emphasis moved from Jewish religious settlements in the West Bank to Israeli fulfillment of its Camp David commitments, nevertheless Israeli actions in the West Bank and Lebanon made Israel seem increasingly pugnacious and militaristic. In Egypt, President Sadat continued to project an image of moderation and statesmanship, though this image sometimes seemed more appreciated abroad than in Egypt itself. Finally, the rest of the Arab world seemed from the U.S. vantage point to remain essentially negative, refusing to offer peace terms or conditions of its own.

The result was almost no movement in American public opinion, despite such sensational events as Israel's bombing of the Iraqi nuclear reactor, the bombing of a residential area in Beirut with the reported loss of 300 lives, and finally the tragic assassination of President Sadat.

Why the Israeli air attacks on the Iraqi reactor and on Beirut had no clear effect on American public attitudes toward either side is suggested by responses to Roper questions in July and August 1981 about each of the bombings. After the bombing of the Osirak reactor, 57 per cent of those polled told Roper interviewers they believed the Iraqis were "planning to make nuclear bombs." After the Beirut bombing, even though 41 per cent told Roper interviewers they disapproved of the Israeli action, only 16 per cent of all respondents said they disapproved strongly.

A CBS/*New York Times* poll released in early July reflected similar results. Of those queried, four-fifths said they had heard about the raid on Iraq. These in turn were evenly divided on whether the Israeli attack was justified. However, they opposed "punishing" Israel by better than three to one. Because the question referred to "punishing" Israel, respondents may have interpreted it to mean severe U.S. actions, rather than limited sanctions such as suspending deliveries of advanced military equipment.

A July 1980 Harris poll found that a plurality of respondents said they would approve "threatening" to withhold economic and military aid from Israel if it became "so unbending that the chances for peace in the Middle East grew much worse." In response to that question, 44 per cent approved such a threat, while 37 per cent disapproved. Responses to another question on the same Harris poll showed the public was disinclined to withhold aid from even a recalcitrant Israel if that meant the "Arabs would have military superiority in case of another war." Responses to that question showed 25 per cent approved withholding aid versus 50 per cent who disapproved.

An indication of where the Arab-Israeli dispute stands in terms of public opinion priorities was provided by a February 1981 Roper poll. It asked respondents about the use of U.S. troops in eight different situations. The poll showed only 26 per cent of Americans would favor use of U.S. troops even in case of an invasion of Israel by Arab countries. The results:

Sending U.S. Troops	Favor	Oppose	Don't Know
If U.S. Embassy employees were taken hostage again in some other country	64%	24%	12%
If Soviet troops invaded Western Europe	51	35	14
If the Soviet Union invaded West Berlin	46	41	13
If Cuban troops were involved in a Communist take-over of a Central American country	42	42	16
If Arab forces invaded Israel	26	58	16
If Soviet troops invaded Poland	23	58	19
If North Korea invaded South Korea	20	63	17
If Soviet troops invaded Iran	17	69	14

The lack of American public support for the Palestinians has long puzzled Arabs familiar with the U.S. tradition of sympathy for the underdog. It is less puzzling if one examines closely the answers to slightly different questions on the subject. The U.S. public is not so basically pro-Israel and anti-Palestinian as superficial consideration might imply. In fact, PLO use of what seem to Americans to be terrorist methods supporting the Palestinian cause, rather than the cause itself, bothers Americans.

In 1977 and 1979 the Roper organization asked: "As you may know, the Palestinian Liberation Organization in the Middle East—known as the PLO—wants to establish a homeland for Palestinians on territory occupied by Israel since 1967. Do you think the PLO is right or wrong in wanting to establish a Palestinian homeland in Israel (in 1980 this was changed to "in Israeli-occupied territory"), or haven't you paid much attention to it?"

The results (in percentages):

	August 1980	Oct-Nov 1979	July 1977
Right	19	26	21
Right, but their methods are wrong (volunteered)	8·	14	9
	(total positive 27)	(total positive 40)	(total positive 30)
Wrong	25	17	20
Haven't paid much attention	31	33	33
Don't know	16	10	17

To the 1980 poll Roper added this question: "If the PLO agreed to recognize the existence of Israel and also stopped its military raids on Israel, do you think Israel should agree to the idea of a homeland for Palestinians on territory now held by Israel, or don't you think they should agree to such a Palestinian homeland?" When the Palestinian homeland was coupled with PLO recognition of Israel, 39 per cent said they thought "Israel should agree." This 39 per cent of respondents was then asked: "Suppose the PLO agrees to recognize Israel and stop its raids, but Israel won't go along with the idea of a Palestinian homeland. In that case, do you think we should or should not reduce U.S. military supplies to Israel until it agrees with the idea of a Palestinian homeland?"

Responses to the two questions:

Israel should agree to a Palestinian homeland if the PLO recognizes Israel	39%	
Favor strong pressure on Israel to accept it		19%
Oppose strong pressure		15
No opinion about pressure		5
Israel should not agree to a Palestinian homeland	21	
No opinion about a Palestinian homeland	40	

From these answers one can reach a number of conclusions about U.S. public opinion and the Palestinians. First, support for a Palestinian homeland peaked in 1979, when it clearly enjoyed the support of a U.S. President (Carter). This was a period close to the Sadat initiative and the generally favorable upturn of American feeling about the Arabs that followed it.

Second, more Americans think the idea of a Palestinian homeland is right than think it is wrong, but only if one includes those Americans who disassociate the idea of a Palestinian homeland from the methods of the PLO.

Finally, if PLO recognition of Israel is included in the question, then Americans favoring a Palestinian homeland outnumber those opposing it by nearly two to one.

Significantly, although Democrats and Republicans hardly differed in their opinions about a Palestinian homeland, those who were better educated, executives and professionals and those who were in higher income brackets were significantly more favorable to the idea. Some 50 per cent of university-educated respondents, of executives and professionals, and of those earning more than $25,000 annually, said Israel should agree to a homeland for the Palestinians if the PLO recognized Israel. About 25 per cent from the same categories said Israel should not agree.

No more than one quarter of any population group approved U.S. pressure on Israel to accept a Palestinian homeland. University-educated respondents, however, were more willing to pressure Israel than those without a university education, by 24 to 15 per cent.

Perhaps the most striking evidence that Americans are moved positively by evidence of conciliation and moderation such as that exhibited by President Sadat in late 1977, and negatively or not at all by pressure such as the Arab oil boycott in late 1973, is provided by a series of Roper polls over a nine-year period. Respondents were asked exactly the same question in each poll:

"At the present time do you find yourself more in sympathy with Israel or more in sympathy with the Arab nations?" The results:

Sympathize	8/81	7/81	4/80	5/78	1/78	3/77	12/74	11/73
More with Israel	39	35	37	35	37	43	41	47
More with Arab nations	10	10	10	9	10	5	5	7
Egypt, but not other Arab nations (volunteered)	3	2	2	1	1	—	—	—
Both equally (volunteered)	10	11	15	15	16	13	13	10
Neither	23	22	21	22	20	23	25	18
Don't know	16	19	15	18	16	16	18	17

These Roper results confirm that between March 1977 and January 1978, spanning the October 1977 Sadat journey to Jerusalem, pro-Israel sympathy declined six points and pro-Arab sympathy rose five points (not including additional pro-Egyptian sympathy), both reaching the approximate levels they still maintained three years later.

NOTES

1. Rosenfeld, Geraldine, "Attitudes of the American Public Toward Israel and American Jews: The Yankelovich Findings," The American Jewish Committee Information and Reference Services, December, 1974.
2. Rosenfeld, Geraldine, "Attitudes of the American Public Toward Israel and American Je   The Yankelovich Findings, January, 1976," The American Jewish Committee Information and Reference Services, March 1976, pp. 1-3.
3. Bureau of Public Affairs, Department of State, memorandum of November, 1978.

PARTISANS OF ISRAEL OR THE ARABS

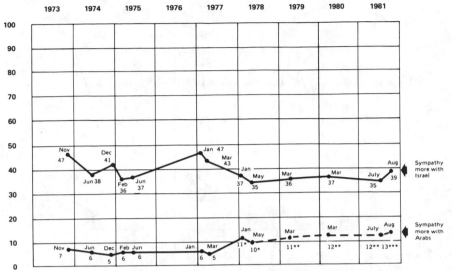

*Includes one percent volunteering sympathy for
Egypt alone, but not the other Arab states.

**Includes two percent volunteering sympathy for
Egypt alone, but not the other Arab states.

***Includes three percent volunteering sympathy
for Egypt, but not the other Arab states.

RESPONDENTS EXPRESSING NO PREFERENCE BETWEEN ARABS OR ISRAELIS

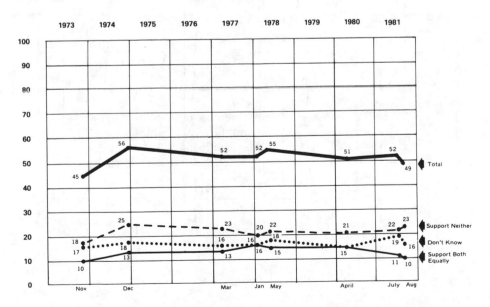

GALLUP POLL RESULTS 1967 - 1981

AMERICAN SUPPORTERS OF ISRAEL OR THE ARABS

Sympathy more with Israel

Sympathy more with Arabs

AMERICAN RESPONDENTS CLAIMING TO BE FOLLOWING MIDEAST EVENTS

June 1967 War

Egypt-Israel War of Attrition 1969-1970

October 1973 War
Arab Oil Embargo
Oct. '73 - March '74
Sinai I - May 74

Shuttle Breakdown
March 1975
Sinai II - May 1975

Sadat to Jerusalem
November 1977
Sadat to US
February 1978
Camp David
September 1978
Egypt-Israel Treaty
March 1979

Index

SMALL TOWN CHICAGO

Kennikat Press
National University Publications
Interdisciplinary Urban Series

General Editor
Raymond A. Mohl
Florida Atlantic University

JAMES DeMUTH

SMALL TOWN CHICAGO

The Comic Perspective of
FINLEY PETER DUNNE
GEORGE ADE
RING LARDNER

National University Publications
KENNIKAT PRESS // 1980
Port Washington, N.Y. // London

For My Parents
Leonard and Bernice DeMuth

Manufactured in the United States of America

Published by
Kennikat Press Corp.
Port Washington, N. Y. / London

Library of Congress Cataloging in Publication Data

DeMuth, James, 1943 –
Small Town Chicago

(Interdisciplinary urban series) (National
university publications)
Bibliography: p.
Includes index.
1. American wit and humor–History and
criticism. 2. Chicago in literature. 3. City
and town life in literature. 4. American newspapers–Illinois–Chicago–History. 5. Dunne,
Finley Peter, 1867-1936–Humor, satire, etc.
6. Ade, George, 1866-1944–Humor, satire, etc.
7. Lardner, Ring Wilmer, 1885-1933–Humor,
satire, etc. I. Title. ~~R003098660~~
PS430.D44   817'.5'20932   79-19853
Library of Congress Cataloging in Publication Data
ISBN O-8046-9252-1

CONTENTS

ACKNOWLEDGMENTS

I wrote my book about Chicago while living in Minneapolis and teaching in Wisconsin. Removed though I was from the city, I was fortunate to receive the support and advice of Professor Joseph Kwiat of the University of Minnesota. His long experience with Chicago and detailed knowledge of the city's cultural history were invaluable; I am indebted to him for his careful reading and perceptive criticism of my manuscript through its several stages of writing and revision.

Other faculty members of the University of Minnesota were also generous with their time and attention. Professor Bernard Bowron introduced me to the principal works of American literary realism and naturalism; I draw upon his ideas in developing my argument in Chapter 5, though I define American literary naturalism more broadly than he. Professor David Noble has shaped my understanding of popular artists; his reading of my original essay on Dunne, Ade, and Lardner was most helpful.

I wish to express my special gratitude to Professor Mary Turpie. My understanding of American Studies has been most influenced by her teaching and her example. Her sensitive reading of my manuscript, and her advice throughout the years, have been extremely valuable. Finally, I want to thank Cornell Jaray, president of the Kennikat Press Corporation, for his suggestions for my manuscript's final revisions.

From beginning to end, my book has taken five years. The work has been satisfying because of the tolerant and intelligent help of my wife Anne. She has carefully read each page from rough draft to final copy, and her advice throughout the course of my work has been indispensable.

SMALL TOWN CHICAGO

James DeMuth is an assistant professor of English at the University of Wisconsin in River Falls, Wisconsin.

INTRODUCTION

Our national humorists have been distinguished artists. They have loosened the nation's tongue and invigorated its literature, have first brought to the printed page and the popular stage the vivid, unschooled speech of their neighbors. The humorists with whom this book is specifically concerned—Finley Peter Dunne, George Ade, and Ring Lardner—initiated an American urban humor. In the years between 1890 and 1920, while working as Chicago journalists, they introduced a national audience to the characteristic speech, mannerisms, and attitudes of various Chicagoans. In reading their syndicated columns, magazine features, and best-selling books, Americans heard a Chicago saloonkeeper, Mr. Dooley, explain that politics "ain't no bean bag," a brash young office clerk from the South Side, Artie Blanchard, affectionately mock the "main squeeze" for whom he worked, and a rookie White Sox pitcher, Jack Keefe, complain about "the rotten support I got that beat me."

Through these comic characters, and others, Americans heard Chicagoans speaking without pretension, without much concern for the proprieties of the schoolmarm or the genteel sensibilities of the literati. Here was a new humor and a new regional American language recorded. However, though the vocabulary was often novel, the image of American society expressed by these humorists was familiar. They represented Chicago as provincial, its people as simple and neighborly. It is this combination of novel language and familiar sentiments which made their humor so entertaining. They made Chicago comprehensible; one could see their comic characters as types of people one had seen, if not exactly heard, before.

Of all the major American cities of the last quarter of the nineteenth century, it is understandable that Chicago should have produced our first nationally popular urban humorists. As a social environment, Chicago contained the same mix of the new and the traditional which they captured in the speech, prejudices, and sentiments of their representative characters. In outward appearance, Chicago in 1890 was not a city but a frontier boomtown, having exploded in population from 368,000 in 1871, the year of the Chicago Fire, to nearly 1,300,000 in 1893, the year of Chicago's World's Columbian Exposition. Much of its population had been drawn directly from the towns and villages of the Old Northwest Territory, the middle South, and the developing Midwest. Its people, while nostalgically retaining their rural habits and attitudes, were also eagerly grabbing for the new riches this boom city offered. To men seeking opportunity, Chicago seemed a horse traders' town on the grandest scale yet, a town of real estate speculators and grain futures gamblers, a rich market which bought, processed, and shipped the meat and produce of a vast region.

Chicagoans, as a people, were on the make, looking for the "main chance." Roughshod, belligerent, and uncultured, this rude city had sprung from the grandiose ambitions of the Davy Crocketts, Mike Finks, Henry Clays, and Stephen Douglases of an earlier frontier, expansionist region. Yet, for all of its frontier swagger, the Chicago of 1890 was distinct from its immediate past. It was cosmopolitan. The city contained a complex, bewildering variety of ethnic cultures. The census of 1890 records 41 percent of the population as foreign-born, with the Irish, German, Bohemian, Polish, and Scandinavians constituting the major groups. It had also begun to create those institutions which would make it cosmopolitan in civilization, as well as in population. The Newberry Library and the Chicago Auditorium were built in 1889, the University of Chicago in 1892, the Chicago Art Institute in 1893, and Orchestra Hall was completed in 1904. Chicago, then, in 1890, was a society of immigrants, widely diverse in cultures, classes, and education, all faced with the experience of creating and understanding a city. This was the kind of novel experience—similar to the expe rience of creating and understanding a democratic nation—which had always been the inspiration for American humorists.

While one can see the general environment of Chicago, in its contrasts, novelties, and extravagances, as conducive to the creation of an urban humor, the young city also provided a more specific medium for its popular artists: the Chicago newspapers. The period from 1890 to 1920 is perhaps the most brilliant and enthusiastic period in all of Chicago journalism. In Chicago newspapers, during this period, the modern style of American sportswriting—anecdotal, dramatic, sentimental, and jocular—was created and refined; in Chicago newspapers, political reporting was frank and critical; in Chicago newspapers, particularly the *Daily News* and the *Daily Tribune*, the arts and entertainment pages were informed and lucid. Among Chicago's distinguished journalists were the daily columnists Eugene Field, Hugh E. Keogh, and Bert Leston Taylor, the reporters Brand Whitlock, Charles Seymour, and Ray Stannard Baker, the art reviewers and critics Wallace Rice, Mary Ives Abbott, Burton Rascoe, Percy Hammond, and Harriet Monroe, the sportswriters Walter Eckersall, Hugh Fullerton, and Charlie Dryden, and the political cartoonists John T. McCutcheon and Thomas E. Powers.

It was within this fertile environment of an intelligent, professional press and a robust, cosmopolitan society that Finley Peter Dunne, George Ade, and Ring Lardner perceived the humor of an American city. Though, in the decades of the 1920s and 1930s, New York City would make urban humor a national art in the vaudeville routines of Al Jolson, Eddie Cantor, and Fannie Brice, the wit of Robert Benchley, James Thurber, and E. B. White, the movies of the Marx Brothers, Katharine Hepburn, Fred Astaire, and Ginger Rogers, and the sophisticated lyrics of Cole Porter and Ira Gershwin, it is Chicago, in the 1890s and early twentieth century, which can claim the distinction of priority. It is the enthusiasm of that first discovery and the excitement of that first success which I want to recover in this study of the lives and works of three Chicago journalists.

1

CHICAGO AND CHICAGO NEWSPAPERS

Chicago in the 1890s was the most dynamic boom city of nineteenth-century America. In the twenty years from 1870 to 1890, its area and population had increased fivefold. At the time of the great Chicago Fire of 1871, the young city encompassed 35 square miles and counted approximately 368,000 people as its citizens; by the opening of the World's Columbian Exposition on May 1, 1893, Chicago had incorporated 185 square miles and grown to nearly 1,300,000 people.

By 1890, Chicago was the second largest and wealthiest city in the nation. In the six decades since its incorporation, it had far outstripped its principal rival, St. Louis, in their competition for the trade and industry of the mid-continent. As a measure of Chicago's economic significance, one can note the city's capacity to store 32,800,000 bushels of grain, the 10,000 manufacturing establishments on its tax rolls, and the $664,567,923 estimated gross value of its manufactured products in 1890. Chicago dominated the extensive national railway system, and, in its South Chicago foundries, produced immense quantities of steel.

Chicago's rise to national prominence had been swift and, in some ways, unexpected. When first settled in the 1830s, the new town seemed very poorly situated: its few buildings lay in the swampy basin of the Chicago River; its people suffered from the extremes of a harsh climate and from the diseases bred in their impure water and inadequate sewerage. Michigan City and Milwaukee appeared more likely gateways to the expanding trade of the Northwest: each was located on higher, drier ground than Chicago; each supported larger populations; each enjoyed superior harbor facilities. However, by dint of several large-scale public enterprises—incredibly ambitious and expensive projects for Chicago's taxpayers—the city dramatically improved its position. Under the mayoralty of "Long John" Wentworth, Chicagoans laboriously raised their commercial buildings twelve feet to fill in the twelve hundred acres of swamp on which they rested. In March 1867, Chicago completed the tunnel under two miles of Lake Michigan to tap the city's first pure water supply. On July 18, 1871, after four years of dredging operations, Chicago successfully reversed the flow of the south branch of the Chicago River ("Garlic Creek") to provide its citizens their first dependable sewer. The most celebrated of Chicago's civic feats, though, was the reconstruction of the city after the Chicago Fire of 1871 had devastated three and one-half square miles of homes and business.

In 1891, the United States Congress recognized Chicago's wealth, energy, and strategic location, as well as the persistent demands of its free-spending citizens' lobby, with the commission to host the World's Fair to commemorate the four-hundredth anniversary of Columbus's discovery of the Americas. The city which prepared to build, in two years, the most extensive World's Fair was significantly different from the city which, two decades earlier, had begun the task of reconstruction after the Chicago Fire. The Chicago of 1871 had been comfortably proportioned and socially attractive. Its people had lived, for the most part, in free-standing, single-family frame homes. Chicago's residential streets, if unpaved, were uncrowded, and its neighborhoods were relatively unsegregated.

The Chicago of 1891 was a different city. The vast increase in population had created a critical housing shortage and an unmanageable demand on municipal services. Over 49 percent of Chicagoans lived in dwellings housing more than ten occupants; one-third of the population had no toilet accommodations other than crude privy vaults; one-half of the children of Chicago died before reaching five years of age. The most dramatic social effects of Chicago's population explosion, though, were not caused by the simple increase in numbers, immense as it was, but by the identity of the new citizens. Chicago's population was swelled by the influx of European immigrants—approximately fifty thousand a year during the 1880s and 1890s—largely drawn from the impoverished and illiterate rural populations of southern and eastern

Europe and Ireland. Of the 1,099,850 Chicagoans in the 1890 census, only 223,206 were native white Americans of native white parents: in the space of twenty years, the percentage of native white Americans in Chicago's population had dropped precipitously from about 50 to 25 percent.

This great increase in foreign population profoundly changed the character of Chicago society. The Chicago citizen of 1871 had been very conscious and proud of his city's intimate cultural ties with New England and the states of the Old Northwest Territory. He counted among Chicago's leading citizens many men who had moved from New England villages and towns with little more capital than their enthusiasm to succeed and their willingness to work long hours. "Long John" Wentworth, Chicago's popular mayor and congressman, had arrived in 1836 from Sandwich, New Hampshire, with a Dartmouth College degree and twenty dollars; William Ogden, the Chicago capitalist who built the city's first western rail lines, had migrated from upstate New York in 1835; George Pullman, builder of the fabulous "Palace Cars," had been a carpenter in Brocton, New York; Marshall Field, Chicago's "Merchant Prince," had managed a small retail store in Pittsfield, Massachusetts; Potter Palmer, the developer of State Street, had come from Albany, New York; Philip Armour was a native of Stockbridge, Massachusetts; Gustavus Swift, the "Yankee of the Yards," hailed from West Sandwich, Massachusetts. Below these business titans were large numbers of managers, salesmen, accountants, and agents who, like their employers, had come to Chicago from the villages and cities of the Northeast.

Chicago in 1871 was a Union, Republican, and Yankee city. It counted among its business leaders Joseph Medill, publisher of the Chicago *Daily Tribune,* who, in 1856, had helped found the Republican party. Abraham Lincoln, Medill's political protégé, had been nominated at the 1860 Republican convention in the Chicago "Wigwam." During the Civil War, Chicago had sent fifteen thousand volunteers to the Union Army and had subscribed heavily to the war bond issues. Chicago was the chief provisioner of the Union cause—Cyrus McCormick's reaper, manufactured in Chicago, greatly increased food production and freed many farm youths to serve in the Union army—and after the war it offered fertile opportunity for Union veterans.

Of Chicago's foreign-born population in 1871, the large majority were of northern and western European stock, easily assimilated by the native population. The 1870 census records 10 percent of Chicago's foreign-born population as English, Scottish, and Welsh in origin, 37 percent from the German states, 10 percent from Scandinavia, and 7 percent from British America. The only intractable foreign-born population in Chicago in 1870 was the Irish, who comprised about 13 percent of the total population. The Irish were separated from Chicagoans by their religion and their politics. They were the largest Catholic population in the city, they were the chief support of the Democratic party, and they had openly sympathized with the Confederate states during the Civil War.

By 1891, the minority social forces represented by Chicago's Irish had grown to considerable importance. A large proportion of Chicago's new European immigrants were Catholic, and they proved an overwhelming challenge to the "Americanization" efforts of Chicago's public schools, settlement houses, and Protestant churches. In addition, they were largely enrolled in the ranks of the Democratic party, often by mass registrations and bloc voting, which violated the native Chicagoan's sense of political "fair play."

By 1891, "Yankee" Chicago was 65 percent Catholic and governed by a Democratic mayor and city council. The city council, especially, was a galling reminder of how the influence of Chicago's native Americans had eroded. The "grey wolves" of the council, led by Johnny "de Pow" Powers, boss of the "Bloody Nineteenth" Ward, openly demanded bribes and favors for the permits, ordinances, and municipal services they delivered. "Hinky Dink" Kenna and "Bathhouse John" Coughlin, the Irish political lords of Chicago's notorious "Levee," the wide-open vice district on the south edge of the Loop, delivered the decisive vote blocs in the mayoral campaigns from 1892 to 1908, with the sole exception of George Swift's narrow 41,000 vote majority in the election of 1896.

The burgeoning foreign population had, in many ways, displaced native Chicagoans from their homes. Large quarters of the city, particularly those political wards immediately surrounding the Loop, were completely given over to the expanding foreign population. The German population, originally a small community on the Near North

Side, had expanded into the Fourteenth, Fifteenth, and Sixteenth wards to the North and Northwest. The Irish had pushed out from their original settlement in "Bridgeport" in the Sixth Ward into the adjacent areas of the Fifth, Seventh, and Eighth wards around the lumberyards, stockyards, and foundries, where they found employment. The blocks between Halsted Street and Ashland Avenue from Chicago Avenue to Sixteenth Street were known as "Pilsen" because of the many Bohemian people concentrated there. There was a "Poor Jews Quarter" of Russian and east Europeans spreading out from the west end of the Twelfth Street bridge; there were "Little Sicilies" in the Twenty-second Ward east of the Chicago River, along Grand Avenue west of the Chicago River, north of Twelfth Street in the "Bloody Nineteenth" Ward and in "The Dive" along south Clark Street and Harrison Avenue.

Chicago's Loop, by 1891, was tightly enclosed by the ghettos of its immigrants. Outside this ring, Chicago's middle-class, native citizens had moved into the new residential districts serviced by the commuter lines. In the center of the ring, along exclusive streets running parallel to Lake Michigan, many of Chicago's wealthy citizens lived in newly built mansions. The separation of Chicago's neighborhoods reflected the strict segregation of classes, ethnic groups, and races which, ever since the 1890s, has marked Chicago's society. In becoming a city of one and one-third million people, Chicago sacrificed the informal heterogeneity of its early expansion; each class, nationality, and race was separate, and the differences among Chicagoans were greatly accented.

Not only had the people and neighborhoods of Chicago changed, the methods by which the city conducted its business were also significantly different from the practices known in 1871 and earlier. Chicago had been known as a "young man's town," with abundant opportunities for young men—particularly young native American men—of talent, ambition, and persistence: "Go to Chicago now," "Deacon" Bross, Chicago's most enthusiastic booster, had exhorted audiences in his tour of eastern United States cities in the weeks immediately after the fire of 1871. "Go to Chicago now. Young men, hurry there! Old men, send your sons! You will never again have such a chance to make money."[1] His appeal was electric. The stories of young men who had risen by their merit to positions of high success abounded in the folklore of Chicago and the nation. Marshall Field had begun his career as an $8.00 a week clerk; Potter Palmer, Philip Armour, Allan Pinkerton, George Pullman, and Cyrus McCormick had all begun their Chicago business enterprises with little or no capital.

Chicago in the 1890s was no longer a "young man's town." The city's labor market was severely depressed. Even in "good times" the great surplus of unskilled foreign laborers depressed the wages of Chicago workers. For those Chicagoans who were particularly ambitious, opportunities in real estate, finance, industry, and sales were restricted. Chicago businesses, like other large businesses in the nation, had developed into powerful trusts. Through rebates, political bribery, and price fixing, they effectively stifled the competition of new enterprises, and within their large organizations, the prospect of rapid advancement was slight.

Not only were jobs and opportunities limited, but employment was insecure. During the latter part of the nineteenth century, in Chicago and throughout the nation, the frequency and duration of economic depressions increased. Chicago suffered a major depression in the middle years of each decade from 1870 to 1900. Each of these depressions was marked by widespread violence as the new labor unions struck to protest layoffs and wage cuts: the railroad strike of July 1877 threw Chicago into ten days of civil disorder; on May 4, 1886, a three-month strike against the McCormick works culminated in the Haymarket Riot; in the summer of 1894, armed mobs roamed Chicago streets in support of the Pullman strikers.

The "good times" between economic depressions did not materially improve the lot of the Chicago worker. Bessie Louise Pierce, the noted Chicago historian, has estimated that food prices increased between 50 and 100 percent and that overall living costs rose between 15 and 40 percent in the prosperous years from 1879 to 1881 while wages remained stationary. She concludes that in those times of prosperity between 1871 and 1893, nearly half of all Chicago workingmen depended on the supplementary wages of women and children to maintain family subsistence.

The demoralizing effects of Chicago's social and economic conditions are perhaps best illustrated in the public response to two closely related events of the 1890s: the World's Columbian Exposition of 1893 and the Pullman strike of 1894. These events are separated by the months of economic depression—the first months of a four-year depression—which are known, in the history of Chicago, as the "dismal winter of 1893." In those winter months, Chicago experienced the full force of the business paralysis which had gripped the nation throughout the summer. The city had no place to house the unemployed, no institutions to relieve their distress, and no budget to employ them. Countless numbers of unemployed men slept in the corridors of City Hall and in the cells of Chicago's prisons. The most ingenious and effective response to their need came not from the city's politicians nor from its business leaders, but from its saloonkeepers. The Chicago saloons dispensed the famous "free lunch" with the purchase of a nickel beer—and often with no purchase—and provided floor space to lodge vagrants at night.*

Chicago's vertiginous descent from the summer of World's Fair prosperity to the "dismal winter of 1893" was particularly marked because the economic and social promise of the fair had been so great. The World's Columbian Exposition was a remarkable American social achievement, especially for a western American city. The new industrial cities of the West—Cincinnati, Detroit, Cleveland, Milwaukee, Minneapolis, Chicago—were disordered, hastily overbuilt, and unhealthy. However, in the buildings, parks, gardens, and lagoons of the "White City" of the Exposition, a distinguished committee of the nation's architects, engineers, and artists had created, in only twenty months, a commodious, clean, and beautiful public facility scaled to accommodate large masses of people. "Today, looking back," Justus Doenecke has commented, "the fair seems to have been . . . the conscious effort to humanize the burgeoning industrial order by enveloping it in pastoral motifs. To an American awed by the advent of technology, shocked by the sheer ugliness of steam engines and turbines, and

---

*"The suffering in the city was very great and would have been very much greater had it not been for the help given by the labor unions to their members and for an agency which, without pretending to be of much account from a charitable point of view, nevertheless fed more hungry people this winter in Chicago than all the other agencies, religious, charitable and municipal, put together. I refer to the Free Lunch of the saloons." William T. Stead, *If Christ Came to Chicago!* (Chicago: Laird and Lee, 1894), p. 142.

apprehensive about the possibility that the new factories would only lead to class war, the exposition served to mollify many fears. By skillful planning, a new era of progress and promise could be revealed."[2]

The heady prophecies of a regenerated city heralded by the fair quickly evaporated in the bank failures and plant lockouts of 1893 and 1894. The widening spiral of economic distress reached its furthest limits in the Pullman strike of 1894, which, at its height in July, incited a series of wildcat strikes that plunged Chicago into seven days of civil disorder. On July 7, 1894, at the very peak of the Pullman strike disorders, the deserted fair buildings were set fire by vandals and burned to the ground.

Of the many effects of the Pullman strike, perhaps the most profound was the general disillusionment of Chicagoans—not only the affected workers, but middle-class Chicagoans as well—in the good faith of their political and economic leaders. In promoting the World's Fair, Chicago's leaders had apparently endorsed the spirit of municipal reform, public planning, and social welfare. The most visionary of the millionaire sponsors was George Pullman, who, in addition to his generous support of the fair, had anticipated its promise of civil order, comfort, and beauty in building the model community of Pullman on the west shore of Lake Calumet in 1881.

During the economic depression of 1893 and 1894, George Pullman grossly violated the enlightened social consciousness he had long advertised. While he exacted only enough in rents and prices from his tenant employees to yield the 6 percent return he expected from his investment, he reduced their wages by 40 percent and laid off a number of them. The Pullman workers, caught between the demands of their landlord and the economy of their employer, struck the Pullman plant on May 11, 1894. George Pullman obstinately refused to meet with them, evicted their leaders, and employed scab labor to run his plant.

In his unyielding response to the strike and to the financial plight of his tenants, George Pullman shattered the illusory optimism of the World's Fair. Public sentiment swung to the cause of the strikers. Pullman was widely castigated for his selfish indifference to the responsibilities he had assumed in building a model community for his employees: "If ye be ill, or poor, or starving, or oppressed, or in grief," Eugene Field savagely began his "Sharps and Flats" column for the Chicago *Daily News,* "your chances for sympathy and for succor from E. V. Debs are 100 where your chances with G. M. Pullman would be the little end of nothing whittled down."[3]

The events of 1893 and 1894 which I have discussed were extreme but not atypical. The dizzying descent from the prosperity of the World's Fair to the depression and strikes of the following months compressed within a short time span the now familiar social pattern of boom and bust that had afflicted Chicagoans each decade since 1870. The challenge facing the Chicagoan of the 1890s, other than the immediate challenges of securing employment and adequate housing, was the challenge of understanding and accepting his city and his place in it. It was a difficult challenge; most of the Chicagoans of the time had not long been urban citizens. The majority of them had either migrated to Chicago from the rural Midwest or had immigrated to Chicago from Ireland, Poland, Italy, or other European countries. If a man had been born in Chicago, it was quite likely that his parents had not.

Chicago in 1890 had few traditions of civilization, and its people lacked a coherent sense of identity and place. The 1890s, and the early decades of the twentieth century, were years of Chicago's gradual self-perception; its people began, hesitantly, to accommodate their habits, ideas, and prejudices to their urban destiny. Mr. Dooley, in one of his early monologues from the Chicago *Sunday Post,* has humorously described this awakening recognition of the city as an acceptable, even attractive, place to live:

> "But I must go back," I says, "to th' city," I says, "where there is nawthin' to eat but what ye want an' nawthin' to dhrink but what ye can buy," I says. "Where th' dust is laid be th' sprinklin' cart, where th' ice-man comes reg'lar an' th' roof garden is in bloom an' ye're waked not be th' sun but be th' milkman," I says. "I want to be near a doctor whin I'm sick an' near eatable food whin I'm hungry, an' where I can put me hand out early in th' mornin' an' hook in a newspaper," says I. [No. 15, p. 49] *

---

*Citations in brackets refer to numbered entries in the Select Bibliography.

As Mr. Dooley's comments lightly illustrate, the Chicago daily news-papers played a significant role in identifying a Chicagoan's place and purpose. It was in the pages of his paper that a Chicagoan was ad-dressed directly and familiarly by such writers as Mr. Dooley; it was in those pages that he found the array of his city acquiring a co-herent form in news reports and editorials; it was the daily paper which amused him and influenced his sentimental, as well as rational, perception of himself as a citizen of the second city in the nation.

Of the Chicago newspapers, the two most significant, and the two on which the national renown of Chicago newspapers rested, were the Chicago *Daily Tribune* and the Chicago *Daily News.* The *Tribune* was one of the earliest Chicago papers, and the first to attain national prominence. Begun on June 10, 1847, only fourteen years after the incorporation of Chicago, the *Tribune* assumed its distinct and in-fluential editorial position eight years later when Joseph Medill, publisher of the Cleveland *Leader,* purchased a third interest. To-gether with Deacon William Bross and John Locke Scripps, Medill shaped the *Tribune* into the vigorous public organ of the Republican party, an effort which culminated in 1860 in the nomination of Abraham Lincoln. From his first days as managing editor of the *Tribune,* Medill promoted the career of State Representative Lincoln: Lincoln's speeches were printed in full text; long editorials commended his public stands; Medill organized a caucus of Illinois editors in 1858, following the Lincoln-Douglas debates, to publicize Illinois's favorite son as candidate for president. With its influence in the Lincoln ad-ministration, and its privileged access to war news, the *Tribune* became the paper which the nation identified with Chicago.

By the 1890s, the *Tribune*'s prestige, though still considerable, was shared and in some measures eclipsed by the *Daily News,* the evening paper begun on January 1, 1876, by Melville Stone; by May 1888, the month in which Stone sold his interests to Victor Lawson, it had at-tained an average paid circulation of 190,700. From its first issues, the *Daily News* was designed to be a paper distinct from the *Tribune* and also distinct from the reporting and editorial practices then common-place among the existing Chicago papers.

The *Daily News* was intended to be a modern and an urban paper. For a year before he ventured into its publication, Melville Stone studied the New York *Daily News* and the Philadelphia *Star* to learn the style and organization of successful one-penny daily newspapers in major cities. The publishing guidelines which Stone adopted were these: the paper must be nonpartisan, with its editorial judgments explicitly identified; moreover, the publisher must have no economic interest other than his newspaper. The strict separation of news and business departments was reflected in the *Daily News*'s reservation of its entire first page to news, a novelty at the time, and by the *Daily News*'s refusal to sell advertising in space committed to news, editorials, or features; moreover, it prosecuted fraudulent advertisers whom it discovered. Unlike that of the *Tribune,* which served its partisan interests by reprinting entire speeches and delivering multicolumned editorials, the style of the *Daily News* was concise: "The idea of its founders," Victor Lawson later commented, "was to give the greatest amount of news in the smallest amount of space for the very least amount of money."[4]

The *Daily News* earned its security and reputation through its prompt, complete, and fair coverage of the great railroad strike of July 1877. Beginning with editorials denouncing the railroads' wage policy—a 10 percent reduction in wages had been ordered by the major rail lines—the *Daily News* continued with full reports of the strikes and riots which were spreading through eastern cities. During the weekend, July 21 and 22, the *Daily News* published several special editions to keep Chicago readers abreast of the rapidly growing national strike. On Monday, a delegation of Chicago businessmen, all advertisers in the *Daily News,* called on Stone and Lawson with a request to suspend publication of the strike reports. This blatant appeal was rejected, and throughout the next weeks, when the strike was in full force in Chicago, the *Daily News* presented its reports. It dispatched reporters on horseback throughout the city to the various centers of disturbance; in its editorials it urged strikers to refrain from violence, but it also continued to denounce the railroads' policy. By the conclusion of the strike, the paper had given full and unusual demonstration of its independence and its sympathy for wage workers.

Building on its reputation gained in reporting the great railroad strike, the *Daily News* quickly set the pace for Chicago papers in the full and responsible coverage of political and economic controversies. One of its methods was unusual and not duplicated by other papers; Melville Stone eagerly and successfully pursued what he called "detective journalism." He personally tracked down and brought to justice several Chicago miscreants, the full exploit of his sleuthing being reported in the *Daily News*. He exposed "King Mike" MacDonald, the Democratic boss, as a jury fixer and police grafter by obtaining the confession of Dick Lane, a burglar then imprisoned in Michigan State Prison. After that he followed the trail of D. D. Spencer, president of the bankrupt State Savings Bank of Chicago, across Canada and western Europe to Cannstatt, where a confession of forgery and embezzlement was obtained. This feat of detection resulted, ultimately, in the passage of an act by the state legislature providing for the inspection of savings banks. Stone continued to engage in these private detections during the whole time he held an interest in the *Daily News.*

Though less sensational, the public-spirited campaigns for political reform which the *Daily News* initiated were of more lasting and general influence. For ten years, from 1888 to 1898, the *Daily News* led the campaign of criticism, exposure, and indictment against Charles Yerkes, the streetcar magnate and corrupt power behind the Democratic party. The issues came to a head when Yerkes obtained from the state legislature an act authorizing the Chicago city council to grant him a fifty-year franchise. With the backing of Mayor Carter Harrison and an aroused public, the *Daily News* intimidated the council into rescinding its approval, secured the defeat of several state legislators, and won the repeal of the state law. In response, Yerkes purchased the Chicago *Inter-Ocean* and for two years conducted a bitter editorial campaign against the "newspaper trust" and its head, "Ricewater" Lawson.

As a result of its efforts against Yerkes, corrupt aldermen, Chicago gamblers, and venal public officials, the *Daily News,* together with the *Tribune* and an association of Chicago business and civic leaders, joined forces to form the Municipal Voters' League in 1896. The executive head of the league was George C. Cole, and his candidate, George Swift, was elected mayor in the 1896 campaign. A further fruit of the *Daily News*'s political efforts, and of its influence on other papers and civic organizations, was its exposure of William Lorimer, congressman and Republican boss elected to the U.S. Senate by the Illinois legislature in 1909. To its credit, the *Tribune* took up the fight against the corrupt Republican and pursued its investigations for two years, finally securing from the U.S. Senate a vote declaring Lorimer's seat vacant. The *Tribune* continued its efforts to reform Chicago's

Republican party throughout the administrations of William Hale Thompson.

Committed to public service and accurate, independent editorial comment, the Chicago newspapers, under the leadership of the *Daily News,* created an environment which stimulated a distinct attitude and style in American letters. Because of their greatly expanding circulations, and the explosive growth of the city, the Chicago papers required many new writers, and it is during this period of the 1890s and early twentieth century that we find employed on the staffs of the Chicago papers, either as reporters, feature writers, or occasional contributors, several of the writers who would create the new style of American realism: Henry B. Fuller, Hamlin Garland, Booth Tarkington, Theodore Dreiser, Harriet Monroe, Carl Sandburg, Ben Hecht, and Sherwood Anderson. "The newsrooms and the men in charge taught the new literature, its subject matter and style, to the young and incoming writers," comments Wilmer Kleinsteuber in an early study of the influence of Chicago's newspapers. He continues:

> The newspapers' reputation for exposing the social injustices in the interest of the public caused the social environment to be the main point of interest. They taught writers to search for the facts which led to better characterization and motivation in novels. The continuing association of the new writers with the social conditions of the average man, required by their newspaper duties, naturally tended to direct these writers to social subjects in their serious writings.[5]

The influence of the Chicago papers on the style of American realism was not only the indirect influence of a stimulating environment, it was the explicit editorial policy of the book and arts review editors. Because of the *Daily News*'s pioneering efforts—it established the first books and art review page in a Chicago paper—and especially because of the generous, enlightened policies of Victor Lawson, there came into being a concentration of Chicago newsmen who believed in literary principles for newspapers. As an indication of the depth of Lawson's commitment to literary excellence, I would note his hiring of Henry Justin Smith as city editor. Smith was an honors graduate of the University of Chicago, having majored in Greek: he was hired for his intelligence, sensitivity, and command of a lucid style. It was Smith who recognized and encouraged Carl Sandburg's genius, allowing the young reporter wide freedom and considerable leisure in pursuing his assignments.

The roster of critics and reviewers employed by the Chicago papers is impressive. Walter Cranston Larned, William Norton Payne, Henry B. Fuller, Henry Blackman Sell, and Ben Hecht reviewed art, literature, and drama for the *Daily News;* Burton Rascoe and Percy Hammond were the leading critics on the *Tribune;* Llewellyn Jones, Francis Hackett, and Charles Collins made the Chicago *Post* an able competitor of its larger rivals. At a time when established papers in eastern cities were either denigrating or ignoring the new writers, American and European, the Chicago critics recognized their value and enthusiastically promoted their works. Furthermore, the Chicago papers contributed materially to the support and publicity of Chicago's distinguished literary magazines of the time, the *Dial, Poetry* and the *Little Review.* In an enthusiastic and typically iconoclastic article, written in 1920, Henry L. Mencken identified Chicago as "the literary capital of the United States," asserting extravagantly, "Go back twenty or thirty years and you will scarcely find an American literary movement that did not originate under the shadow of the stockyards."[6]

The Chicago newspapers fulfilled, very well, their responsibility of making the city comprehensible to its citizens. Though a man might be forced to ride the dirty, rickety streetcars of Charles Yerkes, suffer the high costs of political "rake-offs," and accommodate the rising stench and noise of his overcrowded neighborhoods, he could find in the editorials of his paper, in the columns of investigative reporting, and even in the sensational accounts of Melville Stone's detective exploits, forces competent to deal with the strange conditions of his life. He could follow the affairs of the Municipal Voters' League and recognize his value as a citizen. Furthermore, he could, if sufficiently educated and sensitive, take pride in Chicago's growing distinction as a center of civilization and an impetus in the creation of a distinct American art.

There is one other means, and perhaps it was the most influential, by which the Chicago papers informed and instructed their public. The papers, after all, were addressed to a wide, popular audience; Melville Stone deliberately established the *Daily News* as a one-penny paper. The common denominator in the papers, which appealed across the range of their subscribers, was the entertainment section: the sports page, the reviews of popular theater, and the columnists. It was through these writers that Chicago was made familiar and comfortable to its citizens. In this respect, also, the *Daily News* led its competitors; it employed the first full-time columnist on an American newspaper, Eugene Field. From 1883 until his death on November 4, 1895, Field wrote the entertaining "Sharps and Flats" column for the *Daily News*. In that distinguished column, through sentimental verse, local gossip, humorous parodies, and personal opinions, Eugene Field demonstrated how one man could comprehend, accept, and enjoy the daily rounds of his city.

The popular writers who are the subjects of this book—Finley Peter Dunne, George Ade, and Ring Lardner—were the successors of Eugene Field. Dunne worked briefly with Field on the staff of the *Daily News*, and Ade wrote for the morning edition of Field's *Morning Record*. Ring Lardner had no direct contact with Field, but he knew his work, and by the time Lardner began his career on a Chicago paper the tradition of the daily columnist was well established; in June 1913 Lardner assumed the *Tribune*'s column "In the Wake of the News." These three writers continued and developed the essential motives of Field's popular art. Like Field, they reduced the chaos and complexity of Chicago to the familiar routines, modest ambitions, and homely virtues of its ordinary citizens. They demonstrated, with brief stories of the familiar domestic circumstances in which working-class and middle-class people lived, that Chicago could be understood and that one might find satisfaction and humor in being a Chicagoan.

The appeal of Dunne's, Ade's, and Lardner's stories rests in large measure on their efforts to domesticate the unfamiliar features of Chicago society which disturbed their readers. Through the character of Mr. Dooley, an Irish bartender and ward politician, Finley Peter Dunne confronted and diffused the prejudices of Chicagoans against the enormous foreign-born population in their city. The Irish of Chicago, particularly, had long been castigated for their sympathy with the South during the Civil War, their obstinate loyalty to the Catholic church, and their abuse of power in Chicago's influential Democratic party. Mr. Dooley, however, is a moderate, moral, and patriotic American, and—by dint of his long residence in Chicago— more native than most Chicagoans. Though he spoke with a brogue, he voiced the values Chicagoans esteemed.

George Ade, in the many "Stories of the Streets and of the Town" which he composed for his column in the Chicago *Record,* sympathetically described the earnest efforts of Chicagoans, from young, native-born Americans to the poorest of the foreign immigrants, to find employment, housing, and social acceptance in Chicago. He often reduced the awesome conditions of job competition and economic fluctuation to simple moral vignettes. If one were honest, personable, and ambitious, then, like Artie Blanchard, Min Sargent, Arthur Ponsby, or any number of Ade's other Chicago characters, one could reasonably expect a job, a room, and a welcome in the city. Occasionally, an Ade character will fail, through no fault of his morals or personality; but Ade's emphasis is on the satisfaction which hard work and clean habits will bring.

Though Ade was quite popular with Chicago newspaper readers for his "Stories of the Streets and of the Town," he reached national popularity with his *Fables in Slang.* Ade's *Fables* are characterized by their flippant maxims—"Moral: Never Live in a Jay Town"—and the sharply etched "Chicagoese" slang in which they were written— "She had all the component Parts of a Peach, but she didn't know how to make a Showing, and there was nobody in Town qualified to give her a quiet Hunch." At the time Ade wrote his *Fables,* slang was a disturbing symptom of community decay in the city; it was the language of the streets and underworld, the argot of the prostitutes, gamblers, criminals, and juvenile toughs who infested Chicago's wide-open "Levee" district on the south edge of the Loop. Ade retrieved this language from the underworld and edited its obscene diction. He made it, in this purified form, the exuberant language of office clerks, shopgirls, and small politicians. With his slang, George Ade initiated a wide national audience into the fads and fashions popular with Chicago's young people.

Ring Lardner's effort to present Chicago in a familiar and reassuring light was more tense and self-conscious than that of Dunne and Ade. His intention wavers between satire and sympathy. Lardner's style, therefore, often emphasized Chicago's debasing effect on speech. Dunne and Ade's urban language had been rich and inventive: Mr. Dooley's Chicago-shaped brogue and George Ade's Chicago slang are both exciting and original languages, rich in comic metaphors, puns, and coined words. The language of Lardner's characters, though, is usually flaccid. The habitual grammatical errors, meager diction, and vulgar expletives all reflect the moral debasement of Chicago's middle-class. The dour style of Lardner's satire reflects, it can be said, a general feeling of disappointment noticeable in Chicago writing of the period 1910–30. The 1890s had held great promise of creativity and accomplishment, which declined in the early decades of the twentieth century. Artistically, in the 1890s, Chicago was bubbling with the informal institutions—the Dill Pickle Club, the Cliff Dwellers' Club, the Whitechapel Club—and the men consciously engaged in exploring freshly an American city and an American style of frank, realistic literature. In the 1890s there had been occasion for pride in the creative spirit of the city, symbolized by the World's Columbian Exposition, and in its institutions for social reform, particularly the Municipal Voters' League. By the 1910s the spirit of Chicago had declined; the promises of civic reform were quenched in the administrations of William Hale ("Big Bill") Thompson and the machinations of William ("Billy") Lorimer. Also, this period witnessed the steady migration to New York City of the writers who had made an early reputation in Chicago. From the time of his first substantial success (*You Know Me, Al*–1916), Ring Lardner prepared himself for his move to New York City in 1919.

The tension between Lardner's satire on Chicagoans and his sympathy with his popular audience gives his stories a complexity lacking in Dunne and Ade's stories; but it does not remove them from the traditions of popular humor, which Dunne and Ade had accepted and broadened to include urban themes and characters. Each of these popular writers tried to represent Chicago as a familiar society; each tried to assimilate urban language and urban characters into the conventions and attitudes which had developed in nineteenth-century American humor. In the chapters which follow, I intend to illustrate this common motive and its partial success. I will argue that Dunne, Ade, and Lardner are significant for initiating, in American popular humor, a broad awareness of urban mannerisms and, also, that they are significant for demonstrating the need for a distinctly urban identity. With the popular urban writers and entertainers who follow them, particularly those in New York City during the 1920s, we will recognize that identity. They are decidedly less reverent toward the sentimental conceptions of American village communities and folk characters than were Dunne, Ade, and Lardner; these conceptions, though, did shape the responses of

Dunne, Ade, and Lardner to the city in which they worked and in which they found their initial success. By examining some of their principal early writings, we will find, I believe, that their works reveal an increasing constriction in the vitality of the nineteenth-century traditions which they honored and sought to preserve.

2

FINLEY PETER DUNNE

Finley Peter Dunne* was the only native Chicagoan of our three journalists, and he was one of the few native Chicagoans among the city's prominent newsmen. He was born and raised in St. Patrick's parish on Chicago's near West Side; his family home was on West Adams Street near the intersection of Adams and Desplaines. At the time of his birth (July 10, 1867), St. Patrick's parish was a solidly middle-class, Irish neighborhood; "Pete" Dunne's father, Peter Dunne, owned a small lumberyard and some real estate parcels; the Dunne household included a cook and occasional domestic help. By the time of Dunne's graduation from West Division High School in June 1884, St. Patrick's parish was becoming a blighted neighborhood, spotted with the light industries, warehouses, and transportation facilities of Chicago's commercial district.

It was Peter Dunne's familiarity with Chicago, drawn from a life spent close to the city's center and from a father and relatives who actively worked in their ward's Democratic politics, which became his entry into Chicago journalism. He knew at first hand, and thought them to be commonplace, the political methods of bribery, favoritism, and chicanery. The mechanics of his city's politics—which would appear as a revelation and a disgrace to the "muckrakers" of his day—were, to Peter Dunne, the ordinary topics of his father's and neighbors' conversations.

*Christened Peter Dunne; he added "Finley," his mother's maiden name, to his signature six years after her death.

When the young Peter Dunne sought employment in June 1884, Chicago journalism was a fluid, intensely competitive enterprise of some dozen daily papers. Luckily, Dunne found a position, of sorts, on his first day of application. He was hired by the Chicago *Telegram,* the poorest and most precarious of all the Chicago papers. It survived, its competitors suspected, by blackmailing its regular advertisers. Dunne offered the paper an economical means of covering the local news. He was a young man who knew the Harrison Street police station, the local fire houses, and the county and city courts—and he would work for twelve dollars a week. He was assigned the police beat.

Dunne's career in Chicago journalism, from his humble beginnings with the *Telegram* until 1892, when he began the Irish dialect features for the Sunday edition of the Chicago *Post,* was a record of quick advancement. Building on his initial advantage of being a native son, Dunne rapidly moved from one paper to another as he could interest editors in his knowledge of the city and in his demonstrated ability as a reporter. After nine months with the *Telegram,* he moved on to the *Evening News.* In quick succession, during the next seven years, he worked for the *Times, Daily Tribune, Herald,* and *Evening Post.* While on the staff of the *Times,* at age twenty-one, he was the city editor; for the *Daily Tribune,* he was an editor on the Sunday edition; and for the *Evening Post,* he was the editorial page editor.

The Chicago newspapers were Dunne's university; they even provided him a fraternity, the Whitechapel Club, which he and other young journalists organized as a place to meet, drink, argue, and carouse. The name was inspired by that section of London frequented by Jack the Ripper, and the club met regularly in the backrooms of two Chicago taverns located on "Newspaper Alley" (Calhoun Place). The decorations were ghoulish (weapons from local crimes adorned the walls, the bar was coffin-shaped, and skulls were placed about as centerpieces) and the pranks of the fraternity brothers were occasionally as macabre. Their most notorious escapade, an account of which they sold as an exclusive story to the *Herald* (July 17, 1892), was their cremation of the body of "Club Member Collins" at Miller's Station, Indiana, on the shore of Lake Michigan. Collins, a melancholy, impoverished poet and pamphleteer, had proposed to his fellow Whitechapel Club members a plan of mass suicide to dramatically protest the evils of capitalist exploitation. He then committed suicide by drinking poison and, in the long agonies of his death, composed a fervent last will and testament concluding with the request that the Whitechapel Club cremate his body. The club honored his memory in a gaudy ceremony complete with formal procession, original odes, and eulogies—all of which, they claimed, were inspired by Trelawney's account of the burning of Shelley's body.

Though often juvenile and outrageous in their pranks, the Whitechapel Club members also proved to be an intellectual stimulant for Peter Dunne. Witticism was their favorite sport and the club's highest distinctions went to its "sharpshooters"—those men, Peter Dunne prominent among them, who could best ridicule and silence an honored guest or ambitious member. It is said that the Whitechapel reporters composed their copy with an eye not only for their editors' demands but also for any slips in style or sentiment which might provide ammunition for a "sharpshooter."

The Whitechapel nights formed and tested Dunne's maturing comic style. He was also educated, more formally and charitably, by his senior colleagues on the Chicago papers. While on the staff of the *Evening News,* he worked with Eugene Field and learned from Field that fine balance of sentiment and irony which marks his best work. Dunne's talent for humorous epigrams was encouraged by several editors seeking to enliven their editorial pages and increase their papers' circulation. Cornelius McAuliff of the *Post* would personally read Dunne's copy and then, chuckling over the pages in hand, would walk from his office to the newsroom to read aloud the latest of Dunne's *bons mots.*

One of Dunne's assignments which contributed to his style, particularly in training his ear for the nuances of vernacular speech, was his assignment in 1887 to cover the Chicago White Stockings, then managed by "Cap" Anson and including such colorful players as the great pitcher John Clarkson and the speedy right fielder Billy Sunday. In covering the White Stockings, a championship team the previous two seasons, Dunne, together with Charles Seymour of the *Herald,* largely shaped the modern forms of American sportswriting. Previously, baseball reports had been the dry recitals of turns at bat and inning summaries. Dunne and Seymour, though, made the baseball story coherent and dramatic by highlighting the game's crucial moments and by writing in a familiar, partisan style. They used the ball players' slang as technical terms and thereby influenced the vocabulary by which we now understand baseball. Dunne, specifically, is credited with the introduction of "southpaw," for, in Comiskey Park, left-handed pitchers threw from the south side.

Baseball, editorial witticisms, and "sharpshooter" nights at the Whitechapel Club were part of Dunne's newspaper experience; politics and art completed his education. His political education ranged from an initiation into the criminal feuds of secret Irish nationalist groups to investigations of the "grey wolves" on the city council. The most profound and personally disturbing revelation to Dunne of the corruption and criminality possible in political causes was his discovery of the murderer of Dr. Cronin. Dr. Cronin was a member of the secret Irish nationalist group, the Clan-na-gael; it had been overtaken by Arthur Sullivan and its funds diverted to his personal use. Dr. Cronin openly opposed Sullivan, and on May 4, 1889, he mysteriously disappeared. With the aid of William Pinkerton, police detective Jack Shea, and Patrick Ryan, an ex-detective and close friend of Pinkerton, Dunne pieced together the crime. He discovered and proved that Dan Coughlin, the police inspector in charge of the investigation, was Dr. Cronin's murderer. Then Dunne witnessed the subversion of justice: in the retrial made necessary by the State Supreme Court's invalidation of the original verdict, Sullivan corrupted the public prosecutor and secured a reversal of Coughlin's guilty verdict. The investigation and trial was Dunne's only "scoop" as a reporter, but it formed forever his skeptical distrust of all political causes and politicians.

Apart from politics, which he daily reviewed as an editorial writer, Dunne gained a liberal education in society and the arts as a Chicago newspaperman. One of his close friends, a fellow member of the Whitechapel Club, was the young businessman Robert Hamill, son of a director of the Chicago Board of Trade. Hamill introduced Dunne into select circles of Chicago and acquainted him with their cultural amusements. Dunne's appreciation of the arts, though, as something more than amusement came through his work and friendship with Mary Ives Abbott. An independent, cultured, and widely traveled person, Mary Abbott, after the death of her husband, moved to Chicago and found employment as the arts and book review editor of the *Evening Post.* Dunne, through his professional and personal association with her, acquired the informed taste in literature and theater which was to make his conversation a treasured memory of his many friends.

Peter Dunne, a young man of twenty-five who in 1892 began writing Irish dialect monologues for the *Sunday Post,* was by virtue of his talent, experience, and friendships an exceptional journalist. The opinions of his comic Irish bartenders (first Col. McNeery, then Martin Dooley), though written in low dialect, were informed, intelligent, and incisively phrased. As an example of the clarity of Dunne's mind and the vigor of his expression, his Mr. Dooley monologue on George Pullman is outstanding. Dunne wrote this monologue in the summer of 1894 (August 25) when the Pullman strike had reached grievous levels of class animosity and personal misfortune. George Pullman had locked out his striking workers and evicted their families from his company town, Pullman, Illinois. In thinking about his motives and actions, Mr. Dooley is moved to an intense, controlled rage:

> Mr. Dooley swabbed the bar in a melancholy manner and turned again with the remark: "But wat's it all to Pullman? Whin Gawd quarried his heart a happy man was made. He cares no more f'r thim little matthers iv life an' death thin I do f'r O'Connor's tab. 'Th' women an' childhern is dyin' iv hunger,' they says. 'Will ye not put out ye'er hand to help thim?' they says. 'Ah, what th' 'ell,' says George. 'What th' 'ell,' he says. 'James,' he says, 'a bottle iv champagne an' a piece iv crambree pie. What th' 'ell, what th' 'ell, what th' 'ell.'"[1]

The reception of this Mr. Dooley essay was unique. After the typesetter had run his proof of the entire piece (I have quoted only a small portion of it), he circulated it around the composing room. When Dunne entered the room to check the proof, the typesetters all began to drum their sticks on their cases, and then they broke into a long, sustained applause. It was, Dunne later recalled, the most moving experience of his life.

The popularity of Dunne's comic Chicago barkeep, Martin Dooley, was due both to the outspoken comments he made and to the familiar mold in which Dunne had cast his character; he was the novel embodiment of the crackerbarrel philosopher. Like such predecessors as Jack Downing, Hosea Biglow, Artemus Ward, and Josh Billings, Mr. Dooley exemplified the pride and self-assurance of a satisfied American villager. But unlike the earlier comic characters whom he closely resembled, Mr.

Dooley was not a rustic. His crackerbarrel wisdom expressed the world of a Chicago tavern, and his "village," though as parochial as any New England village or midwestern county seat previously invoked in American popular humor, was the Irish-American Sixth Ward on Chicago's industrialized South Side.

The Sixth Ward, or "Bridgeport," as it was (and still is) more commonly known, was the original settlement of Chicago's Irish, who had come to work on the Illinois and Michigan Canal and had stayed to labor in the mills, foundries, and factories of South Side Chicago. In the preface to his first collection of Mr. Dooley essays, Dunne emphasized for his readers those traditional and unique qualities of Irish culture which distinguished Bridgeport as a community within Chicago:

> In this community you can hear all the various accents of Ireland, from the awkward brogue of the "far-downer" to the mild and airy Elizabethan English of the Southern Irishman, and all the exquisite variations to be heard between Armagh and Bantry Bay, with the difference that would naturally arise from substituting cinders and sulphuretted hydrogen for soft misty air and peat smoke. Here also you can see the wakes and christenings, the marriages and funerals, and the other fetes of the ol' country somewhat modified and darkened by American usage. The Banshee has been heard many times in Archey Road. On the eve of All Saints' Day it is well known that here alone the pookies play thricks in cabbage gardens. In 1893 it was reported that Malachi Dempsey was called "by the other people," and disappeared west of the tracks, and never came back. [No. 11, p. vii]

Dunne's choice of Bridgeport, and Mr. Dooley, was largely accidental. In the first Irish dialect stories which he wrote, Dunne had delivered his opinions through the character of "Col. McNeery," a voluble Irishman whom Dunne had closely modeled after James McGarry, the owner of a prosperous saloon on Dearborn Street frequented by Chicago journalists. Eventually, McGarry became annoyed with his notoriety and appealed to Dunne's publisher for relief. However, another real-life character in the Col. McNeery series, Johnny McKenna, a minor Republican politician in the heavily Democratic Sixth Ward, was delighted with his publicity. When he learned of Dunne's problems with McGarry, he suggested a visit to Bridgeport and an introduction to its people. Dunne accepted McKenna's invitation and soon thereafter created Mr. Dooley; he acknowledged his debt to Johnny McKenna by featuring him, initially, as the most frequent patron of Mr. Dooley's tavern.

Bridgeport immediately appealed to Dunne because it was "shanty Irish," and Mr. Dooley could be allowed a much greater freedom of expression than had been possible with Col. McNeery:

> While I was writing editorials for the *Post,* we became engaged in a bitter fight with the crooks in the city council. McAuliff [Cornelius McAuliff, editor, Chicago *Post*] and I were both municipal reformers but our publisher wasn't so eager. He was nervous about libel suits and loans at banks that were interested in the franchises for sale in the council. It occurred to me that while it might be dangerous to call an alderman a thief in English no one could sue if a comic Irishman denounced the statesman as a thief. [No. 14, p. 270]

Although as a comic editorialist Mr. Dooley promised Dunne immunity from libel, he also posed a significant artistic challenge. Dunne had to represent Mr. Dooley as the authentic spokesman for the Sixth Ward; in so doing, he had to reveal that community, for all its comic shortcomings in social manners and intellectual enlightenment, as the source of Mr. Dooley's assured and sound judgments. Furthermore, in creating Mr. Dooley as a shanty Irish bartender, Dunne had to avoid, without completely denying, the degrading character faults of drunkenness, superstition, and pugnacity which had traditionally identified the Irish buffoon since his initial appearance in American literature as "Teague Oregan" in Hugh Brackenridge's *Modern Chivalry.*

Dunne particularly enjoyed these challenges of representing Martin Dooley as a persuasive public moralist and the Sixth Ward as a worthy community. Frequently he would mock, through Mr. Dooley, the anxieties which a nation of immigrants felt toward the most recent arrivals:

> I was afraid I wasn't goin' to assimilate with th' airlyer pilgrim fathers an' th' instichoochins iv th' counthry, but I soon found that a long swing iv th' pick made me as good as another man

an' it didn't require a gr-reat intellect, or sometimes anny at all, to vote th' dimmycrat ticket, an' befure I was here a month, I felt enough like a native born American to burn a witch. [No. 17, p. 51]

Though Mr. Dooley mocks American excesses, he is a firm patriot. He and his neighbors have found life in America to be a unique opportunity: "I see their sons fightin' into politics," he says, "their daughters tachin' young American idee how to shoot too high in th' public school, an' I thought they was all right" (no. 17, p. 52). Mr. Dooley never denigrates the immigrants' belief in the reality of American opportunity or their efforts, often at great sacrifice, to realize a better life. He reserves his greatest scorn for those native Americans who demean or subvert the institutions and values for which the nation uniquely stood. One of his bitterest indictments was of Ambassador Choate, who, as Mr. Dooley acidly reported, arrived at Buckingham Palace "as fast as his hands an' knees wud carry him" (no. 13, p. vi).

Though appealing to a national audience with his sharp satires on ambassadors, presidents, generals, and business tycoons, Dunne always recalled Mr. Dooley to the subject he knew best: Chicago. For several years, from 1893 to 1898, Mr. Dooley had commented almost solely on local Chicago affairs for Chicago newspaper readers; until Admiral George Dewey entered Manila harbor and prompted Mr. Dooley's widely reprinted speculations about the fate of "Cousin George," Dunne's weekly essays had been published only in the *Chicago Sunday Post* and, later, the *Chicago Journal.* When Dunne became a nationally syndicated columnist in 1900 and moved his family to New York City, Chicago remained Mr. Dooley's enduring concern: it was his permanent home, the limit of his adult experience, and the familiar standard against which he could measure the events, personalities, and fashions of national significance.

The Chicago experience which had first inspired Dunne to write comic essays in Irish dialect was the World's Columbian Exposition of 1893. In the weeks when preparations for the fair were at their peak, Dunne created Col. McNeery, Mr. Dooley's loquacious predecessor. As Dunne presented him, Col. McNeery was keenly amused with the fair because, as the neoclassic "White City," it stood in ironic contrast to the actual city of its builders. While acknowledging Chicago's stupendous and admirable effort in building the fair, Col. McNeery waggishly noted the realities of life in Chicago which the fair planners could not adequately disguise. The fair was broadly and enthusiastically advertised as Chicago's cultural debut; Col. McNeery, however, unerringly perceived the coarsened features of mercantile Chicago beneath the new, ill-fitting fancy dress: "Divvle a word about pothry," he dourly concluded after attending the fair's premier "Lithry Congress." "It was like a meetin' iv th' Bricklayer's Union, it was, so it was, with all th' talk about how th' dirty old book publishers was thrown it into th' poor potes an' grindin' thim down in th' ground."[2]

Just as the "Lithry Congress" convinced Col. McNeery that the World's Fair would not produce Chicago poets where none had been before, a meeting of the "Lady Managers" left him skeptical about the fair's lasting contribution to the movement for women's rights. As Col. McNeery reports this meeting, Chicago's women, notably the committee's chairwoman, Mrs. Potter Palmer, are woefully unsuited for managerial responsibility. The meeting of these newly enfranchised women delegates quickly degenerates into a peevish dispute, replete with tears, between "the 'Naypoltan' ice-crame woman and the "tooty-frooty' Lady Manager":

> "Who'se old?" says th' old lady. "Ye minx," says she. "Ye'er
> a dishturber iv th' peace," she says. "Set down," says all th'
> ladies that do be on th' side iv th' Naypoltan ice-crame lady,
> an' "Thrun her out," says all them that's with th' lady with th'
> white hair. "Ladies," says Mrs. Pammer. "Ordher," she says,
> wallopin' th' table with a fan. "Will ye set down," says th'
> white-haired wan. "Niver," says th' Naypoltan ice-crame wan,
> "till I gets me rights, an' whin I gets home," she says, "I'll
> be tillin' me husband—boo-hoo," says she, cryin' "what a horrid
> way I've been threated."[3]

Broad burlesques of suffragettes, poets, scholars, and other unconventional people reassured Col. McNeery's readers that Chicago was securely immune from the artistic and social renaissance advertised by the promoters of the World's Fair.

Mr. Dooley succeeded Col. McNeery in the last week of the World's Fair (October 23, 1893) when James McGarry's protests convinced

Dunne's publisher that a change of comic character was needed. In
the months and years thereafter, Mr. Dooley would occasionally
reflect on Chicago's grand exhibition, repeating much of Col.
McNeery's mockery and adding his own reflections on the fair's
significance for the working-class Irish of Bridgeport:

> They tell me th' wan we had give an impetus, whativer that is,
> to archytecture that it has n't raycovered fr'm yet. Afther th'
> fair, ivrybody that was annybody had to go to live in a Greek
> temple with an Eyetalian roof an' bay-windows. But thim that
> was n't annybody has f'rgot all about th' wooden island an' th'
> Coort iv Honor, an' whin ye say annything to thim about th'
> fair, they say: "D'ye raymimber th' night I see ye on th' Mid-
> way? Oh, my!" [No. 15, p. 140]

For Mr. Dooley and his neighbors on Archey Road, the Midway was
the World's Fair's significant legacy. The literary congresses, women's
committees, learned symposiums, and grandiose buildings were all
ridiculously foreign to their lives, and the many exhibits celebrating
the progress of mechanical science were too uncomfortably close:

> a wurruld's fair is no rollin'-mills. If it was, ye'd be paid f'r
> goin' there. 'Tis not th' rollin'-mills an' 'tis not a school or a
> machine-shop or a grocery store. 'Tis a big circus with manny
> rings an' that's what it ought to be. [No. 15, p. 140]

On the Midway, away from the stately order of boulevards, temples,
and vistas, the common folk from Bridgeport—"thim that was n't
annybody"—could relax and enjoy themselves. There they were not
edified, patronized, or threatened; they were simply entertained.

The contrast between the vital Midway and the stultifying fair
is broadly analogous, in the Mr. Dooley essays, to the general contrast Dunne draws between Bridgeport and Chicago. In Bridgeport,
the Irish-Americans had evolved a relaxed, satisfying and tolerant
social life which Protestant, Republican Chicagoans tried repeatedly
to reform and uplift. The inviting quality of Bridgeport's social life
is perhaps best illustrated by the balance its citizens comfortably maintain between their saloons and their church. They see this balance as

natural and necessary for a healthy society; "Father Kelly," Mr.
Dooley's pastor, frequently visits Dooley's saloon, and even in his
absence the men in the saloon often discuss the social activities of
their religious fraternities. This easy accommodation, though, offends
the moral sensibilities of reform-minded Chicagoans. In their opposition to the alien culture of the immigrant, as it is represented in the
Mr. Dooley essays, they reveal, ironically, their own contempt for
the civil liberty and democratic equality essential to the American
way of life which they purport to defend:

> Th' rayformer . . . thinks you an' me, Hinnissy, has been watchin'
> his spotless career f'r twenty years, that we've read all he had to
> say on th' evils iv' pop'lar sufferage befure th' society f'r th'
> Bewilderment iv th' Poor, an' that we're achin' in ivry joint
> to have him dhrag us be th' hair iv th' head fr'm th' flowin'
> bowl an' th' short card game, make good citizens iv us an' sind
> us to th' pinitinchry. So th' minyit he gets into th' job he be-
> gins a furyous attimpt to convart us into what we've been
> thryin' not to be iver since we come into th' wurruld. . . .
> His motto is "Arrest that man." [No. 17, p. 168]

The threats to Bridgeport's social equanimity come not only from
the crusades of Chicago's self-righteous reformers, but also, and more
insidiously, from the frivolous fashions of Chicago's urban sophisti-
cates. One strange mode after another is born in Chicago, but nearly
all are squelched in the Sixth Ward. Bloomers and bicycles were
particularly conspicuous examples of Chicago's strange modes. In
one Mr. Dooley essay, Molly Donahue begins riding a bicycle and
wearing bloomers, to the shame of her family and outrage of her
neighbors. Her odd behavior, though, is easily suppressed by Father
Kelly. The worldly-wise priest simply observes, in complimenting
Molly on her attractive bloomers, that he had never before known
that she had bowed legs.

There are many other comic incidents in which the Irish-American
ward confidently deflects the modern challenges to its traditional life.
The "Univarsity Settlement," particularly, is frequently ridiculed as
a source of patently absurd ideas and values:

"Th' question befure th' house is whin is a lie not a lie?" said
Mr. Dooley. "How's that?" asked Mr. Hennessy. "Well," said
Mr. Dooley, "here's Profissor E. Bimjamin Something-or-Other
insthructin' th' youth at th' Chicago Univarsity that a lie, if
it's f'r a good purpose, is not a lie at all. There's th' gr-reat
school down there on the Midway. Ye can larn anything ye
have a mind to in that there siminary an' now they'll have a
coorse in lyin." [No. 15, p. 87]

By confidently ridiculing the strange ideas of the University of Chicago
or the curious fashions of high society, Mr. Dooley warmly affirmed,
for Chicago's ordinary citizens, the contemporary relevance of their
commonsense, conventional tastes and orthodox morality. It is no
surprise, then, that he enjoyed immediate and enduring popularity
from Chicago newspaper readers and, later, the broad audience of
his nationally syndicated newspaper columns and nationally distributed
books.

Mr. Dooley's blithe confidence in his ward's resiliency could, though,
be shaken. The violent criminality of "Petey Scanlan," eldest son of a
pious, sober Irish-American family, for example, prompts Mr. Dooley
to remark, with uncharacteristic resignation, "Sometimes I think
they'se poison in th' life iv a big city." Or, on another occasion, the
desperate suicide of "Timothy Grogan," an unemployed meat packer,
and the degrading poverty into which his widow and children are thrown,
spur Mr. Dooley to bitter denunciations of Philip Armour and his co-
conspirators in the "beef thrust." But these denunciations are infrequent.
Far more often, Mr. Dooley views Chicago with genial tolerance, tem-
pering his satire of unconventional Chicagoans with broad reassurances
to the many ordinary Chicagoans who resembled his neighbors in Bridgeport. In the 1930s, a far different time from the 1890s Chicago of Mr.
Dooley, Dunne looked back, nostalgically, to the Chicago he had known
to observe that "humor, especially political humor, is a privilege of the
innocent and secure."

Dunne perceived innocence and security as the normal conditions
of American life at the turn of the century. In the comic essays he
wrote, these qualities were most evident in the intimate neighborliness of Bridgeport, but they were also characteristic of the general

culture of Chicago. Though he represents Bridgeport as a distinct community within Chicago, it is not a separate, isolated society. For Dunne, the Irish immigrants had found in Chicago the opportunities to build a community which had been denied them in Ireland as the impoverished tenants of landlords. He often contrasts the degradation the Irish had suffered in Ireland with the security and dignity they discovered as Americans. Most frequently he satirizes those exceptional Americans who envy the Old World privileges of Irish landlords and British imperialists. For example, in the Mr. Dooley monologue "On the Servant Girl Problem," Dunne catalogues the many liberating opportunities which Chicago offers an unmarried female immigrant, and he mocks the petty arrogance of those affluent Americans who wish to exploit the new citizens as menial servants:

> But wud ye believe it, Hinnissy, manny iv these misguided women rayfuse f'r to take a job that ain't in a city. They prefer th' bustle an' roar iv th' busy marts iv thrade, th' sthreet car, th' saloon on three corners an' th' church on wan, th' pa-apers ivry mornin' with pitchers iv th' s'ciety fav'rite that's just thrown up a good job at Armours to elope with th' well-known club man who used to be yard-masther iv th' three B's, G, L, & N., th' shy peek into th' dhrygoods store, an' other base lusuries, to a free an' healthy life in th' counthry between iliven P.M. an' four A.M. Wensdahs an' Sundahs. [No. 16, pp. 29–30]

In light of the actual conditions of immigrant labor, as reported, for example, by Mr. Dooley's neighbor on Archer Avenue, Jane Addams, Dunne's version of work and recreation opportunities available in "th' bustle an' roar iv th' busy marts iv thrade" is certainly roseate.* But his purpose is artistic, not sociological. To write effective satire,

---

*Compare Addams's description of sweatshop labor on Halsted Street with Dunne's humorous catalogue of the servant girl's ordinary pleasures. Addams reports: "The visits we made in the neighborhood constantly discovered women sewing upon sweatshop work, and often they were assisted by incredibly small children. I remember a little girl of four who pulled out basting threads hour after hour, sitting on a stool at the feet of her Bohemian mother, a little bunch of human misery." (*Twenty Years at Hull House*, p. 149.)

he needed to broadly define the areas of satisfactory community
life in order to isolate and expose those exceptional men, ideas, and
prejudices which threatened the status quo.

Only once in his career as a public humorist did Dunne seriously
attempt to "correct" his static artistic model of Mr. Dooley's Bridgeport. In 1899 and early 1900, he published in the *Ladies Home Journal* four installments of a projected comic novel tentatively entitled
Molly Donahue; Who Lives across the Street from Mr. Dooley. In
this novel, he withdraws Mr. Dooley from his secure haven behind
the bar of his saloon and introduces him into the actual Sixth Ward
of the 1890s. There Mr. Dooley encounters Molly Donahue, the
eldest daughter of an immigrant family and recent graduate of a
Chicago public high school. She is Bridgeport's "New Woman" who
is zealous for culture, social reform, and women's political rights; she
epitomizes, to an extreme, the "Americanization" expected of second
generation immigrants. As Bridgeport's most modern citizen, Molly
Donahue quickly disrupts Mr. Dooley's tranquillity and thoroughly
undermines his authority.

In each of the four stories, Mr. Dooley leaves his saloon and ven-
tures out to meet his neighbors. He first encounters the Donahues
seated on their front stoop arguing, heatedly, the need of purchasing
a piano; Mrs. Donahue and her daughter Molly insist on its necessity,
while Malachi Donahue vainly protests the exorbitant cost. In the
second installment, Mr. Dooley is invited to Molly's "Musicale," a
bewildering, stifling evening of piano recitals, grand opera arias, and
poetry readings. The third installment finds him eavesdropping on
the meeting of the "Archey Road Woman's Suffrage Club," chaired
by Molly. In the final installment, he reports, at second hand, the
earnest program of Molly's "literary salon."

When confronted with Molly's demands for cultural refinement
and political reform and with her considerable influence over the
women and young adults of the ward, Mr. Dooley flounders pathetically. Instead of representing the settled opinion of his community
on art, politics, the family, and religion, as one might expect from
his venerable status in the Mr. Dooley essays, he is shunted to the
periphery of Molly's activities. From his ignominious position in the
far corner of the Donahue parlor or from behind the closed kitchen
door, he can only weakly protest the strange sentiments which are

influencing his neighbors. When he and other older, perplexed men of the ward request Irish folk tunes at Molly's "Musicale," they are ridiculed for their low taste; when he meets with Malachi Donahue in the kitchen to review the proposed slate of Democratic party nominees, a reform Republican candidate commands the front parlor. Finally, in the fourth installment of the series, he and Malachi flee the threatening women and young people who have overtaken the Donahue home. They retreat to the security of Dooley's rooms above the tavern to share a bottle and to lament their impotence.

In the changed world of Molly's modern Bridgeport of "ginteel" culture, women's independence, and reform politics, Mr. Dooley is exposed as an archaic and prejudiced fool. He has little taste for submitting to the erosion of church authority, family stability, and ethnic pride implicit in her revolt; yet he can only advise her belea-guered father, in the interest of keeping peace in the home, to capitulate to her persistent demands. To restore Mr. Dooley's battered dignity, Dunne removes him from the conflict in the fourth story, and allows him his accustomed philosophic distance as an old, propertied bachelor secure in his rooms with an old friend. Thus restored to his familiar character, Mr. Dooley is never again brought outside the doors of his snug saloon.

The *Molly Donahue* experiment revealed to Dunne the narrow limits of the character he had created. To be an effective satirist, Mr. Dooley required the security of a stable home and the dignity of respected opinions. Only then could he single out the men and events that disturbed his good life and confidently satirize them. In the *Molly Donahue* series, Mr. Dooley temporarily lost this assurance; he be-came a foolish and, indeed, pathetic character. Dunne quickly saw his predicament and restored Mr. Dooley to eminence in a timeless Bridgeport immune from disruptive change. Thereafter, Mr. Dooley spoke with his customary assurance until time had left Bridgeport behind and its spokesman could find less and less to say.

While in his prime, though, in the years from 1893 to about 1910, Mr. Dooley delivered weekly opinions and found many who accepted the reality and contemporary relevance of his Bridgeport. He spoke most frequently and authoritatively on politics, a subject he knew very well from his long experience in the Sixth Ward Democratic party. Dunne endowed Mr. Dooley with a very thorough knowledge of urban machine politics. The venerable saloonkeeper had served his

party for fifty years, the high point of which was his two-year term
as precinct captain (1873-75). In that office he had earned his party's
gratitude by delivering 2,100 Democratic votes from only 500 registered
voters to decisively defeat the reform Republican candidate for alderman. Mr. Dooley, then, knew at first hand the deceit, sabotage, and
intimidation to which politicians ordinarily resorted in winning and
consolidating power. He amused and instructed his readers by revealing
the many similarities between the unscrupulous Democrats he knew and
the other public officials whom he only read about in his newspaper.

Unlike the other topics on which Mr. Dooley commented, politics
allowed no easy contrast between provincial Bridgeport and urban
Chicago; in politics, Bridgeport was inextricably welded to Chicago.
The ward's politicians were conspicuous figures in the general and
persistent corruption of Chicago's political life. As a property owner
and "member of the onforchnit middle class," Mr. Dooley dispassion-
ately observed Chicago's tangled political web and followed its various
strands of culpability to their sources in the downtown council chambers and in his own ward's back rooms.

The most significant political contest for the straight-ticket Democrats of Bridgeport was the biennial aldermanic race; as Mr. Dooley
wryly noted, "Out here we have to pay thim two dollars apiece at
important ilictions f'r aldhermen an' wan dollar whin some minor
office like president is bein' illicted." Chicago's aldermen, particularly
those representing the immigrant wards, had been publicly criticized
for many years for their open and persistent corruption. They had
connived with the various business interests seeking public contracts,
most notably the streetcar entrepreneur Charles Yerkes, to sell out
Chicago's eminent domain for a pittance. "Sandbagging" was their
favorite method of reaping personal profit from public business. Whenever a Chicago business sought an economic privilege from the council,
the "grey wolves," as the corrupt aldermen were known, would organize
a rival company and award the desired privilege to it. This maneuver
forced the legitimate company to buy out the council's paper corporation at great profit to the incorporators. By these flagrant means, the
city council had bankrupted Chicago's treasury and, through long-term,
low-rent leases, had forfeited the city's political authority for decades
to come.

Despite repeated calls for reform, the grey wolves kept returning to
their lair; they served a legitimate political need. For the poor and

immigrant wards, which they represented, political reform held little appeal. Under civil service reform, to choose the most striking example, the poor and ill-educated could never compete for public jobs. But, with a corruptible alderman to bargain for them, they might expect to win a place on the public payroll or a job with a company which was courting the alderman's favor; as "Bathhouse John" Coughlin, alderman from Chicago's notorious Levee, arrogantly explained: "You know, if you ain't a lunkhead, that in wards where the poor have the cinch, next to the priest, the alderman is their guardian angel."[4]

Bridgeport's alderman, in life and in the Mr. Dooley essays, was William J. O'Brien. Mr. Dooley viewed "Willum J." with tolerant respect. And through Mr. Dooley, Finley Peter Dunne educated Chicagoans in the political obligations which Alderman O'Brien diligently fulfilled. In one essay, "On Oratory in Politics," Mr. Dooley illustrates Alderman O'Brien's political function by contrasting him with a high-minded, enthusiastic, and confident reformer. "I'll not re-sort," the reform candidate naively pledges, "to th' ordin'ry methods." "Th' thing to do," he says, "is to prisint th' issues iv th' day to th' voters. I'll burn up ivry precin't in th' ward with me iloquince."

Candidate O'Brien is undisturbed by this innovation in ward politics:

> He niver med wan speech. . . . But he got th' superintendint iv th' rollin'-mills with him; an' he put three or four good fam'lies to wurruk in th' gas-house, where he knew th' main guy, an' he made reg'lar calls on' th' bar-rn boss iv th' sthreet ca-ars. He wint to th' picnics, an' hired th' orchesthry f'r th' dances, an' voted himself th' most pop'lar man at th' church fair at an expinse iv at laste five hundherd dollars. No wan that come near him wanted f'r money. [No. 11, pp. 220–21]

William J. O'Brien does not try to reform his ward; he accepts it, demonstrates his loyalty by attending its picnics, dances, and church fairs; he then works, with what political power he can muster, to sustain his neighbors with jobs, pocket money, and favors. At the campaign's conclusion, he consoles the defeated reformer with this political

advice: "Whin ye've been in politics as long as I have, ye'll know,' he
says, 'that th' roly-boly is th' gr-reatest or-rator on earth,' he says."

As an editorialist for various Chicago papers, Dunne campaigned
against aldermen like William O'Brien, but he respected their political
acumen. In the 1898 council election, for example, he spoke out against
the council leader "Johnny dePow" Powers, but he admonished his
readers to heed the alderman's proven talents:

> If he is defeated it must be by the use of weapons similar to his
> own. The candidate who beats him must be:
>> A friend of the Poor.
>> One whom the people trust to make reform a perceptible
>> benefit.
>> One who wouldn't make reform an affliction and a restraint
>> on personal liberty.
> A candidate who can reform to these specifications may beat
> Powers. For any who can't, to try to beat him will be a waste
> of effort.[5]

For Dunne, the immigrant wards had developed political techniques
appropriate to their needs. In his editorials and in his Mr. Dooley essays,
Dunne did not indict Irish-Americans in his criticism of their aldermen.
The immigrant ward shared in the alderman's "roly-boly," but it did
not provide his funds; aldermen, Mr. Dooley often reminds his readers,
were bought downtown.

While defending the rough political accommodations which Chicago's
immigrants had made, Mr. Dooley repeatedly drew attention to the
real culprit responsible for Chicago's impoverished civic life: the
privilege-seeking businessman.* The moral issue in the corruption of
Chicago's politicians by Chicago's "responsible" businessmen is perhaps best drawn in Dunne's parable of "Martin Dochney":

---

*For a comparison of Dunne's attitude toward business with the ideas of various
"Progressives," see John M. Harrison, "Finley Peter Dunne and the Progressive
Movement," *Journalism Quarterly* 44 (Autumn, 1967), pp. 475–81. At one point,
Harrison notes that "both Dunne and Brand Whitlock dared ridicule that most
persistent of American illusions—that business ethics are superior to political
ethics, hence businessmen must make superior public officials."

'Tis not Hinnissy, that this man Yerkuss goes up to an aldherman an' says out sthraight, "Here Bill, take this bundle, an'
be an infamyous scoundhrel." That's th' way th' man in Mitchi-
gan Avnoo sees it, but 'tis not sthraight. D'ye mind Dochney
that was wanst aldherman here? [No. 12, p. 25]

Martin Dochney, Mr. Dooley explains, was a small contractor on
Halsted Street, "an honest an' sober man" and very popular in the
ward. In his first days on the city council, he is asked to support a
"sandbag" ordinance. When offered a bribe of five thousand dollars,
he angrily assaults his tempter. The next day, though, a close friend
seeks him out to again recommend the ordinance.

"'Tis a plain swindle," Dochney protests. "'Tis a good thing f'r
th' comp'nies," his friend replies, "but look what they've done
f'r th' city," he says, "an' think," he says, "iv th' widdies an'
orphans," he says, "that has their har-rd earned coin invisted."

That night Alderman Dochney ponders the relation between his five-
thousand-dollar bribe and Chicago's deserving widows and orphans.
The money would pay his mortgage and the debt on his new contract. It would buy a new dress for Mrs. Dochney, and besides, he
rationalizes, the ordinance will obviously benefit widows and orphans:

"No wan'd be hurted, annyhow," he says; "an', sure, it ain't
a bribe f'r to take money f'r doin' something ye want to do,
annyhow," he says. "Five thousan' widdies an' orphans," he
says, an' he wint to sleep.

The next day, Alderman Dochney calls on his banker to renew
the notes on his outstanding contract. The banker warmly recommends
the pending ordinance and implies that Dochney's affirmative vote will
satisfy his debt. Dochney votes for the ordinance and continues in his
political career to become a notorious council grey wolf. At the
parable's end, Dunne points the moral of the ward's innocence and
Chicago businessmen's guilt in the corruption of Alderman Dochney:
"He was expelled fr'm th' St. Vincent de Pauls, an' ilicted a director
iv a bank th' same day."

To Mr. Dooley, the crowning irony of Chicago's political life was the identification of reform politics with business methods and ethics: "When a rayformer is ilicted he promises ye a business administhration. Some people want that but I don't." A politician, Mr. Dooley reminds us, usually understands his obligation to serve the immediate needs of his constituents; he may not fulfill this responsibility, but he is aware of it. A businessman, though, in Mr. Dooley's simple contrast, is obliged only to the specific demands of his individual economic interest; serving the dollar, he cannot serve the people. The Mr. Dooley essay "Reform Administration" succinctly illustrates the sharp conflict Dunne sees between political and business habits:

> A reg'lar pollytician can't give away an alley without blushin', but a businessman who is in pollytics jus' to see that th' civil sarvice law gets thurly enfoorced, will give Lincoln Park an' th' public libr'y to th' beef thrust, charge an admission price to th' lake front an' make it a felony f'r annywan to buy stove polish outside iv his store, an' have it all put down to public improvemints with a pitcher iv him in th' corner stone. [No. 17, p. 169]

Though Mr. Dooley often contrasted politicians and businessmen, he did not exempt politicians, or any class of Americans, from the criticism he regularly leveled against businessmen. His criticism of businessmen is frequent and sharp; they often exemplify, in their selfish materialism, moral hypocrisy, and social irresponsibility, the distortion of the democratic spirit which should, ideally, distinguish America as a nation. When Mr. Dooley criticizes other classes of Americans, especially politicians, he criticizes them for emulating or even for tolerating the alien class consciousness of America's new plutocrats. Thus he regularly condemns the war policy of President McKinley ("Mack th' Wanst, or Twict, iv th' United States an' Sulu") for promoting class elitisim as a national principle:

> "In our former war," he [McKinley] says, "we had th' misfortune to have men in command that didn't know th' diff'rence between a goluf stick an' a beecycle; an' what was th' raysult; We foozled our approach at Bull R-run," he says. "Ar-re ye a mimber iv anny

> clubs?" he says. "Four," says Willie. "Thin I make ye a major,"
> he says. "Where d'ye get ye're pants?" he says. "F'rm England,"
> says Willie. "Gloryous," says McKinley. "I make ye a colonel,"
> he says. . . . "Thank Gawd, th' r-rich," he says, "is brave an'
> pathriotic," he says. [No. 11, pp. 26–27]

With similar broad lampoons of public figures like President McKinley, Dunne vigorously affirmed, for two decades, the contemporary relevance of his traditional, crackerbarrel humor. In assessing his political satire, one must conclude that his conscious restoration of such a traditional comic style was commercially successful and artistically advantageous. It allowed him a coherent, familiar moral standard by which to confidently and persuasively measure the men, events, and ideas of his time. By invoking Mr. Dooley's conventional wisdom, Dunne could easily isolate and ridicule those attitudes, ambitions, and principles which were alien to accepted American traditions. He could, for example, decisively separate the imperial ambitions of America's war leaders in the Spanish-American War from the commonplace, domestic concerns of Bridgeport's workers and merchants, or he could sharply contrast the exceptional "public-be-damned" arrogance of some American industrialists and financiers with the ordinary ethical habits expected of Bridgeport's Catholics. By characterizing Bridgeport as a village and Mr. Dooley as its crackerbarrel philosopher, Dunne recovered for his urban audience the familiar values of American tradition: economic self-reliance, informal neighborliness, honest, blunt expression, simple religious faith, and firm community loyalty. Dunne's affirmation of these traditional virtues seemed especially relevant to his time because Mr. Dooley was an immigrant; the Irish barkeep's orthodox patriotism and conventional social attitudes were not the mere residue of habit. They were, rather, the conscious choices of a mature adult.

However, though immediately successful, Dunne's efforts to conserve a traditional comic style were not long sustained. By defining Mr. Dooley as an elderly, opinionated village moralist, Dunne restricted him to social attitudes which became increasingly archaic and eccentric. Mr. Dooley was an independent neighborhood merchant who believed that the bonds of personal obligations, family affiliations, political loyalties, and friendships were sufficient to preserve the economic and social order of his small community. As the urban economy became more large-scaled and technologically sophisticated, and as citizens of cities, towns, and farms became, or aspired to become, more mobile in seeking educational and vocational opportunities, Mr. Dooley's modest social vision of the stable, multigenerational community became less relevant.

Dunne first confronted this possible irrelevancy of Mr. Dooley's social attitudes in his *Molly Donahue* stories of 1899 and 1900 wherein he attempted a realistic, rather than a sentimental, portrait of the Irish-American ward, particularly of the values its second- and third-generation citizens held. In doing so, he undermined Mr. Dooley's confidence and eroded his authority. In drawing the contrasts in character between Molly Donahue and Mr. Dooley, Dunne was carried to the necessary, if unwelcome, conclusion that the Irish-Americans of 1900 would more likely be influenced by Molly's articulate enthusiasms than by Mr. Dooley's stolid common sense. Mr. Dooley, in these stories, discovers that his neighbors prefer Molly's "ginteel" culture to his simple folk songs, poems, and myths of Irish traditions, that they are attracted to her college-educated reform candidate instead of the sturdy, industrious, liquor wholesaler whom he and other Democrats had endorsed, and, most distressingly, that they coveted the status symbols—pianos, carriages, formal drawing rooms, exclusive social clubs—which would set them apart from the common laborers and small tradesmen who had long patronized his tavern. Disturbed by these changes and by the admission that a Mr. Dooley was inadequate to their challenge, Dunne abruptly ended his novel, pleading sudden illness as an excuse, and returned Mr. Dooley to the comfortable security of his "Archey Road" saloon, from which he never again ventured.

The incapacities of the traditional comic model, which Dunne had tentatively explored in his *Molly Donahue* project, were, in the comic art of George Ade, themes of central concern. He worked more persistently than Dunne had to shape the traditional material into an adequate, realistic representation of modern Chicago. Unlike Dunne, who merely appropriated the conventional character of the crackerbarrel philosopher, Ade strove to fashion a distinct contemporary style. He wanted, in his words, "to be known as a realist with a compact style and a clean Anglo-Saxon vocabulary and the courage to observe human virtues and frailties as they showed on the lens" (no. 7, p. 51).

3

GEORGE ADE

A native of Kentland, Indiana, and a graduate of Purdue University, then a ten-year-old land-grant college with only two hundred students and four buildings, George Ade lacked the knowledge of Chicago and familiarity with its manners which Finley Peter Dunne, a native Chicagoan, easily assumed. In his many daily columns and in his three comic novels of Chicago, Ade never created an amiable, assured comic character like Mr. Dooley who could comprehend Chicago in the typical experiences of his home neighborhood. Instead, the characters Ade most frequently described were the fresh immigrants to Chicago, whether European or American, who were somewhat confused and lonely in the strange city, but generally hopeful that they could succeed.

It is important to note that Ade's characters usually do succeed in finding employment, housing, and friends in Chicago. However, Ade was aware that the odds against their success were significant:

> "In 1890," he recalled twenty-seven years later, "Chicago was a mining camp, five stories high. It was owned by the gamblers. What I seem to remember most clearly of that all-night and wide-open time is that the minor courts were controlled by agents of crime. The poor man, unprotected by an alderman, was helpless when the vultures swooped down on him. No wonder we had anarchists." [No. 5, p. 60]

Though well aware that the "poor man" of 1890 Chicago was vulnerable, Ade did not assign him anything like the meager, dispiriting future which Henry Fuller, Will Payne, Robert Herrick, Theodore Dreiser, Frank Norris, and other Chicago novelists had uniformly portrayed. Instead, he perceived, beneath the raw "mining camp" appearance of Chicago in 1890, the nascent structure of a secure, healthy, and satisfying city. By 1917, in the first administration of Chicago's notoriously corrupt mayor William Hale Thompson, Ade believed, quite naively, that Chicago's civic promise had been largely fulfilled:

> The Chicago of to-day, as compared with the Gomorrah of World's Fair year, is a cross-section of the millennium. The courts are beyond the reach of the crooks. The night life consists mostly of going to one's room and reading a book. The voters want good government, whether they get it all the time or not. [No. 5, p. 60]

Ade's method of communicating both his awareness of a Chicagoan's vulnerability and his own optimistic faith in Chicago's moral progress was unique and appealing. In a typical story, Ade will introduce a character as an isolated individual, usually new to Chicago and apprehensive about finding a secure place there. Then, as the story develops, Ade will carefully mute the character's apprehensions about employment, personal security, and social acceptance, which he had initially raised. He will unfold the various means by which an isolated Chicagoan is initiated into a wider and more secure community. Briefly and unexpectedly, a character will be drawn into the lives of his neighbors to discover, if only for a moment, that the routine relationships of a small community are still possible in the large, intimidating city.

Ade's first feature for his column "Stories of the Streets and Town," a brief sketch titled "A Young Man in Upper Life," exemplifies the modest subject and wholesome manner of his comic art. The subject, as in many of Ade's stories, is a young Chicago office employee. Arthur Ponsby—"our Mr. Ponsby," as Ade characterizes him—is a successful copy writer for a Chicago advertising agency. He is generally pleased with his job and himself; and he is particularly pleased with his sixteenth-floor private office with its unobstructed view of Chicago business buildings and Lake Michigan beyond them. His pleasures, though, soon begin to pale. He finds himself isolated within Chicago working alone each day in his office composing, with little variety, the same stale advertising copy which had earned him his initial recognition. In the brief story, Ade suggests, lightly and with amusing detail, the stultifying effect of Arthur Ponsby's routine work; he then contrives an unusual incident to awaken the young man to the variety of work and workers in his immediate neighborhood.

The unexpected, though hardly extraordinary, incident which disturbs Arthur Ponsby's routine is the construction of a new building next to his own. One day when he turned to gaze out his window, he saw, a few feet beyond the window sill, a workman standing atop a steel pillar. For weeks, he intently watches the steelworkers as they nonchalantly balance on the narrow beams, occasionally spit tobacco juice into the infinite space below them, and, at break times, comfortably straddle the girders to leisurely consume their lunch and beer. Finally, one "glad morning," Arthur Ponsby notices the white cap of a mason just above his windowsill:

> For three days he watched the masons with a show of interest which he could not explain. Then the terra-cotta wall went up to greater heights, and Mr. Ponsby, finding some relief in a bare wall, went back to his neglected work. [No. 8, p. 8]

Though construction workers were certainly plentiful in Chicago, Arthur Ponsby's intimate, unhurried observation of their labor and mannerisms was remarkable. He had enjoyed an unusual opportunity to relax, observe, and reflect. This casual, accidental relation between workers in different occupations would be an ordinary part of small town or village sociability, but in Chicago it was uncommon; as Harvey Zorbaugh noted in his pioneering study of Chicago society, *Gold Coast and Slum* (1927), "There is no phenomenon more characteristic of city life, as contrasted with the life of the rural community or village, than that of segregation."[1] The most pervasive condition of urban segregation, according to Zorbaugh, was the minute and rigid division of labor which encouraged social relationships along occupational

rather than community lines. George Ade, in his brief sketch of
Arthur Ponsby, recognized this characteristic occupational segregation of the city and gently deflated its significance and permanence.
Arthur Ponsby was segregated because he had ignored the community
of workers around him. When the steelworker appeared outside his
window, Arthur Ponsby was involved, if at a distance and for only
a short time, in occupations strikingly different from his own routines.

"A Young Man in Upper Life" established the theme and style of
most of the "Stories of the Streets and Town" which were to follow
it. In his brief stories, published six days a week for seven years, George
Ade explored the different circumstances in which Chicagoans were
separated from one another. He often selected a character, similar to
Arthur Ponsby, who had become isolated within the small routines of
his work and home. Then he would describe some unusual event which
disturbed the character's settled habits and awakened him to the wider
and more varied life of his community.

One of the more entertaining of Ade's descriptions of Chicago
community life is the story "The Mystery of the Back-Roomer."
The story is set in Mrs. Morgane's boardinghouse, a modest, three-
story brownstone building with furnished apartments on the top
floors and "a tailoring and cleansing establishment" on the first
floor. Mrs. Morgane had difficulty in renting her small back room
until one day a quiet, neatly dressed man of early middle age accepted the room and, as a mark of his satisfaction, paid his rent two
weeks in advance.

The new boarder soon excited the curiosity of Mrs. Morgane's other
tenants. He seemed unusually secretive, and he kept very strange hours.
All day he remained closeted in his room, and each night he left carrying what seemed to be a small tin cashbox. Mrs. Morgane knew nothing
about the mysterious man; in her haste to rent the room, she had even
neglected to ask him his name. Finally, bowing to the persistent questions of her boarders—some speculated that the man was a burglar or
gambler—Mrs. Morgane stopped him and asked his name and livelihood:

> The next Sunday afternoon the stenographer and the young
> man were present in the parlor as witnesses, when Mrs. Morgane
> by the most urgent methods lured him thither, and, after the
> commonplace remarks, asked: "By the way, what is your pro-
> fession?"

He looked at her reproachfully as he answered: "I am a chiropodist in a Turkish bath."

"A what?"

"He removes corns," explained the department-store young man.

"And bunions," added the professional man. [No. 8, p. 18]

As in other Ade stories, the isolated character is drawn into the community of his neighbors:

They were interested and he told them of the work he did for the night customers. He was a professional man, after all. He became a favored member of the Morgane community and was afterward best man at the wedding of the stenographer and the department-store young man. It was in the morning, and he came around a trifle sleepy, for it had been a busy night.

By emphasizing the chiropodist's isolation—he lives in a single room, works at night, avoids the public rooms of the boarding house—Ade underscored the significance of that character's welcome into the "Morgane community." Even a secretive man of strange habits, Ade suggested, could not easily avoid the sincere and friendly interest of his Chicago neighbors. The Mrs. Morganes, department-store young men, and stenographers of Chicago would preserve and extend the community life of their immediate neighborhoods.

The leisurely pace and modest scale of Ade's "Stories of the Streets and Town," as well as their nostalgic charm, suggest the quiet rounds of life in a small community. Ade described for Chicagoans the picturesque customs and institutions which allowed them to see their city as an intimate, delightful community. Through Ade's daily columns, Chicagoans learned the unique menu of a "plantation dinner" at "Aunt Mary's"; they noticed the quaint appearance of the cobbler shops, tailor shops, and laundries crammed into the four- to six-foot-wide "chinks" between Chicago's commercial buildings; they heard the distinct vocabulary of the boatmen who handled the dwindling traffic on the sluggish Illinois and Michigan Canal; they saw the strange vehicles of Chicago's street vendors, and they laughed at the odd customs of the Chinese on Clark Street. Ade created an attractive, varied

community and invited Chicagoans, represented by his typical characters, Arthur Ponsby or Mrs. Morgane, to become acquainted with their
neighbors.

Of all the Chicagoans Ade portrayed, those who were most isolated
were the new European immigrants. They were removed from the
normal culture of Chicago by their language, poverty and meager education. In several of his daily columns, Ade described the circumstances
of the immigrants and, characteristically, revealed the means by which
they also were being assimilated into the mainstream of Chicago. He
was particularly impressed by the alacrity with which European immigrants seized the opportunity to become self-reliant, property-owning
Americans:

> In this second-hand strip and along the overcrowded streets
> leading off to the west reside many Russian Jews, new to Ameri-
> can privileges, but half-recovered from the persecution which held
> them down for generations. . . . If frugality and untiring industry
> count for anything this district will work out its own salvation.
> The second generation will do business in tall brick buildings
> like those up toward Van Buren Street. In the very heart of
> this populous settlement stands the magnificent Jewish manual
> training school, a voluntary contribution by the representative
> Jews of Chicago to the children of their less favored brethren.
> It combines the common-school features with the modern methods
> of manual training for both boys and girls. [No. 8, pp. 80-81]

The Jewish manual training school was another Chicago institution,
similar to the city's office buildings, boardinghouses, and fraternal
social clubs which served, in Ade's writing, to illustrate the various
means by which Chicagoans were drawn together into communities.
The school was the focus of Chicago's Jewish community, built
entirely from their voluntary contributions, and it was the instrument they used to teach their children the necessary social values and
work skills to become productive, self-supporting, and secure American
citizens.

Ade's intention to reassure his readers that Chicagoans preserved,
in new circumstances, the traditional customs and values long associated
with the community life of American towns and villages is evident even

in his portraits of those Chicagoans who fail to secure a livelihood
in the city. These failures usually find, before they leave Chicago,
one unexpected moment of sympathy to relieve their loneliness and
allow them a comforting memory. John Hazen, for example, a spend-
thrift fool who had wasted his father's inheritance, is staked to meals
and a bed by "Eddie," a Chicago pickpocket. Or Effie Whittlesy, a
naive, unskilled domestic servant discovers that her newest employer,
Ed Wallace, is her old classmate and childhood friend from Brainerd,
Minnesota. Ed Wallace tactfully discusses Effie's loneliness and poverty
with her and suggests that she would be happier at home with her relatives in Brainerd. Buoyed by his interest, Effie decides to return home
and she graciously accepts his offer of train fare. This sentimental and
popular story elicited from William Dean Howells a "thrill of pride in
the higher citizenship which it divines."[2]

Of all Ade's characters who fail to find a home and a purpose in
Chicago, "Doc' Horne" was the most popular with Chicago readers.
Chicago theatergoers immediately recognized Doc' as a familiar
comic character, "an amiable old falsifier, not unlike 'Lightnin', so
delightfully played by Bacon" (no. 7, p. 50). Like the vaudeville
comic on whom he was modeled, Doc' could deftly turn any conversation into a rambling monologue on some fabled incident of his
life; one example was his reputed service as an undercover intelligence
agent for the Union army. These entertaining tall tales were so popular with Chicago readers that Ade collected and revised them into a
novel, *Doc' Horne* (1899).

The principal dramatic interest of the novel is the running conflict
between Doc's affable egotism and his audience's persistent skepticism.
In each chapter, one wonders if Doc's fellow boarders at the "Alfalfa
European Hotel," a cheap rooming house for Chicago transients, will
expose him as the fool and vagrant he apparently is:

> "When I used to go about a great deal in Philadelphia society
> I was counted one of the best waltzers in the city."
> "Phil'delphi! Doc', y're ringin' in a new one on us. When's
> you in Phil'delphi?"
> "I was in Philadelphia the latter part of the 60's," said Doc'
> moving uneasily in his chair. "I don't know that it concerns you,
> but some of the best people in Philadelphia are my friends."
> "D' they know it?" asked the lush. [No. 2, p. 65].

Though Doc's credibility is repeatedly challenged, the motley society of the Alfalfa European Hotel always manages some reconciliation with him. These men, including such disparate characters as a bicycle salesman, a freckle-faced farm boy, an alcoholic realtor, a book agent, and a "lightning dentist,"* are impressed by Doc's dignity and nimble intelligence. Doc's gracious and affable manner draws the men of the Alfalfa European Hotel together into a community; they meet daily in the hotel lobby to converse, relax, and be entertained with another of Doc's tall tales.

The Alfalfa European Hotel and its fragile community epitomize the urban environment and characters of several of Ade's Chicago stories; he would seek out the eccentric and vulnerable places and people to evoke, though with admirable restraint, a general sense of pathos. The hotel and its adjoining ramshackle buildings are maintained by their owner only until a developer will meet his sale price. Before that fateful event, though, Ade allows his odd, weak characters one spirited public defiance: the men of the hotel rally together to defend Doc' when he is implicated in a fraud suit. Doc' had allowed his photograph and signature to be used in advertisements for a patent medicine, and he had been arrested as a partner in the fraud. His fellow boarders hire a lawyer, appear as character and material witnesses at his trial, and then celebrate his acquittal with a banquet in the hotel.

Ade's restrained sentimentality is evident in the novel's conclusion. Doc' is embarrassed by the charges of indigence and vagrancy brought against him by the prosecutor, and he plans his departure from Chicago. In a brief conclusion to the novel, Ade endows Doc' with a $15,000 inheritance and sends him off to Europe. When Doc' returns, he finds that the Alfalfa European Hotel has disappeared:

> When he came back to Chicago in the autumn, on his way to Cincinnati to visit a cousin who was commonly mistaken for Chauncey M. Depew, he wished to go to the Alfalfa European Hotel, but there was no such hotel in Chicago. The old home and the lower houses that propped it up on each side had been

---

*The "lightning dentist" pulls teeth for piece-rate wages at a local dental emporium where scores of his profession are employed.

torn away to make room for a twelve-story office building with
four elevators, and every floor busily inhabited. [No. 2, pp.
291–92]

Doc' Horne, Effie Whittlesy, John Hazen, and the other "losers" in
Ade's Chicago stories characterize his pathetic art. In these stories,
Ade would record the anachronistic people and environments being
overwhelmed in Chicago's growth to industrial maturity, but he would
temper a sentimental response to the loss; he would maintain an
amused, placid distance from his subjects to focus upon their eccentric and endearing features.

Ade's control of sentimentality is also evident in the composition
of his "Stories of the Streets and Town" column. In a typical series
of daily sketches, Ade would mix a few pathetic character studies with
some picturesque accounts of odd places and occupations; then, to
ferment his concoction, he would relate several high-spirited anecdotes about the amusements and fashions of those energetic young
Chicagoans whom one might find, for example, working in the
"twelve-story office building with four elevators" which replaced the
aging Alfalfa European Hotel. For George Ade and his wide audience,
Chicago retained the freshness of its early reputation; it was still the
"young man's town" which drew to its offices, stores, and industries
thousands of hopeful migrants from the farms and small communities
of the Midwest.

Ade's many success stories of young, confident Chicagoans mirrored
his own Chicago experience. He had arrived in Chicago in June 1890
with little money and only vague hopes of employment. Within
eighteen months, he had risen, entirely on his merits, from a
twelve-dollar-a-week cub reporter to a forty-dollar-a-week feature
columnist. When he began his daily "Stories of the Streets and Town"
column in 1893, he selected from the many interviews and observations available to him those incidents and characters which reflected
his own remarkable success as a Chicago journalist.

The most popular of Ade's success stories are those of "Artie
Blanchard," which Ade later published as the popular novel *Artie*
(1898). Artie is a young office clerk distinguished by his rich vocabulary of Chicago slang and by his brash confidence. In the novel, Ade
represents Artie's business office as a moral institution. Through his
work, Artie, the son of a South Side foundry worker, learns business

responsibility, self-discipline, and middle-class propriety. He is fortunate to have gained this opportunity. Ade repeatedly reminds his readers of the ignominious fate which would have befallen Artie had he not found employment in the downtown office. In one incident from the novel, Artie's old friend from the South Side, Billy Munster, a "hanger-on" in city hall, takes Artie out on an all-night drinking binge with two prostitutes. At another time, Artie's alderman tempts him with "boodle" in exchange for campaign support. And, near the end of the novel, one learns that opium smoking had been one of Artie's vices when he ran with the "real dead toughs."

The moral lesson of Artie's deliverance from the corrupt environment in which he had been raised held a very personal meaning for George Ade. Ade had modeled Artie's character and style after Charlie Williams, a young illustrator working in the art department of the *Chicago Record*. George Ade was Charlie Williams's patron. Ade had discovered Williams one winter evening huddled with a group of newsboys over a grating in the alley behind Boyle's Chophouse. He was fascinated by Williams's colorful slang, quick intelligence, and extravagant ambition to become a famous artist. With the assistance of John McCutcheon, Ade secured an apprenticeship for Williams with the *Chicago Record*. Ade's patronage was richly rewarded; Charlie Williams developed into one of the most accomplished and widely known illustrators of his day.

In the opening pages of *Artie,* Ade sets the scene for Artie's eventual assimilation into the moral community of middle-class Chicagoans. Mrs. Morton, wife of Artie's boss, enters the office to sell tickets to a church social. Artie purchases a ticket and then, unexpectedly, finds himself maneuvered by his office mate, Miller, a sober, middle-aged accountant, into actually attending the affair:

> "Sure I'm goin'," he blusteringly answers the amused Mr. Miller. "I've got as much right to go out and do the heavy as any o' you pin-heads. If I like their show I'll help 'em out next time—get a couple o' handy boys and put on a six round go for a finish." [No. 1, pp. 2-3]

Thus Artie is introduced to respectable society. But, unlike his fellow office clerk, the college-educated "young Mr. Hall," Artie is not overwhelmed by respectability. Throughout the novel, Artie retains his distinctive slang and "city wise" irreverence. After the church social, for example, he comically describes Mrs. Morton's reception as an invitation to a back-room poker game:

> "Say, she treated me out o' sight. She meets me at the door, puts out the glad hand and says: 'Hang up your lid and come into the game.'" [No. 1, p. 4]

Artie's unabashed use of slang indicates his innate modesty and honesty; he does not pretend to be anything he is not. This self-honesty allows him a distinct advantage in the personality contests within the office. He can describe, better than anyone else, his own embarrassments and ridiculous postures. For example, when he decides to take up cycling, a sport he had long derided, he entertains the office with a comic description of how he will appear as one of the "club boys":

> "Well, I'm goin' to be one o' them boys," said Artie, after he had seated himself and turned half-way around so that he could see Miller.
> "What boys?" asked Miller.
> "Them bike people with the fried-egg caps and the wall-paper stockins. I'm goin' to be the sassiest club boy in the whole push. You just wait. In about a week I'll come hotfootin' in here with my kneepants and a dinky coat, and do the club yell." [No. 1, p. 154]

Since Artie retains his "tough" street slang, his assimilation of the work ethic maxims of the office is convincing. Ade records this assimilation in a series of incidents in which Artie is pressed to defend the discipline, self-reliance, and prudence valued in the office. And, as the novel progresses, Artie repeatedly appeals to his office superiors, particularly the conscientious Mr. Miller, for moral guidance. For example, when Artie's alderman promises him a share in city hall graft in exchange for campaign support, Artie refers his decision to Miller:

> "Artie, that kind of a man is a thief and that's all you can make of it," said Miller, with presbyterian severity. [No. 1, p. 108]

Artie accedes to Miller's objections. He refuses the easy graft, and a few pages later one discovers him working long hours of overtime to complete an important assignment. Chicago's businessmen, as represented in *Artie,* are a scrupulously moral and productive fraternity.

Artie's success in his office eases his courtship of Mamie Carroll. His promising career impresses her family and gains him the respect of her friends and neighbors. Gradually, Artie is initiated into the Carolls' West Side neighborhood: he shares their front stoops on summer evenings; he brings Miller out to meet Mamie and her family; he serves as best man at the wedding of Mamie's closest friend. The novel concludes, appropriately, with Artie's proposal to Mamie on a warm summer evening in a moonlight-drenched park by the lakefront.

Artie's success, in work and in love, became the moral standard of Ade's Chicago stories. Artie is educated in the discipline and responsibility which ideally characterized American business, and he is welcomed into a respectable middle-class community. His energy, self-assurance, and good-natured generosity were the moral qualities Ade repeatedly endorsed in his several stories of young and successful Chicagoans.

One group of Chicagoans, though, as represented in the "Stories of the Streets and Town," were incapable of fully realizing Artie's virtues. These handicapped Chicagoans were the city's Negroes, whose numbers, in the years from 1890 to 1920, dramatically increased from 14,271 to 109,458. Ade often described, for his amused readers, the innate laziness, sensuality, and limited intelligence of the Chicago Negro, which ordained him for an inferior rank in Chicago society.

The most frequent and popular of Ade's Negro characters was "William Pickney Marsh," a young "cullud boy" who labored at a shoeshine stand in a Chicago barbershop. Ade's characterization of "Pink Marsh" was strongly influenced by the stereotypes of the urban Negro current in Chicago vaudeville. Throughout his adult life, beginning with his introduction to the Grand Opera House in Lafayette, Ade was an enthusiastic patron of vaudeville and the popular stage. In Chicago, in addition to his daily column, he frequently reviewed the new "bills" in the city's various popular theaters. He knew many of the entertainers, and he counted among his closest friends the renowned blackface comics George Thatcher and Willis Sweatman.

The vaudeville image of the urban Negro in the 1890s, it should be pointed out, was significantly different from the earlier minstrel characterization. As Russell Nye comments in his comprehensive survey of American popular arts, *The Unembarrassed Muse:*

> The minstrel show was never sexually suggestive, obscene, or scatalogical. Its humor was occasionally rowdy, but never vulgar. It treated the Negro as an object of amusement, but its racism was never vicious or degrading.[3]

The 1890s, however, introduced a marked change in this image of the Negro. Vaudeville, according to Nye,

> introduced a tough, overtly sexual element into popular music, reflecting the changed manners and mores of an urbanizing, polyglot, acquisitive, and increasingly sophisticated society. This derived partly from the dialect "coon song," from the white minstrel show, and partly from the ragtime songs from Negro honky-tonk low life. The minstrel show developed a comic song based on the caricature of the chicken-stealing, cakewalking, "high yaller" city Negro, done by white men in blackface.... The "coon song" suddenly became a nineties fad (some six hundred of them were written between 1890 and 1900) with one called "Coon! Coon! Coon!" representing the ultimate. Many had ribald, frankly sexual implications—"I Got Mine," "You Don't Have to Marry the Girl," "I Don't Like No Cheap Man," "Pump Away Joseph," or "A Red Hot Member" (who's "cooler than December" and "can surely sting like a bumble-bee").[4]

Ade's portrait of Pink Marsh reflects the caricatures of the Negro by Chicago's blackface comics, "coon shouters," and ragtime musicians. Pink covets the promiscuous "Dearborn Street" women, spends his quarters and half-dollars on "policy," and consumes his every extra dollar in "gin and honey" and craps. At one point in the novel, Pink even entertains his customers and employers by singing, "with his eyes dreamily half-closed," the notoriously degrading "coon song" "All Coons Look Alike to Me":

All a-coons looks alike to me;
I got a new beau, you see,
An' he's-jus as good to me
As you, niggeh, eveh daihed to be,
He's a sutny a-good to me;
He spen's his-a money free.
I do n' like you a-nohow;
All-a coons looks alike to me.
        [No. 6, pp. 117–18]

Ade's purpose in *Pink Marsh,* as it is in *Artie,* is to move his protagonist out of a corrupt Chicago environment, the South Side district of
Artie's youth or the Dearborn Street of Pink's adventures, into a responsible, ordered Chicago community. In terms of the popular
images of Negroes then current, Ade attempts to reform Pink from
a vaudeville "coon" to a minstrel entertainer. The reform is necessary
because the "coon" threatens the moral order of middle-class Chicago.
Ade repeatedly reminds his readers of the anarchic threat which the
"coon" poses. He has Pink frequently refer to the knifings, robberies,
and drunken debauches of the "niggehs" in the Dearborn and Clark
Street ghetto. Ade also reminds his readers that the unreformed "coon"
will be used to undermine all efforts by conscientious Chicagoans to
reform the municipal government: in one incident, Ade describes
Pink's susceptibility to the overtures of "Gawge Lippincott," secretary of the "Milleh In'epen'en Cullud Votehs League," an organization responsible for delivering the Negro vote to Gus Miller, a thoroughly venal Chicago alderman.

In comparing *Pink Marsh* with *Artie,* one notices a significant
difference in Ade's descriptions of the moral reform possible for
each protagonist: Artie Blanchard is rational, while Pink Marsh is
simply sensual. In the course of his employment in a Chicago business, Artie learns the moral requirements for success and decides to
accept them. He chooses to save money and keep regular hours, and
he refuses to accept the bribe his alderman offers. Pink, however, does
not make rational or moral decisions; he simply chooses the easiest
means of satisfying his appetites. He wants a full stomach, a comfortable home, and an easy job. These desires are frustrated in the
violent ghetto along Dearborn and Clark streets. In that area of

Chicago's black district, Pink is cheated of his money, spurned by women in favor of "hot papas" with large bank rolls, and, in one incident, is mobbed and beaten by the "toughs" in a Clark Street tavern. Pink discovers that his appetites will be best satisfied if he marries an older and propertied widow:

> She ain't young as some of 'em otheh babies I had lookin' out faw me, but you 'membeh what I tol' you once, misteh? Cake-walks is good, but you can't eat 'em. You do n' ketch me stahvin'. No, seh! 'At lady I got ain't so wahm on cloze as some of 'em, but she sutny fix up a pohk chop 'at's bad to eat. 'At's love all right, misteh; but Misteh Mahsh sutney got to have his pohk chops. . . . I s'pose I'm pooh. Got my own dooh-step to set on, new suit o' cloze, joined 'e lodge. Do n' speak to 'em cheap cullud people no mo'. [No. 6, pp. 195–96]

In addition to the difficulties Pink must overcome to secure a comfortable place in Chicago (at the novel's conclusion he is a Pullman porter), the dramatic interest of the novel centers on the relation between Pink and the "morning customer," a prosperous Chicago lawyer who frequents Pink's shoeshine stand. In his characterization of the morning customer, Ade salvages his book from the smug stereotypes which had governed his description of Pink. Ade reveals that the eminent Chicago lawyer is merely a patronizing, conceited prig. In a typical situation, the morning customer will condescendingly allow Pink to converse with him and then, for Pink's edification and his own pleasure, he will impress Pink with his erudite vocabulary:

> "Mistah, what is 'at emvalution?"
> "I believe it is defined as a change, by continuous differentiation and integration, from a simple homogeneity to a complex heterogeneity, or something like that." [No. 6, p. 69]

Frequently, the morning customer will mock Pink's confidence in his learning and friendship. For example, when Pink asks him to compose a conciliatory letter to the mother of a girl he is courting, the morning customer, confident that the girl's mother is as ignorant as Pink, cannot resist including in the letter a joke at Pink's expense:

I wish to deny emphatically anything you may hear which is
not derogatory to my character. [No. 6, p. 176]

Though Pink Marsh satisfied Ade's readers as an accurate representation of the urban Negro (Mark Twain wrote William Dean Howells,
"Pink,———oh, the shiftless, worthless, lovable black darling! Howells,
he deserves to live forever"),[5] some readers perceived and resented the
subversion of their settled values in Ade's characterization of the morning customer. A reviewer in *Bookman*, for example, indignantly protested Ade's failure to realize the morning customer's obvious virtues:

> The parade of long words which left Pink openmouthed and
> staring into vacancy produces a sense of shame even in the
> reader. Here was a chance, incidentally and by way of contrast,
> to sketch a gentleman, who should impress Pink by his freedom
> from priggishness and braggadocio. . . . Next time we wish Mr.
> Ade would bestow more attention on his lay figures.[6]

Pink Marsh (1897), *Artie* (1898), and *Doc' Horne* (1899) earned Ade
national recognition. His most prominent and valued admirer was
William Dean Howells:

> Henry B. Fuller and Hamlin Garland had spoken words of en-
> couragement, and there was a letter from William Dean Howells
> which gold could not have purchased. [No. 7, p. 50]

In commenting on Ade's novels, Howells did not perceive any uniquely
Chicagoan style or theme; instead, he appreciated the "unerringly
ascertained average of American life" which they expressed. A review
in *North American Review*, for instance, finds Howells describing Ade
as a droll country cousin who personified the "American spirit":

> In George Ade the American spirit arrives: arrives, puts down its
> grip, looks around, takes a chair and makes itself at home. It has
> no questions to ask and none to answer. There it is, with its hat
> pushed back, its hands in its pockets, and at its outstretched feet
> that whole vast, droll American world, essentially alike in Maine
> and Oregon and all the hustling regions between: speaking one
> slang, living one life, meaning one thing.[7]

In Howells's judgment, Ade was a very promising young American realist and potentially a greater writer than Mark Twain. He noted approvingly that Ade consistently maintained an objective point of view, selected commonplace diction, and employed humor for moral ends. As a measure of his esteem, he invited Ade in 1900 to be one of "twenty leading American and English authors" in a series of new novels he had agreed to edit.[8] Ade, however, despite his respect for Howells, declined the generous invitation; by 1900, he had abandoned his earlier intention to write short stories and novels in a conventionally realist style. He had become, in his words, "the High Priest of American Slang," and he had little time, or economic motive, to write another *Artie* or *Doc' Horne,* even for William Dean Howells.

Ade's success as a writer of slang had begun three years earlier, on September 17, 1897, with the publication of "The Fable of Sister Mae, Who Did as Well as Could Be Expected" in his "Stories of the Streets and Town" column. The impact of Ade's fable was phenomenal:

> Next day the score keepers told me I had knocked a home run.
> The young women on the staff told me the piece was "just killing."
> I found the head editor giggling over the darn fool thing.
> "You've struck a lead," he said. "Follow it up."
> Then I heard from the publisher.
> "Write a lot more of these fables for the paper," he said.
> "Because of the bold type, they are filling; and in a little while we can get out a book." [No. 7, p. 197]

Within a year of the publication of "Sister Mae," Ade was earning eight hundred dollars a week for his nationally syndicated fables. He never returned to the "consecrated job of writing long and photographic reports of life in the Middle West" that William Dean Howells appreciated.

The "Fable of Sister Mae" typifies the impudent humor and brisk, colloquial language of the hundreds of Ade's "Fables in Slang" that were to follow it. It comically describes the different fortunes of two sisters who "lived in Chicago, the Home of Opportunity":

Luella was a Good Girl, who had taken Prizes at the Mission Sunday School, but she was Plain, much. Her features did not seem to know the value of Team Work. Her Clothes fit her intermittently, as it were. She was what would be called a Lumpy Dresser. But she had a good Heart.

Luella found Employment at a Hat Factory. All she had to do was to put Red Linings in Hats for the Country Trade; and every Saturday Evening when Work was called on account of Darkness, the Boss met her as she went out and crowded three Dollars on her.

The other Sister was Different.

She began as Mary, then changed to Marie, and her Finish was Mae.

From earliest Youth she had lacked Industry and Application.

She was short on Intellect but long on Shape. [No. 3, pp. 135-36]

Mae, of course, succeeds spectacularly in Chicago. Of all the men who propose to her, she chooses a "Bucket Shop Man,* who was not Handsome, but was awful Generous." Mae chose wisely. Shortly after her marriage, "Wheat jumped twenty-two points," and Mae moved into a "Sarcophagus on the Boulevard, right in between two Old Families." Eventually, Mae remembered her industrious sister Luella and hired her as assistant cook at five dollars a week. The fable ends with the ironic moral: "Industry and Perseverance bring a sure Reward."

Despite their amusing reversals of moral clichés, Ade's "Fables in Slang," like his popular novels and newspaper columns, were essentially virtuous and uplifting. In his earlier novels, Ade had described the moral reform of young Chicago men; in his "Fables in Slang," he reformed Chicago's street language:

There are niceties of distinction even when out on a slang debauch.

I never referred to a policeman as a "bull," because that word

---

*A "Bucket Shop" was a brokerage firm specializing in small lot orders ("buckets") of commodity futures on the Chicago Grain Exchange.

belongs in the criminal vocabulary, and Mother and the girls are not supposed to be familiar with the cryptic terms of yeggmen.

I never referred to a young girl as a "chicken." The word originated in the deepest pits of white slavery, and it always gave me the creeps. A young girl may be a flapper, a bud, a peach, a pippin, a lolly-paloozer, a nectarine, a cutie, a queen, the one best bet, a daisy, or even a baby doll, without being insulted; but never a "chicken," unless one is writing a treatise on social problems. . . .

Besides, this so-called "slang" that romps so gayly into the homes and offices of the socially important is not slang at all. It is not the argot of the criminal element. [No. 7, p. 51]

As these "niceties of distinction" illustrate, Ade did not reject the aesthetic standards of William Dean Howells in becoming the "High Priest of American Slang"; he continued to seek the "unerringly ascertained average of American life" in separating American slang from vicious, obscene, or degrading Chicago criminal argot. Indeed, if one were to identify the culture of Ade's "Fables in Slang," particularly in light of Ade's background, one would more likely choose Lafayette, Indiana, than Chicago. With the exception of the first fables, published in the "Stories of the Streets and Town" column, few of Ade's fables are set in Chicago or in any identifiable city. Instead, Ade selected for the audience of his widely syndicated feature those communities, characters, and situations which seemed to best represent the national culture. Most of the "Fables in Slang" are set in midwestern villages, small towns, and medium-sized cities. The most frequent characters are farmers, small businessmen, college youth, traveling salesmen, maidens, and housewives. In his "Fables," as Carl Van Doren succinctly noted, Ade consistently ridicules "the reformers, climbers, Bohemians, zealous or shiftless souls of all denominations who secede from the homely circle of the average." His central moral is that "those get along best who best mind their own business."[9]

In 1901, Ade's literary career departed even further from Howells's earlier expectations; as Ade comically described the turn:

While on the sidetrack, trying to get back to the main line, I ran into a second misplaced switch, and finished—where do you suppose? In a gilded playhouse as a comic opera librettist!—two degrees above a professional roller skater and one rung of the ladder below a male hairdresser. [No. 7, p. 198]

The most successful of Ade's comic operas, *The County Chairman* (1903) and *The College Widow* (1904), nostalgically evoke, through stereotyped characters and heart-warming dramatic resolutions, the wholesome "Hoosier" culture of Ade's youth and later manhood. *The College Widow,* for example, boisterously celebrates the adolescent football and fraternity culture of Ade's Purdue University. It describes the elaborate intrigues of the Atwater College football team to lure a star athlete away from their conference rival, Bingham College. The football boys persuade the "college widow," Jane Witherspoon, daughter of the college president, to seduce the rival athlete. Her flirtation succeeds, and Atwater wins the conference championship. At the play's conclusion, President Witherspoon, a haughty, cultured New Englander, becomes a rabid fan, the "college widow" marries the football hero, and the college's principal trustee, Bolton, a self-made millionaire with democratic, folksy manners, treats everyone to a victory party.

The nostalgic, sentimental entertainment of Ade's musical comedies and of his "Fables in Slang" can be seen, despite Howells's repeated protests, as the fulfillment of Ade's original intention to become known as a realist. In commenting upon the style of his works, Ade declared that all of them should be judged in terms of a realist aesthetic:

My early story stuff was intended to be "realistic" and I believed firmly in short words and short sentences. By a queer twist of circumstances I have become known to the general public as a "humorist" and a writer of "slang." I never wanted to be a comic or tried to be one. The playful vernacular and idiomatic talk of the street and the fanciful figures of speech which came out for years under the heading of "Fables in Slang" had no relation whatever to the cryptic language of the underworld or the patois of the criminal element. Always I wrote for the "family trade" and I used no word or phrase which might give offense to mother and the girls or a professor of English.[10]

Ade's consistent desire to write for the "family trade" indicates the essentially sentimental nature of his "realism." He never fully imagined Chicago as a unique subject demanding a fresh and possibly profane treatment. Rather, he would construe the characters, situations, and language suggested by his Chicago experiences to express the conventional attitudes of rural, small-town Americans. "Artie," for example, while using the Chicago slang which was the trademark of his character, could sincerely welcome Miller's country cousin and put him at ease:

> I'm tellin' you, the worst suckers you'll find is some o' these
> city people that know it all to begin with. . . . You couldn't set
> 'em down and tell 'em a thing. Any of 'em that's got himself
> staked to a spring suit and knows the chorus o' "Paradise Alley"
> thinks he's up to the limit. You can make book that them boys'll
> be workin' on bum salaries when they're gray headed, and what's
> more, they'll be workin' for some Reub that came into town
> wearin' hand-me-downs. [No. 1, p. 169]

For Ade's characters, industry, perseverance and good humor will bring them the same rewards in Chicago they could have expected on Main Street. Ade always accented those conditions in which Chicagoans experienced, in their work, recreation, or homes, some familiar feature of small-town community life. He described for his audience the various means by which isolated Chicagoans were drawn into a secure and friendly community of their peers.

Often, however, the sentimental resolutions which Ade attempted were strained and hesitant. In his effort to portray Chicago as a familiar hometown, Ade was restricted to a narrow range of characters and environments. He selected young office workers, independent tradesmen and merchants (cobblers, dry cleaners, vendors, small restaurant owners, barbers, boardinghouse matrons), picturesque laborers (canal boatmen, teamsters, carriage drivers, chiropodists, Bible salesmen, dock workers), and sentimental old men. These characters work in small offices, one-man shops, or in specific, unique districts of Chicago. The intimate scale of their work and associations suggests, often, that they are out of place in Chicago; they are, instead, relics of a culture which is being overwhelmed and dispersed in the steady development of large industries, labor unions, and retail stores. This sense of imminent loss is explicit in the demolition of the Alfalfa European Hotel in *Doc' Horne;* and it is implicit in the closing of Arthur Ponsby's window by a new, tall office building, in the restriction of Artie Blanchard's activities and opinions to the routines of his office, and in the reformation of Pink Marsh into a sober, obsequious train porter.

The "Fables in Slang" and musical comedies, though, were artistic forms which allowed Ade greater freedom in creating his resolutions of traditional attitudes with contemporary expression. In the "Stories of the Streets and Town," he had been restrained by requirements of verisimilitude; he had to shape particular characters to fit specific conditions of work, residence, and recreation in Chicago. In the "Fables in Slang" and musical comedies, however, he could broadly define character types (traveling salesmen, college youths, stolid businessmen, voluble politicians, sentimental girls, and laconic farmers are the characters which most frequently appear), and he was free to imagine situations in which to place and contrast his comic characters. With this freedom, he was able to concentrate on the aesthetic theme which most engaged his enthusiasm and wit: the nuances of the idiomatic language which identified Americans as a distinct and self-conscious people. Some of his characteristic expressions from the "Fables in Slang" are these: "To get a fair Trial of Speed, use a Pace-Maker"; "Say, ain't she the Smooth Article?"; "A New York Man never begins to Cut Ice until he is west of Rahway"; "A Finishing School is a Place at which Young Ladies are taught how to give the Quick Finish to all Persons who won't do." With these and similar expressions, Ade integrated the flip slang of Chicago office clerks and Purdue fraternity brothers with the colloquialisms of Main Street to produce a standard American idiom that was wholesome, entertaining, and refreshingly familiar.

Ring Lardner, Ade's friend and young colleague, was also a sensitive observer of American colloquial language. However, unlike Ade, Lardner was distressed by what he perceived to be a general debasement of colloquial language in Chicago. While Ade could confidently reform Chicago's street language into an entertaining "parlor slang," Lardner found in the language of Chicagoans the symptoms of the city's demoralizing effect on her common citizens. His fiction, written between 1911 and 1920, more closely approximates the critical view expressed in the Chicago novels of Henry Fuller, Robert Herrick, Will Payne, Frank Norris, Robert Morse Lovett, and Theodore Dreiser than do the optimistic comedies of Finley Peter Dunne and George Ade. Though Lardner shared Dunne and Ade's commitment to entertain a popular audience, he could not sustain their comic affirmation; he could not find their healthy, vigorous preserves of small town culture within the industrial, metropolitan Chicago he knew.

4

RING LARDNER

Finley Peter Dunne and George Ade had consciously affirmed the values of the common man; they had transcribed his colloquial language, defended his conventional morality, and respected his sentiments. Their purpose, as popular artists, was to amusingly describe those means by which Irish immigrants and rural midwesterners, foundry laborers and office clerks shaped Chicago neighborhoods into the familiar mold of an American small town. The average Chicagoan, as they represented him, participated in local politics, supported his local church, and carefully maintained a quiet, modestly comfortable home and neighborhood. Their intimate portraits of Chicagoans and Chicago neighborhoods were on the whole emotionally and morally comforting.

Ring Lardner's motives in writing for a popular audience are more ambivalent than Dunne's or Ade's simple affirmations. He often seems to be at once the common man's advocate and his severe critic. His comic writings, especially his many short stories, prompted widely varying reactions from critics and readers. Gilbert Seldes, for example, could claim that "Ring Lardner is, I suppose, the only man in America who can begin, 'Well, friends,'" while Clifton Fadiman, with equal assurance, could insist that "the special force of Ring Lardner's work springs from a single fact: he just doesn't like people."[1] Both reactions are understandable. Ring Lardner exhibits both affection and disdain for the "middlebrow" audience which enjoyed his stories in

Saturday Evening Post, Collier's, The American Magazine, and other mass circulation periodicals.

Lardner engages his reader's sympathy by consistently writing in the first person singular and by adopting, as his own voice, the idiom of the common man. He restricts his language to the ordinary diction of workingmen, well-laced with their colloquialisms, and he composes his writing to reflect the rather haphazard syntax of common speech. Thus, in his essay on Christy Mathewson, published in *The American Magazine,* Lardner expresses his opinions in the following casual manner:

> I s'pose when he broke in he didn't have no more control than the rest o' these here collegers. But the difference between they and him was that he seen what a good thing it was to have, and went out and got it, while they, that is, the most o' them, thought they could go along all right with what they had. [No. 20, p. 27]

Lardner's idiomatic speech, for all its apparent laxity in syntax and grammar, is nevertheless a terse satiric instrument. By adopting the semiliterate idiom of a "wise boob,"* Lardner could express, in the language his popular audience best understood, his sense of the generally debased character of their urban lives. In reading Lardner's fiction, one is always aware of a muffled belligerence threatening to erupt into abuse, complaint, or even obscenity. Notice, for example, the boorish egotism of "Gullible," one of Lardner's early characters who lives in Chicago:

> When we got back to the hotel they was only just time to clean up and go down to supper. We hadn't no sooner got seated when

---

*Lardner defined his characteristic "wise boobs" as follows: "A wise boob; hails from a small town; migrated to Chicago; is convinced that it is the greatest town in the world. A thirty-five dollar a week man with a real sense of humor, reads all the newspapers, *The Saturday Evening Post, The American Magazine,* the Sunday supplements, and an occasional popular novel. Has a faculty for crystallizing any subject he discusses into a few lines, expressed in a manner characteristic of a certain type of American. Never had much use for rhetoric and proves it in his speech. A regular honest-to-god he man. Leads a regular life; has regular friends and is perfectly content to wade through life in a regular way." Donald Elder, *Ring Lardner,* 1956, p. 136.

our table companions breezed in. It was a man about forty-five,
that looked like he'd made his money in express and general
haulin', and he had his wife along and both their mother-in-
laws. The shirt he had on was the one he'd started from home
with, if he lived in Yokohama. His womenfolks wore mournin'
with a touch o' gravy here and there. [No. 19, pp. 62-63]

With his apparently ill-disciplined idiom, Lardner suggests the dis-
integration of moral and social standards in the city; his characters
exhibit little respect for the standards of courtesy, modesty, or good
taste. Their humor is sarcasm and rude practical jokes. Dunne and
Ade, by contrast, had expressed, through their characters' comic
language, a quite different sense of urban culture. For Dunne,
Chicago had stimulated the Irish immigrant to sharpen his folk
dialect into an accurate, humorous, and perceptive urban idiom.
The speech of Mr. Dooley, particularly his concise, ironic aphorisms
("I care not who makes th' laws iv a nation if I can get out an in-
juction," for example), indicates self-control, intelligence, and abound-
ing confidence. George Ade suggests the same qualities in his richly
figurative Chicago slang. And, by his modification of actual Chicago
slang into an appropriate "parlor slang," Ade indicated a keen respect
for the moral scruples of average Chicagoans.

In Lardner's fiction, though, one misses the sense of affirmation,
restraint and propriety which had imbued Dunne and Ade's work.
They had affirmed Chicago as a healthy, moral community by
representing certain Chicago neighborhoods as the novel re-creations
of stable, rural community cultures. Lardner could not sustain their
effort in assimilating the two dissimilar cultures, urban and rural,
industrial and agrarian. Like the Chicago novelists of the 1890s,
Lardner perceived Chicago as a radically unique environment which
incited its people to selfish, immoral, and aggressive behavior. He
translated the novelists' tragic themes of alienation and moral corruption into the modest lives of "thirty-five dollar a week" Chicagoans.
Dunne and Ade had always distinguished the modest citizen from
other Chicagoans; he, if not his economic masters, still preserved
the moral values of an earlier, simpler village culture. Lardner demonstrated that the common man could not be distinguished from the
city in which he lived.

Lardner's first, and still most widely appreciated, urban comic character was Jack Keefe, the "busher" who became a successful pitcher for the Chicago White Sox. Lardner's portrait of professional baseball in *You Know Me, Al* (1916), the epistolary novel of Jack Keefe's two-season career, is detailed and knowledgeable. He drew on an eight-year experience as a sports writer, six years of which he had spent traveling with the Chicago Cubs and Chicago White Sox. In his book he expresses his esteem for baseball and the game's accomplished players through his distinction, scrupulously maintained, between the "bushers" (always fictional characters) and the "regulars" (always actual baseball players). Jack Keefe, a "raw recrut" from Terre Haute of the Central League, is a "busher," inexperienced, overconfident, and irresponsible. It is the duty of the White Sox "regulars"—manager "Cal" Callahan, coach "Kid" Gleason, and veteran pitcher Ed Walsh, principally—to season him into a professional pitcher. The task is formidable, but with patience, insults, fines, and occasional praise, they succeed. In one season, they turn "bonehead" Keefe into the most capable pitcher on the mediocre White Sox team.

The story of Jack Keefe's "education" as a player for the Chicago White Sox is instructive for what it tells us of Ring Lardner's values, attitude, and style as a comic artist. He represents the ball team as a close-knit and responsible community; it is the equivalent, in his work, of Mr. Dooley's "Bridgeport" or George Ade's boardinghouses, offices, and social clubs. As is the case with the neighborly communities evoked by the earlier humorists, Lardner's ball team is humanly satisfying; however, unlike Dunne and Ade, Lardner represents the community of the ball team as artificial, its work as professional entertainment, and its season as short-lived. It does not focus the political and social life of Chicago as Bridgeport does or as Artie Blanchard's office does; the ball team simply has a place and a season within the city.

When Jack Keefe joins the White Sox, he has the obvious talent of a major league pitcher—a strong fast ball and an intimidating curve—but he lacks the necessary modesty and discipline for learning his craft. Throughout spring training and the early season, he infuriates his coaches and teammates by ignoring their instruction and often stubbornly refusing their demands. Predictably, his initial trial as a professional player ends disastrously. He pitches against the Detroit

Tigers, the best team in baseball at the time, and yields sixteen runs in seven innings. Ty Cobb steals four bases; Donie Bush, Sam Crawford, and Bobby Veach steal two each. Keefe walks half a dozen batters, hits two or three more, and bobbles every bunt which the Tigers maliciously push toward him. In the third inning, Cobb bunts directly to Keefe, and Jack falls flat on his face trying to field the ball. Finally, after seven innings, manager "Cal" Callahan decides that Keefe's humiliation is complete:

> I says It's about time you found out my arm was sore. He says I ain't worrying about your arm but I'm afraid some of our outfielders will run their legs off and some of them poor infielders will get killed. He says The reporters just sent me a message saying they had run out of paper. Then he says I wish some of the other clubs had pitchers like you so we could hit once in a while. He says Go in the clubhouse and get your arm rubbed off. That's the only way I can get Jennings sore at me he says. [No. 22, p. 47]

Jack's inept performance earns him his release from the club and assignment to San Francisco of the Pacific Coast League.

The skills Jack learns with the San Francisco club are important because they are the disciplined skills of a team player. Jack had been vulnerable in the Detroit Tigers game with the White Sox because he stupidly threw a hard fastball or curve every pitch, because he often forgot the base runners, and because he had never practiced fielding. Now, humbled by his assignment to a minor league team, he learns to pitch a slow change-of-pace ball, he learns to field his position and hold base runners, and—most important—he learns to obey his catcher, coaches, and manager. In ten weeks he compiles an impressive eleven win, two loss record. The White Sox recall him late in the season and he wins four consecutive starts for them. The next season, after manager Callahan again wisely humbles Jack, this time by assigning him to the second team during spring training, Jack becomes the mainstay of the White Sox pitching staff. He wins thirteen games, loses seven, and concludes the season by winning two of three games in the White Sox–Cubs intercity series.

Professional baseball, as Lardner represents it, is unquestionably valuable for Jack Keefe; the game disciplines him to work with an uncharacteristic dedication, and it justly rewards him on the merits of his performance. Lardner consistently represents the seasoned players and managers, those who have mastered baseball's rigorous competitive standards, as intelligent, fair men genuinely dedicated to serving their team. Obviously, such a portrait glosses over the often ruthless competition which baseball encouraged between veterans and rookies, as well as the petty tyranny in which managers and owners frequently indulged. Many of the players of Lardner's time—Fred Snodgrass, "Wahoo Sam" Crawford, Tommy Leach, "Chief" Meyers, Al Bridwell, and Paul Waner, to name a few of the more outspoken—protested their frustration with the sabotage of their play as rookies. Jealous veterans, they protested, often monopolized practice time or deliberately confused rookies with contradictory instructions; piqued managers and coaches often vented their anger by harassing new players. Paul Waner, for example, has vividly reported how his pitching career was abruptly ended when a martinet coach forced him beyond his endurance:

> The first or second day of spring training we had a little game, the Regulars against the Yannigans—that's what they called the rookies—and I was pitching for the Yannigans. The umpire was a coach by the name of Spider Baum. Along about the sixth inning my arm started to tighten up, so I shouted in, "Spider, my arm is tying up and getting sore on me."
> "Make it or break it!" he says.
> They don't say those things to youngsters nowadays. No, sir! And maybe it's just as well they don't, because what happened was that, sure enough, I broke it! And the next day, gee, I could hardly lift it.[2]

As an experienced sports writer, Lardner certainly knew the abuses rookies frequently suffered. However, he acknowledges these abuses in only two brief incidents in *You Know Me, Al:* manager Callahan's harassment of Jack during his loss to the Tigers and owner Comiskey's shrewd manipulation of Jack into an underpriced, long-term contract. Otherwise, Lardner generously portrays baseball as a productive, moral,

and fraternal activity. His portrait, however, does not appear sentimental or false because the baseball "regulars" express themselves
in an abrasive "wise boob" language of sarcasm and profanity. Manager Callahan and coach Gleason do not solicit Jack's cooperation;
they discipline him with ridicule and, when necessary, with fines
and suspensions. Significantly, the measure of Jack's maturity as a
ball player, after his apprenticeship with the San Francisco team,
is his mastery of the veteran's wit:

> Then Cobb come over and asked if I was going to work. Calla-
> han told him Yes. Cobb says How many innings? Callahan says
> All the way. Then Cobb says Be a good fellow Cal and take
> him out early. I am lame and can't run. I butts in then and
> said Don't worry, Cobb. You won't have to run because we
> have got a catcher who can hold them third strikes. Callahan
> laughed again and says to me You sure did learn something
> out on that Coast. [No. 22, p. 60]

In *You Know Me, Al,* unlike Lardner's later fiction, the wise-boob
language signifies control, self-discipline, and quick intelligence because it is the polished idiom of professionals. As a rookie, Jack
Keefe's language was crude, literal, and abusive—his response to every
joke, criticism, and mishap was the same: "If he ever talks to me like
he done to him I will take a punch at him." With experience, though,
Jack begins to understand and speak—to manager Callahan's surprised
delight—the quick, confident, and sarcastic idiom of a seasoned player;
he is even able to talk down Ty Cobb.

In Lardner's descriptions of Jack Keefe as a ball player, we see that
baseball's discipline is valuable; however, its effect is short-lived. During
the off season, Jack's language degenerates into vulgarity, and his moral
character declines into sloth, greed, and temper. In South Side Chicago,
Jack freely indulges those appetites which the White Sox had carefully
curbed: he sleeps until noon, eats and drinks to excess, wastes all his
money, and on several occasions assaults the waiters, bartenders, and
strangers who, he fancies, have affronted him. It is this degeneration
of character, rather than Jack Keefe's competent performance as a
professional ball player, which has earned *You Know Me, Al* its reputation as an uncompromising satire on the American athlete.

Jack's moral and physical corruption is quickened by his novel experience of freedom and anonymity in Chicago. As a stranger on the South Side, he is freed of the public opinion which, in his hometown of Bedford, Indiana, would have disciplined his behavior much as the vigilant coaches and manager of the White Sox had during the season. It should be noted in Jack's defense, and Lardner carefully establishes this qualification, that he did not seek the moral freedom of living anonymously in Chicago. Throughout his first season, he never questioned the value of a settled domestic life in quiet Bedford. His wife, though, a woman he marries after a five-day courtship at the end of the season, does not share his enthusiasm for Bedford. Instead, Florrie wants swell clothes, "mohoggeny" furniture, jewelry, entertainment, and a hired girl; she wants, and she gets, Chicago.

When Jack marries Florrie, he has $1400 saved from his $1500 salary and $800 intercity series bonus. By February 9, four months later, he is deeply in debt. This swift bankruptcy marks an even more dramatic change in Jack's character. He was, by habits formed in his hometown, an obstinately frugal man, as his scrupulous catalogue of his wedding expenses indicates:

License	$ 2.00
Preist	3.50
Haircut & shave	.35
Shine	.05
Carfair	.45
New Suit	14.50
Show tickets	3.00
Flowers	.50
Candy	.30
Hotel	4.50
Tobacco both kinds	.25

[No. 22, p. 83]

By New Year's Day, though, after only ten weeks of living with Florrie in South Side Chicago, Jack is impulsively and stupidly wasting hundreds of dollars. He buys a complete set of furniture for his already furnished apartment, he indulges Florrie's appetite for clothes and jewelry, and he hires a housekeeper. Goaded by his in-laws, who have moved in with him to conserve their dwindling resources, he pays for several expensive drinking sprees in Chicago clubs and taverns.

The Chicago winter of Jack's corruption ends dismally. Florrie, piqued by his inability to pay her way to spring training, deserts him. To meet his debts, Jack begs a $100 advance from Comiskey and borrows $175 from Al. Comiskey refuses Jack's second request for money, puts him on waivers, and negotiates to sell him to Milwaukee.

During the next season, Jack is reconciled with the White Sox and Florrie: Comiskey signs him to a three-year contract at his original salary and Florrie returns because she is pregnant. Throughout that season, the White Sox management accepts the responsibility of keeping Jack's marriage intact. The greatest challenge comes in the third game of the White Sox–Cubs intercity series. Jack had pitched a shutout in the opening game and seven innings of shutout ball in the third game. Then he looked into the stands and saw Florrie:

> It was Florrie and Marie and both of them claping there hands and hollering with the rest of the bugs.
>
> Well old pal I was never so supprised in my life and it just took all the heart out of me. What was they doing there and what had they did with the baby? How did I know that little Al was not sick or maybe dead and balling his head off and nobody round to hear him? [No. 22, p. 174]

This crisis, as with several other crises in Jack's off-field life, is resolved by Kid Gleason, the White Sox coach specially charged with Jack's care. He privately offers Florrie fifty dollars a day to remain home. Florrie accepts and then reneges on her promise. She hires a baby-sitter, attends all the remaining games, and returns home by cab. After the series, Jack discovers her deception. He vows to divorce her, but then forgives her when she agrees, reluctantly, to return with him to Bedford. They never do return to Bedford, because Jack goes on a barnstorming tour with the White Sox and Giants; before he leaves, he conceals half of his savings in negotiating financial arrangements with Florrie.

You Know Me, Al entertained thousands of readers by confirming familiar and comfortable attitudes about baseball. In Lardner's early comic fiction, as well as in several sports essays, until the stunning revelations of the 1919 "Black Sox" scandal disturbed his opinion, baseball represented an enduring but—regrettably—increasingly anachronistic moral society. It epitomized the values of honest labor, democratic opportunity, self-reliance, and community cooperation ideally associated with the traditional ways of American small towns—particularly, for Lardner, the ways of his hometown of Niles, Michigan. In baseball, a small-town man like Jack Keefe could feel welcome and needed; he worked in a close-knit community of thirty players and coaches, and his talents, proven in fair competition, were essential to the team's success.

In limiting Jack Keefe's competence to baseball, and to the type of traditional community it represented, Lardner established the moral criteria by which he would measure all his urban characters. None of Lardner's Chicago characters, beginning with Jack Keefe, can control the base appetites which the city excited; none, except Jack Keefe, could retreat from the city to compete, without favor or disability, for an honorable place in a secure and fraternal society. Lacking Jack Keefe's exceptional opportunity, Lardner's wise boobs flounder pathetically. They are routinely victimized by the bores, *poseurs,* and phonies whom they attract, and they are scorned by the affluent, fashionable Chicagoans whose recognition they eagerly seek.

The power of Lardner's urban humor, developed first in his satires of ordinary Chicagoans and refined in his many short stories written after moving to New York City in 1919, lies in his deft ability to gradually alter a reader's perception of the wise boob's moral character. When introduced, Lardner's wise boobs are, for the popular audience he entertained, familiar and roughly sympathetic characters. By the usual standards of middle-class achievement, they are comfortably successful people: one is the assistant chief of detectives of the Chicago Police Department; another is a shrewd investor enjoying an early retirement. Lardner's readers, one would imagine, could easily identify with the apparently modest and decent ambitions of his characters. The characters simply desire more comfortable homes; additionally, they desire a wider and more distinguished circle of friends and a social status commensurate with their incomes. One's sympathy is further engaged by the frustration and expense which the characters endure and suffer in pursuing their simple ambitions. Fred Gross, for example, the assistant chief of Chicago detectives, wants to build a house in the suburbs for his growing family. This simple ambition bankrupts him. His architect underestimates the building cost and neglects to design essential features; the contractor defaults on debts; and the workmen do shoddy work. The final cost of the $2,000 house is $5,300. When Fred Gross moves in, he finds that windows won't open and doors won't close; the roof also leaks and the basement floods. In addition to these difficulties, the Gross family lives in their new home from May until August without receiving one visitor.

One's sympathy for Fred Gross and other wise boobs gradually evaporates, though, as one watches envy and greed consume their good sense and modesty. On moving into his new home, Fred Gross immediately understands and covets the snobbish exclusivensss of suburbanites:

> Of corse we miss the Walters & the Arnolds & others that we made frends of them in the city a speshally Grace but . . . this towns got plenty of fine peopl liveing in this town & as soon is we get acquainted we can for get all a bout the peopl we knowed in Chi & not never think a bout them. [No. 21, pp. 36–37]

Though he hungers for their recognition, Fred Gross never gets acquainted with the fine people of his suburb. They shun his overtures and even, at one point, expel him from a local charity ball because, they insolently explain, he could only have received his written invitation by mistake. Hurt and angered by his neighbors' disdain, Fred Gross begins a vendetta against Hamilton, his next-door neighbor and the suburb's leading citizen. He places a quarantine sign on the Hamiltons' porch the night they give a party, he deflates the tires of Hamilton's car, and he arranges with his friend the county sheriff to send deputies to raid Mrs. Hamilton's bridge club as a gambling house.

Gross is encouraged in his petty, juvenile vengeance by Martin, another neighbor whom Hamilton had snubbed. To further incite Gross's anger against Hamilton, Martin warns him to expect retaliation for the raid on Mrs. Hamilton's bridge club. Martin then arranges with some of his friends in the fire department to flood Gross's home in a false alarm. Fortunately, Hamilton recognizes the culprit responsible for this vandalism. He rushes to Gross's house, angrily dismisses the drunken firemen, and promises Gross full reparation from the city council. Gross interprets Hamilton's responsible, if belated, intervention as an overture for his friendship and confidence. Finally, he mistakenly believes, his frustrated social ambitions will be realized:

> Well Charley when Martin comes back I guess he will be surprised to find I and Grace hobbling a round with the Hamiltons and the other high monkey monks hey Charley. [No. 21, p. 123]

A more attractive wise boob than Fred Gross, whose boorish and spiteful behavior soon exhausts one's sympathy, is Gullible, the protagonist of *Gullible's Travels* (1918). Gullible seems mature, quick-witted, and candid; he enjoys, without apology or self-consciousness, his mundane pleasures of spectator sports, gin rummy, and tavern conviviality; and he unerringly sees through the pretensions of others. His sarcastic humor and blunt expression remind one of the confident, ironic banter of Lardner's "regular" ball players. One laughs heartily at Gullible's burlesque summaries of the operas his wife persuades him to attend, and one applauds the success of his clever campaign to rid his home of the unemployed actor courting his sister-in-law. However, when Gullible maneuvers, at his wife's insistence, to ingratiate himself into fashionable society, his rude habits render him a ridiculous, ill-mannered, and vindictive person. He becomes, in effect, the abusive boor Fred Gross became when confronted with the disdain of suburbanites.

The Gullibles' awareness of a fashionable and privileged urban society, sparked by their attendance at a few operas, steadily grows into an obsession. Mrs. Gullible notices, from her avid reading of the newspaper society pages, that many rich Chicagoans vacation in Palm Beach, Florida. Excited by the prospect of socializing with them at a public resort, she wheedles her husband into selling some of his stock to finance a Florida vacation. After two fruitless and distressingly expensive weeks of bribing headwaiters, hotel managers, bartenders, and beach attendants, the Gullibles finally attain, by accident, their coveted opportunity to converse with one of the "E-light o' Chicago":

"What's the matter?" I says, springin' from the lounge.

"Come here!" she says, and went out the door into the hall.

I got there as fast as I could, thinkin' it was a rat or a fire. But the Missus just pointed to a lady walkin' away from us, six or seven doors down.

"It's Mrs. Potter," she says; "*the* Mrs. Potter from Chicago!"

"Oh!" I says, puttin' all the excitement I could into my voice.

And I was just startin' back into the room when I seen Mrs. Potter stop and turn round and come to'rd us. She stopped again maybe twenty feet from where the Missus was standin'.

The Missus shook like a leaf.

"Yes," says she, so low you couldn't hardly hear her.

"Please see that they's some towels put in 559," says *the* Mrs. Potter from Chicago. [No. 19, pp. 149-50]

Chastened and humiliated, the Gullibles return home. Declaring themselves satisfied with their home and old friends, they admit their foolishness in pursuing the Potters, Armours, Fields, and Richardsons— who wanted, above all else, to avoid them and their kind. However, their sobering experience in Palm Beach fades quickly from their memory. They are soon once again scheming to capture a place among the "E-light o' Chicago." When *the* Mrs. Messenger, wife of a prominent local realtor, asks if they play bridge, the Gullibles, with only a vague knowledge of the card game, seize the opportunity to join the exclusive "San Susie Club" of their neighborhood.

During the evening of bridge, Gullible, who had shown some restraint and kindness throughout the Palm Beach fiasco, insults his hosts, abuses his wife, and generally embarrasses everyone. When introduced to Mrs. Messenger, he immediately begins haggling with her over his rent in the apartment building owned by her husband. He then presses his host, Mr. Garrett, to disclose the amount of his rent, persisting in his questioning until the man, reluctantly, admits an approximate figure. During the dinner, Gullible amuses the guests at his table by ridiculing the food, concluding with "Throw some o' the prize money into the dinner; and if they's any skimpin' to be done, do it on the prizes."

During the bridge tournament, Gullible makes a complete ass of himself. He bids each hand ignorantly, and then he complacently annoys his frustrated partner with sarcastic rebuttals: "What kind of a lead was that?" asks Mrs. Garrett after an inept play. "Pretty good one, I guess," smartly replies Gullible. "It fooled you, anyway." Gullible shows no sense of courtesy during the evening. When he is Mrs. Messenger's partner, for example, he baldly calls attention to her weight with the tasteless remark: "Well, pardner, we got 'em out-weighed, anyway." Once, one of his partners stifles a yawn and Gulli-ble, convinced that he is the wit of the party, immediately comments: "I bet you'd perk up if the lady's prize was a mattress. When you're goin' to be up late you should ought to take a nap in the afternoon." He takes greatest liberties, as he believes he is entitled to do, with his wife:

> "Nice work!" I says to the Missus. "You're the Philadelphia Athletics of auction bridge."
> "What was you biddin' no trump on?" she says. "I thought, o' course, you'd have one high heart and some suit."
> "You don't want to start thinkin' at your age," I says. "You can't learn an old dog new tricks."
> Mrs. Nap's husband cut in.
> "O' course," he says, "it's a man's privilege to call your wife anything you feel like callin her. But your Missus don't hardly look old to me."
> "No, not comparatively speakin'," I says and he shut up. [No. 19, pp. 243–44]

Gullible's obnoxious manners finally exasperate his host, provoking an angry, vulgar outburst from Mrs. Garrett, his final partner of the evening:

> "I won't play it! I won't be made a fool of! This poor idiot deliberately told me he had spades stopped, and look at his hand!"
> "You're mistaken, Mrs. Garrett," I says. "I didn't say nothin about spades."
> "Shut you mouth," she says. "That's what you ought to done all evenin'."
> "I might as well of," I says, "for all the good it done me to keep it open at dinner." [No. 19, p. 249]

For Lardner, bridge succinctly dramatized the frustration and inadequacy his wise boobs experienced in trying to establish themselves in an urban society. It is a game which Lardner wholly identifies with urban culture, particularly the culture of those educated and affluent urban citizens who use it as a weapon of invidious social discrimination. The game, relatively new at the time Lardner wrote his stories, is utterly beyond the experience and capacity of the gin-rummy playing "thirty-five dollar a week men" of his stories:

> They told us it was going to be a card party [Fred Gross explains in a letter to his brother], so I and Grace thot of corse they would play cinch or rummy or may be whist but when we got over there they sprung this here game they call auction bridge whist. Mrs. Curtis says if I played whist I wouldent have no trouble lerning this here game but in this game you bid back & 4th. like pitch only you half to say what you biding on & they got a lot of funny sines that means some thing & a man's got to go threw collige to lern all them sines. [No. 21, p. 69]

In Lardner's fiction, bridge symbolizes, in the petty jealousies, vulgar recriminations, and harsh quarrels it inevitably provokes, the breakdown of manners, community, and tradition in the city. Whereas baseball, an accessible, common man's entertainment, had figured prominently in Lardner's early, largely genial fiction and journalism, the strange, intimidating game of bridge appears more frequently in his later, increasingly bitter, stories of the urban middle class. As an urban sport, baseball had reflected the traditional small-town culture of its origins; it had remained an open and leisurely summer's entertainment for fans from all social classes. Unlike bridge, with its esoteric "sines," baseball was common property and an enriching influence on the common language. For Jack Keefe, baseball developed his talent, sharpened his wit and disciplined his impulses. For Fred Gross, Gullible, and a host of later Lardner characters, bridge is a degrading experience; it denies them the pleasure of comfortable social intercourse, it draws out their ill-suppressed greed and envy, and it breaks their fragile self-esteem.

Lardner's generally demeaning characterizations of his wise boobs exhausts the effort of the Chicago popular humorists, beginning with

Finley Peter Dunne, to extend to an urban audience the appeal of a traditional American comic type, the plain-spoken and coarse-mannered rustic moralist. For Dunne, the effort had presented no great difficulty. In all essential features of personality, social status, and experience, Mr. Dooley is simply a transplanted crackerbarrel philosopher. He lives in a parochial community, respects its traditional culture, and is accorded respect because of his age, community service, and property. For Dunne, and the many readers he delighted, the traditional, close-knit Irish-American community of Bridgeport allowed Mr. Dooley to confidently measure and judge the more complex society of Chicago and the nation.

George Ade did not endow his common-folk characters with the full measure of Mr. Dooley's wisdom and confidence, though they embodied, essentially, the same nostalgic values of village domesticity, economic self-reliance, and simple moral rectitude. Unlike Dunne, Ade firmly distinguished himself from his characters; one always recognizes the distinction between Ade, the accomplished storyteller, and the naive characters he describes. This ironic distance between author and subject, not evident in Dunne's generous characterization of Mr. Dooley, was an attitude of general and increasing currency among those humorous Chicago journalists who were contemporaries of Dunne and Ade. Bert Leston Taylor, for years the popular editor of the "Line o' Type or Two" column in the *Chicago Tribune,* amused his readers with condescending, at times snide, comments on the jokes, recipes, poems, aphorisms, advertisements, and anecdotes which contributors submitted for his judgment. He affected a refined, ironic sensibility. Chicago crudity, whether of manners, speech, or opinion, was the favorite subject of his wit. A typical Taylor joke is the following, taken from the February 4, 1901, edition of the *Tribune:*

First Thing Visitors Notice

Clark—   I knew Miss Kenosha was a stranger to Chicago before you told me.

Dearborn— So? How?

Clark—   She noticed that all the men in the car had soiled collars on.

Eugene Field, his brother Roscoe Field, Franklin P. Adams, and George Phair, among others, also entertained Chicago readers with witty burlesques of middle-class manners and ambitions. In Eugene Field's "Sharps and Flats" column, for example, a meeting of the "West Side Literary Lyceum" prompted the following wry report:

> At a meeting of the West Side Literary Lyceum last week, the question, "Are Homer's poems better reading than Will Carleton's?" was debated. The negative was sustained by a vote of forty-seven to five. On this occasion Miss Mamie Buskirk read an exquisite original poem entitled "Hope; or, The Milkman's Dream."[3]

In Lardner's characterization of the wise boob, the irony separating the Chicago humorist from the common Chicagoan expands dramatically. His characters, introduced as self-satisfied and practical-minded people, quickly alienate the reader's sympathy as they succumb to envy and ill temper. For Lardner, the city—Chicago, later New York City—was responsible for the moral degeneration of its common citizens. By exciting the wise boobs' dormant appetites for privilege and conspicuous consumption, the city denied them the stability, intimacy, and modesty which they had known in the small hometowns they had left.

In his many short stories written after his move to New York City in 1919, Lardner repeated, with little variation, the moral characterization of Chicago and its wise boobs. The only significant difference between Lardner's later stories (excepting *The Big Town,* written in 1920) and his Chicago stories is, occasionally, the image of the American small town. In Lardner's Chicago fiction, and in *The Big Town,* the small hometowns of the urban characters—Bedford, Indiana; South Bend, Indiana; St. Joseph, Michigan—are nostalgically described as stable, comfortable, and moral communities. The people of Bedford, as Jack Keefe's wife Florrie knows and dreads, would influence Jack by their moderate habits and discipline him by their public opinions. In Lardner's later fiction, however, the distinct, nostalgic, moral quality of the American small town occasionally dissolves and disappears. "Haircut," generally considered Lardner's masterpiece, is a bitter indictment of the sleazy morality which small towners could accommodate. In the story, a vicious, jealous practical joker, Jim Kendall, is tolerated and envied by his more cautious confederates in the town's barber shop. The moral standards of decency and responsibility, which small towns had embodied in Lardner's earlier fiction are in "Haircut" only enforced when the town half-wit murders Kendall for exposing the gentle and virtuous Julie Gregg to public ridicule.

Lardner's stories of urban boobs and, occasionally, of small town brutes parodied, with devastating effect, the worn conventions of nineteenth-century American popular humor. Reviewing Lardner's work in her influential *American Humor,* published shortly before Lardner's death, Constance Rourke grimly evaluated his fiction as the "final product of a humor that had worn away idiosyncrasies, taking with it all the edged elements of character."

> All his stories turn on humor; practical jokes make the substance of many situations as in an earlier day, but in the end the brutality which underlies them is exposed. That innocence which once was made a strong strain in American portrayals is seen uncombined with shrewdness and revealed as abysmal stupidity.[4]

The innocent yet shrewd folk character whom Rourke lamented did survive into the twentieth century, most notably in Will Rogers's stage character, but his customary appeal was diminished and tenuous. Urban humorists, particularly, recognized the need for developing new comic *personae.* Damon Runyon, the Marx Brothers, Leo Rosten, and Sidney J. Perelman created profane, street-wise, and nimble-witted city characters. These new urban comics either ignored or grossly burlesqued the conflict between America's rural traditions and its urban future, which had shaped Lardner's view. Instead, they embraced the city on its own terms and directly expressed its exciting vitality. In their humor, the city emerges as a stimulating environment which inspires an original "hip" language, a manic comic irreverence, and a sophistication utterly beyond the reach of Lardner's isolated, anxious, and ignorant urban misfits.

5

CHICAGO LITERATURE

Of the popular Chicago writers, Ring Lardner received most attention from literary critics and artists. During the 1920s, his short
stories and baseball saga were appraised by Clifton Fadiman, Edmund
Wilson, Gilbert Seldes, H. L. Mencken, Carl Van Doren, F. Scott
Fitzgerald, and Sherwood Anderson. Lardner's critics all identified
the slack language and petty materialism of his characters as significant and unusual qualities in popular literature; they debated whether
his conception of character was authentic or contrived. To some,
Lardner was a major artist for opening American writing to speech
and characters which had been censored or sentimentalized by the
governing literary sensibilities, particularly those of William Dean
Howells. He was regarded as an original, frank, and native voice;
indeed, Virginia Woolf saw Lardner as the seminal American writer
of the twentieth century:

> Mr. Lardner does not waste a moment when he writes in think-
> ing whether he is using American slang or Shakespeare's English;
> whether he is proud of being American or ashamed of not being
> Japanese; all his mind is on the story. Hence, incidentally, he
> writes the best prose that has come our way. Hence we feel at
> last freely admitted to the society of our fellows.[1]

Lardner was quite uncomfortable with the formal appraisals of his
writing. He thought them overstated, for he had always considered

his writing modest and journalistic, written for money and under the pressure of magazine and newspaper deadlines. Also, he was disturbed by what he perceived as a misreading of his intention; he did not see himself as a disaffected critic of American values but, rather, as an entertainer whose finest tools were irony and parody and whose greatest endowment was a sensitive ear.

This tension in Lardner's work, between the entertainment he intended and the moral criticism others found him producing, can be seen as the refined product of three decades of vigorous and original activity among Chicago's popular and formal artists. Though H. L. Mencken's designation of pre-1920 Chicago as the "literary capital of the United States" is extreme, it is not wholly inaccurate. The popular works of Dunne, Ade, and Lardner, and the changing character of those works, were stimulated by an artistic environment which also nurtured the *Dial, Little Review,* and *Poetry* magazines, the Chicago Symphony and Opera, the Art Institute, and several significant American novelists.

To highlight the distinct character of Dunne, Ade, and Lardner as popular writers, and define the motives which focused their perceptions of Chicago, we should examine this larger artistic environment; the most revealing comparison is that between these popular writers and their fellow "serious" novelists who created, in the three decades preceding 1920, the "Chicago novel." Their realistic novels are some of our prime examples of literary naturalism. In them, we find that those dominant social and economic features of late nineteenth-century Chicago which I have reviewed—Chicago's unstable economy, the enormous increase in its foreign population, the increasing consolidation of its industry—had profoundly affected the authors' moral attitudes. For these writers—Henry Fuller, Will Payne, Robert Herrick, Theodore Dreiser, Hamlin Garland, and Frank Norris are the most significant figures—Chicago became a compelling symbol of social evil. The literary historian Bernard Duffey, in his excellent study *The Chicago Renaissance in American Letters,* identifies their perception of alienation, corruption, and loss as the essential meaning of the "Chicago novel":

The young man, or woman, at odds with a world he never made—
one which threatened to undo him by forcing him into the power
of foreign and hostile circumstances: this was the great preoccupa-

tion of Chicago realism. Small wonder the novels it produced were, above all, testimonies of outraged sensibility. They were, as analyses, overhasty; and as programs for action or definition, they scarcely existed. But they did record the depths of confusion into which Chicago—the immediate and inescapable symbol of a horribly triumphant world—could throw one who had been formed by a friendly, humane, hopeful, and orderly culture.[2]

This central theme of alienation found varied expression in the "Chicago novels." Hamlin Garland, in *Rose of Dutcher's Cooly* (1900), for example, tempered his heroine's disappointments with common sense. Rose, a wholesome, idealistic migrant to Chicago from a small town, must adjust her naive romantic vision of a daring and handsome artist to fit the actual character of her Chicago suitors. After several disappointments, she finally marries a journalist, stolid in his habits though cynical in his attitudes.

Other Chicago novelists were not so temperate. Will Payne, in *Jerry the Dreamer* (1896) and *Money Captain* (1898), defined an absolute conflict between the business culture of Chicago and the moral aspirations of his protagonists. He does not resolve the conflict as Upton Sinclair does in *The Jungle* (1906) with Jurgis Rudkus's enrollment in the Socialist party; rather, he insists on the necessary capitulation of his protagonists. Jerry gives up his work on the Socialist newspaper *The Call* to satisfy his wife's insistent demand that he make money; Nidstrom, a private secretary to the "money captain" Dexter, the powerful overlord of Chicago utilities, accepts Dexter's selfish and corrupt materialism as his only hope of securing a place in Chicago.

Perhaps the most extreme rejection of Chicago business culture is expressed in the novels of Robert Herrick. Like Garland, Fuller, and Norris, Herrick structures his novels around a heroine's choice between competing suitors. The *Gospel of Freedom* (1898) finds Adela Anthon choosing John Wilbur, a Chicago businessman, over Simon Erard, an expatriate critic and artist. But she leaves Wilbur when she understands that his business success and personal vitality were only possible in the moral vacuum he had accepted. Herrick's later novels *(The Web of Life, The Common Lot, The Memoirs of an American Citizen)* repeat this Chicago drama. Each novel concludes with the wholesale rejection of Chicago and its business culture.

To best illustrate this central theme of alienation, and the range of characters, situations, and images in its expression, I will take up three major novels written between 1895 and 1902: *With the Procession* (1895), *Sister Carrie* (1900), and *The Pit* (1902). These three novels are diverse: in *With the Procession,* Henry Fuller describes Chicago through the sensibilities of its social elite; *Sister Carrie* views Chicago through the eyes of a simple rural migrant; *The Pit* concentrates on the trading floor and the brokers' rooms of the Chicago Grain Exchange.

Henry Fuller, a native Chicagoan of old family, introduces his reader to the social "procession" of charity balls, debuts, derby days, expensive dinner parties, and exclusive premiers through which Chicago's millionaires assert their privileges. The novel describes the efforts of one prominent "settler" Chicago family, the David Marshall family, to recover the social distinctions they had let lapse. Their decision is prompted by their sobering discovery, in an emotional family conference, of their exclusion from the invitation list for the annual Pacific Hotel game dinner, an event which had traditionally been the principal social occasion for Chicago's families of established wealth. In reviewing the invitation list published in the evening paper, the family realizes that the annual commemoration of "the smaller town and the earlier day" of pre-Civil War Chicago will be celebrated by a motley assortment of old and new Chicagoans chosen, it seems, by no criteria except wealth and notoriety: "Yes they'll all be there— the Hubbards, the Gages, and the whole crowd of Parmelees, and Kittie Corwith and her father, and all the rest, and—and the Beldens! The Beldens—there!" (no. 18, pp. 36-37).

The Beldens' social success was particularly offensive; that family owed what distinction it could claim to its parasitical hold on David Marshall's business and reputation. In the financial panic of the mid-eighties, Marshall had been forced to solicit Belden's aid, and Belden had then pushed his advantage. He joined the Marshall Company as head of a department. Then, in what Fuller describes as a series of blackmail demands, he became a partner and then a co-owner; finally, he forced Marshall to reorganize the firm as a stock company. And now, capping all his successes, Belden had displaced his patron from the invitation list for the Pacific Hotel game dinner.

Throughout the novel, Fuller emphasizes the differences between Chicago's newcomers and its "settlers." Belden's greed and immorality stand in sharp contrast to Marshall's generosity and concern; unburdened by Marshall's scruples, he can profit from the periodic "busts" in Chicago's economy and force a family business into a new stock corporation. Of all the images in this novel of the valuable but sadly anachronistic traditions of Chicago's "settler" past, perhaps the most poignant is the garret bedroom which Mrs. Granger Bates, an old-time acquaintance of David Marshall, maintains in an obscure corner of her new Lake Shore Drive mansion. In that small, oddly furnished room, she can escape the stiff formalities of her music room, library, Louis Quinze salon, and "Sala de Los Embajadores"—Fuller emphasizes the divorce of these rooms from any native Chicago tradition—to relax and daydream amid the relics of her girlhood home. It is to this room that she leads Jane Marshall, David Marshall's eldest daughter, when the girl calls to reopen the acquaintance between the two "settler" families. The woman and the girl ease into the comfortable intimacy of this room furnished with a cracked and peeled mahogany bureau, a shabby writing desk, a threadbare Brussels carpet, and a small upright piano. Together they rediscover the openhanded hospitality and robust humor of an earlier, smaller Chicago. Sue Bates pounds out "Dan Tucker" and "Java March" on her old piano while Jane sings spiritedly and dances the old-time country reels. They sentimentally indulge in memories of old Chicago and firmly cement the neglected bonds between their families.

The private, nostalgic reunion of Sue Bates and Jane Marshall is opposite, in every respect, to the invidious "procession" of Chicago's high society. That "procession" is the public scramble of Chicago's newly affluent families for social status. The Marshall family had remained aloof from this competition. While other businessmen grabbed large fortunes from real estate and other commercial speculations, David Marshall had tried, despite Belden's nagging objections, to simply satisfy the customers of his wholesale grocery business. While other prosperous Chicago families had moved out to Gold Coast or Prairie Avenue mansions, David Marshall had remained in his original Near North Side homestead. The Marshalls did not participate in the social season, and, until omitted from the Pacific Hotel dinner, were indifferent to the public recognition they had forfeited.

When the family resolves to join the "procession"—ironically, they are aided by their fellow "settler," Sue Bates—they initiate a train of demoralizing consequences. The youngest daughter, Rosamund, caps her social debut by impetuously marrying the foolish son of a knighted Englishman, a boy with neither talent nor fortune; the youngest son, Truesdale, is exposed as a knave; the oldest son, Roger, compromises one after another of his moral principles to salvage the family's failing fortune; the father, David Marshall, prematurely dies from the exhaustion of overwork and the anxieties of his newly complicated business and social ambitions. By the end of their adventure in pursuing the prizes of Chicago's "procession," the Marshall family has disintegrated. In the novel's last chapter, Eliza Marshall, David Marshall's widow, is alone in the chill, damp rooms of her new Prairie Avenue mansion fending off the insinuating questions of Mrs. Belden.

The vanity and greed which the millionaire's "procession" aroused did not, alone, undermine the security and affection of the Marshall family. The family dissolved under the pressure of another and allied "procession," the sordid growth of business and political corruption which had divorced contemporary Chicago from the simple community of the pre-Civil War years. David Marshall is harried beyond endurance by the financial and emotional demands of fighting this gorgon. He cannot obtain settlements of outstanding accounts in the venal municipal courts; he cannot secure police protection (all the police in this novel are Irish) from the vandals and thieves in his neighborhood; and, finally, he cannot control his partner's reckless speculation. For David Marshall, contemporary Chicago is an alien and inhuman force. It crowds in on his home with industries and railroad spur lines; it blights his peace with noise, smoke, and petty criminality. In the face of these conditions, he sells the home of his father to make room for a warehouse.

The measure of Chicago's corrupting influence in *With the Procession* is the extent of moral compromise exacted from the Marshall family. Truesdale Marshall repudiates the strict morality of "settler" Chicago by blithely refusing to marry the girl whose child he had fathered. To prevent a court case, David Marshall bribes her family

and buys a substitute groom. When bankruptcy threatens the
Marshall and Belden Company, David Marshall is again forced to
a painful compromise. He allows his son, Roger, a Chicago lawyer,
to invest the remaining family capital in several nefarious speculations which yield windfall profits. The tainted money restores the
family's fortune; but it is a hollow security. In the end, David
Marshall's survivors have only his money. They divide the inheritance
and scatter. Chicago, the "Black City," as Fuller names it in the novel,
has overwhelmed one of its first families. He dramatically contrasted
the "urbs in horto" of Chicago's settler years with the "Black City"
of the 1890s: "the urbs in horto of the earlier time existed only in
the memory of 'old settlers' and in the device of the municipal seal,
while the great Black City stood out as a threatening and evil ac-
tuality" (no. 18, p. 10).

With the Procession, and Fuller's earlier novel, *The Cliff Dwellers*
(1893), outlined for future Chicago novelists the typical pattern of
a Chicago tragedy. Fuller defined the essential meaning of life in
his city as the conflict between an individual's moral nature—reflect-
ing the values of a simpler society—and his craven appetites, which
were excited by the prospect of success in Chicago. When an individual decides to compete for the wealth and distinction Chicago
offers, he compromises his morality and initiates his ruin. In the
dissolution of the Marshall business and the Marshall family, Henry
Fuller expressed his sense of Chicago's loss of the vision and decency
of its "settlers," among whom one of the most prominent had been
his grandfather, Henry ("Judge") Fuller.

The Chicago novelist's alienation from his city, announced in
the early novels of Henry Fuller, receives a very poignant expression
in Theodore Dreiser's novel *Sister Carrie.* His is a poignant expression
because, for Carrie Meeber, Chicago is a liberating and potentially
satisfying environment. Dreiser does not exploit, to the extent which
Fuller and Norris do, the simple contrast between rural virtue and
urban vice. Had Carrie remained in Columbia City, Wisconsin, she
would have stagnated; the Wisconsin town is dull, and Carrie eagerly
flees its routines. In Chicago, once she escapes her sister's South Side
tenement and the degrading factory labor that had been available to
her, her personality and confidence expand. Chicago stimulates the
development of Carrie's innate grace and talents. As Charles Drouet's

mistress, she becomes a very attractive and self-assured woman. She learns the fashionable taste in clothes and furniture; she imitates the bearing and manners of impressive women; she executes, quite well, her opportunity to perform in an amateur play; and she begins to perceive the limits, narrower than her own, of Drouet's mind and taste.

However, Carrie is tempted, like the Marshall family and like Curtis Jadwin, the conservative businessman in *The Pit,* to reach beyond the security of her comfortable circumstances to grasp the richer prizes of Chicago: she reaches for George Hurstwood. Chicago, as represented by Hurstwood, the self-important manager of Fitzgerald and Moy's fashionable club, upsets the balance of Carrie's life. He makes Carrie aware of the absolute differences which separate Chicagoans, and he incites her to covet the wealth and manners which distinguish him from Drouet.

Carrie's receptiveness to Hurstwood's advances releases forces which destroy forever the trust, affection, and security she had enjoyed in Chicago. Her flirtation drives Drouet from their apartment and goads Hurstwood's wife to initiate divorce proceedings. Though Hurstwood is the seducer—even to the extent of abducting Carrie from Chicago—Carrie is far from blameless. She is excited by the wealth and pleasure Hurstwood represents, and she coyly encourages his passion. It is this excitation of base appetite which Dreiser, as well as Fuller and Norris, stresses as the irresistible appeal of Chicago. Each author then proceeds to demonstrate how the city, once it has awakened the protagonist's appetite, frustrates his ambitions and destroys his illusions. Carrie covets the finely dressed, important Hurstwood and ends, with him, as an anonymous refugee in New York City.

Carrie's move to New York City is a sobering education. In Chicago, she had enjoyed many comforts which New York City denies her. Her modest Chicago apartment, for example, bordered a very pleasant city park; her first New York City apartment, though larger and more expensive, offers only a distant glimpse of the treetops in Central Park. In Chicago, Carrie had been protected and petted. Her affair with Hurstwood had been a sentimental indulgence in clandestine meetings, leisurely country rides, and poetic declarations of passion. New York City, though, has none of the beauties and pleasures which had

heightened Carrie's life in Chicago. As represented in *Sister Carrie,*
New York City is harsh, competitive, and impersonal.

With Carrie's move to New York City and, in the final chapters
of the novel, with the movement of all the principal Chicago characters
there, too, Dreiser implies that Chicago's future lies in New York
City—the second city in the nation will become, in time, like the
mature first city. That fate is ominous. In New York City, Carrie
watches Hurstwood, the proud symbol of Chicago prestige, crumble.
The rapid wasting of his small capital, and the deadening frustration
of his limited energy, jar Carrie to an awareness of his real impotence, which his Chicago success had obscured.

Through diligent efforts and the luck of circumstances, Carrie
saves herself from Hurstwood's fall. She finds employment as a chorus
girl in a Broadway musical; within a year, she has vaulted to stardom.
Her success, though, like the success of Roger Marshall in restoring
his family's fortune, is empty. The city has forced her into painful
moral compromises—she deserts Hurstwood when his money runs
out—and it has exposed the cheap value of its rewards:

> Friends there were, as the world takes it—those who would bow
> and smile in acknowledgement of her success. For these she had
> once craved. Applause there was, and publicity—once far off,
> essential things, but now grown trivial and indifferent. Beauty
> also—her type of loveliness—and yet she was lonely. In her
> rocking-chair she sat, when not otherwise engaged—singing and
> dreaming. [No. 9, p. 476]

Carrie's pathetic loneliness in her luxurious Waldorf suite resembles
Eliza Marshall's loneliness in her new Prairie Avenue mansion. Both
Dreiser and Fuller emphasize the loss of human satisfaction which
success in the city exacts.

The constriction of affection, energy, and faith which the protagonist of the "Chicago novel" suffers in his pursuit of wealth and distinction is most dramatically portrayed by Frank Norris in *The Pit.* By
comparison with this novel, *With the Procession* and *Sister Carrie*
are temperate books. Fuller and Dreiser had carefully modified the
degrading experiences of their protagonists. In *With the Procession,*
for example, Jane Marshall contributes her inheritance to an endow-

ment fund of the University of Chicago. Mrs. Granger Bates, the
society leader who had launched the Marshalls on their quest for
social distinction, offers to restore their fortune when she learns of
the Marshall and Belden Company bankruptcy. Her aid is unneeded,
but her generous concern is gratifying. In *Sister Carrie,* Hurstwood's
crushing failure is balanced by Carrie's incredible success; his moral
decay is balanced by her emotional maturity. In her struggle for
security in New York City, Carrie outgrows her vanity. She begins
to comprehend the responsibilities of her talent and sympathies:
she listens to Ames's recommendations of substantial literature and
serious drama; she declines the self-indulgence and gaudy display
she had once envied; she generously supports charities.

By accenting the maturity and generosity of Jane Marshall, Mrs.
Granger Bates, and Carrie Madena, Fuller and Dreiser temper their
indictments of the city. They demonstrate that exceptional characters can endure the city's trials and finally resist its enticements.
Frank Norris is not so temperate. He propels his protagonist, Curtis
Jadwin, through an incredible "boom" and then smothers him in
a total "bust." At the novel's conclusion, Norris allows Jadwin no
accommodation with Chicago: his fortune is entirely consumed in
the failure of his "corner" on September wheat; he flees Chicago
to start a new life in "the West."

Norris's diction is as intemperate as his conception of success
and failure in Chicago. He blazons Curtis Jadwin's financial career
with inflated rhetorical banners:

> Was this upheaval a revolution that called aloud for its Napoleon?
> Would another, not himself, at last, seeing where so many shut
> their eyes, step into the place of high command? [No. 23, p. 259]

Such full-blown rhetoric found some justification in the actual conditions of speculation on the Chicago Board of Trade. Norris had based
his drama of Jadwin's "corner" on May and September wheat on
reports of Joseph Leiter's 1898 attempt to "corner" the commodity
market on May wheat. Leiter's speculation had failed; Philip Armour
undersold him with wheat he had transported from Duluth and stored
in special warehouses he had hastily constructed on Goose Island. The
magnitude of Leiter's failure and the daring and expense of Armour's

opposition were of the titanic scale of the battle Norris describes between the "Great Bull," Curtis Jadwin, and the "Great Bear," Charles Crookes. Chicago's business, it seemed, was as sensational and disruptive as Norris represented it to be.

Norris creates his most flamboyant effects in the novel when he depicts the Chicago Board of Trade as a malevolent force of grim vitality and power. Often he compares the building to a sinister pagan idol, "bleak, monolithic, crouching on its foundations like a monstrous sphinx with blind eyes, silent, grave" (no. 23, p. 421). This theatrical representation of the Board of Trade as a self-willed, malevolent force is essential to Norris's purposes as a naturalistic writer; as Professor Charles Walcutt has noted, "The intent of denouncing the Pit as an unsocial force represents the idealistic branch of the divided stream of naturalism—its reforming zeal, its passionate belief in a moral law which ought to prevail."[3] Professor Walcutt argues that the tension, often unresolved, between materialism and moralism constitutes the dramatic power of American literary naturalism. The principal writers in this tradition—Hamlin Garland, Stephen Crane, Jack London, Frank Norris, Winston Churchill, Theodore Dreiser, Sherwood Anderson, and James T. Farrell—intend, paradoxically, to portray man as both a passive creature shaped by his environment and as an innately moral being in conflict with certain perverse forces of the environment. This paradox is often resolved, rhetorically, by endowing the principal characters of a naturalistic novel with two environments, rural and urban, or, in the case of Henry Fuller, "settler" and modern. Conventionally, the rural environment accounts for the characters' moral nature, and the urban environment submits that nature to severe stress.

In *The Pit,* the conflict between rural and urban environments is simple and absolute. Curtis Jadwin was raised on a small farm in Ottawa County, Michigan. That farm symbolizes the dignity of simple possessions, the generous affection of a close-knit family, and the satisfying discipline of physical labor. Norris's evocations of this ennobling environment are embarrassingly sentimental:

> Sam, do you know, I can remember the time, up there in
> Ottawa County, Michigan, on my old dad's farm, when I
> used to have to get up before daybreak to tend the stock,

and my sister and I used to run out quick into the stable and
stand in the warm cow fodder in the stalls to warm our bare
feet. . . . She up and died when she was about eighteen—galloping
consumption. Yes, sir. By George, how I loved that little
sister of mine! You remember her, Sam. Remember how you
used to come out from Grand Rapids every now and then to
go squirrel shooting with me? [No. 23, p. 200]

As a businessman in Chicago, Jadwin had striven to preserve the
virtues of his rural home. Throughout the first half of the novel,
Norris underlines Jadwin's abiding moral concerns; he repeatedly
notes Jadwin's sponsorship—inspired by a Dwight Moody sermon—
of a Sunday school for poor immigrants, his generous patronage of
honest, industrious young men, and his moderate personal habits.
The man seems indelibly moral. When Laura Dearborn accepts his
marriage proposal, he exclaims "May God bless you! May God bless
you!" (no. 23, p. 161).

However, Curtis Jadwin, the moral and sympathetic businessman-
hero, is no match for the "monstrous" influence of the Board of
Trade. He is attracted by its dynamic activity and begins to covet
its prize, the "corner" on the commodity market. Norris emphasizes the immorality of Jadwin's ambition by spotlighting his
gamble against a background of pathetic, broken speculators who
had tried "corners" before him: the book opens on the day of
Helmick's colossal failure; Jadwin's best friend, Charlie Cressler,
repeatedly warns Jadwin against the temptation to which he, years
earlier, had yielded and been nearly ruined; Jadwin justifies his first
"corner" as, in part, a noble philanthropy to restore the health,
sanity, and fortune of Hargus, a broken speculator who lives off
the charity of Jadwin's broker.

Despite the ominous warnings of his friend, despite the lesson of
the ruined men who move in the shadows of his consciousness, and
despite the obvious immorality of interfering in the distribution of
foodstuffs, Jadwin cannot resist trying for the highest prize in
Chicago's business world. He enters the commodity market cautiously and succeeds easily. Emboldened by his first success, he begins
to study the market. He perceives that the wheat price is depressed
and the crop supply is short. In an ecstatic flash he understands

the great opportunity before him: "Sam," he shouted, "do you know—great God!—do you know what this means? Sam, we can corner the market" (no. 23, p. 268).

Jadwin's successful corner of Chicago's May wheat supply exacts a severe toll on his time, health, and sanity. He abandons his Sunday school and philanthropies, he neglects his business, and he alienates his wife. When his expensive gamble succeeds, it offers him no satisfaction. He had intended to defeat C. H. Crookes, the "Great Bear" of the exchange. Instead, he ruined his best friend, Charlie Cressler. Cressler had joined the Crookes' investment clique—they solicited him for the window-dressing appeal of his well-known business sobriety—and he had been left with enormous debts when his confederates deserted him. In despair, he commits suicide. Melodramatically, Laura Jadwin, in her attempt to restore the neglected social relations between the two families, finds Cressler dead in his library.

Incited by the tragedy of Cressler's death and confident of his own ability to control the commodity market, Jadwin madly resolves to "corner" September wheat. Before the demands of this doomed project, his moral nature disintegrates. He criminally bribes freight haulers; he buys out trade journals to publish false crop estimates; he finds sadistic pleasure in the despair of the men he ruins; and he spurns his wife, who despondently accepts the advances of her long-time suitor, Corthell Hull.

To Norris's imagination, Chicago, symbolized by the Board of Trade, is an inexorable and evil force. When a businessman—Helmick, Cressler, Hargus, Jadwin—yields to its influence, the city completely ruins him. There is no possible moderation. Chicago arouses a man's basest appetites and draws him to the limit of his greed. Norris concludes Jadwin's Faustian career as the "Great Bull" of the Chicago Board of Trade by having him completely repudiate Chicago. With his wife, he leaves the city to seek, in the redeeming rural "West," the modest security and simple satisfactions Chicago had denied him.

The Chicago novelists described the ruinous excesses which Chicago incited: successful men were drawn to the extremes of greed and selfishness; broken men were driven to suicide or pathetic resignation. In writing their strong indictments of the city, these novelists emphasized the disruptive and alien elements which had grown to prominence in Chicago's explosive transformation from the medium-sized city of 1870 to the metropolis of 1890. In their books, one often finds degraded foreign immigrants; one encounters irresponsible, undisciplined businessmen; one sees the demoralizing conditions of factory labor, unemployment, and labor violence.

In the face of the pessimism of their novelists and the unsettling conditions of their lives, the Chicago reading public hungered for the familiar; they sought reassurance that their city was comprehensible and their lives were significant. The major Chicago novelists had asserted that Chicago was a strange and dangerous social environment which necessarily alienated man from his values, his labor, and his neighbors. Finley Peter Dunne, though, in his "Mr. Dooley" essays, presented the Chicagoans of the city's Sixth Ward as confident and generally secure and satisfied citizens.

For Dunne and his readers, the community of the Sixth Ward became the ethical standard by which to judge Chicago businessmen, politicians, reformers, socialites, and ordinary citizens. In this close-knit immigrant community, Dunne discovered the language, personalities, and institutions needed to support one of the most popular folk moralists of the American comic tradition: "Mr. Dooley of Archey Road," philosopher, bartender, and political sage. Like Jack Downing and Hosea Biglow before him (with whom he was often compared) Mr. Dooley understood America as essentially a village society; he demonstrated that the ordinary people of Chicago, even the city's newest immigrants, preserved their habits of intimate sociability and maintained the values of political participation and individual initiative long associated with the democratic life of an American village. This demonstration was persuasive because it appeared realistic and modest. Unlike the novelists, Dunne does not define symbolic characters and dramatic conflicts; instead, his characters are ordinary, their neighborhood is authentic, and their politics are described honestly. Mr. Dooley's sharp judgments and many references to actual people and events firmly set Bridgeport in a real Chicago.

A Mr. Dooley monologue which illustrates very well the appeal and quality of Bridgeport is "On the Popularity of Firemen," reprinted in Dunne's first book-length collection of Mr. Dooley pieces,

Mr. Dooley in Peace and in War (1898). Mr. Dooley begins by asserting that the Irish-Americans of Bridgeport are responsible and productive citizens:

> They'se an Irishman 'r two on th' fire departmint an' in th' army, too, Jawn, though ye'd think be hearin' some talk they was all runnin' prim'ries an' thryin' to be cinthral comitymen.

Mr. Dooley then illustrates Bridgeport's esteem for its honest and conscientious workingmen by describing the affection which "Clancy," a Chicago fireman, enjoyed from his neighbors and friends:

> All th' r-road was proud iv him, an' faith he was proud iv himself. . . . All th' people looked up to him, an' th' kids followed him down th' sthreet; an' twas th' gr-reatest priv'lige f'r anny wan f'r to play dominoes with him.

Repeatedly, Dunne emphasizes Clancy's pride in the respect of his community and, conversely, his respect for the moral values and social customs of his neighbors. He carefully integrates Clancy's specific duties as a fireman with his other, equally important, community obligations. For example, Dunne evokes the sense of Clancy's devout Catholicism by describing his call away from a baptism to answer an alarm:

> Why, wanst whin Clancy was standin' up f'r Grogan's eighth, his son come runnin' in to tell him they was a fire in Vogel's packin' house. He dhropped th' kid at Father Kelly's feet, an' whipped off his long coat an' wint tearin' f'r th' dure, kickin' over th' poorbox an' buttin' ol' Mis' O'Neill that'd come in to say th' stations.

The essay concludes with Mr. Dooley's account of Clancy's death. He died in "wan iv thim big, fine-lookin' buildings that pious men built out iv culluloid an' plasther iv Paris." With poignant, restrained sentiment, Dunne describes the effort of Clancy's widow to maintain the composed dignity her husband would have expected: "I seen thim

bringin' him home; an' th' little woman met him at th' dure,
rumplin' her apron in her hands."

The simple, quiet style of "On the Popularity of Firemen" is
appropriate for Dunne's conception of Bridgeport as an intimate
and stable community in which a fireman or a bartender or a common laborer could find dignity, responsibility, and affection. By
consistently representing Bridgeport as a parochial community, Dunne
established a coherent, familiar moral standard for Mr. Dooley. Since
Mr. Dooley knew his moral obligations and social status as a Bridgeport merchant, politician, and parishioner, he could confidently
judge the significant men and events of his day. He could, for
example, vigorously condemn the Chicago "beef trust" by simply
contrasting its greed and arrogance with the modest needs and industrious habits of his neighbors:

> Whin they tilt th' price iv beef to where wan pound iv it
> costs as much as manny th' man in this Ar-rchey Road'd
> wurruk fr'm th' risin' to th' settin' iv th' sun to get, they
> have no thought iv th' likes iv you an' me. "Tis aisy come,
> aisy go with thim; an' ivry cint a pound manes a new art
> musoom or a new church, to take th' edge off hunger. [No.
> 12, pp. 67–68]

With the humorous sketches and stories of George Ade and Ring
Lardner, originally addressed to a Chicago newspaper audience as
Dunne's Mr. Dooley essays were, one notices, by comparison with
the Bridgeport characters, a tightening constriction in the range of
knowledge, experience, and influence of the "common man" characters portrayed. While Mr. Dooley is a confident spokesman for the
settled opinions of Bridgeport, the working-class and middle-class
Chicagoans portrayed by Ade and Lardner are insecure. Unlike the
people of Bridgeport, they lack firm ties with an established community within Chicago; they are usually represented as recent migrants to Chicago from the rural Midwest. Their self-confidence,
traditionally the most conspicuous feature of American character
in the writings of nineteenth-century popular humorists, is either
hesitant and muted or obnoxiously belligerent. They do not exhibit
the calm, assured identity which Mr. Dooley projects as an Irish-

American, a Catholic, a Democrat, and an established neighborhood merchant; instead, their anxieties and frustrations place them within the ranks, though in modest positions, of the alienated urban characters in Chicago novels.

Ade's short character sketch "From the Office Window," reprinted in *Chicago Stories* (1963), illustrates his conception of the limited community life available to Chicagoans. In the story, an office worker is moved to a desk near a back window which overlooks an alley and offers a limited view of the back windows of another building. One of these windows opens on a small carpenter's shop; another opens on the apartment of a woman and her daughter, both seamstresses. The office worker, as so often happens in Ade's stories, is gradually drawn into the modest lives of his neighbors across the alley. He paces his work to the carpenter's repertoire of popular songs, loudly whistled each day, and he observes the courtship of the young woman by two policemen, one red-haired, the other dark-haired. Some time later, when he returns from an extended business assignment, he glances through his familiar window and notes that the carpenter's shop is vacant and that the young woman, "a little older and not quite so merry-faced," is nursing a red-haired infant.

This brief story gently conveys a sense of social isolation; the tentative, distant relations among the office worker, the carpenter, and the young woman suggest a frustrated longing for community. In this story, and in several similar to it, Chicagoans are separated by alleys, jobs, neighborhoods, or individual routines. Though Ade would frequently evoke this sense of isolation in order to portray, sentimentally, the ingenuous means by which ordinary Chicagoans would overcome their barriers to create the welcome and responsibility of genuine community—the moral reform and business and romantic success of Artie Blanchard is the paradigm of this intention—his typical characters and their social relations are limited. By comparison with the citizens of Bridgeport, Ade's Chicago characters are naive and reticent people. Their relationships lack the stability and purpose of Mr. Dooley and his neighbors, and their opinions lack the informed confidence of Mr. Dooley's long political experience.

This constriction of a character's experience, responsibilities, and confidence is more explicit and extreme in the fiction of Ring Lardner. For Lardner, the traditional models of American character and community, so vigorously reaffirmed by Finley Peter Dunne, could only serve to explain the special communities of professional baseball teams. On the Chicago White Sox, Jack Keefe lives in a fraternal society, works in a challenging, highly skilled craft, and earns a status commensurate with his proven talent. Other Chicagoans portrayed by Lardner have little relation with this kind of intimate community and responsible work. Lacking the ball players' exceptional opportunities, they become bored with the dull company of their few friends and frustrated with the petty routines of their jobs. With a pathetic, absurd intensity, they covet the leisure, wealth, and privileges of the "E-light of Chicago."

The final scene in *Gullible's Travels, Etc.* (1917) sharply portrays the frustration, jealousy, and boorish conceit typical of Lardner's urban characters. The scene begins on the morning after Gullible and his wife had been rejected from the "San Susie" bridge club for their incompetent play and vulgar manners. Lardner presents them at their breakfast table complacently discussing whether to introduce the Hatches to the bridge club they had been asked to leave:

> "Why didn't you tell 'em about the Hatches? They're right here in the neighborhood and can play bridge as good as anybody."
> "I wouldn't think o' doin' it," says she. "They may play all right, but think o' how they talk and how they dress!"

The next Tuesday evening, as the Gullibles are leaving to attend a movie, they meet the Hatches outside the home of the bridge club president. The Hatches, they learn, have been invited to replace them. Finally, they clearly see that they are alone and unwelcome in their Chicago neighborhood.

As is evident in *Gullible's Travels, Etc.,* Lardner found few attractive resources among middle-class Chicagoans; in his stories, the common man is a wise boob, a character to be satirized, ridiculed, and isolated. Earlier comic characters in American popular humor (Jack Downing, Hosea Biglow, Major Jones, Huckleberry Finn, Josh Billings, Artemus Ward) had been ideal characters; they had expressed, in an amusing, rough-hewn folk idiom, the moral and social ideals which characterized the distinct national identity of Americans.

"Josh Billings" (Henry W. Shaw), for example, could express the characteristic initiative, enterprise, and practicality of Americans in the following comic aphorism: "An Amerikan luvs tew laff, but he don't luv tew make a bizzness ov it; he works, eats and haw-haws on a canter."[4] Lardner's characters, though, lack the wit and self-assurance of "Josh Billings" or other early comic spokesmen. In his humor, Lardner constantly emphasizes the insecurity and vulgarity of his characters by allowing them only a garbled, debased language: "I would have a whole lot better time, and you could too," Mrs. Gullible says, "if we could get acquainted with some congenial people to go round with, people that's tastes is the same as ourn." The discrepancy in diction between "acquainted with some congenial people" and "people that's tastes is the same as ourn" accents the "dissociation" of Mrs. Gullible from an appropriate, indigenous culture–she, unlike "Josh Billings," can neither accept her identity nor express, in a coherent idiom, the values she shares with other Americans. She can only express, in an impulsive, ill-considered manner, her selfish motives and feelings.

The common intention which links Dunne, Ade, and Lardner, and which distinguishes their comic art from the Chicago novelists, is their attempt, realized by Dunne and finally abandoned by Lardner, to interpret Chicago in the familiar and nostalgic terms of a small American community. In trying to reconcile Chicago, a city of more than one million people, with the popular conception of an American community, the humorists viewed the city from a distinctly different perspective than we find in the major novelists. While the novelists sought out the centers of wealth and influence in Chicago—the ostentatious mansions of Lake Shore Drive and Prairie Avenue, the exclusive clubs of Chicago's business titans, the frenzied trading pit of the Chicago Grain exchange—to expose the forces which tragically overwhelmed Chicagoans, the humorists searched the city's ethnic neighborhoods, anonymous office buildings, small retail shops, board-inghouses, baseball teams, and suburbs to find the autonomous societies in which Chicago's ordinary folk preserved the habits and values of their rural heritage.

The broad distinction between the characteristic attitude of the Chicago novelist and Chicago humorist, by which I mean the contrast between disaffection and affirmation, became blurred in the comic stories of Chicago which Ring Lardner wrote between 1911 and 1919. Dunne had affirmed that Chicago, for all its faults of civic corruption, was yet a hospitable environment for separate, stable communities. George Ade had limited the scope of this affirmation—the communities he portrayed were single offices, boardinghouses, small shops—and noted the occasional misfits who could find no place in Chicago; but still he represented in his brief stories the idea that Chicago usually offered its various newcomers opportunity for economic security and social intimacy. Ring Lardner, though, except in his representation of the Chicago White Sox baseball team, does not affirm that Chicago nourishes or even tolerates the best impulses of its citizens.

Lardner writes about the same kind of characters as Dunne and Ade had selected, but, apart from the White Sox veterans whom he admired, he denies to them any pleasing distinction in language, manners, and ambitions. Lardner's Chicago characters do not embody, as Dunne's and Ade's characters often did, the familiar virtues of America's rural past. Instead, they keenly envy the new pleasures and privileges of Chicago's social, business, and political elite. They earnestly try, by vacationing in Palm Springs or by moving to a suburb or by joining a bridge club, to break from the stultifying company of their neighbors and to ingratiate themselves into the society of people who desire, above all, to completely avoid them.

Lardner's stories are comic and entertaining because his characters do not suffer the severe consequences of death, bankruptcy, social ostracism, and isolation which afflict the protagonists of several Chicago novels. Nevertheless, they do suffer embarrassment, loneliness, and ridicule. His humor stands as a protest against the conditions of urban life which exhaust the common man's dignity and assurance. He translates into the modest lives of Chicago's common people the alienation and disappointment which Chicago novelists had described as the price ambitious Chicagoans paid for their success.

6

CONCLUSION

The significant development revealed in our examination of Finley Peter Dunne, George Ade, and Ring Lardner is their gradual exhaustion of a traditional concept of American character. That concept, as succinctly defined by Constance Rourke in her influential book, *American Humor: A Study of National Character,* was the definition of the American as "indefatigably rural, sharp, uncouth, witty."

> Plain and pawky, he was an ideal image, a self-image, one of those symbols which peoples spontaneously adopt and by which in some measure they live. . . . He was a symbol of triumph, of adaptability, of irrepressible life—of many qualities needed to induce confidence and self-possession among a new and unamalgamated people.[1]

I believe that the art of Finley Peter Dunne, George Ade, and Ring Lardner marks the dissolution of a coherent tradition in American popular humor. They did not sustain the sense of triumph, confidence, and self-possession of the "plain and pawky" common American so vigorously asserted in the Bridgeport sketches of Finley Peter Dunne, nor did they inspire in future urban humorists their nostalgic vision of the small, rural American community as an appropriate moral standard by which to measure urban experience. Though Ring Lardner remained a popular writer throughout the 1920s, his vision of a debased and demoralizing urban culture, initially welcomed by some critics as a daring and authentic conception in popular literature, came to be recognized as extreme and eccentric: Carl Van Doren characterized Lardner's stories as among "the most skeptical, most cynical, most heartless universes ever invented," and Elizabeth Bibesco described Lardner's imagination as that of "an entomologist observing, collecting, annotating and showing his insects."[2] While other popular humorists in the 1920s and 1930s—notably Damon Runyon, Sidney J. Perelman, Robert Benchley, Don Marquis, Ogden Nash, James Thurber, and Leo Rosten—amusingly expressed the variety and uniqueness of urban language, Lardner insistently repeated the flat, monotonous idiom of his Chicago wise boobs. He neither perceived nor expressed any hope that the city could foster a culture that might engage the minds and spirits of Americans for purposes higher than self-indulgence.

The styles of urban humor to become prevalent in the 1920s were confidently, even arrogantly urban—the *New Yorker,* quite unabashedly, was "not edited for the old lady in Dubuque. It will not be concerned in what she is thinking about."[3] This conscious rejection of a rural style was widespread; the popular urban entertainers of the 1920s (Bert Savoy, Eddie Cantor, "Keystone Cops," W. C. Fields, Eubie Blake, Ira and George Gershwin, Cole Porter, Florence Moore, Fanny Brice, Joe Cook, Franklin P. Adams, Henry Morgan) did not exhibit the vested emotional interest in defending an American rural tradition which is evident in the work of Dunne, Ade, and Lardner. Their experiences were urban—many of them were the sons of Jewish immigrants in New York City—and their audience was urban. Their art, whether in the polished essays of Benchley, Thurber, and White, or in the ebullient "darktown" musicals of Noble Sissel and Eubie Blake, measured and extended the rhythms of the city they knew.

The usual "rhythms" expressed in popular urban entertainment of the 1920s reflected the fast pace, excitement, and complexity of the city, particularly New York City. The early silent films of Mack Sennett's Keystone Company, for example, brilliantly exploited an urbanite's awareness of and interest in machines. Their elaborate chase scenes and split-second pratfalls were mechanically intensified by an intentional speeding of the camera; their favorite prop, used with wild, confident abandon, was the new automobile. This recognition, often a comically irreverent recognition, of machines and mechanical rhythm was pervasive in the popular urban arts of the 1920s. Among the more original and elaborate expressions of this aesthetic were the complex choreographies of Florenz Ziegfeld's "Follies." A "Follies" production, as Gilbert Seldes observed,

> shows a mania for perfection; it aspires to be precise and definite; it corresponds to those de luxe railway trains which are always exactly on time, to the millions of spare parts that always fit, to the ease of commerce when there is a fixed price; jazz or symphony may sound from the orchestra pit, but underneath is the real tone of the revue, the steady incorruptible purr of the dynamo.[4]

On humbler scales than Mr. Ziegfeld's lavish revues, the aesthetic of mechanical precision was also apparent. Vaudeville skits, for example, were precisely coordinated: each skit was short, economical, and efficient. Vaudeville audiences did not expect or tolerate leisurely elaborations or digressions from their entertainers. They applauded exact timing, rapid repartee, and energetic dancing. They came to the theaters to witness the forces dominant in their urban lives—machines, time-tables, complex divisions of labor—transformed into stimulating entertainment.

Finley Peter Dunne, George Ade, and Ring Lardner had attempted a different style of urban humor. They had tried to represent Chicago as a familiar and ordinary community. They had measured their characters' language and personalities against the traditional model of the simple, ill-educated but honest and moralistic American democrat who was proud, self-reliant, and rural. The discrepancy between their conception of an appropriate urban culture and the actual character of the city grew steadily: in Dunne's comic essays, the characters live in a coherent community; Ade's characters can discover only remnants of that community in boardinghouses, small offices, and among their immediate neighbors; Lardner's characters can find no community within Chicago. The only communities with which Lardner's characters can maintain relations, by entertaining visiting relatives or by making emergency appeals for personal loans, are the rural hometowns they have left.

· The promise of an urban humor announced in the Mr. Dooley essays is not completely fulfilled in the popular art of George Ade and Ring Lardner. Though Dunne modeled Bridgeport after the traditional and sentimental conceptions of an American village, he did communicate, through Mr. Dooley's wide-ranging and confident comments on the affairs of his city, the sense of Chicago as a unique and satisfying social environment. It is significant that Dunne endowed Mr. Dooley with a long and active experience of Chicago; Mr. Dooley is comfortable in his city. George Ade and Ring Lardner do not communicate this sense of comfort: a poignancy undercuts each of Ade's sentimental affirmations of Chicago, and a dourness imbues Lardner's attitude toward the wise boobs—who are entertaining, often, because they are insensitive to embarrassment.

There are, I believe, two significant reasons for the differences among these writers, apart from the general influence which the conception of Chicago as a symbol of social evil, defined and repeated by the Chicago novelists, exerted upon them. Much of the difference between Dunne and Ade can be accounted as essentially a difference in personality and background. They share the same motive—to present Chicago as an appealing and entertaining environment—but they differ in temperament. Ade was never comfortable in Chicago. Though he made his reputation as a Chicago journalist and, later, as a Broadway playwright, Ade always considered himself a Hoosier. When he had earned independent wealth, he immediately purchased a large tract of land outside his hometown, built a spacious, rambling estate, and spent the remaining forty years of his life alternately entertaining his friends at Hazleton and, during the winter months, traveling abroad. Ade consistently perceived Chicago in those small units which bore some resemblance to the Indiana villages or the Purdue fraternity which he knew; he usually suggested, in his Chicago stories, the necessary barriers to social intimacy which were the condition of life in the city.

The difference between Dunne and Lardner is not as personal as that between Dunne and Ade. Though Lardner admired Dunne, and occasionally met him when both lived on Long Island in the 1920s, he did not know Dunne as a colleague and contemporary, as George Ade had. Nor did Lardner know Dunne's Chicago. Dunne's Chicago was the Chicago of the World's Fair and the Municipal Voters' League, the Chicago of the ethnic Democrat and the reform Republican; Lardner's Chicago was the Chicago of William Hale Thompson and "Boss"

Billy Lorimer. The promises of reform, creativity, and civic pride which were building in Dunne's era seemed abandoned in Lardner's, especially by 1919, the year of the "Black Sox" scandal and the summer race riots. Like Dunne, Lardner measured Chicago against the model of a neighborly community, but he perceived Chicago as a diminished environment, a condition of life which eroded discipline, fellowship, and pride. He dramatized this perception in the vulgarities of his characters and the meager sensuality and materialism of their ambitions.

The potential for a rich urban humor, evident in Mr. Dooley's irreverent wit, in George Ade's slang, and in Ring Lardner's accurately nuanced idiomatic speech, reached fruition in another city and another time. In New York City, in the 1920s and 1930s, one finds a full and coherent urban humor. In Clarence Day's burlesques of "Father's" old-fashioned prejudices, in silent film scenes of automobiles wildly careening through city traffic, in the profane wit of Groucho Marx and the sexual exuberance of Harpo Marx, in the "street" idiom of Damon Runyon, and the clever, risqué lyrics of Cole Porter; in these and similar examples, modern urban humorists would announce their separation from the homely attitudes of Finley Peter Dunne and George Ade, and from the narrow discontent of Ring Lardner.

The significance of Dunne, Ade, and Lardner is in their exploration of urban speech, prejudices, institutions, and character types as the resources for a modern American humor. However, in their attempts to accommodate the traditional characters, attitudes, and values of nineteenth-century American humor with the novel experience of Chicago, they illustrated a widening discrepancy between the ideal of the parochial community and the actual character of urban experience. They were popular in their time, one may speculate, because the disparity between attitude and experience depicted in their writings elicited an empathetic response from a general audience. They gave form to the feeling that traditional habits of mind were inadequate for the comprehension of urban experience. Their comic art reveals, within the realm of entertainment and popular journalism, the broad reach of the "watershed" dividing the agrarian republic of nineteenth-century America from the urbanized and industrialized nation state of twentieth-century America.

NOTES

1. CHICAGO AND CHICAGO NEWSPAPERS

1.   Lloyd Lewis, *Chicago: The History of Its Reputation* (New York: Harcourt, Brace and Company, 1929), p. 137.
2.   Justus D. Doenecke, "Myths, Machines and Markets: The Columbian Exposition of 1893," *Journal of Popular Culture* 3 (Spring, 1973), pp. 535-36.
3.   Ray Ginger, "A Compulsory Heaven at Pullman," *Altgeld's America* (New York: Funk and Wagnalls, 1958), p. 164.
4.   Charles H. Dennis, *Victor Lawson: His Time and His Work* (Chicago: The University of Chicago Press, 1935), p. 38.
5.   Wilmer Kleinsteuber, "The Influence of Chicago Newspapers upon American Literature" (University of Minnesota: unpublished M.A. thesis, 1955), pp. 66–67.
6.   Henry L. Mencken, "The Literary Capital of the United States," quoted in Harry Hansen, *Midwest Portraits* (New York: Harcourt, Brace and Company, 1923), p. 192.

2. FINLEY PETER DUNNE

1.   Finley Peter Dunne, "What Does He Care?" originally published in the Chicago *Sunday Post* (August 25, 1894), reprinted in Elmer Ellis, *Mr. Dooley's America* (New York: Alfred A. Knopf, 1941), pp. 84-86.
2.   W. Irving Way, "Mr. Martin Dooley of Chicago," *The Bookman* 9 (May, 1899), p. 218.
3.   Ibid.
4.   Lloyd Wendt and Herman Kogan, *Bosses in Lusty Chicago* (Bloomington, Indiana: Indiana University Press, 1971), p. 208.
5.   Ellis, p. 95.

3. GEORGE ADE

1.   Harvey Zorbaugh, *Gold Coast and Slum* (Chicago: The University of Chicago Press, 1927), p. 232.
2.   William Dean Howells, "Our National Humorists," *Harper's Magazine 134* (February, 1917), p. 444.

3.   Russell Nye, *The Unembarrassed Muse* (New York: The Dial Press, 1970), p. 164.

4.   Ibid., p. 317.

5.   Mark Twain, letter to William Dean Howells, July 22, 1908, reprinted in *One Afternoon with Mark Twain* (Chicago: The Mark Twain Society of Chicago, 1939), pp. 8-9.

6.   "Pink Marsh: review," *Bookman* 6 (September, 1897), p. 74.

7.   William Dean Howells, "Certain of the Chicago School of Fiction," *North American Review* 176 (May, 1903), p. 739.

8.   Jack Brenner, "Howells and Ade," *American Literature* 38 (May, 1966), p. 200.

9.   Carl Van Doren, "Old Wisdom in a New Tongue: George Ade, Moralist in Slang," *The Century Magazine* 105 (January, 1923), pp. 472, 475.

10.   George Ade, "Autobiography," *Letters of George Ade,* ed. Terence Tobin (West Lafayette, Indiana: Purdue University Studies, 1973), pp. 14-15.

4. RING LARDNER

1.   Gilbert Seldes, *The Seven Lively Arts* (New York: A.S. Barnes and Company, 1962), p. 121. Clifton Fadiman, "Ring Lardner and the Triangle of Hate," *The Nation* 136 (March 22, 1933), p. 315.

2.   Lawrence S. Ritter, *The Glory of Their Times* (New York: Macmillan Company, 1966), p. 281.

3.   Francis Wilson, "Eugene Field, The Humorist," *Century Magazine* 64 (July, 1902), p. 448.

4.   Constance Rourke, *American Humor* (Garden City, New York: Doubleday and Company, 1953), p. 229.

5. CHICAGO LITERATURE

1.   Donald Elder, *Ring Lardner* (New York: Doubleday, 1956), p. 119.

2.   Bernard Duffey, *The Chicago Renaissance in American Letters* (Ann Arbor, Michigan: The Michigan State College Press, 1954), p. 110.

3.   Charles Walcutt, *American Literary Naturalism, A Divided Stream* (Minneapolis: The University of Minnesota Press, 1956), p. 153.

4.   Henry W. Shaw, *Josh Billings on Ice* (New York: G. W. Carleton and Company, 1868), p. 183.

6. CONCLUSION

1.   Constance Rourke, *American Humor: A Study of the National Character* (originally published New York: Harcourt, Brace and Company, 1953); Anchor edition, pp. 25, 35.

2.   Carl Van Doren, "Beyond Grammar; Ring W. Lardner: Philologist among the Low Brows," *Century Magazine* 106 (July, 1923), p. 475. Elizabeth Bibesco, "Lament for Lardner," *Living Age* 345 (December, 1933), p. 367.

3.   Harold Ross, "The New Yorker: A Prospectus," quoted in *A Time of Harvest,* ed. Robert Spiller (New York: Hill and Wang, 1962), p. 55.

4.   Gilbert Seldes, *The Seven Lively Arts* (New York: A. S. Barnes and Company, 1962), p. 133.

BIBLIOGRAPHIC ESSAY

I began my research for this study with what I thought would be a limited purpose: I wanted to place the career and works of Finley Peter Dunne, whose political irreverence I have long enjoyed, within the broader context of Chicago at the turn of the century and the tradition of American popular humor. Since that beginning, my purposes have multiplied and my field of research has expanded. I offer this bibliographic essay as a traveler's report of the highlights and byways of a satisfying journey.

Any reader interested in a further investigation of the three principal figures in this study will find several valuable biographies available. Ring Lardner has received most attention from biographers; his life is recounted and artistic view defined in *Ring Lardner* by Donald Elder (1956), *Ring Lardner and the Portrait of Folly* by Maxwell Geismar (1972), and two stimulating recent books, *The Lardners* by Ring Lardner, Jr. (1976), and *Ring* by Jonathan Yardley (1977). I recommend the books by Geismar and Yardley for their critical appraisals of Lardner's art and the memoir by Ring Lardner, Jr., for its special insight into the Lardner home. Of all the biographies, though, my favorite is the first; Donald Elder's study is rich in its full and sympathetic exploration of the family, professional, and private fabrics of Ring Lardner's intense life.

For George Ade, there is a delightful, generous biography by a friend (Ade had hundreds): *George Ade: Warmhearted Satirist* by Fred Kelly (1947). A more concise account of Ade's life and a deeper critical exposition of his art is the biography *George Ade* by Lee Coyle (1964). And finally, to return to the subject with which I began, Finley Peter

Dunne, his circles of work and friends, and "Mr. Martin Dooley of Archey R-road" are thoroughly explained in what I consider to be a model biography: *Mr. Dooley's America* by Elmer Ellis (1941). Of more recent studies, *Mr. Dooley's Chicago* by Barbara C. Schaaf (1977) is a valuable introduction to Dunne's art (a topically organized anthology of Chicago *Sunday Post* and *Evening Post* selections with a running commentary on social issues and specific men and events); by contrast, *Mr. Dooley and the Chicago Irish* edited by Charles Fanning (1976), also an anthology, is of interest to someone very knowledgeable about Dunne (Mr. Fanning identifies all the topical references in the Mr. Dooley essays he reprints). A unique book in the Dunne collection is the collaborative memoir of Finley Peter Dunne and his son Philip, *Mr. Dooley Remembers* (1963).

Chicago as a subject has not been as thoroughly researched as I had expected it would be when I began my study. We are indebted to Professor Bessie Louis Pierce for her comprehensive and lucid *History of Chicago*, of which I used primarily the first volume (1957). Most other studies of Chicago history are anecdotal. The best of these is *Bosses in Lusty Chicago* by Lloyd Wendt and Herman Kogan (1967). Others in which interesting and entertaining points of information can be found are *Fabulous Chicago* by Emmett Dedmon (1953), *Chicago: The History of Its Reputation* by Lloyd Lewis (1929), and *Giants Gone: Men Who Made Chicago* by Ernest Poole (1943). Two special studies of Chicago history which I found invaluable in understanding the full scope of experience during my time period are *Gold Coast and Slum* by Harvey Zorbaugh (1927) and *Black Chicago: The Making of a Negro Ghetto, 1890–1920* by Allan Spear (1967).

Two other subjects remain within the range of my expedition: American humor and American literary naturalism. *Native American Humor* by Walter Blair (1937), *American Humor* by Constance Rourke (1931), and *Crackerbox Philosophers in American Humor and Satire* by Jennette Tandy (1925) are classics in this field of study. Of more recent works, I find *The Rise and Fall of American Humor* by Jesse Bier (1968) a challenging book whose thesis is too insistent, while *Humor in America* by Enid Veron (1976) is the overview of our comic tradition which I recommend to everyone. For American literary naturalism, my views were clarified by *The Beginning of Naturalism in American Fiction* by Lars Ahnebrink (1961), *Henry Blake Fuller of Chicago* by Bernard Bowron

(1974), *The Chicago Renaissance in American Letters* by Bernard Duffey (1954), *The American City Novel* by Blanche Gelfant (1954), *The Progressive Mind* by David Noble (1970), *Five Novelists of the Progressive Era* by Robert Schneider (1965), and *American Literary Naturalism, A Divided Stream* by Charles Walcutt (1956).

In the Select Bibliography which follows, I first identify those primary sources which I noted in brackets within my text. I do not list all the primary sources which I studied, since there already exist comprehensive bibliographies for George Ade and Ring Lardner: *A Bibliography of George Ade* by Dorothy Ritter Russo (Indianapolis: Indiana Historical Society, 1947) and *Ring W. Lardner: A Descriptive Bibliography* by Matthew J. Bruccoli and Richard Layman (Pittsburgh: University of Pittsburgh Press, 1976). A bibliography of Finley Peter Dunne has not yet been compiled, but the reader will find the bibliography in *Mr. Dooley's Chicago* by Barbara C. Schaaf a useful beginning. The second part of my Select Bibliography is intended as a guide to those secondary and background sources which I found most instructive.

SELECT BIBLIOGRAPHY

PRIMARY SOURCES (cited in brackets in text)

1. Ade, George. *Artie*. Chicago: Herbert S. Stone, 1898.
2. ———. *Doc' Horne*. Chicago: Herbert S. Stone, 1899.
3. ———. *Fables in Slang*. Chicago: Herbert S. Stone, 1899.
4. ———. *Fables in Slang and More Fables in Slang*. New York: Dover Publications, Inc., 1960.
5. ———. "Looking Back from 50." *American Magazine*, February 1917, pp. 7-9.
6. ———. *Pink Marsh*. Chicago: Herbert S. Stone, 1897.
7. ———. "They Simply Wouldn't Let Me Be a Highbrow." *American Magazine*, December 1920, pp. 50-51, 197-99.
8. *Chicago Stories*. Ed. Franklin J. Meine. Chicago: Henry Regnery Company, 1963.
9. Dreiser, Theodore. *Sister Carrie*. New York: W. W. Norton and Company, 1970.
10. Dunne, Finley Peter. *Dissertations by Mr. Dooley*. New York: Harper and Brothers, 1906.
11. ———. *Mr. Dooley in Peace and War*. Boston: Small, Maynard and Company, 1898.
12. ———. *Mr. Dooley in the Hearts of His Countrymen*. Boston: Small, Maynard and Company, 1899.
13. ———. *Mr. Dooley on Ivrything and Ivrybody*. New York: Dover Publications, Inc., 1963.
14. ———. *Mr. Dooley Remembers*. Ed. Philip Dunne. Boston: Little, Brown and Company, 1963.
15. ———. *Mr. Dooley's Opinions*. New York: R. H. Russell, 1901.
16. ———. *Mr. Dooley's Philosophy*. New York: R. H. Russell, 1900.
17. ———. *Observations by Mr. Dooley*. New York: R. H. Russell, 1902.
18. Fuller, Henry Blake. *With the Procession*. New York: Harper and Brothers, 1895.

19.   Lardner, Ring. *Gullible's Travels, Etc.* New York: Charles Scribner's Sons, 1917.

20.   –––. "Matty." *American Magazine.* August 1915, pp. 26–29.

21.   –––. *Own Your Own Home.* Indianapolis: Bobbs-Merrill, 1919.

22.   –––. *You Know Me, Al.* New York: Charles Scribner's Sons, 1916.

23.   Norris, Frank. *The Pit: A Story of Chicago.* New York: Doubleday and Company, 1903.

SECONDARY AND BACKGROUND SOURCES

1.   Ahnebrink, Lars. *The Beginnings of Naturalism in American Fiction.* New York: Russell and Russell, 1961.

2.   Bier, Jesse. *The Rise and Fall of American Humor.* New York: Holt, Rinehart and Winston, 1968.

3.   Blair, Walter. *Horse Sense in American Humor.* Chicago: University of Chicago Press, 1942.

4.   –––. *Native American Humor.* 2nd ed. San Francisco: Chandler Publishing Company, 1960.

5.   Bowron, Bernard. *Henry Blake Fuller of Chicago.* Westport, Connecticut: Greenwood Press, 1974.

6.   Commager, Henry Steele. *The American Mind.* Yale University Paperback. New Haven, Connecticut: Yale University Press, 1950.

7.   Coyle, Lee. *George Ade.* New York: Twayne Publishers, 1964.

8.   Dedmon, Emmett. *Fabulous Chicago.* New York: Random House, 1953.

9.   Dennis, Charles H. *Victor Lawson: His Time and His Work.* Chicago: The University of Chicago Press, 1935.

10.   Duffey, Bernard. *The Chicago Renaissance in American Letters.* East Lansing, Michigan: The Michigan State College Press, 1954.

11.   Elder, Donald. *Ring Lardner.* New York: Doubleday and Company, 1956.

12.   Ellis, Elmer. *Mr. Dooley's America.* New York: Alfred A. Knopf, 1941.

13.   Friedrich, Otto. *Ring Lardner.* Minneapolis: University of Minnesota Press, 1965.

14.   Geismar, Maxwell. *Ring Lardner and the Portrait of Folly.* New York: Thomas Y. Crowell, 1972.

15.   Gelfant, Blanche Houseman. *The American City Novel.* Norman, Oklahoma: University of Oklahoma Press, 1954.

16.   Ginger, Ray. *Age of Excess: The United States from 1877–1914.* New York: Macmillan, 1965.

17.   –––. *Altgeld's America.* New York: Funk and Wagnalls, 1958.

18.   *The Glory of Their Times.* Ed. Lawrence S. Ritter. New York: Macmillan, 1966.

19.   Hansen, Harry. *Midwest Portraits.* New York: Harcourt, Brace and Company, 1923.

20.   *Humor in America.* Ed. Enid Veron. New York: Harcourt, Brace and Jovanovich, 1976.

21.   Jones, Howard Mumford. *The Age of Energy: Varieties of American Experience, 1865–1915.*

22.   Kelly, Fred. *George Ade: Warmhearted Satirist.* Indianapolis: Bobbs-Merrill, 1947.

23.   Kleinsteuber, Wilmer. "The Influence of Chicago Newspapers upon American Literature." Unpublished M.A. thesis, University of Minnesota, 1955.

24.   Lardner, Ring, Jr. *The Lardners: My Family Remembered.* New York: Harper and Row, 1976.

25.   *Letters of George Ade.* Ed. Terence Tobin. West Lafayette, Indiana: Purdue University Studies, 1973.

26.   Lewis, Lloyd. *Chicago: The History of Its Reputation.* New York: Harcourt, Brace and Company, 1929.

27.   McCutcheon, John. *Drawn from Memory.* Indianapolis: Bobbs-Merrill, 1950.

28.   Marx, Leo. *The Machine in the Garden.* Oxford Paperback. New York: Oxford University Press, 1972.

29.   Masson, Thomas L. *Our American Humorists.* New York: Moffett, Yard and Company, 1922.

30.   May, Henry F. *The End of Innocence: A Study of the First Years of Our Own Time, 1912-1917.* Quadrangle Books. Chicago: Quadrangle Books, Inc., 1964.

31.   *Mr. Dooley and the Chicago Irish.* Ed. Charles Fanning. New York: Arno Press, 1976.

32.   *Mr. Dooley Remembers.* Ed. Philip Dunne. Boston: Little, Brown and Company, 1963.

33.   *Mr. Dooley's Chicago.* Ed. Barbara C. Schaaf. Garden City, New York: Anchor Press, 1977.

34.   Noble, David. *The Progressive Mind.* Rand McNally Paperback. Chicago: Rand McNally, 1970.

35.   Nye, Russell. *The Unembarrassed Muse.* Dial Press Paperback. New York: Dial Press, 1970.

36.   Pierce, Bessie Louise. *A History of Chicago: The Rise of a Modern City, 1871-1893.* New York: Alfred A. Knopf, 1957.

37.   Poole, Ernest. *Giants Gone: Men Who Made Chicago.* New York: McGraw-Hill, 1943.

38.   *Ring around Max: The Correspondence of Ring Lardner and Max Perkins.* Ed. Clifford M. Caruthers. DeKalb, Illinois: Northern Illinois University Press, 1973.

39.   Rourke, Constance. *American Humor.* Anchor Books. Garden City, New York: Doubleday and Company, 1953.

40.   Schneider, Robert. *Five Novelists of the Progressive Era.* New York: Columbia University Press, 1965.

41.   Seldes, Gilbert. *The Seven Lively Arts.* 2nd ed. Perpetua Books. New York: A. S. Barnes, 1962.

42.   *Some Champions: Sketches and Fiction by Ring Lardner.* Ed. Matthew J. Bruccoli and Richard Layman, with a Foreword by Ring Lardner, Jr. New York: Scribner, 1976.

43.   Spear, Allan. *Black Chicago: The Making of a Negro Ghetto, 1890-1920.* Chicago: University of Chicago Press, 1967.

44.   Stead, William T. *If Christ Came to Chicago!* Chicago: Laird and Lee, 1894.

45.   Stone, Melville E. *Fifty Years a Journalist.* Garden City, New York: Doubleday, 1921.

46.   Szuberla, Guy. "Urban Vistas and the Pastoral Garden: Studies in the Literature and Architecture of Chicago (1893-1909)." Unpublished Ph.D. dissertation, University of Minnesota, 1972.

47.   Tandy, Jennette. *Crackerbox Philosophers in American Humor and Satire.* New York: Columbia University Press, 1925.

48.   Thorp, Willard. *American Humorists*. Minneapolis: University of Minnesota Press, 1965.

49.   Walcutt, Charles. *American Literary Naturalism, A Divided Stream*. Minneapolis: University of Minnesota Press, 1956.

50.   Wendt, Lloyd, and Herman Kogan. *Bosses in Lusty Chicago*. Bloomington, Indiana: Indiana University Press, 1967.

51.   *The W.G.N.* Chicago: The Tribune Company, 1922.

52.   Wiebe, Robert. *The Search for Order, 1877-1920*. New York: Hill and Wang, 1967.

53.   Yardley, Jonathan. *Ring: A Biography of Ring Lardner*. New York: Random House, 1977.

54.   Yates, Norris. *The American Humorist: Conscience of the Twentieth Century*. Ames, Iowa: Iowa State University Press, 1964.

55.   Zorbaugh, Harvey. *Gold Coast and Slum*. Chicago: University of Chicago Press, 1927.

INDEX